THE FORMS OF THE OLD TESTAMENT LITERATURE

*Now available

2 KINGS

BURKE O. LONG

The Forms of the Old Testament Literature
VOLUME X
Rolf P. Knierim and Gene M. Tucker, editors

WILLIAM B. EERDMANS PUBLISHING COMPANY
GRAND RAPIDS, MICHIGAN

For my wife, Judy,
and my children,
Melissa and Timothy

Copyright © 1991 by Wm. B. Eerdmans Publishing Co.
255 Jefferson Ave., S.E., Grand Rapids, MI 49503

Printed in the United States of America

Library of Congress Cataloging-in-Publication Data

Long, Burke O.
2 Kings / Burke O. Long.
pm.   cm.   — (The Forms of the Old Testament literature ; v. 10)
Includes bibliographical references.
ISBN 0-8028-0535-3 (pbk.)
1. Bible. O.T. Kings, 2nd — Commentaries.   I. Title.
II. Title: Second Kings.   III. Series.
BS1335.3.L663   1991
221'.540663 — dc20   91-36766
                                                            CIP

CONTENTS

ABBREVIATIONS AND SYMBOLS

I. MISCELLANEOUS ABBREVIATIONS AND SYMBOLS

B.C.E.	before common era
ca.	*circa* (about)
cf.	compare
ch(s).	chapter(s)
col(s).	column(s)
Diss.	Dissertation
Dtr	Deuteronomic source
DtrH	Deuteronomistic Historian
Dtr^N	Nomistic Deuteronomistic source
Dtr^P	Prophetic Deuteronomistic source
ed(s).	editor(s), edited by; edition
e.g.	for example
esp.	especially
et al.	*et alii* (and others)
Eng.	English
Eng. tr.	English translation
Fest.	*Festschrift*
f(f).	following verse(s), pages(s), line(s)
Hebr.	Hebrew
i.e.	*id est* (that is [to say])
lit.	literally
LXX	Septuagint
LXX^B	Codex Vaticanus
LXX^L	Codex Lagardiana
MS(S)	manuscript(s)
MT	Masoretic Text
n(n).	note(s)
NT	New Testament
OT	Old Testament

p(p).	page(s)
pl(s).	plate(s)
plur.	plural
PN	personal name
repr.	reprint
rev. ed.	revised edition
RN	royal name
RS	Ras Shamra
s.	singular
T. 12 Patr.	Testaments of the Twelve Patriarchs
tr.	translator(s), translated by
v(v).	verse(s)
vol(s).	volume(s)
VS(S)	the ancient version(s), or translation(s), of biblical literature
§(§)	section(s)
+	plus, and
√	the root or stem of a word
→	cross reference to another section of the commentary.

II. PUBLICATIONS

AB	Anchor Bible
AfO	*Archiv für Orientforschung*
AmstCah	*Amsterdamse Cahiers voor Exegese en Bijbelse Theologie*
AnBib	Analecta biblica
ANEP	J. B. Pritchard, ed., *The Ancient Near East in Pictures Relating to the Old Testament* (2nd ed.; Princeton: Princeton University Press, 1969)
ANET	J. B. Pritchard, ed., *Ancient Near Eastern Texts Relating to the Old Testament* (3rd ed.; Princeton: Princeton University Press, 1969)
AOAT	Alter Orient und Altes Testament
ARE	J. H. Breasted, ed., *Ancient Records of Egypt* (5 vols.; Chicago: University of Chicago Press, 1906-1907)
ARI	A. K. Grayson, *Assyrian Royal Inscriptions* (2 vols.; Wiesbaden: Harrassowitz, 1972-1976)
ARM	Archives royales de Mari. Transcriptions et traductions
ASTI	*Annual of the Swedish Theological Institute*
ATANT	Abhandlungen zur Theologie des Alten und Neuen Testaments
ATD	Das Alte Testament Deutsch
BARev	*Biblical Archaeology Review*
BAT	Die Botschaft des Alten Testaments
BBB	Bonner biblische Beiträge
BDB	F. Brown, S. R. Driver, and C. A. Briggs, *Hebrew and En-*

glish *Lexicon of the Old Testament* (rev. ed.; Oxford: Oxford University Press, 1957)

BethM	*Beth Miqra*
Bib	*Biblica*
BibOr	Biblica et orientalia
BJRL	*Bulletin of the John Rylands University Library of Manchester*
BJS	Brown Judaic Studies
BKAT	Biblischer Kommentar: Altes Testament
BR	*Biblical Research*
BWANT	Beiträge zur Wissenschaft vom Alten und Neuen Testament
BZ	*Biblische Zeitschrift*
BZAW	Beiheft zur *Zeitschrift für die alttestamentliche Wissenschaft*
CBQ	*Catholic Biblical Quarterly*
CBQMS	Catholic Biblical Quarterly Monograph Series
ConB	Coniectanea biblica
CrozQ	*Crozer Quarterly*
EBib	Études bibliques
EHAT	Exegetisches Handbuch zum Alten Testament
ErfTS	Erfurter theologische Studien
EstBib	*Estudios Bíblicos*
EvT	*Evangelische Theologie*
FOTL	The Forms of the Old Testament Literature
FRLANT	Forschungen zur Religion und Literatur des Alten und Neuen Testaments
GKC	*Gesenius' Hebrew Grammar,* ed. E. Kautzsch, tr. A. E. Cowley (2nd ed.; Oxford: Clarendon, 1910)
HKAT	Handkommentar zum Alten Testament
HSM	Harvard Semitic Monographs
HTR	*Harvard Theological Review*
ICC	International Critical Commentary
IDB	*Interpreter's Dictionary of the Bible*
IDBSup	Supplementary volume to *IDB*
IEJ	*Israel Exploration Journal*
JANESCU	*Journal of the Ancient Near Eastern Society of Columbia University*
JAOS	*Journal of the American Oriental Society*
JBL	*Journal of Biblical Literature*
JJS	*Journal of Jewish Studies*
JNES	*Journal of Near Eastern Studies*
JPS	*Jewish Publication Society Version*
JSOT	*Journal for the Study of the Old Testament*
JSOTSup	Journal for the Study of the Old Testament Supplement Series
JSS	*Journal of Semitic Studies*
JTS	*Journal of Theological Studies*
KAI	H. Donner and W. Röllig, *Kanaanäische und Aramäische In-*

	schriften (2nd ed.; 3 vols.; Wiesbaden: Harrassowitz, 1966-1968)
KHC	Kurzer Hand-Commentar zum Alten Testament
KJV	*King James Version*
NEB	*New English Bible*
NedTTs	*Nederlands theologisch Tijdschrift*
NJPS	*New Jewish Publication Society Version*
OLZ	*Orientalistische Literaturzeitung*
Or	*Orientalia*
OTL	Old Testament Library
OTS	*Oudtestamentische Studiën*
POS	Pretoria Oriental Series
PRU	*Le Palais royal d'Ugarit*
PTMS	Pittsburgh Theological Monograph Series
RivB	*Rivista biblica*
RLA	*Reallexikon der Assyriologie* (Berlin and Leipzig, 1932-)
RS	Ras Shamra
RSV	*Revised Standard Version*
SANT	Studien zum Alten und Neuen Testament
SBFLA	*Studii biblici franciscani liber annus*
SBLDS	Society of Biblical Literature Dissertation Series
SBLMS	Society of Biblical Literature Monograph Series
SBLSBS	Society of Biblical Literature Sources for Biblical Study
SBS	Stuttgarter Bibelstudien
SBT	Studies in Biblical Theology
ScrHie	Scripta Hierosolymitana
SEÅ	*Svensk exegetisk årsbok*
SJT	*Scottish Journal of Theology*
TAik	Teologinen Aikakauskirja
TBü	Theologische Bücherei
TDOT	G. J. Botterweck and H. Ringgren, eds., *Theological Dictionary of the Old Testament* (Eng. tr. of *TWAT;* Grand Rapids: Eerdmans, 1974-)
ThStK	*Theologische Studien und Kritiken*
TTZ	*Trierer theologische Zeitschrift*
TUAT	*Texte aus der Umwelt des Alten Testaments*
TWAT	G. J. Botterweck and H. Ringgren, eds., *Theologisches Wörterbuch zum Alten Testament* (Stuttgart: Kohlhammer, 1970-)
TZ	*Theologische Zeitschrift*
VT	*Vetus Testamentum*
WMANT	Wissenschaftliche Monographien zum Alten und Neuen Testament
ZAW	*Zeitschrift für die alttestamentliche Wissenschaft*
ZTK	*Zeitschrift für Theologie und Kirche*

Editors' Foreword

This volume completes Burke Long's treatment of the Books of Kings in the FOTL series. Since it follows the objectives and format of the series as described in the previously published volumes, including Long's volume on 1 Kings, the reader is invited to consult the editors' foreword in those volumes for pertinent information.

As in any work such as this series, which extends over decades, it is inevitable that the individuality of its different authors as well as the ongoing developments in research must be taken into account. History does not stand still, even in the field of form-critical studies. However, it can be said that the original design of the project, which focuses on the literary nature of the extant texts as the point of entry and primary focus of form-critical work, has thus far stood the test of time. Indeed, for a variety of reasons it has represented a common ground from which diverse exegetical approaches can be undertaken. Burke Long's introduction to this volume and his exegesis well document this fact.

The editors wish again to express their appreciation for the various kinds of support received at the two centers of the project. Both Claremont Graduate School and Candler School of Theology at Emory University provide financial support. The Institute for Antiquity and Christianity at Claremont provides facilities. For this volume, the editors are especially indebted to Marilyn Lundberg and Michael Phelps, Old Testament Ph.D. students at Claremont Graduate School and research associates to the project, for their conscientious and sustained work, which represents the largest part of the editorial process.

ROLF P. KNIERIM
GENE M. TUCKER

PREFACE

The aim of this book and its companion volume, *1 Kings with an Introduction to Historical Literature* (FOTL IX), is to present a sustained form-critical analysis of the books of Kings.

Recently, increasing numbers of biblical scholars of both the First and Second Testaments have turned their energies away from the essentially reconstructive tasks of analyzing oral tradition and the history of written sources toward investigating literary features of the received canonical texts. If anything, this development has strengthened the decision I took in 1984 to follow a similar course for *1 Kings*. The reader will note that I have not ignored matters of literary history, but have given them considerably less emphasis than is customary for commentaries on the Bible. This has entailed a deliberate decision to redefine somewhat the classical categories of form criticism (formal structure, genre, setting, and intention) in the light of their application to a substantially unified written work of historiography. For further orientation, I refer the reader to the preface of *1 Kings*.

Throughout the commentary, I have imagined 1–2 Kings as a writing produced during Israel's experience in the Babylonian exile after 587 B.C.E. This general setting constitutes the primary historical dimension of the analysis. However, the reader should be aware of some of the limitations under which I, and I believe all modern critics, must work. The notions of unity, formal coherence, and meaning I take not so much as qualities somehow contained within the text, awaiting discovery. Rather, I look upon them as aids to making sense of what I read. Furthermore, terms that suggest a creative mind behind the biblical text, such as "intention," "Deuteronomistic historian" (DtrH), "writer," or "author" (the last three are used interchangeably for the most part), are partly misleading. They encourage us to ignore our active involvement in reading, analysis, interpretation, and criticism. These images of a single writer, or even multiple editors, are really shorthand codes for an authorial presence which is implied in my experience of 1–2 Kings as coherent shape and rhetorical force. Of course, this point of view does not exclude the possibility, or even the likelihood, that the text as we read it today has resulted from a long process of literary development. I merely mean to say that I have chosen a different theoretical point from which to view the task of literary analysis. I hope the results demonstrate the usefulness of that decision.

Bibliography, selected according to the aims of the commentary, is provided at appropriate points. In the body of the work, I refer to standard commentaries by author and abbreviated title. Full information on these frequently cited publications will be found in a special section at the front of the book.

To the list of those persons and institutions who were acknowledged as important for the completion of *1 Kings,* I gratefully add the following: the Lily Endowment Visiting Scholar Program for support during 1988 while in residence at Candler School of Theology; the Dean of Bowdoin's faculty, Alfred H. Fuchs, who facilitated a series of generous research grants and who granted released time; Bowdoin's President, A. Leroy Greason, for a recent grant from the Sumner T. Pike Fund which enabled Jeffrey Kuan, a graduate student at Emory University, to handle a host of tedious and technical details connected with the manuscript; my students at Bowdoin over the years, and especially the graduate students at Emory who, during my most recent visit during 1988, provided me with a forum for testing and tempering many of the ideas contained in this book.

I dedicate this work to my wife, Judy, and to my children, Melissa and Timothy. They offered not only love, and hence support, for the task, but also good-humored realism during my decade-long obsession with memories of old kings.

August, 1989   BURKE O. LONG

BIBLIOGRAPHY

FREQUENTLY CITED COMMENTARIES

I. Benzinger, *Die Bücher der Könige* (KHC IX; Freiburg: Mohr, 1899); C. F. Burney, *Notes on the Hebrew Text of the Books of Kings* (Oxford: Oxford University, 1903; repr. New York: KTAV, 1970); M. Cogan and H. Tadmor, *II Kings* (AB 11; Garden City, NY: Doubleday, 1988); K. D. Fricke, *Das zweite Buch von den Königen* (BAT 12/2; Stuttgart: Calwer, 1972); J. Gray, *I & II Kings. A Commentary* (2nd ed.; OTL; Philadelphia: Westminster, 1970); H. Gressmann, *Die älteste Geschichtsschreibung und Prophetie Israels* (Die Schriften des Alten Testaments II/1; Göttingen: Vandenhoeck & Ruprecht, 1921); G. Hentschel, *2 Könige* (*Die Neue Echter Bibel* 11; Würzburg: Echter, 1985); T. R. Hobbs, *2 Kings* (Word Biblical Commentary 13; Waco: Word, 1985); R. Kittel, *Die Bücher der Könige* (HKAT I/5; Göttingen: Vandenhoeck & Ruprecht, 1900); B. O. Long, *I Kings with an Introduction to Historical Literature* (FOTL IX; Grand Rapids: Eerdmans, 1984); J. A. Montgomery, *A Critical and Exegetical Commentary on the Books of Kings* (ed. H. S. Gehman; ICC; Edinburgh: T. & T. Clark, 1951); R. Nelson, *First and Second Kings* (Interpretation; Atlanta: John Knox, 1987); J. Robinson, *The Second Book of Kings* (Cambridge Bible Commentary; Cambridge: Cambridge University, 1976); A. Šanda, *Die Bücher der Könige* (EHAT IX; Münster: Aschendorff, 1911-12); W. Wifall, *The Court History of Israel: A Commentary on First and Second Kings* (St. Louis: Clayton, 1975); E. Würthwein, *Die Bücher der Könige* (ATD XI; Göttingen: Vandenhoeck & Ruprecht, 1977/84).

2 KINGS

Chapter 1

INTRODUCTION TO 2 KINGS

BIBLIOGRAPHY

See the list of frequently cited commentaries, provided on p. xiii, and the bibliography in Long, *1 Kings*, 2-3 and 11-13.

P. Buis, "Rois (livre des)," Supplément au Dictionnaire de la Bible 10,56 (Paris: 1982) 695-740; T. Fretheim, *The Deuteronomic History* (Abingdon: Nashville, 1983); G. Gerbrandt, *Kingship According to the Deuteronomistic History* (SBLDS 87; Atlanta: Scholars Press, 1986); A. D. H. Mayes, *The Story of Israel Between Settlement and Exile: A Redactional Study of the Deuteronomistic History* (London: SCM, 1983); J. McConville, "Narrative and Meaning in the Book of Kings," *Bib* 69 (1988) 31-49; S. McKenzie, "The Prophetic History and the Redaction of Kings," *Hebrew Annual Review* 9 (1985) 203-20; M. O'Brien, *The Deuteronomistic History Hypothesis: A Reassessment* (Göttingen: Vandenhoeck & Ruprecht, 1989); B. Peckham, *The Composition of the Deuteronomistic History* (HSM 35; Atlanta: Scholars Press, 1985); I. Provan, *Hezekiah and the Books of Kings* (New York: de Gruyter, 1988); M. Rose, *Deuteronomist und Jahwist: Untersuchungen zu den Berührungspunkten beider Literaturwerke* (Zurich: Theologischer Verlag, 1981); H. Weippert, "Das deuteronomistische Geschichtswerk," *Theologische Rundschau* 50 (1985) 213-49.

Structure

I. Account of the divided kingdom
    (continued from 1 Kings)   1 Kgs 22:52 (*RSV* 51)–2 Kgs 17:41
    A. The reign of Ahaziah   1 Kgs 22:52 (*RSV* 51)–2 Kgs 1:18
    B. Between the reigns: Elisha
        succeeds Elijah   2:1-25
    C. The reign of Jehoram of Israel   3:1–8:15
    D. The reign of Jehoram of Judah   8:16-24
    E. The reign of Ahaziah   8:25–9:29

The books of Kings were originally one, as the artificial interruption of Ahaziah's reign at 1 Kgs 22:52 (RSV 51) clearly indicates. Thus, the first verses of the book traditionally known as 2 Kings draw the reader into the midst of an ongoing account of an Israelite people divided against itself. Virtually all segments of time are demarcated by introductory and concluding regnal summaries, and, when the divided kingdom is in view, nearly every ruler is related synchronistically to his counterpart in the opposite kingdom. This is the dominant structural feature of the book. In 2 Kings it is disturbed only at 8:25–11:20, when violent events and personages so impinge upon one another that neat divisions between north and south are impossible to maintain (see detailed discussion below).

The historian of 1–2 Kings selects events salient to his purposes, evaluates them, and leads the reader through various regnal epochs. At the point where 2 Kings begins, the writer continues the story of an Israelite kingdom divided since the death of Solomon (1 Kings 12). Ahaziah is on the throne. The author takes the reader from this king's religious condemnation and death through a similarly interpreted dissolution of the whole line of northern kings during the reign of Hoshea (I, 2 Kgs 1:1–17:41). The focus then shifts to the kings of Judah alone, whose regencies are followed until, at the last, even the southern kingdom perishes (II, 18:1–25:30).

Throughout, the subject of the account is royal history, but its theme is the moral and religious failure that led to the loss of national identity and autonomy. In the turmoil following the destruction of Jerusalem, the writer, who is taken by many scholars to be the Deuteronomistic historian (see Long, *1 Kings,* 14-21), draws a warning from the catastrophe. The DtrH possibly hints that hope for the future, or at least comfort for those in anguish, might be nurtured by a tiny morsel, the favorable treatment accorded the last Judean king who lived on in captivity (2 Kgs 25:27-30)

For further discussion of structural and thematic features peculiar to the books of Kings, the reader is referred to Long, *1 Kings,* 11-30.

Genre, Setting, and Intention

Second Kings and the Deuteronomistic work of which it is a part (see Long, *1 Kings*, 14-19) is an example of HISTORY, an extensive written composition in which an ancient author, who by implication claims to be bound by the facts, draws upon a variety of sources to produce a work unified by chronology and particular interpretive concerns. The books of Kings were composed in exile after 586 B.C.E., probably by scribes in Babylon. The main intention would have been to narrate the story of the Hebrew monarchy in such a way as to explain the disaster of exile while speaking to dispossessed royalists (and loyalists of Yahweh) who were in need of a revised sense of self-understanding. For full discussion see Long, *1 Kings*, 30-32.

Chapter 2

THE INDIVIDUAL UNITS

THE REIGN OF AHAZIAH: CANONICAL FRAMEWORK, 1 Kgs 22:52 (*RSV* 51)–2 Kgs 1:18

Structure

I. Introductory regnal resumé	1 Kgs 22:52-54 (*RSV* 51-53)
II. Events during reign	2 Kgs 1:1-17a
A. Notice of rebellion	1
B. Legend of Ahaziah's death in confrontation with Elijah	2-17a
III. Concluding summary	17b-18

The reign of Ahaziah extends across the conventional division of Kings into two separate books. However, it is clear from the literary structure of the material that no such division was originally intended by the Dtr author who compiled this history of the monarchy. With the reign of King Ahaziah, the writer follows his usual paratactic design. That is, most regnal periods are presented as separate blocks of tradition introduced and concluded with formulaic summaries related to accession and succession to the throne. Within such frameworks and arranged in chainlike series, one finds a variety of materials selected for their pertinence to the particular reign and the didactic purposes of the whole composition (see Long, *1 Kings*, 21-30).

The report of the reign of Ahaziah opens with a formulaic introduction and theological appraisal (see discussion at 1 Kgs 22:52-54). With a simple conjunction, *wāw,* serving as transition, the author-editor then relates a first event in standard reportorial style: "And Moab rebelled against Israel following the death of Ahab" (II.A, v. 1; the *RSV* reverses these two clauses and obscures the simple parataxis by which this event is joined to the regnal summary). Immediately, without any transition, the subject which will largely characterize this reign comes into view: Elijah's harsh confrontation with the king and his emissaries, which issues at the last in a prophecy-fulfilling, but otherwise unex-

7

plained, death (II.B, vv. 2-17a). Providing this ignoble and abrupt end with a cover of normalcy, familiar formulas close out the report of the reign (III, vv. 17b-18).

Genre

Since this unit comes from the hand of an exilic writer, we may not specify a genre with any precision. Within the whole, however, one may observe the typical REGNAL RESUMÉ (1 Kgs 22:52-54 [*RSV* 51-53]). The form-critical features of the concluding summary in vv. 17b-18 are more unusual. The SUCCESSION FORMULA, "Jehoram his brother became king in his stead" (1:17b), and the CITATION FORMULA, "Now the rest of the acts . . ." (v. 18), are entirely at home in a concluding REGNAL RESUMÉ (see full discussion at 1 Kgs 14:21-31). Yet the normal sequence of these two formulas is reversed (the LXX shows the more usual word order, v. 18 before v. 17), and the SYNCHRONISTIC ACCESSION FORMULA with its additional explanation (v. 17b) normally belongs to the opening of a reign rather than to its conclusion. For reasons which escape us, some dislocation has occurred in the transmission or editing (the LXX adds at v. 18 the regnal information from 3:1). In any case, the basic purpose seems to have been to close out the reign of Ahaziah with summary information. Apart from 2 Kgs 1:1, which is a simple NOTICE, the remaining material in vv. 2-17a belongs to the genre of LEGEND. See below for detailed discussion.

Setting

We must look to the work and times of the exilic Dtr historian for the most important setting of this composition. Even though the notice of Moab's rebellion (v. 1) may have been drawn from some sort of chronistic record (Gray, *Kings,* 459; but cf. Montgomery, *Kings,* 438) and the legend of Ahaziah's death (vv. 2-17a) from popular tradition, the literary setting in the books of Kings remains the crucial consideration.

Several features in the composition are worth noting. First, the brief remark about Moab's rebellion in v. 1 is repeated in 3:5 (the situation so simply stated receives a full literary realization in 3:6-27). Such motival repetition is better seen here as a technique of synchronous narration than as an instance of clumsy editing (see B. O. Long, "Framing Repetitions in Biblical Historiography," *JBL* 106 [1987] 385-99). A writer breaks off one sequence of action (Moab in rebellion) while opening a second; then, with repetition of the first action (3:5), forward motion in the "primary" story resumes. In this way, the Dtr writer provides a distinctive setting for the final deed of Elijah's career (1:2-17a) and the designation of his successor (ch. 2): they stand forth against the canvas of Moab's concurrent rebellion. Moreover, Moab's revolt will prove to be only the first in a series of challenges to Israel's and Judah's imperial claims (3:5-27; 5:1; 6:24; 8:20-22; 10:32-33; 12:17-18). When the kings' orderly succession is under threat, continuity in prophetism nonetheless persists.

Second, a geographical ordering of material extends the reader's vision beyond the strict limits of Ahaziah's reign. Action begins in Samaria (1:2), moves to a mountain nearby (1:9), and thence continues down to the valley of the Jordan (2:6-14). At the close, Elisha, now fully empowered by his master's spirit (2:14, 15), returns to the mountain (Carmel) and finally to Samaria (2:25). Although the symmetry of movement is less than perfect (against Lundbom), and the episodes along the way not clearly "balanced" in theme (against Hobbs), one nonetheless is drawn into a closed loop of travel conveyed in a spatial image: "going down" and "going up" *(yrd* and *'lh)*. Elijah "went down" to King Ahaziah (1:15), "down" to Bethel (2:2), thence to the environs of Jericho, from which he "went up" and returned to Samaria (2:23). Note, too, that fire "came down" while Elijah refused to "go down" to Ahaziah. Eventually, amidst a "fiery" vision, Elijah will "go up" from Elisha and the other prophets (2:11).

These wider literary connections lead the reader to draw analogies among distinct parts of the larger Dtr history. It does not seem accidental that most of these links are forged with traditions that fill a pausal moment, ch. 2, between the reigns of two kings. Elsewhere such lapses in the forward chronological movement of reign-by-reign sequence are occasions for the Dtr historian to lift up material of particular thematic importance to the whole work (see 1 Kgs 2:12b-46; 12:1-20; 2 Kgs 13:14-25; 17:7-41; and Long, *1 Kings,* 26-28).

Intention

From this sense of setting, one may perceive nuance of purpose. Clearly, the writer means this unit to epitomize the reign of Ahaziah. In brief, the events illustrate and justify the initial appraisal of his rule (1 Kgs 22:52-54 [*RSV* 51-53]), and thus contribute to the ongoing recital of failure among the northern kings. At the same time, the towering presence of Elijah in Ahaziah's reign seems clearly related to, if not preparatory for, his role in ch. 2, a moment between this reign and the next. In the latter, Elijah will be taken from his companions — and removed from the historian's story. Yet his greatness, his power in double measure, still courses among lesser mortals through Elisha, whose person and deeds recall the master as no one else does (see Hobbs, 333). The reign of Ahaziah, then, prepares the way for our accepting Elisha into this ongoing recital of apostasy in Israel. The image of fire expresses prophetic continuity: a mighty conjurer of consuming flame from above leaves his spirit to a successor-prophet in a vision of fiery chariots. If transgression begets its generations of apostasy, so too, prophecy spawns successors who guard exclusive devotion to Yahweh. At least this center holds against ongoing threats to the kingdom.

Bibliography

T. R. Hobbs, "2 Kings 1 and 2: Their Unity and Purpose," *Studies in Religion/Sciences Religieuses* 13 (1984) 327-34; J. Lundbom, "Elijah's Chariot Ride," *JJS* 24 (1973) 39-50.

AHAZIAH'S DEATH (IN CONFRONTATION WITH ELIJAH)
1:2-17a

Structure

I. Setting (Ahaziah's initiative toward Baal)	2
A. Ahaziah's sickness	2a
B. Commission to messengers *(mal'ākîm)*	2b
1. Messengers sent	2bα
2. Instructions: inquire of Baal	2bβ
II. Prophecy for Ahaziah (Yahweh's initiative toward Ahaziah)	3-8
A. Commissioning of Elijah	3-4
1. Narrative introduction *(mal'āk)*	3aα
2. Instructions	3aβ-4bα
a. Concerning the mission	3aβ
b. Message: prophecy of punishment for Ahaziah	3b-4bα
1) Accusatory question (reason for punishment)	3b
2) Announcement of punishment	4a-bα
3. Narrative conclusion: commission taken up	4bβ
B. Consequence of Elijah's actions: prophecy received	5-8
1. Messengers' *(mal'ākîm)* report to Ahaziah	5-6
a. Narrative introduction	5
b. Commissioning by a man of God	6
1) Description of circumstances	6aα
2) Commission	6aβ-b
a) Concerning the mission	6aβ
b) Message: prophecy of punishment for Ahaziah	6b
(1) Messenger formula	6bα[1]
(2) Accusatory question: reason for punishment	6bα[2]
(3) Announcement of punishment	6bβ
2. Ahaziah's reactions to prophecy	7-8
a. King's query: who is the prophet?	7
b. Answer: description of man of God	8a
c. King's declaration of recognition	8b
III. The missions of fifty (Ahaziah's initiative toward Elijah)	9-14
A. First mission	9-10
1. Dispatch of men to Elijah	9a
2. Relaying of king's orders	9b

Scholars dispute the original unity of this piece, but not its outer bounds. Many have argued essentially that vv. 9-16, which seem digressive and excessively repetitious, are a later expansion of an earlier tradition about Elijah's prophecy against Ahaziah (vv. 2-8, 17a; e.g., Gunkel, *Elias,* 30; A. Schmitt, *Gottesbescheid,* 59-60; Steck, "Erzählung," 546-56; Fohrer, *Elia,* 42-43; Koch, 183-88; Gray, *Kings,* 461; Würthwein, *Könige,* 267). Other critics, fewer in number, consider the reasons given for disunity as spurious and thus defend the literary integrity of the unit on stylistic and structural grounds (e.g., Montgomery, *Kings,* 348; Šanda, *Könige* II, 7; Rofé, *Prophetical Stories,* 33-37; De Vries, 61-63). Evidently, stylistic and source-critical arguments have not proven decisive in settling the dispute. Largely overlooked until very recently have been structural and rhetorical patterns which suggest unity — if not in some original version, then surely in the redacted text before us (e.g., Begg; Licht, 55-59;

Hobbs, *2 Kings*, 4: "the first story embraces the second and places it in a new context"). In view of the impasse in these matters, it seems the more productive course to analyze the received form of the text.

The main plot may be stated very simply. A crisis — the king is ill — raises the question of recovery. When the matter is referred to the oracles of Baal-zebub, Yahweh intervenes and announces the impending death of the king. This same God stands behind the oracle's fulfillment, as the narrator notes that Ahaziah died "according to the word of the Lord" (v. 17). At this level of abstraction the account seems roughly congruent with a common narrative sequence: a crisis, an oracle in response to inquiry or divination, and its fulfillment which resolves the crisis (cf. 2 Kgs 8:7-15; 1 Kgs 14:1-18; 22:1-38; 2 Kgs 3:4-27; Long, 342-45; cf. Culley, 169-77, who compares this story with others on the basis of a simplified action sequence: wrong action, punishment announced, and punishment realized).

Yet this sense of linear plot hardly conveys the complexity of the actual narrative in 2 Kings 1. The path to fulfillment is marked by puzzling repetitions, ellipses, and unclear motivations. For example, Yahweh's oracle against the king is repeated three times (vv. 3-4, 6, 16); and why does the writer describe the mission of the fifty three times with little change or movement in narrative development? Is there literary point to the ellipsis between vv. 4 and 5 which requires the assumption that Elijah's commission of vv. 3-4 has been carried out? Moreover, various motivations are ambiguous. The writer gives no reason for Ahaziah's throwing more and more men into fiery confrontation with Yahweh's prophet (vv. 9-14); nor do we know why the messenger of Yahweh suddenly sends Elijah to the king after these incidents occur. In short, we may state the plot in general terms, but the details of the narrative resist easy integration into it.

The key to understanding the structural coherence of this unit lies not so much in the narrated action as in several related patterns of repetition. It is plainly unsatisfactory to rest one's inquiry on the commonplace claim that patterns of three were favorites of popular storytellers. Even if that were true, one must go on to examine the literary effects of such repetition. In this particular narrative, the author-narrator manipulates various literary possibilities to suggest aspects of Elijah's character while portraying a struggle between opposing powers: God, whose authority flows through the divine messenger, or "angel" *(mal'āk)*, and King Ahaziah, whose power extends to others through military "messengers" *(mal'ākîm)*. By exploiting the double meaning of *mal'āk* and developing the confrontation, the author dramatizes Elijah's (God's) unquestionably superior and dangerous power, and connects it with the prophet's (God's) oracle (see Begg; Licht; Vater, 376-77). Also, repeated motival and thematic tethers recall another time in Samaria (1 Kings 17–19) and anticipate the moment of succession in prophetical leadership (2 Kings 2). The story evokes repetition-memory of Elijah's confrontations on Mount Carmel, and, in images of heavenly fire, boils and concentrates Elijah's mysterious powers, as though drawing off sufficient volatile essence to ignite fervor in his successor (cf. 1:11-14 and 2:11).

A first significant structure emerges in the thrust and parry of dramatic initiative. The main characters are three: Elijah, King Ahaziah, and — offstage — Yahweh, God of Israel. One Hebrew word, *mal'āk*, translated variously as "angel" (of Yahweh) and "messenger" (of the king), weaves the action into cloth. The king reaches out first to inquire of Baal-zebub through royal "messengers" (*mal'ākîm;* I, v. 2). Abruptly, Yahweh responds. He sends a divine messenger (*mal'āk,* "angel") whose charge turns Elijah into an obstacle to the king's inquiry. Even Ahaziah's own emissaries (*mal'ākîm,* v. 5) subvert their mission and bring back, in effect, an oracle from Yahweh, not Baal-zebub (II, vv. 3-8).

Suddenly, dramatic energy flows in the opposite direction. The king now pursues Elijah, repeatedly sending royal militiamen to summon the prophet from his place on a hill in Samaria (III, vv. 9-14). The military officers act and speak precisely as royal emissaries, i.e., as *mal'ākîm* without the title (cf. vv. 9b, 11b with 2 Kgs 18:19, 29; Gen 32:4). Their mission finally succeeds — but hardly by any power of their own — and the initiative shifts once again. Yahweh faces Ahaziah as before in a doubly staged confrontation. He sends a messenger (*mal'āk,* "angel") to Elijah with the command to comply with the king's stubborn, relentless demands to "come down" and, we must presume, he sends another prophecy, a repetition of the first one. But this time, as things turn out, the word is delivered directly to Ahaziah by Elijah (IV, vv. 15-16). The meeting is nearly unmediated confrontation, as though Yahweh himself at last stands face-to-face with this earthly ruler. Dénouement follows quickly: Ahaziah dies, as prophesied (V, v. 17a). The narrator shows no interest in the circumstances or physical causes.

These alternating initiatives seem calculated to convey ironic perspective on events. The king means to solicit the power of foreknowledge from the god of Ekron, and when thwarted in his efforts, he fixes on Elijah. However, since Elijah really is a kind of *mal'āk* for Yahweh, King Ahaziah repeatedly summons Yahweh, the God of Israel, while obsessively calling down Elijah the Tishbite. For his part, Yahweh seems determined to confront Ahaziah. In the end the king meets this God, or rather his oracle-bearing emissary, having set out to inquire only of Baal-zebub.

This irony sharpens the unexpectedly disruptive quality of Yahweh's intervention. Just as Elijah earlier emerges from the penumbra of obscurity as little more than a name, a vague paternity, and a suggestion of troublesome movement at the behest of private voices (see esp. 1 Kgs 17:1), so Yahweh bursts onto stage without warning. Indeed, the writer seems to have manipulated a biblical *topos,* or folkloristic "type scene," to heighten this implicit comparison. Other occasions on which a prophet inquires of the deity establish for us the schematic model: a crisis, a representation to the deity to "inquire" (*dāraš*) about its outcome, followed by the results. Usually events follow a script which is presaged in an oracle (e.g., 2 Kgs 8:7-15; 22:18-38; see 1 Kgs 14:1-18 in Long, *1 Kings,* 153-57, for fuller discussion of the literary pattern). Contrary to this convention, but perhaps according to another narrative template wherein transgression must be punished (see Culley), the inquiry launched by Ahaziah never reaches its target, and the god of Ekron never delivers an oracle. Yahweh suddenly intervenes and supplants the message sought from Baal-zebub; it is Yahweh's prophet who presides from his remoteness, calls down consuming fire, and at last unburdens himself of an oracle that Ahaziah most likely would prefer not to hear.

The controlling initiative obviously belongs to Yahweh. Most assuredly there is a God in Israel. (The rhetorical questions in vv. 3, 6, and 16 surround and penetrate those events which supply the answer. Between narrative characters the questions accuse and find fault, but to a reader they sharpen an ideological claim embedded in the act of narration.) One sees the tracings of God in Elijah's (or God's) sudden, imperious assault upon a king who has sought other powers. And Yahweh's triumph is the grander for Ahaziah's foolishness.

A second important structural feature is the twice-triple repetition of two motifs, the prophecy and the mission of the fifty (see the outline, II + IV and III, vv. 4, 6 + 16 and 9-14). The narrator repeats these nearly verbatim, but in a broken series which produces a sort of limping chiasmus. We may visualize the pattern as follows (cf. Licht, 56-57):

> Introductory exposition (king's sickness) [v. 2]
>> Prophecy (spoken by *mal'āk*) [v. 4]
>> Prophecy (spoken by *mal'ākîm*) [v. 6]
>>> Mission of the fifty
>>> Mission of the fifty [vv. 9-14]
>>> Mission of the fifty
>> Prophecy (spoken by Elijah) [v. 16]
> Conclusion (king's death) [v. 17]

Seen as a structure of repetition, this narrative lacks many of the elements which lend action and drama to more fully realized narration. Repeated elements in an AA/BBB/A pattern, set within the conventional motif of someone's illness leading to death, give the illusion of time passing without much forward movement. This sense of stasis contrasts with the energy of insistent intervention, disruption, and voracious fire conjured from heaven. In short, stasis-in-repetition contrasts with the struggle for allegiance between personages in the story.

One effect of this repetition is that words and perceptions of others, including the word of God, mediate the character of Elijah in the story. First, consider the prophetic oracle. Its first instance occurs in familiar narrative dress: the narrator reports the commission to deliver a prophecy, which is quoted, and then its delivery (see Vater, 376-78). However, the royal messengers convey the word, and thus assume the role of prophet (or Elijah's messengers) before the king. Not once falling from Elijah's lips, the double utterance is a kind of surrogate prophet, indeed the only information Ahaziah has at the moment. But it is enough, as the king concludes, without direct sight, "It is Elijah, the Tishbite" (vv. 7-8). In short, Elijah recedes behind his own oracle.

Something similar holds for the final repetition of prophecy in v. 16. The structures that have indirectly mediated character drop away. Elijah moves on command of the angel (v. 15), confronts King Ahaziah directly, and delivers the oracle of death. Yet, as before, attention falls to God's word itself, with the added image of abject surrender to its insistent urging. Elijah is present as repeated oracular speech — direct address, accusatory, judging — as though he were some sort of ocular and aural sign, a visible oracle for the royal messengers, King Ahaziah, and perhaps the reader as well.

The thrice-repeated mission of the captain and his fifty men, vv. 9-14, also contributes to the characterization of Elijah. Like a grim experiment, events repeat with slight but significant variations. The first captain addresses Elijah, "O man of God, the king says, 'Come down'" (v. 9). The second mission leader, who sounds slightly more officious, perhaps impatient, puts the command with urgent formality: "O man of God, thus says the king, 'Immediately come down'" (v. 11b). Then in a complete reversal of style and tone, a third officer solicits mercy with grandly adulatory and courtly petition (vv. 13b-14). In fact, his twice-repeated plea, "let my life be precious in your sight," wraps itself around allusion to the disastrous fate of his predecessors. The captain forgets about the king's order, and indeed seems to abandon the whole mission. He seeks only life for himself and his charges, and he masks his surrender in elevated speech.

These changes in the midst of repetition convey shifts in attitudes, from imperious control to surrender in the face of Elijah's overwhelming power. Earlier the king's messengers who have been sent to inquire of Baal-zebub turn about and become in effect the bearers of Elijah's (Yahweh's) word (vv. 2b, 5-6). Here, the king stubbornly seeks to counter Elijah's strange authority with his own. The king fails at this when the last of the royal emissaries abandons his mission (vv. 13-14; see Begg, 78-79). Even the descriptive remark that Elijah is "sitting on the top of a hill" (v. 9) contributes a visual correlate to the prophet's unassailable position: the militiamen must "go up" (ʿālâ, vv. 9, 11, 13), and Elijah can only "go down" (yārad, v. 15) to meet this temporal, and lesser, royal authority. The prophet's attention is not to be imperially commanded, but deferentially courted. And Yahweh's designs are not blocked by controlling his prophet.

Indeed, through this repeated military mission, one realizes that Elijah embodies supraordinary power. He is a bundle of harsh, unyielding responses — a conduit for heaven's oracles or fire-on-demand. If Elijah's person is hidden in oracle (vv. 3-4, 6; also v. 16), it is no less recessive in this picture of preternatural force repeatedly unleashed upon those who carelessly approach. (For other images of God's consuming, punishing fire, cf. Num 11:1-3; 16:28-33; Deut 4:24; 9:3.)

Thus the pattern of twice-triple repetition intimates the prophet's essential character. At the same time, repeated alternation of dramatic initiative, while lending structure to the action, offers ironic perspective on events. King Ahaziah seeks Baal-zebub, but when diverted, his determined pursuit of Elijah yields — as if by conjury — Yahweh's awesome power in fiery word instead. Like that great contest on Mount Carmel (1 Kgs 18:20-40), the struggle still seems at bottom to be between Yahweh, God of Israel, and Baal, god of Canaan, or between their earthly stand-ins, Elijah and a misguided king. In the reader's experience this ideological combat takes body from these patterns of repetition, and with significant alteration to convention lies sprawled across the narrative path that leads, typically, from divine oracle to actualization, to that moment when King Ahaziah dies (v. 17a).

Genre

This unit is clearly LEGEND, a narrative concerned primarily with the wondrous, miraculous, and exemplary (so Koch, 186, but only for a presumed original vv. 2-8, 17a; Rofé, *Prophetical Stories,* 34-40, "epigonic legenda"; Lundbom, 40-41, and Fohrer, *Elia,* 42-43, seem to agree substantially). Attempts to be more precise have not proved notably more advantageous. Steck favors "didactic story," but only for the presumed more original vv. 2-8, 17a; De Vries (p. 55) studies the whole as a subgenre of legend, "supplicatory power story," but mistakenly denies the story's ambiguities in the search for a precise, and narrow, functional definition.

Many of the building blocks for this legend are conventional literary forms. The typical ORACULAR INQUIRY shapes in part a reader's expectations and leaves its imprint in some of the narrative's features (see 2 Kgs 8:7-15; 1 Kgs 14:1-8). Note also the report of the prophet's COMMISSION (vv. 3-4; cf. Isa 22:15-25 and full discussion at 1 Kgs 12:22-24 in Long, *1 Kings,* 138-40; note how Elijah's commission is attenuated in v. 15). V. 2 records a similar commissioning of messengers. Not surprisingly, the king's emissaries (vv. 9-12) and Elijah, emissary of Yahweh, all preface their words with the usual MESSENGER FORMULA (vv. 9, 11, 16). The third captain of fifty, however, utters a PETITION, vv. 13-14 (see discussion at 1 Kgs 3:14-15 in Long, *1 Kings,* 62-67). Of special note is the artful form of this petition. Identical petitionary phrases ("let my life be precious in your sight") frame a citation of earlier precedent (v. 14a) which justifies the petition. The speech is courtly, formal, rounded, and conveys in grandiose style the earnest turnabout which characterizes the third mission to Elijah. The oracle given in commission, reported to the king, but only once put in Elijah's mouth, is a typical PROPHECY OF PUNISHMENT (vv. 3b, 6b, 16). This example begins with a reproachful question, really an accusation in rhetorical form (but cf. v. 16), which then leads into the announcement of punishment. See Isa 22:16-18; Jer 22:13-19; 1 Kgs 21:19; cf. an oracle from Mari (ARM xiii, 23; *ANET,* 625). For full discussion see Long (*1 Kings,* 143-52) concerning 1 Kgs 13:21-22. The legend concludes with a simple report of ORACLE FULFILLMENT, v. 17a (see 1 Kgs 16:34; 17:16).

Setting

One may reasonably assume that in oral tradition legends would have originated with the folk and been preserved in many different societal settings. Scholars have often suggested that legends about prophets belonged especially among groups of prophets (e.g., De Vries). Perhaps this particular example stems from disciples of Elijah, even the "sons of prophets" (so, e.g., Koch, 186, but only thinking of a presumed original version; see Fricke, *2 Könige,* 17). However, there is little reason to so restrict the popularity and social function of such narratives. In any case, reliable evidence for these conjectures is unavailable.

Consequently, the literary setting of this biblical legend should be our most important consideration. Clearly this example stands at the center of the Dtr writer's coverage of Ahaziah's two-year reign. Aside from the brief notice about Moab's rebellion, v. 1, this narrative is the only incident reported for the reign. Curiously, the writer recounts not how the king ruled but how he died! Owing to the literary patterns which suggestively recall aspects of other Elijah traditions, and perhaps turn our sights forward to the prophet's disappearance in ch. 2, we must view this incident in Ahaziah's reign as solidly embedded in a larger view of Elijah which transcends somewhat the structure of regnal epochs in the books of Kings. It is a speculative and largely moot point whether the legend was originally transmitted in some independent collection of prophetic narratives (see Hentschel).

Intention

In oral tradition those who created and retold legends would have held various but usually religious intentions according to occasion and circumstances of narration. From what has just been said, the question of intention should be raised primarily as authorial purpose now implied in the final shape of the Dtr history. First, the writer seeks to characterize Ahaziah's reign as disastrous — publicly (Moab rebels) and privately (the king pays for apostasy with his life). There may even be a bit of ironic wordplay in the presentation. The reference to Baal-zebub ("Baal of the Flies"), if not an allusion to Baal-zebul (Ugaritic *zbl b'l ars*, "Prince, Baal of the earth") and related instead to Ugaritic *dbb*, "flame" (Fensham), might suggest that Ahaziah seeks out a kind of Canaanite firepower only to provoke Elijah's (Yahweh's) consuming fire from heaven. In any case, Ahaziah's very short rule seems a kind of divine punishment. At the very least it illustrates the negative evaluation given him in the introductory summary, 1 Kgs 22:52-54 (*RSV* 51-53). The DtrH viewed the situation as entirely typical of those kings who went the way of Jeroboam and in this case, it is singularly noted, the path of Ahab and Jezebel (1 Kgs 22:53 [*RSV* 52]: "the way of his father and in the way of his mother").

The allusion to these archetypes of Israelite apostasy suggests that the personal fate of Ahaziah be seen as part of the persistent struggle between Yahweh and Baal for religious allegiance in the northern kingdom. Ahaziah's fate is also symptomatic of the sickness at the heart of Israel, a sickness which will lead in time to national death (see 2 Kings 17). It is not accidental, then, that the situation narrated here recalls Elijah's meeting with Ahab. By analogy, what was true of Ahab (and Jezebel) was true of Ahaziah. One must assume that this king sees a challenge to himself in Elijah's prophecy of punishment, and so pursues the messenger, as with Ahab before him (1 Kings 18). And like Ahab, Ahaziah dies in opposition to Yahweh and Yahweh's prophet (see 1 Kgs 22:1-38). In this regard, Elijah's (Yahweh's) accusatory question, "Is it because there is no god in Israel?" forms a kind of leitmotif of intent: the king's apostasy and the struggle between the gods epitomize Ahab as well as his son Ahaziah, and encapsulate the address from writer to reader which occurs in the act of reading. There is a god in Israel, and this poses sharply the question of loyalty

— for Ahab as for Ahaziah — or whether there can be a people of Yahweh in the midst of Israel (see Hobbs, *2 Kings,* 12-13).

This legend also adds to the picture of Elijah given in preceding materials (1 Kings 17–19; 21). There, he is characterized as the archetypal meddler, the triumphal intervenor who rears up suddenly with a word or a miracle. We now know him as the mysterious prophet who is given definition in a divine oracle or in a flaming manifestation of supernatural power. Prophetical person and authority seem too awesome to capture; instead, the legend approaches the nexus of numinal power in repeated oracles (vv. 3, 6, 16), twice-done deadly conjury (vv. 9-12), and the courtly deference of a militiaman who cannot prevail against Elijah (vv. 13-14).

While reporting the end of Ahaziah, the narrative also weaves a legend of irresistible prophetic power, in its own way more startling than anything Elijah has done heretofore. (Cf. his challenge for Yahweh to send fire down onto Mount Carmel, 1 Kgs 18:30-38.) This power, symbolized in fire and suggesting something capricious if not personally vainglorious, also foreshadows a prophetic succession yet to be told. It will be Elisha, to this point just barely known by the reader (1 Kgs 19:19-21), who will ask for a double portion of Elijah's spirit, and who will receive it amid the fire of visionary chariots and horses (2:11).

Bibliography

C. Begg, "Unifying Factors in 2 Kings 1:2-17a," *JSOT* 32 (1985) 75-86; R. Culley, "Punishment Stories in the Legends of the Prophets," in *Orientation by Disorientation: Studies in Literary Criticism and Biblical Literary Criticism (Fest.* W. A. Beardslee; ed. R. A. Spencer; PTMS 35; Pittsburgh: Pickwick, 1980) 167-81; S. De Vries, *Prophet Against Prophet* (Grand Rapids: Eerdmans, 1978); F. Fensham, "A Possible Explanation of the Name Baal-Zebub of Ekron," *ZAW* 79 (1967) 361-64; G. Fohrer, *Elia* (ATANT 53; 2nd ed.; Zürich: Zwingli, 1968); H. Gunkel, *Elias, Jahve und Baal* (Religionsgeschichtliche Volksbücher II/8; Tübingen: Mohr, 1906); G. Hentschel, *Die Elijaerzählungen* (ErfTS 33; Leipzig: St. Benno, 1977); K. Koch, *The Growth of the Biblical Tradition* (tr. S. M. Cupitt; New York: Scribner's, 1969) 183-95; J. Licht, *Storytelling in the Bible* (Jerusalem: Magnes, 1978) 55-59; B. O. Long, "2 Kings iii and Genres of Prophetic Narrative," *VT* 23 (1973) 337-48; J. Lundbom, "Elijah's Chariot Ride," *JJS* 24 (1973) 39-50; A. Rofé, "Baal, the Prophet and the Angel (2 Kings 1): A Study in the History of Literature and Religion," *Beersheva* 1 (1973) 221-30 (Hebr. with Eng. summary); idem, *The Prophetical Stories* (Jerusalem: Magnes, 1988 [tr. of 1986 Hebr. ed.]); A. Schmitt, *Prophetischer Gottesbescheid in Mari und Israel* (BWANT 114; Stuttgart: Kohlhammer, 1982) 59-64; O. H. Steck, "Die Erzählung von Jahwes Einschreiten gegen die Orakelbefragung Ahasjas," *EvT* 27 (1967) 546-56; A. Vater, "Narrative Patterns for the Story of Commissioned Communication in the Old Testament," *JBL* 99 (1980) 363-82.

BETWEEN THE REIGNS: ELISHA SUCCEEDS ELIJAH, 2:1-25

Structure

Regnal summaries completely enclose and distinguish this unit from the reigns of Ahaziah and his brother Jehoram (1:17b-18; 3:1-3). Seen in relation to the whole book of Kings, the material fills a "pausal moment" between the sequentially rehearsed reigns. At this point, the Dtr writer introduces material of thematic importance to the entire Dtr history. (For fuller discussion, see Long, *1 Kings,* 26-28; cf. 1 Kgs 2:12b-46; 2 Kgs 17:7-41.)

This unit stands at the head of what may have originally been one or more cycles of Elisha traditions (H.-Chr. Schmitt), or even part of a pre-Dtr "prophetic record" still visible in 1 Sam 1:2–2 Kgs 10:28 (A. Campbell, *Of Prophets and Kings. A Late Ninth Century Document* [CBOMS 17; Washington: Catholic Biblical Association, 1986]). Now intertwined with accounts of various royal affairs in 2 Kings 3–13, the prophetic career of Elisha lives in material of diverse character, genre, and age — including brief legends of the prophet's miracles (e.g., 2 Kgs 2:19-22, 23-25; 4:1-7, 38-45), and more artistically developed but hardly less legendary narratives (2 Kgs 3:4-27; 4:8-37; 5:1-27; see fuller discussion at the reign of Jehoram, 2 Kings 3–9).

Given the obscure origins and history of this prophetical tradition, we can only discern with reasonable assurance something of the logic behind its final arrangement in the Dtr history. Having been introduced in 1 Kgs 19:19-21 and then pushed far from sight, Elisha now emerges as a full character between the reigns of Ahaziah and Jehoram. He participates variously in events during the years of Jehoram, Jehu, Jehoahaz, and Jehoash. In 2 Kgs 13:14-21, another pausal moment between regnal periods, the Dtr author reports Elisha's death and a miracle attributed to his bones. The latter tradition and 2 Kings 2 form a kind of enclosure around four regnal periods, reputedly 73 years, while marking, like a superstructure over the times of these kings, the beginning and end of Elisha's work as an independent prophet in the north.

Many scholars have held that originally independent traditions still visible in 2:1-15 (perhaps vv. 16-18), 19-22, and 23-24 were knit together over time by one or more redactors. Some critics pursue detailed reconstructions of the forms of tradition that lie behind the present text (e.g., Reiser, 328-31; H.-Chr. Schmitt); others are skeptical, or emphasize its present unity (e.g., Carlson).

One must admit to literary tensions in the account. Vv. 16-18 do not join very smoothly to the preceding material, while vv. 19-22 and 23-24 seem essentially unrelated to each other and to vv. 1-15 (but cf. Carlson).

Nevertheless, there may be in the explicit geographical markers a sign of deliberate, or at any rate resultant, unity (Foresti; Lundbom; cf. Hobbs, *2 Kings,* 17-18). If one plots the places actually named in the narratives, an organized pattern emerges:

A From Gilgal to Bethel (2:1b-2)
  B Bethel (2:3-4)
    C Jericho (2:5-6)
      D Jordan River (2:7-8a)
        E Crossing (2:8b)
          F Transjordan (2:9-14a)
        E' Crossing (2:14b)
      D' From the Jordan to Jericho (2:15-17)
    C' Jericho (2:18-22)
  B' Bethel (2:23-24)
A' _ _ _ _ _ _ _ _ _ _ _ _ _

The chiastic structure is not perfect, of course. Elisha does not return through Gilgal, and he continues beyond Bethel to Carmel and Samaria (v. 25). The latter note may reflect an editor's attempt to bring Elisha (and the reader) full circle to the entry point of ch. 1, where Elijah is shown active in and about Samaria, presumably on Mount Carmel (1:9). Alternatively, v. 25 may simply make a catchword transition to 3:1 where the next regnal summary mentions Samaria.

Foresti regards Gilgal as a cultic site near Carmel, and so saves in religious connotation the imperfect geographical chiasmus: Elijah goes out from holy ground (Gilgal) and Elisha returns to that same holy ground, retracing his mentor's steps (Carmel). Lundbom (pp. 41-42) extends the limits of the chiasmus backwards to 1:2-16, but the geographical references in ch. 1 are noticeably vague by comparison and much less important in bringing coherence to the narrative elements. (Hobbs, *2 Kings,* 18, also observes a literary retracing of Elijah in his successor through loose motival associations of 1:1-8, 16-17 with 2:19-22 and 1:9-15 with 2:23-24.)

These attempts to find structural links between chs. 1 and 2 are not very successful. One is left with ch. 2, a self-contained pause between the reigns, with a strongly delineated sense of ordered journey. The result is more affective than informational. Small events repeated stage by stage build suspense on the way toward the climactic moment when Elijah leaves the earth. The translation to heaven is clearly set apart. Not only does the writer-narrator anticipate the main idea with a thematic statement (v. 1a), but he also frames the moment with identical images: miraculous crossings of the river Jordan (vv. 8b and 14b) and "sons of prophets" who look on from afar (vv. 7, 15a). Following Elijah's departure into the heavens, narrative movement resumes, but with considerably less dramatic effect and structural integrity (see detailed analysis below). Only a circumstantial clause, a passing comment, signals after the fact Elisha's movement back to Jericho where he awaits the search party (v. 18); the itinerary notes in vv. 23, 25, in contrast to those in vv. 2, 4, 6, 9, 14, seem to be superficial connectors between independent reports of miracles.

It is clear from the way in which geographical notations mark the central dramatic moment that they serve mainly to focus and unify narrative content. Having learned of the impending translation of Elijah, one watches the progression — all in one day — to that moment when the crack between eternity and temporality opens to Elisha's visionary sight (the vocabulary and style at vv. 10-12a suggest the conventions of vision reports, as in Judg 13:19-21; 2 Kgs 6:17; Tob 12:15-21). Having been privy to the private conversations between master and follower, the reader is aware that Elisha has inherited Elijah's "spirit." His actions demonstrate the gift (v. 14), and later events confirm its presence for those onlookers who are then transformed from fellow travelers and distant observers to "servants" of Elisha (vv. 7, 15). The succession of prophetic authority is sure (cf. Num 27:18-23). The mysterious prophetic power, for good (II.A, vv. 19-22) or ill (II.B, vv. 23-24), is now manifest in concrete deeds (though perhaps not so precisely identifiable as Carlson, 404-5, argues).

Genre

Since this unit is very likely an editorial composition, we may not specify a genre with great precision. ITINERARY, a formal structure given to accounts which relate movement by stages, seems to have provided something of a literary skeleton upon which independent traditions have been hung (cf. Exod 17:1–18:27; 1 Kgs 19:1-18). The concluding v. 25 is best called an ITINERARY NOTICE. Within the whole, one may note at least three examples of LEGEND (vv. 1-18, 19-22, 23-24). See the full discussion below.

Setting

This unit has probably resulted from editorial or authorial design; therefore, we must consider its setting in the work of the DtrH, who compiled a history of the monarchy for his early exilic audience. This particular series of incidents is arranged in a digression between the reigns of Ahaziah and Jehoram. By analogy the material relates to both reigns, to the preceding Elijah traditions in 1 Kings, and to the Moses-Joshua saga before that. At the same time, the unit opens onto later events in which Elisha is to play sometimes dominant, sometimes minor, roles (see fuller discussion below).

21

Intention

By assembling these traditions into a pausal moment between the reigns, the DtrH meant to account for the departure of Elijah from his history. Like Moses (Deut 34:6b), who was also seen by some tradents as a "prophet" (*nābî*, Deut 34:10), Elijah leaves earth and story without a trace. And as with Moses, a legacy remains in the person of a successor. Elisha takes up the mantle of leadership as Elijah departs. Elisha demonstrates his new power and position, as did Moses' successor Joshua, in visionary sight (v. 12; cf. Josh 5:13-15), miracle (v. 14; cf. Josh 3:11-17), and reality-creating speech (vv. 19-22, 23, 24; cf. 1 Kgs 16:34; Hobbs, *2 Kings,* 19; Gray, *Kings,* 475; Montgomery, *Kings,* 354). The literary pattern is deeply rooted in folkloristic thinking and customs of *rites de passage:* the (successor) man of God withdraws, gains sacred power, and returns to his former society to work wondrous deeds (cf. 1 Kgs 17:17-24; Luke 4:1-15; and analysis at 2 Kgs 2:1-18 below).

This pausal moment thus captures a momentous change in religious leadership. Just as Elijah represented for the DtrH an authentic voice for Yahwism in the apostasy-prone Omride northern kingdom, so Elisha will be a similarly presented prophetic power in the waning years of that same dynasty (2 Kgs 3:1–10:17). Moreover, as the transition from Moses to Joshua assured continuity in Yahweh's guidance, so Elijah-Elisha, analogously portrayed, are steady voices for Jerusalemite Yahwism in a kingdom laboring under the shadow of Jeroboam and the successor Omrides. Elisha himself will bring this phase in the history to an end by inspiring Jehu's conspiracy against the Omride house (2 Kgs 9:1-3; 10:28).

Bibliography

K. Baltzer, *Die Biographie der Propheten* (Neukirchen: Neukirchener, 1975) 99-105; L. Bronner, *The Stories of Elijah and Elisha as Polemics against Baal Worship* (POS 6; Leiden: Brill, 1968); R. Carlson, "Élisée — Le Successeur D'Élie," *VT* 20 (1970) 385-405; G. Fohrer, *Prophetenerzählungen* (Die Propheten des Alten Testaments 7; Gütersloh: Gütersloher, 1977) 80-108; F. Foresti, "Il rapimento di Elia al cielo," *RivB* 31 (1983) 257-72; E. Frerichs, "Elisha: A Problem in Legend and History" (Diss., Boston, 1957); H. Gunkel, *Geschichten von Elisa* (Meisterwerke hebräischer Erzählungskunst I; Berlin: Curtius, 1925); J. Lundbom, "Elijah's Chariot Ride" (→ 1 Kgs 22:52–2 Kgs 1:18, Canonical Framework); J. Miller, "The Elisha Cycle and the Accounts of the Omride Wars," *JBL* 85 (1966) 441-54; W. Reiser, "Eschatologische Gottessprüche in den Elisa-Legenden," *TZ* 9 (1953) 321-38; G. Rösch, "Elias. Eine Studie," *ThStK* 65 (1892) 551-72; H.-Chr. Schmitt, *Elisa. Traditionsgeschichtliche Untersuchungen zur vorklassischen nordisraelitischen Prophetie* (Gütersloh: Gütersloher, 1972); H. Stipp, "Elischa — Propheten — Gottesmänner; die Kompositionsgeschichte des Elischazyklus und verwandter Texte, rekonstruiert auf der Basis von Text- und Literarkritik zu 1 Kön 20.22 und 2 Kön 2–7" (Diss., Tübingen, 1984).

THE ASCENSION OF ELIJAH AND THE EMPOWERING OF ELISHA, 2:1-18

Structure

The beginning of this unit clearly stands apart from the concluding regnal summaries in 1:17b-18; its ending is somewhat more problematical. Persistent voices have argued against the originality of vv. 16-18 (e.g., Gunkel, *Elisa,* 32; Galling, 141-42; Haag; A. Schmitt, 56-71; Spronk [who also takes vv. 2-6 as secondary]; Würthwein, *Könige,* 274; H.-Chr. Schmitt, 105, posits vv. 16-18 as part of a hypothetical reconstruction of stages in the history of redaction). The request to confirm Elijah's disappearance (v. 15) seems odd, so the reasoning goes, in view of vv. 3, 5 and the admission made in v. 15. Other scholars disagree, or assume the unity of vv. 1-18 (see, e.g., Šanda, *Könige* II, 77-78; Gray, *Kings,* 466; del Olmo Lete, *La Vocación del Líder,* 165-78; Carlson; Lundbom; Rofé, "Classification," 436). Indeed, there is no stylistic incongruity between vv. 1-15 and 16-18, and the presumed incoherence in content disappears if one assumes that the prophets only wanted to find the corpse. Literary convention may also help us grasp their motivation. The onlookers see nothing of that intimate visionary moment beyond the Jordan (see Acts 9:7, where bystanders do not share the vision); they know only that Elisha has crossed the Jordan and returned to them alone. The spirit may play tricks after all, as Obadiah earlier suggests of Elijah's mysterious comings and goings (1 Kgs 18:12). Hence one must test appearances and confirm inferences (v. 15), even while knowing beforehand that Elijah this day will depart (vv. 3, 5).

The structure of the plot is plain to see. Anticipating his main subject (v. 1a), the narrator builds through movement and dialogue (I, vv. 1b-6) to his central event, the translation of Elijah into heaven (II, vv. 7-15). The aftermath or dénouement underscores Elisha's rightful place as successor to the master when the other prophets confirm for themselves that Elijah's body really is nowhere to be found (III, vv. 16-18).

The dominant structural feature, often overlooked, and when observed, insufficiently studied, is the carefully marked geographical progression. The narrator takes us toward the Jordan River (with three highly repetitive dialogues), to the bank of the river itself, across the river and back again, and finally away from the river toward Jericho and Bethel from whence the action began. Each stage is marked with a brief notation as, for example, "(they) went from Gilgal" (v. 1b, *RSV* "were on their way from . . ."); "they went down to Bethel" (v. 2b); "they came to Jericho" (v. 4b; see vv. 6b, 8b, 14b, and v. 18a, "while he tarried at Jericho"). Moreover, the narrative climax comes at the furthest point in the journey, where repeated words and images frame the vision of Elijah's ascension. Onlookers stand silently at some distance, separated from the important event by a prophet's cloak and a river which must be miraculously parted (vv. 7-15). One may visualize the structure as follows:

> A   Sons of prophets afar off (v. 7)
>   B   River divided, Elijah and Elisha cross over (v. 8)
>   C   Vision in Transjordan (vv. 9-12)
>   B'   River divided, Elisha crosses back (vv. 13-14)
> A'   Sons of prophets at some distance (v. 15)

Note the number of repeated details which mark this concentric structure. The "fifty men of the sons of prophets" (v. 7a) who were "at Jericho" (v. 5a) are surely the same ones mentioned in v. 15a. Somewhat obscure in the *RSV*, the identification is clear in the Hebrew, for v. 15a, "and the sons of the prophets who were from Jericho watched him from a distance" (*minneged*; cf. 2 Kgs 4:25; Ps 38:12 [*RSV* 11] corresponds to v. 7a; "fifty men . . . went and stood at some distance" [*minneged merāhôq*]). The phrase "the two of them crossed over" (v. 8b) exactly balances v. 14b, even to the use of the same verb, *'br*; the parting of the river is repeated verbatim, vv. 8b and 14b, nicely marking both spatial distance and physical separation as Elijah and Elisha carry on their business apart from the others. In fact, v. 7 pointedly describes the distance between Elijah and Elisha and the fifty prophets who watch from afar, just as vv. 15b-16 bring them together again.

Carefully integrated into this itinerarylike concentric structure are three scenes of dialogue, each of which closes with a statement that the characters move on to another location (I, vv. 2-6). Obviously, in their tedious repetition these dialogues offer no particular or new information. They seem neither a "test" of Elisha's fitness to succeed Elijah (against De Vries, 82-83) nor a clear balance in chiastic fashion to the dialogues of vv. 16-18 (against del Olmo Lete). Yet to delete them as superfluous additions seems arbitrary (against Würthwein, *Könige*, 274). Instead, these little scenes might be explained as literary devices to build suspense (cf. Licht, 105-6).

At the outset, everyone is apparently aware that Elijah is to be taken away: Elisha, the "sons of prophets," who are perhaps members of a guild or more simply personal followers of Elisha (Hobbs, *2 Kings*, 25-27), and Elijah himself (v. 9). The narrator's statement in v. 1a informs even the reader. Contrary to A. Schmitt, H.-Chr. Schmitt, Würthwein, and others, this statement need not be seen as a clumsy editorial remark. Rather, one may take it as a typical antici- patory device of Hebrew narration. (See Gen 22:1; 18:1; for heavily redacted materials, see 1 Kgs 11:14a, 23a, 26a; N. Sarna, "The Anticipatory Use of Information as a Literary Feature of the Genesis Narratives," in *The Creation of Sacred Literature* [ed. R. E. Friedman; Near Eastern Studies 22; Berkeley:

University of California, 1981] 76-82.) Such an anticipatory statement establishes a hierarchy among possible readings of the narrative and thus defines at the outset one particular view, that of the writer, as the preferred view. In 2 Kings 2, everyone who is aware of Elijah's impending departure shares an omniscience toward events which, in biblical narrative, is usually the prerogative only of the narrator-writer and reader.

Nevertheless, the narrator has withheld important information. No one, not even the reader, knows the time and place of Elijah's departure. As though avoiding the thought of inexorably approaching trauma, the characters repeatedly suppress conversation about the event while steadily approaching it. Elijah's and Elisha's exchanges dramatize the latter's tenacious resolve to follow the former to the final moment; members of a growing entourage repeat with urgent insistence the same question: "Do you not know that today the Lord will take away your master?" Elisha repeatedly bids them to cease their questioning, all the while that his master Elijah, like a seaman standing watch on the prow, cries out the next move, stage by stage. All march inexorably toward that event foreseen in its main character, except its time and place. In fact, Elijah's sounding of the journey and the narrator's itinerarylike notices which follow (vv. 2, 4, 6) are the principal variants in an otherwise unvarying sequence (see Lundbom, 45-46). So the question is not *what* will happen, or whether it is anticipated, but the unspoken anxiety which arises from realizing that one knows at once too much and too little: *where?* and *when?* will Elijah leave us? The literary device of repeated dialogue rivets one's attention to the *fact* of movement, and builds the chilling impatience of steady, inevitable closure with mystery.

The literary pattern ceases with the report of the arrival at the Jordan River, and the narrator marks the change stylistically. The customary *wāw* conversive (*wyqtl*) sequence gives way to a perfect tense verb (*qtl*) with its subject displaced to the head of the sentence. "Fifty men of the sons of prophets also went (on to the Jordan)," but now they are onlookers "from afar" rather than partners in suspenseful dialogue (v. 7). The travelers pause; they stand before a space, a time, an event, into which only the specially set apart may enter. Exactly at this point, through repeated "setting" motifs, the narrator defines a private moment beyond the Jordan (II.A, C, vv. 7-8, 13-15). The waters part; Elijah and Elisha pass over dry of foot into a region physically and temporally closed to the sons of prophets — like a holy thing shut away from sacrilege. The Transjordan seems less a physical place than a trope for that liminal space between the ordinariness of prophetic community and the numinous circumstances of Elijah's translation from earth.

Not yet ready to relieve suspense, the writer provides yet another dialogue (II.B.1, vv. 9-10). From one point of view more talk means further delay in the progress of events. Yet, unlike the dialogues which preceded it, this last exchange in this set-apart space offers the surprise that the departure of Elijah has also to do with the empowering of *Elisha*. As the Jordan marks divisions among the prophets, so this new information creates a kind of gnostic bond between Elijah and Elisha. With the reader, they now share knowledge that is denied those prophets left behind at the thresholding river. The reader is privy to a parting wish, a suggestion of the gift of spirit, of visionary sight to come and now expects that Elijah will not leave Israel bereft of its prophetic voice. But the where? and the when? remain as impenetrable as before. Elijah's and Elisha's portentous exchange seems in no way to have alleviated the peculiar kind of tension which the narrator has built to this point. In fact, when the journey resumes, a Hebrew durative style (infinitives and participles) again wraps movement in watchful anticipation: "And as they went on and kept on talking . . ." (v. 11).

Suddenly Elijah ascends to the heavens in a numinal storm (cf. Job 38:1; 40:6; Jer 23:19). The reader sees with Elisha's eyes, in a vision. A fiery specter in fact divides Elisha from the one he swore never to abandon. The Hebrew is graphic and immediate: "And behold, a fiery chariot and horses of fire! And they parted the two of them" (*wayyapridû bên šĕnêhem* v. 11; Lundbom's historicizing interpretation, that this event reflects Elijah's being kidnapped by soldiers in royal chariots, misses the literary point and completely ignores the characteristic language of visionary experience). Both image and sound transport us back to v. 8b: "and the two of them crossed over" (*wayyaʿabrû šĕnêhem*).

As the Jordan separates "sons of prophets" from the two prophets, as knowledge creates its own powers of distinction, so too this new sight is given to Elisha and reader alone. Visionary space, and indeed Elijah and Elisha it seems, belong to a numinal realm set apart from the ordinary. Religious feeling and narrative convention require that the prophet confront the holy in isolation and preserve its sacrality from contamination. Such is the way to bring the benefits of divine power into human community (see comments at 1 Kgs 17:17-24, in Long, *1 Kings*, 184-87; cf. Exod 19:10-13; the temptations of Jesus, Luke 4:1-15; the initiatory rites for shamans and other spirit intermediaries discussed in M. Eliade, *Shamanism* [tr. W. R. Trask; Bollingen Series 76; Princeton: Princeton University Press, 1964]).

Elisha reacts to the vision with an outcry and gestures of grief as though overcome with distress (v. 12; cf. Gen 37:34; 2 Sam 13:31; Josh 7:6; Judg 11:35; Esth 4:1). Yet the matter is really not so easily penetrated. His words perhaps attribute a title to Elijah ("My father, my father! the chariots of Israel and its horsemen" [so J. Williams, "The Prophetic 'Father',", *JBL* 85 (1966) 344-48]; cf. 2 Kgs 13:14; see Cogan and Tadmor, *II Kings*, 32). Or is it a description of numinal hosts surrounding the master (see 2 Kgs 6:17; also 2 Kgs 13:14; and M. A. Beek, "The Meaning of the Expression 'The Chariots and the Horsemen of Israel'," *OTS* 17 [1971] 1-10)? One is left wondering whether Elisha grieves for his departed mentor or shrinks from some awesome sight glimpsed on the edge of the natural. In any case, the final parting of the two men — the last image of division and separation in the narrative — seems irrevocable and caught in a linguistic emphasis: "he rent them [his clothes] *into two pieces*" (v. 12b). The usual expression reports more simply the tearing of garments (*qrʿ bgdyw*, 1 Kgs 21:27; Josh 7:6; 2 Kgs 22:11; Esth 4:1; cf. 1 Kgs 11:30). But here *lišnayim qĕrāʿîm*, "into two pieces," alludes to *šĕnêhem*, "the two of them together," of vv. 6, 11, and suggests the depth of change wrought by the trajectory from Gilgal to Transjordan.

The climax finally having been achieved, the narrator quickly reverses field. Elisha moves decisively to demonstrate that he stands in Elijah's stead.

Duplicating the miracle of liminality, he crosses the barrier between sacred and profane. Now emphasizing integration rather than separation, the writer mentions the master's cloak twice in seemingly superfluous detail (vv. 13, 14) and recounts nearly verbatim Elijah's earlier parting of the waters (v. 14b; cf. v. 8b; apparently in the interest of English literary style, the *RSV* obscures the repetition in the Hebrew). Such repetition is significant in so spare a narrative idiom as the Bible, and helps the reader to focus symbolic senses: Elisha takes up the trappings of power, the mantle that has caught him unawares in the past (1 Kgs 19:19-21), performs a deed which makes that power his own, and retraces exactly the steps of the departed Elijah back into ordinary space.

Reassertion of the ordinary comes as the sons of prophets who have stood in the distance pay homage to this man returned from the beyond. Their response is unequivocal and conventional, and confirms that the numinal man with Elijah's special powers has reestablished his ties to human society. The sons of the prophets come out to meet Elisha, in effect overcoming their estrangement from those events they have witnessed from afar, and they offer homage as to a king or divine being (cf. Gen 42:6; 43:26; 18:2; 1 Kgs 2:19).

Away from the Jordan and heading toward Jericho, however, matters of the spirit seem less assured. Though paying the highest respect to Elisha (he is now their "lord" and they his "servants," v. 16), his followers seem to know the tricks of the spirit, as did Obadiah before them (1 Kgs 18:7-12; see also Ezek 3:12, 14; 8:3; Bel 36, 39). Apparently only witnesses to the fact of Elisha's return, they want or need to assure themselves that he is truly alone, that Elijah will not reappear somewhere to demand again his habitual due. Or they may wish to look for the corpse, having known all along that the Lord would take Elijah away (vv. 3, 5; Rofé). Apparently a search which turns up no trace of the departed master satisfies them and confirms their homage giving, that whatever exactly happened in the Transjordan, Elijah's spirit has now come onto another. Elisha upbraids the hapless prophets, as though this time (and a rare case at that) things *are* what they seem to be. The succession has occurred, Elijah has gone, and the prophets' homage to a new master is justified and properly offered (Rofé, "Classification," 438). A subtle play on words makes the point: those "strong men" *(bĕnê-ḥayil)* who carry out the search should also be understood at the end as "loyal and upstanding" men, worthy of another's trust. (See 2 Sam 2:7, where the phrase is equivalent to *'îš ḥayil* of 1 Kgs 1:42, and *ben-ḥayil* of 1 Kgs 1:52. See also 2 Sam 13:28; Deut 3:18, and the plural *'anšē-ḥayil* in Gen 47:6; Exod 18:21, 25.)

The narration breaks off abruptly: "Did I not say to you, 'Do not go?' " (v. 18). There is no indication of Elisha's tone or demeanor. One must guess at the point of this concluding scene "while he [Elisha] tarried at Jericho." One may be *meant* to guess. Like Elijah, the successor prophet seems self-determined, aloof, cold, and unfathomable. Yet this sense of character is formed for the reader only *after* Elijah's disappearance into the heavens; or as the reader, and not the other prophets, knows, after Elisha has received a double portion of spirit and brandished its power in miracle. In contrast, Elisha's outcry on seeing the vision beyond the river seems spontaneous and deeply emotional — the despair of an orphaned disciple (Rofé, "Classification," 438). The image of human warmth arouses memory of poignant conflict between familial bonds and devotion to Elijah which the reader has carried from 1 Kgs 19:19-21. But if this impression is correct, in the end Elisha seems very changed and somewhat enigmatic. Observe, too, the curious detachment from emotion, even a lack of emotion, in the anecdotes which follow (vv. 19-22, 23-24), and the moral sensibility which must be awakened in Elisha by a bereaved mother in 4:8-37. Perhaps the narrator suggests that possessing, or being possessed by, the spirit of Elijah (note the passive sense in v. 15), as distinct from more excessive emotionalism (cf. 1 Sam 19:23-24), really makes for this strange asceticism of character. Those in the narrative who encounter Elisha, and those who read about him, confront the same ambiguity — the unnatural in the midst of the natural.

Genre

This narrative is a LEGEND, a story concerned primarily with the wondrous, miraculous, and exemplary (see Montgomery, *Kings,* 354; cf. Gray, *Kings,* 466; Plöger, 50, speaks of "miracle story").

Despite many attempts, it has proved difficult to reach a more precise identification. De Vries (p. 54) designates this unit a "Prophet-Legitimation Narrative," a type of legend that justifies the nature and scope of a prophet's power. He cites only one other possible example, 1 Kgs 17:17-24, hardly suffi-cient to establish a "type"; in any case, the notion of legitimation, presumably for Elisha in this instance, seems too restrictive. After all, the story has to do as much with Elijah as Elisha; in fact, it is the heavenly aspect of Elijah which ignited the imagination of later Jewish storytellers and interpreters (A. Wiener, *The Prophet Elijah in the Development of Judaism* [London/Boston: Routledge, Kegan & Paul, 1978]).

Rofé ("Classification," 436-39; *Prophetical Stories,* 41-51) supposes 2 Kgs 2:1-18 to be a portion of *vita,* or "legendary (→) biography," but in so doing he ties the narrative to an untested and perhaps untestable theory of literary history. Similarly, Baltzer (pp. 101-2) thinks of biography, and describes 2 Kgs 2:1-18 as a prophet's "installation" on the model of certain Egyptian texts. Quite apart from the difficulty in using biography to describe any OT materials (this works against Rofé as well), it is questionable whether the author or storyteller really speaks of "installation," as presumably he might have done with the literary conventions of Num 27:17-23. Despite a few parallels with (→) vocation accounts, the term "call narrative" does not fit this particular legend, which fails to mention divine mission (as in, e.g., Jeremiah 1; Isaiah 6; and Ezekiel 1–3; against del Olmo Lete, *La Vocación del Líder,* 290-92; idem, "La Vocación de Eliseo," 165-78; also A. Schmitt, 129). Finally, the generic term "didactic nar-rative" (Haag, 31) is at once too restrictive, perhaps even anachronistic (Haag associates the genre with disciples engaged in theological reflection), and too broad (any number of folk narratives might serve didactic purposes for particular persons on particular occasions).

Influential in the composition of this legend would have been the conven-tions of ITINERARY (cf. Exod 17:1–18:27; 1 Kgs 19:1-18). In the author's hands, a rhetorical structure used to organize movement by stages has been transformed artfully to build suspense and focus. One may also note the shaping influence of literary elements most at home in VISION REPORTS (vv. 11-12; see B. O. Long, "Reports of Visions Among the Prophets," *JBL* 95 [1976] 353-65). The author marks the beginning of Elijah's ascension by the characteristic "and behold" *(wĕhinnēh)* followed by a brief vision sequence, i.e., a series of descriptive images conjured up linguistically with nominal clauses (cf. Jer 38:21b- 22; 1 Kgs 22:19; Isa 6:1). Note the conventional usage of the verb "see" (v. 12a, *r'h*, here in a participial form) as part of the vision's content (see Jer 4:23, 24, 25; 1 Kgs 22:19; Ezek 1:1). Finally, the author closes the scene of Elijah's ascension with a simple declaration, v. 12b, "And he saw [*r'h*] him no more." It is a closure with many parallels in reports of visions (e.g., Judg 6:22; 13:20-21; Tob 12:21; 2 Macc 3:34 [*RSV* 33]; Mark 9:8; Acts 8:39). Yet in this instance the usage also points beyond vision to the permanent disappearance of Elijah from the earth.

Several minor formulaic expressions may be noted in passing: the OATH (vv. 2, 4, 6; see 2 Kgs 4:30; 1 Sam 20:3; 25:26); the stereotyped description of distress (v. 12; see 1 Kgs 21:27; Gen 27:34); and a conventional image of respectful submission to authority (v. 15b; see Gen 42:6, 43:26; 1 Kgs 2:19).

Setting

Legends by their very nature are widely dispersed creations of the popular imagination. Thus their settings would have been quite varied, depending on circumstances of origin and occasions of use. This particular example about two great prophets may have originated with folk storytellers or with groups of prophets (Gray, *Kings*, 466; Plöger, 28; De Vries, 53). Some scholars point to followers of Elisha (A. Schmitt, 130-31; Miller, 441-47). The legend, lacking telltale vocabulary, hardly seems a Deuteronomic composition, against Foresti. Rofé plausibly suggests, though without significant biblical evidence, that the extant story is the result of a late attempt to create an orderly account of the prophet's life from scattered and diverse legendary traditions. We lack assured grounds for choosing any one of these several possibilities. In the light of this fact, it seems more important to consider carefully the *literary* setting of the narrative in the book of Kings. The legend now stands "between the reigns," at the beginning of a series of accounts about the northern kingdom in which Elisha will play a role, though not always a central one. It also stands at the end of a somewhat fragmented series of similar accounts involving Elijah (1 Kings 17– 19; 21; 2 Kgs 1:2-17). Thus the narrative is pivotal to Elijah and Elisha, to the reigns of Ahaziah and Jehoram, and to the wider Dtr history which includes this pausal moment in the midst of the ongoing account of the northern kingdom.

Intention

In keeping with the popularity of the legends, we must suppose that the tellers of legends would have had different intentions according to varying circumstances. Consequently we should not unduly restrict what might have been the case for this particular example. A fascination with the marvelous, and with explaining the beginnings in glory of a religious virtuoso, surely would have been important purposes behind this legend (see Rofé, "Classification"; idem, *Prophetical Stories*). The desire to legitimate the successor to Elijah (De Vries, 54) also might have played a role. Thus we may plausibly suggest a storyteller's impulse akin to a biographical interest, but one which was satisfied with legendary materials (cf. the Talmudic legends of the sages; or the 17th-century collections of the legends of Baal Shem Tov; Rofé).

As part of the exilic Dtr history, one important purpose must have been to portray the empowered succession from one prophet to another as symbolic of an epochal transition — the passing from Elijah's conflict with the early Omrides to Elisha's efforts toward that dynasty's dissolution (2 Kgs 6:24–10:36). Yet this flow of the generations, and the peculiar words and images used to describe it, evoke a wider canonical archetype, the passing from Moses to Joshua. The latter was "minister" and deputy to Moses (*mĕšārēt;* sometimes "servant" in the *RSV,* e.g., Exod 24:13; 33:11; Num 11:28). Similarly, Elisha first appears in the Dtr work as one who "ministered" to Elijah (*šārat,* 1 Kgs 19:21). Over time, the "minister" Joshua is marked as one who will take up Moses' preeminent position. In him the "spirit" dwells (Num 27:18); he is commissioned, or "commanded" *(ṣwh),* as successor to Moses (Deut 31:7-8, 14-23), and is reaffirmed in this position by God himself after Moses' death (Josh 1:1-9). So, too, Elisha receives the "spirit," steps into Elijah's place, and is confirmed by divine vision and public events (2 Kgs 2:1-18). Moses dies in the Transjordan near Jericho, and without a trace remaining ("No man knows the place of his burial to this day," Deut 34:6). Quickly the narrator remarks that Joshua, who has already been commissioned, is "full of the spirit of wisdom" (Deut 34:9), and shows that he succeeds marvelously at working mighty deeds, the first of which is a parting of the River Jordan (Josh 3:11-17). So too, Elijah disappears without a trace (2 Kgs 2:11-12), and Elisha, having had the spirit of Elijah settle on him, parts the Jordan waters to take his place as leader among the prophets (cf. 2 Kgs 2:8, 14 and Exod 14:21 with Josh 3:11-17; see Foresti). And like Moses after crossing the sea, Elisha's first wondrous deed is to purify drinking water (2 Kgs 2:19-22; see discussion below; cf. Exod 15:22-25).

If Moses-Joshua represent a paradigm of transition for an earlier formative period in Israel's history, then Elijah-Elisha appear to serve a similar purpose for the DtrH. As Moses-Joshua stand for continuity in Yahweh's faithfulness and *tôrâ* giving, and constancy in obedient partnership, so Elijah-Elisha represent steady voices for Jerusalemite-styled Yahwistic allegiance in a kingdom laboring under the pernicious shadows of Jeroboam and Ahab. It was probably a long view from exile which took up this sweeping panoramic vision and suggested such special enhancement of Elisha's status. The pausal moment between reigns gave the opportunity for such analogical image making, and constrained the reader to make new associations with the paradigms that had always made theological sense of national memory.

At the same time, one is fully and properly introduced to Elisha. The spirit which now rests upon him is a double portion of Elijah's terrifying power which had been beamed at the hapless royal emissaries (2 Kings 1). Its stern militancy, which can consume an army or energize visions of fiery armament, horses, and chariots, recalls the very first mention of Elisha in the Dtr history as destined for uncompromising zealotry: "and him who escapes from the sword of Jehu shall Elisha slay" (1 Kgs 19:17). This pausal moment serves as a suggestive station on the way from that proleptic hint of Yahweh's victory over Baal to its consummation in an Elisha-inspired military slaughter (1 Kgs 19:15-18; see discussion at 2 Kings 9–10).

Bibliography

See bibliographies at 2 Kgs 1:2-17a; 2:1-25. K. Baltzer, *Die Biographie* (→ 2 Kgs 2:1-25); C. Canosa, "Eliseo sucede a Elías (2 Re 2:1-18)," *EstBib* 31 (1972) 321-36; K. Galling, "Der Ehrenname Elisas und die Entrückung Elias," *ZTK* 53 (1956) 129-48; P. Severin Grill, "Die Himmelfahrt des Elias," *BZ* 24 (1938-39) 242-48; E. Haag, "Die Himmelfahrt des Elias nach 2 Kg 2:1-15," *TTZ* 78 (1969) 18-32; C. Houtman, "Elia's hemelvaart. Notities over en naar annleiding van 2 Koningen 2:1-18," *NedTTs* 32 (1978) 283-304; J. Licht, *Storytelling in the Bible* (Jerusalem: Magnes, 1978) 105-6, 130-33; G. del Olmo Lete, "La vocación de Eliseo," *EstBib* 26 (1967) 287-93; idem, *La Vocación del Líder en el Antiguo Israel* (Bibliotheca Salmanticensis 3; Salamanca: Pontifical University, 1973) 165-78; O. Plöger, "Die Prophetengeschichten der Samuel- und Königsbücher" (Diss., Greifswald, 1937); A. Rofé, "The Classification of the Prophetical Stories," *JBL* 89 (1970) 427-40; A. Schmitt, *Entrückung-Aufnahme-Himmelfahrt: Untersuchungen zu einem Vorstellungsbereich im Alten Testament* (Forschung zur Bibel 10; Stuttgart: Katholisches Bibelwerk, 1973) 47-139; K. Spronk, "2 Koningen 2. Een onderzoek naar ontstaan en opbouw van de tekst en naar de achtergrond van de daarin vermelde tradities," *Gereformeerd Theologisch Tijdschrift* 88 (1988) 82-97.

LEGENDS OF ELISHA'S DEEDS OF POWER, 2:19-24

Structure

I. Miracle of good water from bad   19-22
   A. Setting: bad water   19
      1. Narrative introduction   19aα
      2. Request to Elisha for help   19aβ-b
   B. Resolution   20-21
      1. Preparations   20
         a. Elisha's instructions   20a
         b. Execution of instructions   20b
      2. Miracle: good water from bad   21
         a. Elisha's action   21a
         b. Oracle   21b

There is a virtual consensus among scholars that this unit consists of two originally independent traditions (e.g., Gray, *Kings,* 466, 477-79; Šanda, *Könige* II, 77-78; Gressmann, *Geschichtsschreibung,* 289-91; H.-Chr. Schmitt, 106; Fricke, *2 Könige,* 27-28, reads 2:1-25 as a literary unit). The narrated incidents are quite distinct in content, and the pieces join with one another very loosely (e.g., v. 23a, "And he went up from there"). The Dtr writer has apparently related them specifically to the wider context through geographical allusions (i.e., "to Bethel," v. 23a) and thereby brought the material into the itinerarylike schema of ch. 2 (see discussion at 2:1-25). In addition, the mention of "men of *the* city," v. 19a, appears to make a specific reference to Jericho of the preceding vv 15-18.

The first section, vv. 19-22, sets up a crisis (I.A, v. 19) which is resolved through an action of the prophet (I.B, vv. 20-21). The narrator then notes the continuous realization of miracle with the typical oracle fulfillment formula (I.C, v. 22; cf. 2 Kgs 4:42; 1 Kgs 17:8-16).

The second tradition turns on words of mockery which also seem to constitute a grave offense against this man of God (II.A, v. 23). Elisha responds with a curse "in the name of the Lord" (II.B, v. 24a), and as though propelled by the words, bears fall upon the boys and rip forty-two of them to shreds (v. 24b).

Despite the simplicity of the narratives, one should note their compact expressivity. The Jerichoites' plaint and Elisha's oracle combine vivid metaphor with euphony, at least in the traditional Masoretic pronunciation. The water is bad, and the earth gives misbirth *(wĕhammayim rāʿîm wĕhāʾāreṣ mĕšakkālet),* but after the miracle neither death nor miscarriage comes forth *(māwet ûmĕšakkālet),* vv. 19 and 21. The second incident rings with repeated sounds of "go up" (*ʿōleh,* v. 23a) and some small boys cheered, as though picking up the words of the storyteller, *ʿălēh qērēaḥ, ʿălēh qērēaḥ,* "Go up, you baldhead! Go up, you baldhead!" (v. 23b).

In all this, the narrative achieves a sense of artful play in the telling and of gravity in the tale. Elisha is a helper who brings healing with action and word, and a bad-tempered wizard who strikes immediately at those who belittle him. Together, the two images suggest the ambiguity of sacred power (see 1 Kgs 17:7-24).

Genre

This unit consists of two short PROPHET LEGENDS. Each one is a rudimentary story which emphasizes the wondrous and miraculous in a simple miracle among anonymous folk. The prophet is venerable for his great and easily stirred power, not memorable for his personality. The other personages are shells, barely more than possibilities laid before the miracle worker, who manipulates their inherent ordinariness (e.g., sticks, salt, flour, a glance of the eye) to bring about a miracle. The wonders themselves seem only little more than ordinary in this understated world. See Rofé ("Classification," 430-33), "simple *legenda*," and Robinson (*Kings,* 28), "legendary folktale." (Cf. De Vries, 53-54, "power demonstration narrative," a type of legend.)

The first legend, vv. 19-22, follows a pattern similar to 2 Kgs 4:38-41; 6:1-7; Exod 15:22b-25a. A crisis or problem leads to action (in this case accompanied by an oracle) which in turn resolves the crisis. The conclusion consists of a note that a miracle has occurred "according to the word spoken by PN." Thus the storyteller emphasizes the prophetic word as the miraculous means by which change, usually rescue of some sort, comes about (see discussion at 1 Kgs 17:2-16). These legends seem to be variants of a more general pattern in which a problem brought to the attention of someone with power to help elicits divine intervention, which in turn results in a miracle that solves the problem (Culley, *Narrative,* 72-75; see 2 Kgs 4:38-41; 6:1-7; Exod 15:22-25).

The second legend, 2 Kgs 2:23-25, differs only slightly. A prophetic word (in this case, a curse) still carries power to achieve miraculous effect. We may compare 1 Kgs 16:34 where the oracle fulfillment formula precisely describes the working out of Joshua's curse on Jericho. This short legend also is similar to a larger narrative pattern in which one tells of a wrong committed and how that transgression is finally punished through curse or divine intervention (see Culley, "Punishment Stories," 169-70; idem, *Narrative,* 100-101). For parallels, see Num 11:1-3; 21:4-9; 2 Kgs 5:20-27; 2 Kgs 1:2-17a (contains the oracle fulfillment formula), and 1 Kgs 13:1-32, especially vv. 20-26 (v. 26 is close to the oracle fulfillment formula).

One should also note some important formulaic elements in these legends: a PROPHECY OF SALVATION, v. 21b, introduced by the typical prophetic MESSENGER FORMULA, "Thus says the Lord." There is also an ORACLE FULFILLMENT FORMULA, v. 22, but given in this case a for-all-time sense by the addition of the TESTIMONY FORMULA, "until this day," which collapses the distance between the act of narrating and the time frame of the story world.

Setting

In oral tradition, legends would have been created and circulated in many different social settings, and would have had many occasions for use depending upon the circumstances and aims of storytellers. The brevity and austere simplicity of these particular examples suggest to Rofé ("Classification," 432-33; see also idem, *Prophetical Stories,* 13-26) that they are skillfully reduced written versions of longer oral legends. They may have belonged originally to prophetic groups (see De Vries, 54), perhaps followers of Elisha in Gilgal (Gray, *Kings,* 477) or in Jericho (H.-Chr. Schmitt, 180). Given the complete absence of reliable evidence on these matters, the most important consideration must be the *literary* setting of these legends in the book of Kings. They tell of the first miracles performed by Elisha after the disappearance of Elijah, and hence belong to the account of a change in prophetic leadership "between the reigns." (See discussion at 2 Kgs 2:1-25.)

Intention

Among the people, these legends would have been told for many reasons, depending on the occasions and circumstances of telling. We may think generally of demonstrating the powers of this prophet Elisha for the enjoyment and edification of his followers (so De Vries, *Prophet,* 53-54) or for the awe of children (H.-Chr. Schmitt, 182, commenting on vv. 23-24). These opinions, however, are simply vague speculation. We lack real information on the social background of these stories, and because of their brevity, it is difficult to gain a complete understanding apart from their present literary setting.

In context, however, a main purpose must be to illustrate Elisha's power, which he holds from Elijah and God. Carlson ("Élisée," 405), takes the number 42 (v. 24) to mean "almost all" (2 Kgs 10:14; Judg 12:6) and thus equivalent to the "double portion" of v. 9. When Elisha is on center stage, his actions seem to confirm the succession, to legitimate its power, and to add further emphasis to the Moses-Joshua model already suggested by the translation of Elijah into the heavens (see discussion at 2:1-18). Elisha's act to purify the waters near Jericho recalls Moses' similar deed at Marah (Exod 15:22-25a), and the release of a powerful curse echoes a similar tradition of Joshua (1 Kgs 16:34).

An impulse akin to the writing of biography must have lain behind this collection of legendary materials in ch. 2. The reader now knows more fully that Elisha is a successor in the line of Moses, Joshua, Elijah; one has seen his power — for weal *and* woe, whether or not the matter is congenial to modern tastes (see Gray, *Kings,* 466, who calls 2:23-25 "in every respect a puerile tale"). Implicitly, one understands that the duty of guarding the reverence due Yahweh now falls to Elisha, who will finish out his "life" mostly with the Omride dynasty in Israel (chs. 3–13). If Elijah represents to the Dtr writer the authentic voice for Yahweh worship in the apostasy-prone northern kingdom, then this pausal moment between the reigns of Ahaziah and Jehoram closes with a newly confirmed voice, the power-laden activity of a new prophet and successor, Elisha.

Bibliography

See bibliographies at 2 Kgs 1:2-17a; 2:1-25. R. Culley, *Studies in the Structure of Hebrew Narrative* (Philadelphia: Fortress, 1976) 72-75; A. Rofé, "Classification" (→ 2 Kgs 2:1-

18); Y. Zakovitch, " 'Go up, Baldhead! Go up, Baldhead'; Rings of Commentary in a Biblical Story," *Jerusalem Researches in Hebrew Literature* 7 (1985) 7-22 (Hebr.).

THE BEGINNING OF THE REIGN OF JEHORAM, 3:1-3

Structure

I.	Synchronistic accession formula	1a
II.	Length of reign	1b
III.	Theological appraisal	2-3

This unit is a typical Dtr introduction to a northern regnal period. The information having to do with accession is briefer and more compressed than that given for Judean kings. Name, place of reign, and accession date reckoned with the years of a Judean counterpart appear as one statement; then follows a note on the length of reign. (See 1 Kgs 16:29; 22:52 [*RSV* 51]; 2 Kgs 15:13; and cf. the longer formula for Judean kings, 1 Kgs 14:21; 22:41-42.) The religious judgment on the king follows the stereotyped pattern for all Israelite kings after Jeroboam: Jehoram did "what was evil in the eyes of the Lord," and moreover, he "clung to the sin of Jeroboam." This statement seems less a limitation on the preceding assertion (as *RSV* "nevertheless," translating *raq,* implies) than something additional to be said (see Josh 1:17, 18; 2 Kgs 14:4). Of note are the specific mitigations added to this judgment: the king did evil, but "not like his father and mother," and he "put away the pillar of Baal which his father had made." Jehoram carries out some degree of reform, and yet the shadows of his father (Ahab) and mother (Jezebel) linger with unusual vividness among the blander formulaic summaries (cf. also 1 Kgs 22:53 [*RSV* 52]). It may not be accidental that in the first incident related about Jehoram, a prophet frequently associated with the king's predecessor refers again to those same infamous royal parents (3:13; the words "prophets of your mother" are absent in the early Greek VS of this verse).

This opening to Jehoram's rule actually begins a compendium of tradition that runs to 10:34-36, where a conventional summary closes out the reign of Jehu, a military commander who wrests the throne from Jehoram. Jehu murders both Jehoram and the Judean king Ahaziah, thus bringing to an end two regnal periods and launching his own brief rule. The literary problem for the Dtr writer was to take account of this fateful meeting of three kings and still follow the preferred technique of presenting each regnal period as an enclosed block of tradition, with introductory and concluding summaries. The solution was to begin conventionally with an introduction to Jehoram of Israel (3:1-3), recount events during his time (3:4–8:15), and without formally concluding Jehoram's rule, resume the sequence of Judean kings (8:16-24), getting quickly to Ahaziah (8:25-27). Jehu murders this Judahite while simultaneously revolting against Jehoram of Israel (8:28–9:29). In this way, Dtr presents the end of both Jehoram and Ahaziah and the rise of Jehu as an occurrence within the regnal period of Ahaziah. From these circumstances, the writer goes on to recount incidents during Jehu's reign (9:30–10:33) and ends with the usual concluding summary (10:34-36).

Elisha is placed at or near the center of all these events. Most of what the DtrH considers relevant to Jehoram's reign is drawn from freely circulating stories or collections of tales about Elisha (3:4–8:15). Even the destructive energies of Jehu are presented as having been commissioned and legitimated by Elisha (9:1-10).

Thus, the opening onto Jehoram's regnal period is fraught with implications. The archetypes of Baalistic unfaithfulness ("father and mother") and a hint of reform ascribed to Jehoram ("put away the pillar of Baal") set forth in brief the essential dynamics of the Dtr writer's view of Israelite history. It is really a struggle between true Yahwism (represented by the prophets who destroy the icons of Baalism) and apostates, who worship the deities of the people roundabout. The end of Jehoram expresses a victory of sorts for the Yahwists. He will die in the midst of violent revolution instigated by Yahweh, foreseen by Elijah (1 Kgs 19:17), commissioned by Elisha (2 Kgs 9:1-3), and carried out by Jehu (8:28–10:27).

Genre

This unit is an Introductory REGNAL RESUMÉ, an editorial device used frequently by the Dtr writer of the books of Kings. See full discussion at 1 Kgs 14:21-31 in Long, *1 Kings,* 158-65.

Setting

This resumé most likely derived from the activity of the Dtr historian in the early exilic period, although he may have drawn on certain royal sources for some of the information and formulas (see discussion at 1 Kgs 14:21-31, in Long, *1 Kings,* 158-65).

Intention

The writer intended to summarize the rule of Jehoram, to evaluate it, and to introduce the narratives of events during his reign. Though condemned, this king already seems to be a forerunner of Jehu (Hoffmann, 84-86). Jehoram initiates the single, though small, act which in the DtrH's eyes counts as reform in the north. He "put away the pillar of Baal which his father had made." This tentative step will find its full stride in the succeeding reign of Jehu (2 Kings 9–10, esp. 2 Kgs 10:28). Of no other Israelite king will the DtrH speak so positively. (His opinion of Judean kings is another matter altogether.) At the same time, the unexpected allusion to Jezebel suggests that this Phoenician queen to the Omrides, whom we last heard about in a summarized prophecy (1 Kgs 21:23), is still a presence in the ongoing "story" of monarchy in the north.

37

Bibliography

H.-D. Hoffmann, *Reform und Reformen: Untersuchungen zu einem Grundthema der deuteronomistischen Geschichtsschreibung* (ATANT 66; Zurich: Theologischer Verlag, 1980).

JEHORAM'S CAMPAIGN AGAINST MOAB, 3:4-27

Text

In v. 24b the Hebrew is uncertain; the *RSV* and *NJPS,* "they advanced, constantly attacking the Moabites," basically follows the lead of the Greek. See Cogan and Tadmor (*II Kings,* 46).

In v. 25 *RSV* "till only its stones were left in Kirhareseth" covers a number of textual problems. Semantic and grammatical difficulties were compounded when the early VSS failed to recognize a city name in *baqqîr ḥărāśet* (cf. Isa 16:11; Jer 48:31, 36). The sense seems to be that only (the stones of) the fortress city Kirhareseth remained, the other cities having been already demolished stone by stone (vv. 25a, 19). See Montgomery (*Kings,* 362-63).

Structure

I. The main crisis	4-5
A. Background exposition: Moab a vassal to Israel	4
B. Moab's rebellion	5
II. Response to crisis: preparation for retaliation	6-8
A. Israelite muster	6
B. The making of alliances	7-8
1. First diplomatic exchange (dialogue)	7
a. Proposal to Jehoshaphat: war pact	7a
b. Jehoshaphat's reply: declaration of alliance	7b
2. Second dialogue (diplomatic exchange)	8
a. Jehoshaphat's query	8a
b. Jehoram's reply	8b
III. Secondary crisis on way to battle	9-12
A. The crisis: no water	9
B. The king's responses	10-12a
1. Jehoram's cry of distress	10
2. Jehoshaphat's actions to secure divine guidance	11-12a
a. Query for a prophet	11a
b. A servant's answer: Elisha	11b
c. Jehoshaphat's response: affirmation of Elisha	12a
C. Result: journey to Elisha	12b
IV. Resolution of secondary crisis	13-20

This unit may be easily distinguished from the Dtr writer's introductory resumé (3:1-3), and from the tradition at 4:1 which begins a new subject in the typical style of a self-contained narrative (cf. 1 Kgs 21:1; 1 Sam 1:1; 2 Sam 13:1). Even though the remaining 3:4-27 reads relatively smoothly, certain oddities hint at a prior literary history. First, a prophetic announcement finds fulfillment in vv. 25-26 as one expects (cf. vv. 19 and 25), but then is substantially qualified, if not contradicted, by v. 27 (cf. v. 18), and in a way which suggests that a Moabite god (probably Chemosh) displays powers in battle which rival Yahweh's (cf. 1 Kgs 20:13-20). Second, the narrator begins with explicitly identified kings, vv. 4, 6, 7, develops a personalized focus in vv. 10-14, but then shifts in the end to a sweeping vision in which an unnamed king of Moab rules the impersonal drama of large warring groups (vv. 21-27). Third, the narrative offers an unusual double prophetic oracle, with duplicated messenger formula, in vv. 16-17, and a miracle which seems to have a double purpose (vv. 17, 22-23).

Some scholars explain these incongruities as having appeared when prophetic material was added to an earlier account of battle (H.-Chr. Schmitt, 34; see also Würthwein, *Könige,* 281; cf. Reiser, 329-31). Alternatively, a prophetic narrative may have received a new context with the addition of vv. 4-5a and 25b-27 (De Vries, 122-23). These hypotheses have not achieved any consensus. Other scholars, while allowing for redactional developments, treat the material finally as substantially unified (e.g., Šanda, *Könige* II, 81-82; Montgomery, *Kings,* 358-59; Gray, *Kings,* 468-69; Fricke, *2 Könige,* 42-43; Hobbs, *2 Kings,* 33-34; Long, 340-41). In the most thorough recent study of these matters, Schweizer (35-42) finds no major disruption in the textual unit, and even incorporates v. 27 as an intentional negative judgment on Elisha's prophetic activity.

As it now stands, the unit consists of a complex of speech-events framed by two action sequences. There are three dialogues, vv. 7-8, 10-12a, and 13-15a, and a longer prophetic address, vv. 16-19 (see Schweizer, 78-80). The narrator quickly describes action leading into and away from these central moments (vv. 4-6, 20-27; the stylized collective utterance in v. 23 neither slows the action nor disturbs the reportorial style). Where narrated time slows, dialogue carries important themes and sets many of the reader's expectations.

The larger plot is straightforward: a crisis precipitated by Moab's rebellion against her overlord Israel (I, vv. 4-5) leads to retaliation. (Cf. the structural outline by De Vries, 66, which obscures these connections in the plot; Schweizer, 78-81, emphasizes formal alternation of speech with action.) Jehoram, the Israelite king, bands together with the kings of Edom and Judah (II, vv. 6-8) and wages a military campaign but with less than totally victorious results (V, vv. 21-27). This larger movement opens with a statement of background which, through participial phrase and inverted word order (subject + *hāyâ* and participle), suggests an enduring state of affairs: "Now Mesha, king of Moab, was a sheep breeder, and he [habitually] brought to the king of Israel a hundred thousand lambs" (v. 4). Sequential time begins only in vv. 5-6 with Moab's rebellion (note the conventional *wyqṭl* style) and comes to rest in v. 27bβ when the narrator restores the original equilibrium: "and [they] returned to [their own] land." Between this main crisis and its qualified resolution the narrator develops a secondary problem, the lack of water for troops and animals (III, vv. 9-12). Overcoming this second difficulty requires the aid of Elisha, whose double promise of both water and military victory leads to a miracle of double duty: water comes to slake thirst and to confuse the enemy (III-IV, vv. 9-20 and 22-23).

The narrator enriches this simple plot by developing other themes in dialogue and prophetic speech. (See a similar technique in 1 Kings 20 and 22.)

The first such event, reported in vv. 7-8, is a conventional scene of international relations stylized as diplomatic missions between kings (cf. 1 Kgs 5:15-23 [*RSV* 5:1-9]; 15:18-19; 20:2-6, 9-11; 2 Kgs 16:7; 18:14). The narrator encloses this scene with a repeated verb, "[he] went" (*wayyēlek*, vv. 7aα [missing, however, in some VSS] and 9aα). The device suggests that two actions — the one described by these enclosures, and the other within the frame — happen simultaneously. Note the same use of repetition in 1 Kgs 20:16-18 and 2 Sam 13:34-38; see full discussion at 2 Kgs 4:8-37. Thus, while Jehoram is going to war, a formal diplomatic exchange unfolds through letters or messengers: "and he sent [word] to Jehoshaphat" (*wayyišlaḥ 'el* . . . , a technical phrase as in 1 Kgs 5:15, 16, 22 [*RSV* 5:1, 2, 8]; 20:2; 2 Kgs 16:7; 18:14). However, the author prefers the illusion of informal dialogue. So transmitted messages and diplomatic exchange dissolve into face-to-face question and answer, vv. 7b-8. Jehoram makes a proposal (v. 7a) and Jehoshaphat agrees. The language in v. 7b expresses solidarity and formal commitment between the kings (cf., e.g., 1 Kgs 15:19; 22:4; 2 Kgs 16:7; on a similar idiom in Ugaritic from a king to his overlord, see Cogan and Tadmor, *II Kings,* 44). Thus two kings, their plans, their declaration of alliance, and their fates stand before us in dialogue (cf. Vater, 379-80). This selective narrowing of focus to Jehoram and Jehoshaphat makes the sudden introduction of the king of Edom into the narrative completely unremarkable (v. 9a). He is blended into the background of the writer's assumptions (see vv. 12, 26).

A second speech event, vv. 10-12a, portrays these two kings still opposite each other. Circling about in the parched steppelands of Edom, Jehoram and Jehoshaphat each react to the lack of drinking water. The narrator again constructs the scene as simple conversation and suspends it as before between nearly identical phrases (vv. 9a and 12b). Conversations occur en route. This time Jehoram has no name. He is simply the "king of Israel" who decries his fate. His words explode out of despair ("Alas!" ['ăhāh]; cf. Judg 6:22; 11:35; 2 Kgs 6:5) and intimate that he views his plight as an unfair perversion of divine election for the Lord's war. It was the prophetess Deborah who "called" (*qr'*) Barak and sent him on a divinely appointed mission to defeat Sisera, of whom Yahweh said, "I will give him into your hands" (Judg 4:6-7). Here the king of Israel laments that he and his allies seem called (*qr'*) only to find that Yahweh has turned that customary cry of victory completely around: the allied kings are to be given "into the hand of Moab," instead of the Moabites into theirs (cf. vv. 10b and 18a; Josh 7:7). In contrast, and less self-pityingly perhaps, Jehoshaphat asks for a prophet through whom Yahweh might be consulted (v. 11). And as though further to diminish Jehoram in the reader's eyes, a servant, not the king himself, quickly suggests Elisha, casting him as protégé, as one who ministered to his master (1 Kgs 19:21b) during those days of Elijah's struggle with Ahab and Jezebel (1 Kgs 18:1–19:18). Elisha himself will make a similarly recollective allusion in v. 13. Jehoshaphat brings the matter to a quick end by acknowledging Elisha's authority: "He has the word of Yahweh" (*RSV* "The word of the Lord is with him"; cf. 1 Kgs 17:24). In effect it is the Judean Jehoshaphat who drives events, who presses his ally to seek audience with Elisha. The narrator adds his own congruent emphasis in

v. 12b: three kings "went down" to Elisha, but only one, Jehoshaphat, is named (cf. v. 9a).

A third speech-event, vv. 13-19, belongs almost entirely to Elisha. The larger narration to this point has followed a conventional pattern: (1) a crisis leads to (2) meeting with a prophet wherein one requests and receives an oracle that looks toward ending the problem (cf. 2 Kgs 8:7-15; 1 Kgs 14:1-18; 20:13-14; 22:5-6). Yet the narrator surmounts the requirements of type by continuing to exploit evaluative contrast and suggestive allusion.

A threefold exchange between the king of Israel and Elisha persuades the prophet to seek guidance from Yahweh, vv. 13-14. While functionally equivalent to the request for an oracle in the type scene (cf. 2 Kgs 8:8-9; 1 Kgs 14:2; 22:5-6, 15), this dialogue transcends mere conventionality. Jehoram, whom the narrator still avoids calling by name, meets with unexpected hostility. In unusually strong and direct language Elisha rejects the request implicit in the king's presence: "What have I to do with you . . . ?" (*mah-lî wālāk*, v. 13a). Like the colloquial English expression, "what *is* this . . . ?" the question implies not only that the prophet holds contrary opinions and values in this situation (see 2 Sam 16:10; 19:23) but that he also demands that Jehoram explain himself (see Judg 11:12; 1 Kgs 17:18; 2 Chr 35:21; cf. O. Bächli, "Was habe ich mit Dir zu schaffen? Eine formelhafte Frage im AT und NT," *TZ* 33 [1977] 69-80). Elisha later sarcastically dismisses the king and at the same time evokes recollections: "Go to the prophets of your father and the prophets of your mother" (v. 13aα), or to the Baalistic prophets who served Ahab and Jezebel (cf. v. 2 and 1 Kgs 18:19ff.). Jehoram seems defensive, and repeats his despairing outburst made in private (cf. v. 10), but now with a different connotation. It is *Yahweh,* not the gods of father and mother, who has threatened this campaign against Moab, and it is to a prophet of this same God that one should turn for advice. In response, Elisha finally voices the contrast which the narrator has been building hitherto with allusion and innuendo: for the sake of Jehoshaphat, who after all has urged this consultation, he will deal with the king of Israel (v. 14b). The idiom "have regard for" *(nś' pānîm),* which is mostly used as a legal term in the Bible, suggests that one looks upon another's request already predisposed to act favorably (Num 6:26; Gen 19:21; 2 Sam 2:22; cf. 2 Kgs 5:1; Isa 3:3; 9:14 [*RSV* 15]; Schweizer, 124-41).

So three allied kings have come down to Elisha. Only one, Jehoram, takes on narrative body: he speaks, is rebuked, and, though unnamed by the narrator, is given his character — his name — by allusion to apostate father and mother. The other personages fall silent, and one of them, Jehoshaphat, is given life by name, by implicit contrasts, and by a prophet's "regard."

Immediately Elisha turns to secure an oracle from Yahweh (vv. 15-19). Here the narrator delivers a last major speech-event and returns to the mainspring of the plot. With intrusive directness relatively rare in biblical prose, it is explained that this moment, unlike the others, has its origin in the mysterious rush of supernatural power, for "whenever the minstrel played, the hand of the Lord came upon him" (v. 15; we retain the Hebr. *wĕhāyâ* plus participle in its frequentative sense; music and prophecy are associated in 1 Sam 10:5; for the "hand of God," meaning prophetic inspiration, see 1 Kgs 18:46; Ezek 3:22; 8:1).

The prophet's first utterance (v. 16) is cryptic, consisting only of a messenger's verbal signature, "thus says the Lord," and five short words: "Make[ing] this wadi pools, pools." (Cf. Jer 14:3; Cogan and Tadmor, *II Kings*, 45, take the word *gēbîm* to mean depressions on wadi floors that remain full of water after a flooding torrent has passed by. Note another compressed Elisha oracle in 2 Kgs 4:43bβ, "Eat[ing] and left over.") From somewhere beyond the ordinary, Yahweh declares his intention and answers the kings' pursuits. A second prophecy, v. 17, also introduced with a messenger formula, explains the first (note the conjunction "for" [*kî*]). Drawing sense out of that initial rush of obscure words, Elisha offers two promises. There will be water, but its wellspring is as hidden as that which yields up jumbled speech. From some mysterious place beyond wind and rain, drink will appear for man and beast (cf. vv. 17 and 9b). With wordplay Elisha adds a second promise. Filling this streambed *(nahal)* with water is an easy thing *(nāqal)* for God to do. Much harder it is to turn a reprobate king's complaint completely around. Nonetheless, "the Lord will give the Moabites into your [plur., keeping *all* the kings before us] hands" (v. 18).

These several speech-events in vv. 9-20 are no ordinary series of ornamental dialogue between characters. Clearly they serve as steps on the way to the final event, the battle with Moab (V, vv. 21-27bα). Yet, they slow the pace of action dramatically and draw one's attention elsewhere. Out of word and allusion the narrator builds a contrast between Jehoram and Jehoshaphat and hints that Jehoram's purposes have within them some vestige of father and mother, Ahab and Jezebel. Indeed, Jehoram seems a man of uncertain allegiance. He puts together the machinery for suppressing a Moabite rebellion, but when lack of water threatens the success of the campaign, he decries his fate as though he were called out to be a *victim* of Yahweh. In so brusquely and sarcastically dismissing him, Elisha reveals the king's deeper loyalties, which will not be falsified by any subsequent events. He belongs with father and mother, and, by implication, to their prophets, their lord, their Baal. In contrast, Jehoshaphat the Judahite, without the slightest trace of self-pity, suggests guidance through a Yahwistic prophet, affirms Elisha as having "the word of the Lord," and retreats into the background. Apparently the merit of Jehoshaphat alone justifies Elisha's, and presumably Yahweh's, concern. In any case, these three speech-events seem calculated to win the reader's sympathy for Jehoshaphat while denying it to Jehoram. At the same time the narrator characterized the relationships between kings and prophet as essentially involving a struggle between contradictory religious devotions (cf. 1 Kgs 18:20-40). Yet, despite all, Elisha says, Jehoram's defeatist outcry (v. 10) will be turned around to signal victory (v. 18b). With this promise, the narration resumes the action sequence begun in vv. 4-6.

Not surprisingly, prophecy will have its fulfillment. The land fills up with water and presumably the armies are refreshed (v. 20). This miracle is a first installment on final victory. Yet the path from prophetic word to its actualization is neither simple nor conventional. The tale is told, rather, with indirectness and ironic distance. While the kings seek out Elisha, the Moabites have already massed on the border (v. 21; cf. "were called out" [Niphal of *ṣˁq*] in Judg 6:34, 35; 10:17; 12:1; Schweizer, 149; note v. 21 is a circumstantial aside, using inverted word order with verbs in perfect tense [*qtl*], which takes the reader back slightly in time). Waiting in this sandstone red land *('ĕdôm),* the Moabites mistake blood-red water *(mayim 'ădummîm)* for blood *(dām).* They think their enemies have struck each other (the verb seems related to "sword") and so, bemused, they themselves are struck and routed (vv. 24-25).

There is chauvinistic humor in these wordplays and disastrous miscalculation, because one knows Elisha's promise and already expects its fulfillment (cf. a similar use of ironic distance in 1 Kgs 20:13-15, 23-30; 18:20-40). However, the urgently paced narration quickly dashes that confidence. The prophecy of victory (vv. 18-19), seemingly on its way to complete fulfillment (v. 25; note the similarity of wording to v. 19), is strangely denied its ultimate actualization when the Israelite armies abruptly withdraw from their assault on Kirhareseth (v. 27bβ). If the narrator previously shared his ironic amusement at those Moabites who mistake saving waters for death-flow, now he falsifies expectations and makes a victim of the reader's own calculations. Not only does victory appear less than victorious, and prophecy less than fulfilled, but the circumstances under which events occur are completely ambiguous. Is it the punishing outbreak of Yahweh's "wrath" *(qeṣep)* which falls upon Israel? (For this usual sense of *qeṣep* see Num 18:5 and 17:11 [*RSV* 16:46]; Josh 22:20 [cf. Josh 7:6ff.]; Deut 29:27 [*RSV* 28]; Isa 60:10; Jer 21:5.) Or does the Moabite god, Chemosh, respond to the firstborn sacrifice and strike out at the besiegers? (See Šanda, *Könige,* II, 24; the background in Canaanite culture for this motif is illustrated by an Ugaritic text that promises relief from siege if prayer-petition and sacrifice, including child sacrifice, are offered to Baal in the prescribed manner; see Margalit.) Or does fearful trembling grip the Israelites as they witness the horror of human sacrifice? (So Montgomery, *Kings,* 364, with several early Greek and Latin VSS; Schweizer, 168; Margalit; cf. 2 Kgs 16:3.) Or is it perhaps all three? Events turn on the anger of Chemosh *and* the hysteria-stricken Israelites (so, apparently, Gray, *Kings,* 490). In any case, ultimate triumph eludes Jehoram, Jehoshaphat, and the king of Edom (and, presumably, the Moabites, who lose all but one city).

Something shakes the reader's mastery of these events as well: the narrator creates this world, arouses expectations by allusion and pattern, and then turns one about at the end. (See a similar narrative strategy in 1 Kgs 22:1-38; see Long, *1 Kings,* 232-37.) Accepting this narrative as it now stands — whatever one may construe of its earlier history — one cannot escape the conclusion that the omniscient narrator employs ambiguity and surprise to confound kings, prophet, and reader alike.

Genre

The genre of this unit is not easy to describe precisely. There are features of both (→) legend and (→) historical story. A significant portion, vv. 5-25, follows not only the pattern of (→) battle story, but also a convention of theological didacticism: crisis, oracle promising relief, and fulfillment of divine word (see Long, 347, calling this section "oracle-actualization narrative"). If one leaves aside generic identifications for reconstructed earlier stages of the present narrative (e.g., De Vries, 65-66; II.-Chr. Schmitt, 34, 51-52), it seems best to speak of PROPHETIC BATTLE STORY, a type of (→) historical story largely concerned with an imaginative telling of military conflict, but in a way which gives a central place to one or more prophets who assume dramatic and interpretative importance. (See Montgomery, *Kings,* 358, "prophetic popular story of an actual historical event"; and Gray, *Kings,* 469, "historical narrative" in which Elisha plays a subsidiary role; Šanda, *Könige* II, 81, stresses "historical narrative.") For close biblical parallels, see 1 Kgs 20:1-34; 2 Kgs 18:17–19:36; 2 Chr 20:1-30; also cf. 1 Kgs 22:1-39, which gives rather more emphasis to the prophetic elements.

An important formal element in this narrative is the schema of (→) oracular inquiry. The inquiry begins with a problem to be addressed by divine word, and includes an audience with a prophet wherein an oracle is sought ("inquire of the word of Yahweh" [*dāraš 'et-děbar yahweh*]), the oracle itself, and finally an account of its fulfillment. (See Long, *1 Kings,* 156, and full discussion.) In 2 Kgs 3:4-27, Moab's rebellion, a threat exacerbated by an army run out of water (vv. 5, 9-10), is sufficient crisis to require guidance by God through Elisha. (The technical divinatory phrase, "inquire of Yahweh," appears in v. 11; Cogan and Tadmor, *II Kings,* 45, refer to Mesopotamian diviners who accompany armies in the field.) Two oracles, vv. 16, 17-19, and their fulfillments, vv. 20, 21-25, quickly follow. (Cf. 2 Kgs 8:7-15; 1 Kgs 14:1-18; 2 Chr 20:13-20; Long, 343-45.) As the narrative now stands, this literary convention primarily shapes the heart of a longer (→) battle story, but is obviously undercut by the surprising turnabout in vv. 26-27.

Formulaic elements worth noting are: CRY OF DISTRESS, v. 10, with its typical exclamatory interjection, "Alas!" (*'āhāh*), and brief reason for the distress (see 2 Kgs 6:5 and full discussion with parallels); CONVEYANCE FORMULA, "he (the Lord) will give the Moabites into your hands," v. 18b, a typical feature of battle accounts (cf. 1 Kgs 20:13, 28; 22:6) and Deuteronomistic summaries, as in Judg 3:8; 4:2 (see Schweizer, 116). The narrator in 2 Kings 3 has employed this formula with some irony. Typically it signifies victory for Israel, as in v. 18. However, the distressed Jehoram had already turned it against himself (v. 10), and later events, vv. 26-27, despite the prophecy, burden the formula with an ambiguity it usually does not carry. What does it mean in *this* situation that God promises to give Moab into Israel's hands? Also note the PROPHETIC EMPOWERING FORMULA, "the power [lit., 'hand,' *yād*] of the Lord came upon him," v. 15, which expresses the seizure of the prophet through God, and announces to the reader that oracle and/or vision is to come forth (see 1 Kgs 18:46; Isa 8:11; Ezek 1:3; 3:14, 22; 8:1; 37:1; 40:1; Schweizer, 141-48; and, above all, Walther Zimmerli, *Ezekiel 1* [Hermeneia; Philadelphia: Fortress, 1979] 117-18). There is a fragmentary OATH in v. 14, "As the Lord of hosts lives . . ." (*hay yahweh şĕbā'ôt*), perhaps here just an exclamation, since no actual statement of what will be undertaken follows (cf. 1 Kgs 17:1; 18:15; 2 Kgs 5:16; Schweizer, 118). The phrase which is linked to this oath formula, "the Lord . . . *whom I serve"* (lit. "before whom I stand," *'ăšer 'āmadtî lěpānāyw*) appears elsewhere only in the Elijah and Elisha narratives (1 Kgs 17:1; 18:15; 2 Kgs 3:14; 5:16) and adds solemnity to the speech as well as motival continuity between Elijah and his

45

successor. Finally, a DECLARATION OF ALLIANCE appears in v. 7b (see 1 Kgs 22:4b; 1 Sam 14:7b; cf. 2 Sam 5:1).

Setting

There is insufficient evidence to suggest a typical societal setting for prophetic battle story. Nor are we any better able to guess at the circumstances in which this particular example may have originated or been transmitted. Montgomery (*Kings*, 358) implies a popular folk setting. Certain connections with cultic "holy war" contexts (e.g., the conveyance formula [v. 18b], the mustering of troops [v. 21], and mention of "burnt offering" [v. 27]) remind Schweizer (p. 171) of a priestly origin with an anti-Elisha cast; H.-Chr. Schmitt (44-45) believes both the original folkloristic battle account and its expanded prophetically edited version came from Judah and were part of a larger postexilic collection which included 1 Kings 20 and 22. (Šanda, *Könige* II, 81, also notes these literary affinities.) De Vries (pp. 122-23) argues for an origin in the later Jehuite period. Given the disarray of scholarly opinion and the slim evidential base, it seems wisest to give primary weight to the present literary context in the books of Kings.

This prophetic battle story is the first incident related about King Jehoram's reign; it presupposes the note about "peace with Israel" during Jehoshaphat's time (1 Kgs 22:45 [*RSV* 44]), and brings into the foreground of the Dtr history that Moabite trouble which was only background for Jehoram's predecessor, Ahaziah (2 Kgs 1:1). Since prophets and their activities, particularly those of Elijah and Elisha, were of great importance to this exilic historian, it may be that this story ought to be seen as some kind of sequel to the pausal moment between reigns, ch. 2, which focuses on Elijah and Elisha together. Here in ch. 3, the reader gains a full picture of Elisha operating independently of his predecessor, but recalling in word and allusion the latter's relationships with the earlier members of the Omride family.

Intention

In context, the Dtr writer meant to relate a first incident in the reign of Jehoram. The story portrays both victory and defeat; it tells of a king whose successes, clearly emphasized, are mitigated by an opponent's power (v. 27) and a prophet's hostility (v. 13). This mixed evaluation of Jehoram corresponds inversely to the formulaic condemnation, qualified with a positive remark, which he receives in the introductory summary (v. 2).

The author recounts Moab's rebellion and its nearly total suppression, as though finally to deal with a problem first mentioned as backdrop to Ahaziah's reign and death (2 Kgs 1:1). Yet, the DtrH also allows one to question whether Yahweh actually provides the means to victory. The kings in their own ways dispute the matter, and by shrinking prophesied victory to indeterminate outcome, especially one that hints at a rival god's powers, the narrator seems to equivocate (see discussion by Cogan and Tadmor, *II Kings,* 51-52). At the least, his way of telling the tale, or perhaps leaving its original form untouched, undermines a reader's simplistic ideological appropriation of it, just as was the case when Ahab a generation earlier consulted the prophets (1 Kgs 22:1-38; see Long, *1 Kings,* 233-36). Moreover, contrasting images of the Hebrew kings and reference to Elisha's serving Elijah recall that same generation of Jezebel and Ahab, when Yahwistic prophets struggled against a royal line infatuated with the Baals (1 Kings 22). Clearly not limited to Jehoram alone, the historian presses a number of analogies and pushes a simple story to the level of paradigmatic event, timeless in its evocation of fundamental conflicts among religious affirmations.

Jehoram seems most lame when suspecting Yahweh's intention. The king initiates military action against Moab. When the plans flounder in the dry steppelands of Edom, he feels himself a victim of God whom he did not call upon, and whom — in the writer's opinion — Jehoram has neglected throughout his reign (vv. 2-3). Moreover, Jehoshaphat's bearing in the story reflects negatively on Jehoram. Seeking after prophetic guidance (vv. 11-12) and declaring military solidarity with Jehoram (v. 7b), Jehoshaphat's actions recall another time and place (1 Kgs 22:4-9) when he seeks divine guidance, and with attitudes pointedly contrasted to those of an Israelite king, Ahab, who, like Jehoram, has been tossed aside by the historian's negative introductory summary (16:29-33). Elisha stirs those recollections in the reader (v. 13) as though to declare that even now the season has not turned, that those ideological struggles for religious devotion persist among Ahab's heirs.

Jehoshaphat, a foil for one's memory, has already been evaluated positively by the Dtr writer in 1 Kgs 22:43a. Here he asks for divine guidance through a Yahweh-prophet whom the reader knows to be the fully empowered successor to Elijah (ch. 2). This king's initiatives for turning vassal control into God's war seem approved. It is not Jehoram but Jehoshaphat who seems "called," and the latter's piety enables at long last the containment of Moab's threat to Israel.

One might suppose that this positive outcome to events correlates with the DtrH's favorable attitude toward Jehoshaphat and Judah. Yet victory is not as complete as one would have expected from the conventions of biblical accounts of battle. Perhaps this ambivalence expresses the Dtr writer's attitude toward Jehoram. This king loses his place to a Judean ally and the shadow of his parents nearly eclipses Elisha's impulse to intercede. Perhaps Jehoram's moral disadvantage even compromises the fulness of victory at the end (cf. Cogan and Tadmor, *II Kings,* 52, n. 8).

In this light, one may suggest that Jehoram's self-pitying claim (v. 10) that he is a victim elected for defeat captures the narrator's ironic vision. God gives victory that is also failure, a call that is also a mark of retribution. In the reader's ken, Jehoram — judged on the wrong side of God from the beginning — sees truly, if not quite with full realization, that his destiny comes from God, just as Micaiah son of Imlah claims that confusion among Ahab's prophets is God-sent. The kings, even Elisha, speak as though they have a grip on their fate, but in the concluding action sequence, where there is no speech, they lose initiative and control. Their actions, expectations, and understanding, and those of the reader, seem shaken and falsified. The story subverts a simplistic view of the didactic association between piety and success, impiety and failure, even as its introductory framework speaks otherwise.

Bibliography

See bibliographies at 2 Kgs 1:2-17a; 2:1-25. K. H. Bernhardt, "Der Feldzug der drei Könige," in *Shalom: Studien zu Glaube und Geschichte Israels* (*Fest.* A. Jepsen; ed. K. H. Bernhardt; Stuttgart: Calwer, 1971) 11-22; B. Margalit, "Why King Mesha of Moab Sacrificed His Oldest Son," *BARev* 12/6 (1986) 62-63, 76; H. Schweizer, *Elischa in den Kriegen. Literaturwissenschaftliche Untersuchung von 2 Kön 3; 6:8-23; 6:24–7:20* (SANT 37; Munich: Kösel, 1974).

MULTIPLICATION OF A WIDOW'S OIL, 4:1-7

Structure

I. Audience with Elisha: petition and response	1-4
A. Woman's speech (petition)	1
1. Narrative introduction	1a
2. Speech	1b
a. Declaration	$1b\alpha$
b. Attestation	$1b\beta_1$
c. Declaration	$1b\beta_2$
B. Elisha's first response (investigating how to solve problem)	2
1. Elisha's query	2a
2. Woman's reply	2b
C. Elisha's second response: instructions concerning oil	3-4
II. The problem solved	5-7
A. Multiplication of oil	5-6
1. Opening narration: continuous pouring	5
2. Dialogue: no more jars	$6a\text{-}b\alpha$
3. Conclusion: flow stopped	$6b\beta$
B. Results	7
1. Elisha informed	$7a\alpha$
2. Elisha's response: instructions to woman	$7a\beta\text{-}b$

This unit is clearly separate from 3:4-27. The abrupt introduction of a new character and situation, and the inverted word order in the Hebrew (v. 1a, subject + verb in perfect tense) are both typical features of independent, popular narrative (cf. 4:38a, 42a; 1 Kgs 1:1a; 13:1; 21:1; 2 Sam 13:1). The outer limit is defined by 4:8, which opens onto a different incident in a new situation (note the idiomatic *wayhî hayyôm* [*RSV* "one day"] in 4:8, 11, 18, which ties this material together stylistically). Within 4:1-7 there are no signs of literary disorder.

The literary structure is straightforward. The narrator reports a woman's problem and Elisha's determination of a means to help her (I, vv. 1-4). Then oil appears miraculously (II.A, vv. 5-6), and through the prophet's words the reader infers that this event will solve the woman's problem (II.B, v. 7). More abstractly, the plot follows a pattern common to other tales of miracle: (1) a party in a problem situation requests help, (2) a helper responds by taking action to extend help, (3) a miracle results and removes the problem (see Culley, *Narrative*, 91-92, who cites examples in 2 Kgs 4:38-41; 6:1-7; 2:19-22; Exod 15:2-27; 17:1-7; 1 Kgs 17:17-24).

The narrative consists mainly of three scenes formed primarily by direct speech (I, vv. 1-4; II.A, vv. 5-6; II.B, v. 7). Indeed, the essential elements of narrative plot — a conflict and its resolution — emerge only in words spoken by the woman and Elisha (vv. 1b, 2-4, 7). Spare prose narration charts dialogue, describes the flow of oil (largely as execution of what is given in direct speech, vv. 4, 5-6), and marks its abrupt cessation (two words only, v. 6bβ). The characters are only slightly realized.

The first scene consists of nested dialogues. A woman reveals her troubles to Elisha, v. 1b, and receives his definitive response only in vv. 3-4 after a secondary exchange, v. 2, has taken place in which the prophet settles on a means of helping her. The woman is vaguely identified as "a certain woman (wife) from among the women (wives) of the sons of the prophets." (The *RSV,* with the LXX, has lost something of the indefiniteness in the MT, which gives the impression that this woman emerges out of dim obscurity.) She offers two declarations: that her husband is dead, and that creditors threaten her son's freedom. Between these assertions, the widow attests to her husband's piety: "*You*, you know [the Hebrew is emphatic] that your servant has always revered the Lord" (v. 1bβ$_1$, *hāyâ yārē*᾽ has a durative sense). Her words imply a petition and suggest the moral basis on which it might be favorably granted (see Gen 30:26, 29; Exod 32:22; Num 20:14; 1 Kgs 5:17, 20 [*RSV* 3, 6]). Thus in this first speech we learn with Elisha of this woman's particular problem and that she means to ask him for help. Elisha responds accordingly, searching in dialogue, v. 2, for a means to help her, and finally issues his direct instructions, vv. 3-4.

The second scene (II.A, vv. 5-6) involves only the widow and her sons. Her actions, which carry out to the letter Elisha's instructions, suggest the mystery of wondrous things happening in secret: "she shut the door upon herself and her sons; they were bringing [vessels] and she was pouring out [oil]" (the Hebrew participial clause suggests continuous activity). The narrator stresses the impersonal quality of the miracle. In a brief verbal exchange, woman and son discover that no jars remain — and immediately, expressed with two words, the narrator provides closure, "the oil stopped." Neither by action of this widow and her sons, nor by Elisha's direct manipulation of the tools of miracle (cf. 4:41; 2:21), nor by God's words (cf. 3:17-20) does the flow of oil cease. One observes simple serendipity clothing hidden calculus: a single jar of oil by chance in the house, many jars to be filled (the number is not fixed), and when there are no more, the flow ceases.

The third scene (II.B, v. 7) reports that Elisha, having been told of the surfeit of oil, now instructs the woman how to resolve her difficulties. Thus, the crisis which was revealed only in her retrospective plea, v. 1b, finds its resolution — at least in prospect.

These three scenes carry within themselves a larger "plot," the difficulty and its solution, only in retrospect and prospect. The narrator seems rather more concerned to convey the immediacy of encounter between prophet and woman. In this light, meeting-in-direct-discourse is really the significant narrative event, as it was in the narrative of Solomon discovering a child's true mother (1 Kgs 3:16-27).

Genre

This narrative is a PROPHET LEGEND, a narrative which focuses on a prophet as the main character and exemplar of power, divine favor, or wondrous deed (see Rofé, "Classification," 430, "simple *legenda*"; H.-Chr. Schmitt, 91-99, anecdotal "Miracle story"; Plöger, 50-51, "prophetic-act story"; and De Vries, 53, "power demonstration narrative," a legend which shows the prophet's charismatic power). Hobbs's doubts about the suitability of the word "prophetic" for this story seem too restrictive, and his alternative, a "problem to solution" story type, is not sufficiently determinative (*2 Kings*, 45-46).

Setting

Legend belongs to the world of folk storytellers (see Haller, 109, who stresses the "folktalelike" [*märchenhaft*] features of 2 Kgs 4:1-7). Legends would have originated and flourished in many different societal settings among different peoples, and would have found various occasions for use depending on the circumstances and aims of their narrators. Because of its central interest in a prophet, many commentators have speculated that this particular example arose among prophets in ancient Israel (e.g., Gray, *Kings*, 466-67; De Vries, 53) or perhaps with Elisha's disciples at Gilgal (see H.-Chr. Schmitt, 157-58). However, one may not so easily rule out the more ordinary person, who also would have had some interest in repeating legends about specially revered holy men. This particular story may at one time have found a setting in an early oral or written collection of traditions about Elisha (Gray, *Kings;* H.-Chr. Schmitt).

Since evidence for these matters is so slim, the more important question has to do with the literary setting of this legend in the books of Kings. The narrative is associated with vv. 8-37 by similarity of motif, Elisha helping a woman in distress, and by literary *topos* (cf. vv. 4, 5 with v. 33). More importantly, the narrative is one of several incidents which bring Elisha into full view, while ostensibly recording events of importance to Jehoram's reign.

Intention

Prophet legend would have been told primarily to celebrate the wondrous power and exemplary deeds of a prophet, and so to inculcate awe and devotion in the hearer. In its present literary context, this particular example now seems to serve mainly the purposes of the Dtr writer. Elisha cares for his "God-fearing" (v. 1) band of followers apart from the royal house and its king, Jehoram, who, despite occasional dealings with the prophet, nonetheless remains at a strained distance (3:14). Indirectly, one sees that this king is ineffectual and ignorant of Yahweh's power in Israel (5:7; 6:26-31).

Bibliography

See bibliographies at 2 Kgs 1:2-17a; 2:1-18. R. Culley, *Narrative*, 91-92 (→ 2 Kgs 2:19-24); Eduard Haller, "Märchen und Zeugnis: Auslegung der Erzählung 2 Könige 4:1-7," in *Probleme Biblischer Theologie* (*Fest.* G. von Rad; ed. H. W. Wolff; Munich: Kaiser, 1971) 108-15; H.-Chr. Schmitt, *Elisa* (→ 2 Kgs 2:1-25).

REVIVAL OF A SHUNAMMITE WOMAN'S SON, 4:8-37

Structure

There are certain stylistic features within this unit which link it to the literary milieu of 4:1-7 (e.g., a variant feminine suffix, vv. 2, 3, 7, 16, 23; the similarity of Elisha's musing questions, 4:2 and 4:13; the echoes of 4:4-5 in 4:21, 33). Yet, 4:8 abruptly begins an entirely new incident in a new locale, with new characters opposite Elisha, and with a rare idiomatic expression, *wayhî hayyôm* (*RSV* "one day") situated only in 4:8, 11, 18 (cf. 1 Sam 1:4; 14:1; Job 1:6, 13; 2:1). Moreover, the unit's literary sophistication contrasts with the relative simplicity of 4:1-7. The same is true when one compares this narrative with the material which follows in vv. 38-41. There the narrator begins with the inverted Hebrew word order characteristic of self-contained narration (v. 38a; cf. vv. 1aα, 42a; 1 Kgs 1:1a; 13:1) and relates a separate incident in an entirely new location (the reference to Gilgal presupposes a context of narration unrelated to vv. 8-37).

Many scholars treat vv. 4-37 as a unified whole (e.g., Rofé, "Classification," 433-35; idem, *Prophetical Stories,* 27-33; Montgomery, *Kings,* 371, who argues against an earlier view that vv. 12-15 are secondary insertions; Gray, *Kings,* 467; cf. Šanda, *Könige* II, 29-33). Yet A. Schmitt, who agrees substantially with H.-Chr. Schmitt (pp. 93-101), has determined that vv. 13-15 and 29-30a, 31, 32b, 35 are later editorial additions, and thus analyzes a hypothetical original narrative (vv. 8-12, 16-28, 30b, 32a, 33-34, 36-37). (Note the quite arbitrary judgments of Würthwein, *Könige,* 290.) One may doubt that the use of *na'ar* to mean both "servant," Gehazi (vv. 12, 19, 22), and the woman's "son" (vv. 29-35), as opposed to *yeled,* "son," elsewhere (vv. 18, 26, 34, 35), offers sufficient data for redactional theories, especially if one grants an ancient author the freedom to use language imaginatively. Nor need one assume that Gehazi's intermediarial role in vv. 12-15 is problematic, since that is precisely his position in other portions of the narrative which are presumed to be "original" by A. Schmitt (vv. 25b-26, 27, 36 [Würthwein simply pronounces everything having to do with Gehazi as secondary]). Furthermore, the repetitions in vv. 12b and 15 need not have resulted from clumsy editing; they may just as well portray one action (dialogue between prophet and servant) as happening simultaneously with another (the woman awaiting Elisha's business with her). See 1 Sam 19:12, 18; 20:27, 29; and full discussion below. In view of the ambiguity of such evidence as may be adduced for claims about redaction history, it seems preferable to deal with the narrative as it now stands without denying the possibility of editorial activity during some earlier stage of development.

One may easily discern the main lines of narrative structure. After the background exposition, which suggests something of the main characters and setting for incidents to follow (I, vv. 8-11), the drama plays itself out in three movements mostly built of speech and dialogue: in fulfillment of prophecy, a son is born to a Shunammite who was without child and whose husband was old (II, vv. 12-17); the son sickens and dies, creating a crisis for both mother and prophet (III, vv. 18-25aα); Elisha's miraculous intervention restores the boy to life (IV, vv. 25aβ-35). Dramatic intensity drains away in a brief and final meeting between prophet and woman (V, vv. 36-37).

The dénouement completes a thematic and structural symmetry in the narrative. The Shunammite appears first in deferential respect toward Elisha (vv. 8-10); she questions and pleads, even rebukes him, while demanding his help (vv. 16, 27- 28), and now at the end, she falls at his feet (she had earlier grabbed hold of them in petitionary abandon, v. 27). Indeed, the woman seems nearly to worship this man of God (v. 37, *tištaḥû 'ārṣâ;* cf. Gen 18:2; 19:1; 1 Kgs 1:23; 2 Kgs 2:15). At the close, Elisha in effect declares her son restored (v. 36bβ) as earlier he had announced his birth (v. 16). Occurring only as part of annunciation (vv. 14-17, 28) and restoration (v. 36), this "son" motif spans the narrative's main action: a son is given in promise, lost in sickness, and restored by the mother's pursuit of a holy man's power.

The narrative opens with a carefully constructed exposition (I, vv. 8-11) consisting of repeated framing motifs (vv. 8aα₁, 11a) which enclose unusually detailed description. One may visualize the structure as follows:

Framework	"one day Elisha crossed to Shunem"
v. 8aα₁	*(wayhî hayyôm wayya'ăbōr . . .)*
	Description (vv. 8aα₂-10)
	"and there, a wealthy woman . . ."
	(wĕšām 'iššâ gĕdôlâ . . .)
Framework	"One day he came there . . ."
v. 11a	*(wayhî hayyôm wayyābō' šammâ)*

Narrated time (v. 8aα₁) stops, then resumes in v. 11a. In the pause, retrospective suggestions of character and past relationships emerge in a network of repeated images. (Note 1 Sam 1:3a, 7a; 2 Kgs 7:5b, 8a — other examples of repetition which demarcate a place at which the narrator fills a gap in the reader's information. See Long, "Framing Repetitions.") The characterization begins with a brief nominal sentence, "and there, an esteemed [*gĕdôlâ*] woman," v. 8aα₂ (cf. 5:2; 10:6, 11; Jonah 3:7). One hears of her customary actions in past days: "and she (habitually) urged him to eat food, and whenever he passed by, he would turn aside there to eat food" (v. 8b; note the durative temporal sense of *wayhî middê* + infinitive, *'obrô,* "whenever he passed by"; see 1 Kgs 14:28a;

1 Sam 1:7; 18:30). The verb "pass by" *('br)* links the habitual past to the singulative action in the present with which the story began, v. 8aα₁. Then follows an explanation of how this habit developed: "and she (had) said to her husband . . ." (vv. 9-10). Note the repeated words which tie Elisha's customary action, v. 8b, to the Shunammite's plan to care for him: "pass by" *('br)*, "turn (go) in there" *(yāsūr šammâ)*, repeated in vv. 8bβ, 9, 10. Finally, with some of these same expressions, "turn in" *(wayyāsar)*, and "there" *(šammâ)* the author turns habitual past into present, and slides back into the incident about to unfold in *this* moment, when Elisha "came there" *(wayyābō' šammâ*, v. 11aβ). Note that the latter phrase recalls the Shunammite's intentions, who envisioned that he would "come" *(bô')* to her home, v. 10bα. At the same time, this verb, along with *wayhî hayyôm*, marks the resumption of the main narrative sequence.

This intricately constructed opening exposition gives the reader a palpable sense of the Shunammite. She is "wealthy" *('iššâ gĕdôlâ*, v. 8aα₂; cf. 1 Sam 25:2; 2 Sam 19:33) but, one imagines, also greatly esteemed (cf. 2 Kgs 5:1). She confesses her awe before Elisha ("this is a holy man of God"; cf. 1 Kgs 17:24) and summons the means to provide lavishly for him (note the narrator's descriptive fullness, "chamber with walls . . . a bed, a table, a chair, and a lamp . . ."). Man of God and Shunammite woman now meet in *this* narrative moment, vv. 8aα₁ + 11a, with background, obligations, and relationship long since established.

Yet for all the suggestion of familiarity between them, their meeting on this new occasion seems curiously indirect (II, vv. 12-17). One must visualize a conversation between Elisha and his servant Gehazi *about* the woman (whom he calls only "this Shunammite," cf. v. 25b) while she stands by, having "presented herself" *(watta'ămōd lĕpānāyw* [*RSV* "stood before him"]; see Montgomery, *Kings,* 368). Contrary to the opinion of many critics, the text demands no alterations. Nearly identical phrases in vv. 12 and 15 simply bracket this conversation and set it forth as occurring while the frame-action, the woman's standing nearby, continues. (Cf. vv. 25b, 27a; see 1 Sam 3:1, 19; 19:12, 18; 2 Sam 13:34, 37; Exod 20:18, 21; Talmon, 9-26. Cf. also A. Berlin, *Poetics and Interpretation of Biblical Narrative* [Bible and Literature Series; Sheffield: Almond, 1983] 126-28.)

Thus, after Gehazi has summoned the Shunammite and while she stands by, perhaps moving closer "in the doorway" (v. 15b), the two men discuss Elisha's business with her. As in 4:1-7, Elisha gropes for the raw materials of miracle. How shall he reward her awe-filled service *(hărādâ,* RSV "all this trouble") to him? He puts this first musing inquiry (v. 13; cf. 4:2) as a charge for Gehazi to ask the woman if Israel's king or army commander might be of some help. Apparently overhearing, the Shunammite injects herself into the conversation. Yet the narrator's way of telling suggests that she intrudes tentatively, as though speaking to no one in particular. She declares simply, "I dwell among my own people" (v. 13b). As though hearing but not acknowledging her reply, Elisha inquires directly of Gehazi, v. 14a, who nudges the man of God toward a solution: perhaps he can give the gift of a son to this woman who has none, and who — with an aged husband — has no hope of one (cf. Abraham and Sarah, Gen 18:10-12).

Suddenly, oblique communication shifts to declaration and response. Turning to the Shunammite, Elisha announces a simple promise, v. 16a, that "at this time next year" she will "embrace a son." (In view of Akkadian parallels, the *RSV* "when the time comes round" [*kāʿēt ḥayyâ*] should not be understood as referring to a period of pregnancy; it simply means "next year." R. Yaron, *"Kaʿeth ḥayyah* and *koh leḥay,"* VT 12 [1962] 500-501.) Instantly, the Shunammite reacts rudely, without thought of protocol and with words that rebuke the prophet as much as convey her skepticism, v. 16b. Seeming to mock her emotional outburst, the writer immediately invokes a standard formula of conception and birth (v. 17), and thus closes the scene with the disinterested tone of a reporter. The event occurs essentially as Elisha had predicted.

This first section of the narrative recalls a conventional annunciation scene (see Gen 18:10-14; 16:11-14; Judg 13:3-5; Luke 1:11-20, 26-36; cf. Alter, 125-26; Neff). However, departures from convention reveal more than conformity with it. It is not an "angel" *(malʾāk)* or other supernatural emissary who announces imminent birth (as Gen 16:11; Judg 13:3; Luke 1:30), but Elisha, a "man of God," acting on his own initiative. The Shunammite woman, true to type, is skeptical. She expresses doubt, even protest, at this promise which must seem cruel in view of its chances of fulfillment. So doing, in the reader's ken, the woman puts herself on the side of Sarah, who laughed at her own similarly announced prospects (Gen 18:12), and against Elisha; her adulation (v. 9), after all, has commonsense limits, and she seizes the right of protest. For his part, Elisha does not parrot the usual annunciatory formula, but suggests an unusual image: she will "embrace" a son (cf. Gen 29:13; 33:4; 48:10; Song of Songs 2:6; 8:3). This woman will not simply bear a child and thus overcome barrenness or present the world a hero. (The boy is in fact only an anonymous child whose sole function in the narrative is to be born, die, and be brought back to life.) Rather, Elisha hints at the Shunammite's future transformation into a fully realized mother. The woman's response adds yet another particularity to convention. She protests strongly but politely, "No, my lord, O man of God, do not lie ['*al-těkazzēb*] to your maidservant," and thus infects the habitual decorum between prophet and hostess with moral accountability. The disorder will later erupt in demand and indignation (v. 28).

The next scene (III, vv. 18-25aα) tells quickly of the crisis that disturbs the symmetry of promise and fulfillment; it is also the catalyst which reorders Elisha's relationship with this woman. As quickly as one learned of conception and birth, one now reads of childhood and death in short sentences paced by action verbs: "and the child grew . . . and he went out . . . and he said, 'My head, my head!' . . . and he (the servant) lifted him and brought him . . . and he sat . . . and he died" (vv. 18-20). The child's cry elicits no word of comfort, and the mother's efforts to hold back the night are simply swept away by a one-word obituary, *wayyāmōt,* "and he died." Nothing stills the rush of events. The woman entombs her son among the effects of the man of God, and turns immediately to arranging a journey. Her speech discloses the urgency: "that I may quickly go . . . and return again," v. 22; "Urge the beast on, do not slacken the pace . . . ," v. 24. She turns aside her husband's uncomprehending restraint, v. 23, with one word, *šālôm.*

The narrator transports us through tremendous space and time: from birth to death without a significant childhood; from mother to sonless mother cheated of motherhood; from parent showing no conventional signs of grief to a woman singlemindedly fixed on some undisclosed aim. The Shunammite is clearheaded and purposeful in her urgent concentration. Her husband, something of a foil, seems only a mystified bystander beside this burst of "maternal passion" (see Rofé, "Classification," 433-34). She speaks only to get what she needs, to demand the haste she requires, and to refuse explanation in one-word triviality, šālôm, "It will be well" (v. 23bβ).

Indeed, in the next scene (IV.A, vv. 25aβ-30) the Shunammite's intense pursuit of her aim propels her right past every obstacle, including those formalities which kept Elisha at some remove in vv. 12-15. While she approaches the man of God on Carmel (note the framing repetitions which mark out synchronous events, "and she came to the man of God," vv. 25aβ, 27aα), Elisha orders Gehazi to send her greetings. As in vv. 12-13, the woman responds to this private exchange between Elisha and servant as if she has overheard, or in this case, as though she has so quickly covered the ground between them and her as to make the sending of a messenger quite superfluous. (On the parallels in literary structure with vv. 12-17, see van Daalen.) Clearly nothing will stand in her way. The woman returns the polite, unsuspecting greetings with her by now familiar one-word disguise of intent and determination, šālôm, "It is well" (v. 26). She may hint at her confidence in the outcome of her mission. In any case, she thrusts protocol aside, grabs hold of Elisha's feet, and explodes with confrontational, accusatory questions (v. 28). Not even Gehazi, who rises to push her away, can restrain her. This mother denied will be satisfied only by the assistance Elisha alone can offer. But he, like Gehazi, is ignorant of what lies behind this headlong intrusion onto Mount Carmel. In words that recall Hannah's similar anguish (cf. 1 Sam 1:10), Elisha acknowledges her distress, but then admits (to Gehazi) a blindness rarely confessed among the prophets: "The Lord has hidden it from me and has not told me" (v. 27; cf. 1 Kgs 14:5-6). One may suppose that the Shunammite's passion includes anger, indignation, and grief. However, the narrator shows us only the outward persona of a determined woman, transformed into a mother by a prophet's word, pressing herself upon the first cause of her troubles.

Her rhetorical questions in v. 28 rebuke Elisha, and, remarkably, imply to the reader that the man of God lacks more than merely God's private revelation. (See A. Schmitt, 17-18, who comments on the woman's doubts about Elisha.) *She* has been wronged in this business; it is *her* son who is dead, and it is *this* man of God who somehow should assume responsibility. The woman had said, "do not lie to your maidservant," and what now can Elisha's promise possibly mean? How can Elisha's self-initiated reward for her now bring any delight? The woman, perhaps shaken by the promise of motherhood, and surely buffeted by the wind of death, must now, with a new gale, be tearing loose her moorage. It is not the formerly generous Shunammite whom one sees now, but a desperate mother bereft of her son. She demands (without knowing Elisha's view that second sight was withheld from him) that he accept responsibility for what his miracle making has wrought in her life (cf. Rofé).

In the Shunammite's extremity, she perceives Elisha as a god who holds sway over life and death. Yet ironically, the aggrieved victim, like Job, must break through protocol and raise the issue of moral accountability. To her, Elisha's first response must have seemed, at the very least, insensitive. Even if Gehazi, armed with his master's staff and urgent charge, were able to harness apotropaic powers (cf. Exod 7:20; 8:1-2, 12-13 [*RSV* 5-6, 16-17]; 17:5, 9), it may be too feeble a gesture. And in any case, sending a servant seems less than the mother's sense of restitution demands. Her second word to Elisha, formally an oath (v. 30a), really rejects the prophet's response and demands implicitly that he deal personally with the situation. (Note how in v. 30 the narrator refers to the Shunammite as "mother of the child," perhaps to signal that one is reading from her point of view.) She will not be thrust aside either physically or procedurally (v. 27), and certainly not in this matter of moral accountability. Elisha seems to understand, although he still speaks nothing directly to the woman. The narrator tells us simply, "he arose and followed her." However, one has been shown a clearheaded "mother of the child" up against a somewhat obtuse, not fully informed man of God who must be pushed to action in this crisis. The picture strongly contrasts with the Elisha who dominates the beginning of the narrative. There, when there was no crisis, he volunteered to reward the Shunammite's solicitous actions toward him.

The mother's insistence finally seems vindicated by events (IV.B, C, vv. 31-35). While Elisha and the Shunammite are en route, Gehazi goes ahead, tries to revive the boy, and fails completely. Marking this incident as circumstantial "meanwhile" (the Hebrew word order and syntax shifts), the writer depicts a valley from which Elisha takes his ascent. Gehazi carries out the instructions perfectly. Yet, as the Baal prophets once shouted their imprecations to a deaf sky (1 Kgs 18:26-29), so Gehazi lay his master's staff on unresponsive flesh: "There was no sound or sign of life" (*wĕʾên qôl wĕʾên qāšeb,* v. 31a; cf. 1 Kgs 18:29b). The miracle cure requires more than a servant and the master's staff, it seems, and this the Shunammite foresees completely.

Against this image of failure, the narrator plays out the climactic scene, IV.C, vv. 32-35. Briefly, one looks with Elisha's eyes. He arrives, "and behold [*wĕhinnēh*], the youth lay dead on his bed," v. 32. (*hinnēh* + participle often marks a shift to a character's vantage point; see A. Berlin, *Poetics and Interpretation of Biblical Narrative* [Bible and Literature Series; Sheffield: Almond, 1983] 59-63; and 1 Sam 19:16; Judg 4:22.) Then, reverting to the narrator's position of omniscient observer, we gaze upon a world of curative magic and Elisha's step-by-step efforts at resuscitation. Set apart from ordinary space, locked away in the roof-chamber-become-tomb, Elisha prays to Yahweh and stretches himself like a curative template over the corpse. He lays mouth to mouth, hand to hand, and eye to eye, and "pants over him." (The *RSV* "stretched himself upon him" is based on v. 34a; *wayyighar,* v. 34aβ, has caused confusion in the VSS and among critics. See R. Mach and J. Marks, "The Head Upon the Knees: A Note to 1 Kings 18:42," in *The World of Islam* [*Fest.* Philip Hitti; ed. J. Kritzeck et al.; London: Macmillan, 1959] 68-73; in private communication, J. Greenfield suggests additional support in the Targum for translating √*ghr* as "breathe strongly" or "pant." But cf. 1 Kgs 18:42, where one would think more naturally of "lean down" or "crouch.")

Warming flesh seems to mark the end of a first phase in the curative procedure. Elisha disengages and walks "one time to and fro." The phrase *'aḥat hēnnâ wĕ'aḥat hēnnâ*, which only occurs here, suggests prescribed action. Then he "goes up" again, breathes heavily *(wayyighar)* over him as before, and life returns. The youth sneezes *(wayzôrēr;* see Burney, *Notes,* 276; cf. G. R. Driver, "Ancient Lore and Modern Knowledge. 2. Resuscitation," in *Hommages à A. Dupont-Sommer* [Paris: Librairie Adrien-Maisonneuve, 1971] 280-82). And he sneezes seven times, as though to suggest the mysterious powers attending the number "seven" (cf. 1 Kgs 18:43). The boy opens his eyes, and the second phase is over. There remains only the presentation of the wonder to the anxiously waiting mother.

In sharp contrast to the other major sections of the narrative which build drama in discourse, the climactic scene is impressive for its descriptive detail and lack of direct speech. One senses the silent, intense effort somehow set apart from shrill demands, a private place where the master of mysterious curative powers, or the conjurer of Yahweh's powers, may breathe life from himself into inert flesh (see Gen 2:7). Elisha's actions now are every bit as determined as the Shunammite's and suggest that he has fully accepted her moral claims on him and his powers. It seems a moment of self-aware, conscientious action at a time when Yahweh has offered no revelation.

In the dénouement (V, vv. 36-37), Elisha grandly presents the woman with her restored child. His words "take up your son" (v. 37) not only announce the miracle, but tap the memory of that annunciatory moment: "you shall embrace a son" (v. 16). The promise of birth and this short declaratory command are Elisha's only *direct* words to the Shunammite mother. Taken together, the utterances evoke Elisha's view of their relationship. In *giving* the son, Elisha plays the part of the emissarial miracle worker who dispenses largesse among his patrons. In *restoring* the son, he merely works his magic again. Yet these words of closure seem to suppress but not quite deny the moral and human transformations which this woman demands of him.

The Shunammite responds effusively, falling at Elisha's feet and "bowing to the ground" as though before royal or divine authority (v. 37). The narrator quickly concludes: "she took up her son and went out." Though narrative equilibrium returns, one cannot any longer view the Shunammite as awe-filled patron to this man of God (cf. vv. 8-10). For, unlike her first son, she demands this second or restored one as her morally just recompense. She is a victor even if Elisha does not quite admit openly to his vulnerability. While being transformed by circumstance into an aggrieved mother pursuing restitution, she herself forces a change in Elisha. The prophet was and still is a miracle worker, though perhaps he summons up the power with unusually rigorous effort. (Contrast the remarkably similar deed of Elijah, but told with far less suggestion of sheer difficulty.) Yet Elisha also responds, if somewhat hesitantly, to a moral claim put by another human being. In this change one may detect a certain maturation of character, as compared with the dispenser of curse in 2 Kgs 2:23-24 or the flatly conceived benevolent miracle worker in 4:1-7, 38-44; 6:1-7 (see Rofé, "Classification," 433-34). Moral responsibility seems to be a means by which prophetic power may be channeled into the human realm.

Genre

Leaving aside generic terms for supposed earlier stages of this narrative (e.g., A. Schmitt, 23, "prophetic narrative" for vv. 8-12, 16-28, 30b, 32a, 33-34, 36-37), one can clearly designate this narrative as a whole as a PROPHET LEGEND, i.e., it is a story which portrays a prophet or similar holy person as a main character and exemplar of supernatural power working, divine favor, and sometimes piety and virtue. Hobbs (*2 Kings*, 45) resists the designation as "prophetic," but on inadequate grounds (see above at 2 Kgs 4:1-7). Rofé ("Classification," 434; *Prophetical Stories*, 31-34) rightly observes the literary and psychological sophistication of this narrative as compared with, e.g., 2 Kgs 2:19-22 or 4:1-7, and thereby speaks correctly about artistic elaboration of oral *legenda*. One may accept the observation without accepting his theory about religious, moral, and literary *development* over time, for which the evidence is less than adequate. S. De Vries (p. 53) agrees with the designation "legend," but by defining it functionally as "power demonstration narrative" he unduly restricts the literary facts, which imply reflection on a moral limitation of such power. (See the similar legend told of Elijah in 1 Kgs 17:17-24 [Kilian]; also John 11:1-45; R. Bultmann, *The History of the Synoptic Tradition* [tr. J. Marsh; Oxford: Blackwell, 1963] 233-34.)

An important element in this legend is the ANNUNCIATION SCENE, whose stereotyped elements announce the birth of a child destined to be a great leader, hero, savior, and the like. Typically a divine emissary appears (Niphal of *r'h*, as in epiphany) and announces that a barren or otherwise troubled woman will "conceive [*hrh*] and give birth [*yld*]," or simply "have a son," whose special significance is marked by name, unusual features, or heroic destiny. The parent-to-be reacts frequently with disbelief, fear, and even skepticism, all of which are overridden by a subsequent report of conception and birth, just as forecast. (See Gen 16:11-14; 18:10-14; Judg 13:3-5; Lk 1:11-20, 26-36.) The writer has adapted the convention in 2 Kings 4 to suit the particular aims of prophet legend (see detailed discussion above). The fulfillment of the announced birth is reported in a prophetic mode as well, for v. 17b, "as Elisha had said to her," seems closely analogous to the (→) oracle fulfillment formula, as, e.g., in 1 Kgs 16:34; 17:16; 2 Kgs 1:17 (see A. Schmitt, 20; and H.-Chr. Schmitt, 94).

Literary patterns from ritual texts may lie behind vv. 33-35. The measured detail of Elisha's actions imply ritual, either fancifully imagined by popular narration or based upon real experience with prophetic figures. The boy's sneezing "seven times" corresponds to the number seven in other literary reflexes of ritual, e.g., priestly texts that prescribe purification rites (Lev 16:13, 19; 4:6; 14:7, 16, 27, 51; Num 19:4) or narratives about miracle working (Josh 6:4, 15; 1 Kgs 18:43; 2 Kgs 5:10, 14). The motifs "mouth upon his mouth . . . eyes upon his eyes . . . hands upon his hands" are strikingly paralleled in two (→) incantations from Babylonia in which a priest breaks demonic spells by reciting "your head upon his head, your hand upon his hand, your foot upon his foot, you (the evil spirit) shall not place" (Daiches, 492).

Of course, the words in 2 Kgs 4:34-35 are not words of incantation but a narrative rendering of healing ritual which was perhaps meant to include special words (Elisha is said to have "prayed to the Lord" in v. 33) in order to attain the release of the patient from dire circumstances. If this is a correct understanding, a literary analogy may be found in the ritual text associated with the Babylonian *šurpu* ("burning" for purification) series of incantations and prayers (Reiner). The text (Reiner's tablet I, pp. 11-12) prescribes for the practitioner various operations keyed explicitly to incantations and prayers to be spoken (Reiner's tablets V-VI, pp. 30-35). To combine word and action in prescribed ways is to release the sufferer from spells or calamity. See also Meier (pp. 57-64) for a ritual text which belongs with the *maqlû* series of incantations, and Laessøe for ritual ablutions. A much later Seleucid text, the "Aramaic incantation in cuneiform" (Gordon), deserves mention because of its unusual storylike account of someone's breaking an evil spell. However, its relevance to an understanding of 2 Kgs 4:33-35 is slight at best.

Finally, one may note several other literary conventions: OATH, v. 30a (see 1 Kgs 29-30; 17:11); formulaic DESCRIPTION OF HOMAGE, v. 37a ("came [*bô'*] bowing to the ground [*hištahăwû 'ārṣâ*]"; see Gen 18:2; 42:6; 43:26; 2 Kgs 2:15); GREETING, v. 26, "Is it well with . . . ?" (see 2 Kgs 5:21; 9:11, 17, 18, 19, 22; Gen 29:6; 2 Sam 18:32).

Setting

In oral tradition, prophet legends would have flourished among the people, and possibly among prophets themselves (see 2 Kgs 8:4); they would have been told on various occasions depending on the aims and circumstances of the storytellers. This particular example may have originated in northern Israel (events are set at Mount Carmel; see Gray, *Kings*, 467), perhaps among followers of Elisha (De Vries, 56-57; A. Schmitt, 24). These are matters for speculation, however. More to the point is the literary setting of this Elisha legend in the Dtr history. It is one of a series of prophetic traditions representing for the author-editor the reign of Jehoram, and one of several which depict Elisha as a worker of miracles for those in particular need (4:1 7, 38-42).

Intention

Legend seeks to edify and instruct, to inspire awe and emulation by focusing on wondrous deeds, special virtues, and miraculous powers. This particular example of legend clearly shows in the end that Elisha really is a "holy man of God" who, out of compassion, cares for individuals in distress (Hobbs, *2 Kings*, 54; A. Schmitt, 24-25). The legend illustrates "what a model prophet can do" (De Vries, 53). In these aims, the narrative keeps company with, e.g., 2 Kgs 4:1-7; 6:1-7, or 1 Kgs 17:17-24.

Yet the narrator's skill subverts such uncomplicated sentiment with ironic juxtaposition. The Shunammite grows into an aggrieved mother with sufficient assurance and moral conviction to challenge Elisha's dominance and expose the limits of prophetic power. The writer probes the substance of this holy man of

God; he draws the human, male shape of wonder-worker in Jehoram's kingdom over against an unnamed, assertive woman who turns aside protocol and moral obtuseness. Perhaps one is meant to temper that unreflective awe before the prophet whose power and authority have seemed unquestioned to this point. The legend begins with that respectful attitude (vv. 8-10) and ends with it intact (v. 37). But along the way, one's adulation is cooled by the mother's experience of loss and the knowledge of Elisha's astonishing blindness. Even God does not tell all to his prophet — and that is information consciously given the reader. Elisha knows less than he needs to know, and does less than he is able to do, or than might be expected in heroic circumstances. In the end, with strenuous labor and prayer, he manages to turn the miracle trick, but at what cost to his prestige and authority (cf. Alter)? Homage is due this prophet, but also reserve, for his power has seemed in need of moral restraint and his knowledge has seemed deficient. As a sort of new miracle, Elisha is taught the lesson (or does he get the point after all?) by a woman without lineage, emboldened only with passion and determination born of her desperate bereavement. The legend is about the prophetic successor to Elijah, but also about the "grand figure of a woman" from Shunem ('iššâ gĕdôlâ, v. 8; see Long, "Figure at the Gate").

Bibliography

R. Alter, "How Convention Helps us Read: The Case of the Bible's Annunciation Type-Scene," *Prooftexts* 3 (1983) 115-30; S. Daiches, "Zu II. Kön iv,34 (Elišas Handlung durch babylonische Beschwörungstextstellen erklärt)," *OLZ* 11 (1908) 492-93; A. Deem, "The Great Woman of Shunem," in *Proceedings of the Eighth World Congress of Jewish Studies; A: The Period of the Bible* (Jerusalem: World Union of Jewish Studies, 1982) 21-24; S. De Vries, *Prophet* (→2 Kgs 1:2-17a); C. Gordon, "The Aramaic Incantation in Cuneiform," *AfO* 12 (1938) 105-17; R. Kilian, "Die Totenerweckungen Elias und Elisas — eine Motivwanderung?" *BZ* 10 (1966) 44-56; J. Laessøe, *Studies on the Assyrian Ritual and Series bît rimki* (Copenhagen: Ejnar Munksgaard, 1955); B. O. Long, "Framing Repetitions in Biblical Historiography," *JBL* 106 (1987) 385-99; idem, "A Figure at the Gate: Readers, Reading, and Biblical Theologians," in *Canon, Theology and Old Testament Interpretation: Essays in Honor of Brevard S. Childs* (ed. G. Tucker et al.; Philadelphia: Fortress, 1988) 166-86; G. Meier, *Die Assyrische Beschwörungssammlung Maqlû* (*AfO* Beiheft 2; Berlin: 1937); R. Neff, "The Annunciation in the Birth Narrative of Ishmael," *BR* 17 (1972) 51-60; E. Reiner, *Šurpu: A Collection of Sumerian and Akkadian Incantations* (*AfO* Beiheft 11; Graz: 1958); A. Rofé, "Classification" (→ 2 Kgs 2:1-18); idem, *Prophetical Stories* (→ 2 Kgs 1:2-17a); A. Schmitt, "Die Totenerweckung in 2 Kön 4:8-37," *BZ* 19 (1975) 1-25; H.-Chr. Schmitt, *Elisa* (→ 2 Kgs 2:1-25); S. Talmon, "The Presentation of Synchroneity and Simultaneity in Biblical Narratives," in *Studies in Hebrew Narrative Art Throughout the Ages* (ed. J. Heinemann and S. Werses; ScrHie 27; Jerusalem: Magnes, 1978) 9-26; A. G. van Daalen, "Onderzoek naar de compositie van 2 Kon 8:1-6 en 4:8-37," *AmstCah* 1 (1980) 51-61; idem, "De opbouw van 2 Konigen 4:12-17 en 25-28 en hun onderlinge samenhang," *AmstCah* 2 (1981) 41-49.

TWO MIRACLES AMONG THE PROPHETS, 4:38-41, 42-44

Text

On the basis of Ugaritic *bsql,* which means "plant" or "herb," translate *wĕkarmel bĕsiqlōnô* in v. 42 as "plants from his orchard" instead of the *RSV* "fresh grain in his sack" (Gray, *Kings,* 501). The latter was based on ancient VSS's attempts at understanding and a modern emendation (see Burney, *Notes,* 277-78).

Structure

I. First episode: bad food made good   38-41
  A. Narrative setting (famine)   38a
  B. The problem   38b-40
    1. Elisha's instructions to prepare food   38b
    2. Contamination of food   39-40
      a. Preparation (addition of poison)   39
      b. Discovery of contamination   40
  C. Resolution of problem (the miracle)   41
    1. Elisha's action   41a-bα
    2. Result: food is restored   41bβ
II. Second episode: abundance from scarcity   42-44
  A. Narrative setting (bringing of food offerings)   42a
  B. The miracle   42b-44
    1. Elisha's instructions   42b
    2. Servant's demurring question (the problem)   43a
    3. Elisha's response   43b
      a. Instruction   43bα
      b. Explanatory oracle   43bβ
    4. Result   44
      a. Instructions carried out   44a
      b. Statement of oracle fulfilled (miracle)   44b

    This unit consists of two brief, simply structured narratives which probably had separate origins (cf. H.-Chr. Schmitt, *Elisa,* 99-100, who views vv. 42-44 as a redactional supplement to vv. 38-41). Following vv. 8-37, the first episode marks an abrupt shift to Gilgal and a change in both subject matter and characters. The second narrative is similarly separated from 5:1-27. Both feature Elisha with his "men" or "sons of prophets" in situations involving food (cf. *ṣaq lāʿām,* v. 41, and *tēn lāʿām,* vv. 42-43). Yet each incident sets the master in a distinct situation. Lacking significant transition between them, each episode opens with simple perfect tense and inverted word order, the stylistic sign of new beginnings.

    The structure of the first episode, vv. 38-41, is uncomplicated and basically determined by the plain sequence of action. With circumstantial nominative sentences, the narrator first establishes significant background: "and [there was] famine in the land, and the sons of prophets were sitting before him [Elisha]."

One hears Elisha's instructions, therefore, as actions taken in extremis. He orders food prepared for his followers, the mixture is inadvertently poisoned, and upon hearing the prophets' cry of distress, Elisha takes action to restore its whole-someness. The general structure is comparable to other short accounts of miracles wherein a problem is brought to the attention of a helper who responds by doing something that leads to a miraculous solution (Culley, *Narrative*, 75-78; cf. 2 Kgs 2:19-22; Exod 15:22-27). Nowhere in this episode is the miracle directly described. Rather, events around it emerge in direct discourse, briefly reported action, and the narrator's gradual release of critical information — the background circumstances (v. 38a), the herb gatherer's ignorance (v. 39bβ), the poisoned food (v. 40bβ), and its restoration (v. 41bβ). Perhaps on the outer edges of this narrative there is a wordplay between "famine" *(hārāʿāb)* and "harm" *(dābār rāʿ)*.

The second episode, vv. 42-44, follows a slightly different literary pattern (see Culley, *Narrative*, 96-100). Having received gifts of food, Elisha orders that his entourage be fed. His servant objects on the grounds that the supply is insufficient, whereupon Elisha repeats his instructions and adds a divine oracle. This time the prophet's wishes are followed, and the narrator directly reports the miracle: everyone eats, with food to spare, "according to the word of the Lord." The key element which sets this episode apart from vv. 38-41 is the divine oracle and its function in portraying the disparity between Elisha's and others' view of reality (see 1 Kgs 17:8-16 and discussion there). The servant demurs, v. 43, by his natural lights; Elisha commands on the basis of the supranatural, a divine word which he announces only when challenged: "Give the men [the food] that they may eat because [*kî*] thus says the Lord, 'Eat(ing) and leav(ing) over.'" In effect, this oracle — a clipped pair of infinitive absolutes (cf. 2 Kgs 3:16; Hos 4:2) — reinforces the mystery and special position of Elisha. He is attuned to a level of reality missed by ordinary folk, including his servant who presumably is among the "sons of prophets." Elisha is likened implicitly to Elijah, who in 1 Kgs 17:8-16 similarly overwhelms lesser percep-tions with a Yahweh oracle that foresees miracle.

Genre

This unit consists of two PROPHET LEGENDS, each of which is a rudimentary story emphasizing the miraculous power of the prophet among his followers (see Rofé, "Classification," 430-33; De Vries, 53-54; on Hobbs's misgivings [*2 Kings*, 45-46]), see above at 4:1-7). As in 2:19-22, the prophet is held in awe for his great powers, not his winsome personality.

The first legend, like 2:19-22; 6:1-7; and Exod 15:22b-25a, is character-ized by a typical structure: (1) a problem is brought to one perceived as having the power to help, (2) the helper elicits divine intervention, which in turn leads to (3) a miraculous solution (see Culley, *Narrative*, 72-78).

The second episode is a variant on this pattern and finds a parallel in 1 Kgs 17:8-16 (Culley, *Narrative*, 96-100). In both cases, the problem demanding attention is defined a little more in terms of human perception than objective circumstances. The oracle from God announces the miracle, as it does in 2 Kgs 2:19-22, but it also dramatizes disparate angles from which the characters view their particular situations. The second legend includes an abbreviated version of the typical ORACLE FULFILLMENT FORMULA, v. 44b. The oracle itself opens with the usual MESSENGER FORMULA.

Setting

Legend belongs to the world of folk storytellers, and would have found various occasions for use depending on the particular circumstances and aims of narrators. These particular examples may have had their main home among the prophets who were associated with Elisha, perhaps at Gilgal or other shrines (De Vries, 53; Gray, *Kings,* 466). In terms of present literary setting, these legends, together with vv. 1-7, provide a short-subject framework for the more complex narrative in vv. 4-37. They are part of a series of incidents which feature Elisha, often in analogous circumstances to his master Elijah, extending various kinds of help to people great and small.

Intention

Among the people and perhaps "sons of prophets," prophet legends would have been used for many different reasons. One may perhaps safely assume that such narratives would have demonstrated the prophets' supernatural powers for the entertainment and instruction of lesser mortals. The legends aim to instill attitudes of wonder and awe toward this "man of God," a term used interchangeably with "prophet" in these stories.

It is difficult to discern a specific intention within the DtrH's presentation of Jehoram's reign. These brief legends provide accent for the overall picture of Elisha, of course. Perhaps in addition, the DtrH suggests that despite its apostate kings and people (both working assumptions of the DtrH), God's power is yet available through Elijah's successor. In case there was doubt in any reader's mind, there really is a prophet in Israel, and that means that there really is a God whose steady press of moral demand shapes human actions (see 5:8; 3:11). This point of view, which of course is characteristic of the DtrH's evaluative summaries of all the kings, comes to explicit narrative expression in chs. 5–7, and especially in ch. 9. There, after the end of Jehoram's reign, Elisha empowers Jehu to carry out a violent purge of Baalists from the northern kingdom.

Bibliography

R. Culley, *Narrative* (→ 2 Kgs 2:19-24); S. De Vries, *Prophet* (→ 2 Kgs 1:2-17a); A. Rofé, "Classification" (→ 2 Kgs 2:1-18); H.-Chr. Schmitt, *Elisa* (→ 2 Kgs 2:1-25).

THE HEALING OF NAAMAN AND THE AFFLICTION OF GEHAZI, 5:1-27

Structure

The length and complexity of this unit stand in sharp contrast to the unidimensional traditions which precede and follow (4:38-41, 42-44; 6:1-7). In these stories, simple miracles meet the material needs of Elisha's followers. Yet, the account of Naaman's healing and Gehazi's moral lapse presses beyond miracle to its moral consequence, and it does so with narration of international horizons, dramatic power, and vivid characterization of personages.

The unit opens with the inverted word order (subject plus verb in perfect tense) so typical of shifts in scene, or of beginnings of self-contained narrative (cf. 4:1, 38, 42; 6:8; 1 Kgs 20:1; 21:1). It concludes with a succinct closure that, like a circle, joins beginning with end. Naaman was leprous *(mĕṣōrā')* and became clean, but now Gehazi, who was clean, becomes "leprous as snow" *(mĕṣōrā' kaššāleg).*

Many critics argue for or assume the internal unity of vv. 1-27 (e.g., Šanda, *Könige* II, 84-85; Montgomery, *Kings,* 373-76; Fohrer, *Erzählungen,* 100-101; Gressmann, *Geschichtsschreibung,* 297; Gunkel, *Geschichten,* 45; most recently, DeVries, *Prophet,* 54; Rofé, "Classification," 145-48; idem, *Prophetical Stories,* 108-12, who also cites Zakovitch; Cohn; Zakovitch was unavailable to me). Other scholars suppose Naaman's confession of Yahweh and Gehazi's subsequent deception and punishment to be some sort of addendum. Some take the Gehazi episode, vv. 20-27, as a secondary expansion (e.g., Fricke, *2 Könige,* 68; Hentschel, 11-12; Schult; Gray, *Kings,* 502; G. von Rad, 541, considered vv. 20-27 as an "unedifying counterpart" to the narrative which precedes). H.-Chr. Schmitt (pp. 78-79) and Würthwein (*Könige,* 298-303) viewed an original vv. 1-14 as having been supplemented by two separate expansions.

Yet, many features in the narrative cannot be easily dismissed as secondary (see esp. Cohn; also Hobbs, *2 Kings,* 59-61; on the original status of vv. 19b-27, see Smelik). The sudden appearance of Gehazi, catching the reader unprepared, need not be a mark of clumsy editing (against Hentschel and others), for this character elsewhere strides into view at a stroke, as though the writer assumes always that Gehazi hovers close by Elisha, ready to be summoned onstage (see 2 Kgs 4:12; 8:4). Moreover, details of language and style link parts of the text that some scholars have identified as independent redactional layers (for what follows, see esp. Cohn, and also Rofé). Already mentioned is the rounding effect of *mĕṣōrāʿ* (leprous) in vv. 1 and 27: Naaman's "festal garments" *(hălîpôt bĕgādîm)* and treasures, v. 5, have a function in the narrative only in relation to v. 23; the oath formula, *hay-yahweh* ("as the Lord lives," v. 16), has its counterpart on Gehazi's lips (v. 20); the narrator's description of urgent petition, "and he urged him" *(wayyipṣar-bô),* v. 16, occurs again in v. 23 (the Hebrew requires only a slight but plausible emendation); v. 19b, "And he went from him a short distance [*kibrat-ʾāreṣ*]" is hardly what one would expect to close a self-contained narrative (cf., e.g., Gen 18:33; 32:1; 2 Sam 12:31b; 2 Kgs 3:27). The phrase rather more implies that further action involving these characters will yet occur (see the similar usage in Gen 35:16; 48:7). Finally, one may note the unifying effect of motival reversals: the proud foreigner turns humble Yahweh worshiper, the servant of a prophet emerges as arrogant deceiver, the leper becomes clean, and one who was healthy becomes a leper. Also, contrasting characterizations, such as weak king over against powerful prophet, or generous Naaman as against greedy Gehazi, suggest that an integrative, moralizing vision lies behind the narrative (see Gressmann, *Geschichtsschreibung,* 297-98).

In these discussions of literary unity, the main concern of scholars has been to satisfy a modern reader's implicit criterion for coherence. Defenders of disunity and supplementation use a model of narrative flow from tension to resolution, and, applying this metaphor as a measure, they find it violated in this story. Cohn sees that difficulty, but finds coherence instead in purposeful shifts in narrative foci. The narrative comprises "three distinct units, each centering on a different character" (vv. 1-14, Elisha; vv. 15-19, Naaman; vv. 20-27, Gehazi), each extending the meaning of the preceding unit (Cohn, 171-72; cf. Hobbs, *2 Kings,* 59, who thinks of a drama in three acts).

I should like to suggest a slightly different model in order to exploit to their fullest potential the motival links between Cohn's "units." Let us imagine a series of waves undulating along a line, each one containing within itself the energy that gives rise to the next.

The first wave carries Naaman from leprosy to cure (I-II, vv. 1-14). A problem that emerges as part of the background summary, v. 1, is addressed throughout subsequent scenes in Aram and finds its resolution such that the flesh of this "great man" (*'îš gādôl,* v. 1) becomes like that of a "little child" (*na'ar qāṭōn,* v. 14).

Latent within this first movement is the energy for another. Our knowledge that the God of Israel has given Naaman his success (v. 1) stands in contrast to Naaman's intransigently arrogant and misguided attitudes toward Elisha, Yahweh, and the land of Israel (vv. 11-12). The writer is emphatic about this point and thus suggests to the reader that Naaman's attitude is in need of reform (cf. Cohn, 177). Our expectations are met when Naaman, healed, "his flesh turned back" (*wayyāšob bĕśārô,* v. 14), subsequently "turns back" (*wayyāšob,* v. 15) to Elisha and speaks as a convert (cf. use of *šûb* in the sense of religious conversion at Isa 55:7; Hos 6:1; Jer 4:1).

A third wave gathers its strength out of this second one. After the fact, one learns that Gehazi has witnessed the scene of confession, the pressing of gifts, and Elisha's refusal to profit from his own or Naaman's piety. Gehazi misunderstands the situation, or rather his latent opportunism draws energy from misapprehension, and so gathers a third wave to roll forward (v. 20). He goes off to sully this high moment of physical and spiritual transformation by turning it to self-serving advantage (see Rofé, "Classification," 146). Therefore he stands accused, as Elisha says: "Was this a suitable time to take money and to take garments?" (v. 26b; *RSV* "accept" misses the ironic double entendre in the verb *lāqaḥ,* which can mean "accept" a gift [vv. 16, 20, 23] and "take something unlawfully" as here and in 2 Sam 12:4).

Read in this way, the narrative offers a series of climactic moments, each one a rising and falling that carries within itself the tendency toward another upswell. The waves roll toward a shoreline, where originary energy subsides, and a last glimpse of leper whiteness returns the reader to that initial image, "he was a leper," v. 1.

Obviously a structural outline is inadequate to capture the metaphor of rolling waves. Nonetheless, I attempt to suggest the narrative's integrative complexity with strategically placed words. Sections I and II, vv. 1-14, describe the problem of Naaman's leprosy and the steps taken toward its eventual miraculous cure. Yet in its midst, vv. 11-12, Naaman's "ignorant arrogance" confronts us and will be transformed in III.A, vv. 15-19. This turnabout in Naaman has its own generative power as Gehazi's disease erupts as punishment for his profaning that moment of spiritual healing (III.B, vv. 20-27). Hentschel's division of vv. 1-19a into scenes determined simply by shifts in locale misses this generative fluidity of plot; cf. Cohn (pp. 171-73), who sees three units — vv. 1-14, 15-19, 20-27 — as interdependent phases in unified narration.

Beginning with inverted Hebrew word order, the writer first suggests people, contrasts, relationships, and situations. Naaman's personage spills forth: "commander of the army of Aram [*RSV* 'Syria'] . . . great man with his master

. . . in high favor . . . a mighty man of valor . . ." Then, a single blighted leaf: he also is "leprous." It seems that Naaman is as famous for his accomplishments as for his disease. Beyond this fact, we learn a secret "truth" about his fame. It is the God of Israel who has given victories to Aram through this afflicted hero. If Naaman's status among his people is mitigated by his disease, so is his prowess diminished in the reader's eyes, because the cause of his fame is unknown to his admirers and perhaps hidden even from himself.

The writer clusters a second set of oppositions around the anonymous maid in Naaman's household (see Cohn). She is an Israelite, he an Aramean; she is a "little maiden" *(na'ărâ qĕtannâ)*, he a "great man" *('îš gādôl); she is a* captive servant, he a commander; he has fame in the king's estimation, "before his lord" *(lipnê 'ădōnāyw;* cf. Gen 7:1; 1 Sam 20:1), she has none, for she simply "waited upon" ("was before," *wattĕhî lipnê)* Naaman's wife (cf. Deut 1:38; 1 Sam 19:7).

When narrative time begins to run in v. 3, one realizes that these contrastive images, which mostly seem like fortuitous circumstances, really carry within them a mysterious generative power. The humble maiden wishes that Naaman was in Samaria with its Israelite prophet, for there her master would find a cure. She speaks privately to her mistress, and her Israelitish sentiments begin a series of events that will result in a healing and an unexpected tie between Naaman and Israel. Her wish is taken as suggestion and quickly transmitted to the king (the Hebrew and Greek differ as to who bears her words). The monarch immediately orders Naaman to set out to see the ruler of Israel. As the scene closes with Naaman going to the land of Israel, the narrator reverts to the public symbols of this leprous commander's status: he carries with him riches and fine garments, presumably to reward the one whom he seeks (v. 5; see v. 15). That same wealth will in time be transformed into Gehazi's badge of transgression (v. 23).

Countering the sense of urgency conveyed in vv. 3-5, the writer builds a series of delays, obstacles, and diversions in what might have been an uncomplicated journey from sickness to cure. First, Naaman is sent to the king of Israel, not the prophet of Samaria. He stands on the soil which has given up a "little maiden," in proximity to her revered prophet and to the God who has, unbeknownst to him, made him victorious in old battles. And yet Naaman must follow "channels," as though the medical arts exist under royal patronage (see Montgomery, *Kings,* 374), or as though the Israelite king himself possesses special curative powers. Second, the king of Israel interprets the request written in the letter (v. 6b) as some kind of threat. He reacts as though confronting deep troubles ("he rent his clothes"), pleads his powerlessness ("am I God to kill and to make alive?" [cf. Deut 32:39]), and invokes the politics of international suspicion ("consider and see"). As though consulting his advisers, the king impugns the Aramean's intention without the slightest trace of diplomatic delicacy: "this [one] sends to me . . . Consider . . . how he seeks an occasion [for trouble]." See Judg 14:4 and 1 Kgs 20:7. Somehow a servant's quiet wish and confidence in the prophet from Samaria have become entangled with the egoistic inhibitions of state politics.

Perhaps the writer mocks this pilgrimage for healing at Samaria's royal court (Cohn, 175). Perhaps tension is built up — how is Naaman after all to receive his cure if royal bureaucracy stands astride the path? Suddenly the prophet, who has seemed somehow inaccessible to Naaman while uppermost in our expectations, intervenes to break the impasse. Elisha, "man of God" (the phrase is missing in some Greek VSS), sends a message chiding the king for his wrongheadedness. In effect the prophet requests Naaman's case (v. 8).

So, the energy released by the Israelite maiden might be directed properly after all. But a new unexpected impulse develops, too. Elisha injects an ideological element into the situation. He will see Naaman not merely to cure him, but that he "may know there is a prophet in Israel." What Naaman looks for, what the Israelite woman wishes, and what Elisha intends, do not quite coincide. Herein lies the energized matter from which subsequent dramatic action will take form.

In the next section of narrative (II.B, vv. 9-14), the writer relates how Naaman finally takes his cure and thus completes the first major movement of the tale. Although the Aramean soldier is mostly in view, it is really Elisha who drives the action. Once again the path to cure seems blocked. Naaman arrives at the prophet's house amid symbols of social status ("with his horses and chariots"), and yet he stands outside like the solicitous woman from Shunem (2 Kgs 4:15). Elisha sends him instructions at a distance, and the narrator suggests an affront of some kind, a conflict between what *is* and what Naaman thinks *ought* to be. To Elisha's instructions, Naaman reacts with anger and pique. Narrative pace slows, and we glimpse something rare in biblical narrative — the preserve of private thought and emotion, realized here as a bundle of habitual attitudes rooted in success and royal favor. Repeated descriptions (vv. 11a, 12b) surround Naaman's private thoughts (vv. 11b-12a); anger burns hotly and continuously while Naaman, muttering to himself, turns away. The scene of departure forms a perfect chiasmus:

A   Description of angry departure v. 11a
     (wayyiqṣōp . . . wayyēlak)

  B   Speech (thought) vv. 11b-12a

A'   Description of angry departure v. 12b
     (wayyēlek běḥēmâ)

If the literary structure emphasizes Naaman's feelings, so too the word order in vv. 11b-12a. The position of *'ēlay,* "to me," is emphatic, and the infinitive *yāṣô',* "come out," also adds stress. "I thought, 'to [such a man as] me ['ēlay] he would surely come out [yēṣē' yāṣô']. . . .'" Then, as though soured with bitterness at having to stand outside with retinue in hand, Naaman adds, "'and stand [before me].'"

Apparently Naaman expects pomp and ceremony. Or perhaps, as might be read by a Yahwistic partisan, he sought that "cloudy vapor and magical twilight" so attractive to the unenlightened (von Rad, 50). In any event, Naaman looks for curative therapy, for Elisha to "wave his hand over the [affected] place

71

(and) call upon the name of the Lord his God" (see H. A. Brongers, "Die Wendung *běšēm jhwh* im Alten Testament," *ZAW* 77 [1965] 1-20). What he gets is an order, an insult in its simplicity, a silly directive to wash in the Jordan River. The proud leper resists with heated rhetoric, and again the Israelite woman's wish seems blocked.

As before, an unexpected figure intervenes to break this new impasse. Prodding their master's chauvinism with naive good sense, Naaman's servants gently, politely, strike the target with persuasive force: "My father, [if] the prophet [had] commanded you [to do] a great thing, would you not have done it? How much more, then, when he says to you, 'Wash, and be clean'?" (v. 13). This man of great repute, an *'îš gādôl,* stands convicted of misplaced pride by talk of a small washing in a tiny river distant from the great waters of Damascus.

Carrying this ironic tone into the report of Naaman's healing (v. 14), the writer describes the cure with nonchalance, as though it really were a routine matter to dip oneself seven times in the Jordan just as Elisha has directed, and be made well. (Note the number seven, 2 Kgs 4:35.) Only a small descriptive simile exceeds slightly this understatement: Naaman's flesh becomes "like the flesh of a little child" (v. 14b). With this, the narrator brings closure. As a "little maiden" *(na'ărâ qěṭannâ)* initiated this series of events, so now Naaman is figuratively transformed into a "little child" *(na'ar qāṭōn).* At first introduced as great in reputation *('îš gādôl),* then shown to be arrogant in his expectations, the military hero has now submitted to Elisha's quiet authority (Cohn, 177).

Yet, one may wonder. Has Naaman altered his harsh chauvinism after all? Has Elisha realized his intent that Naaman recognize a prophet in Israel? And what of the narrator's remark that it is Yahweh who gave Naaman his earlier success? Is this latest victory also to go misattributed? Leprosy has been cured, but other energies, or rather, unanswered questions press the flow onward.

As Naaman's flesh is "restored" *(wayyāšob,* v. 14), so he turns about and returns *(wayyāšob,* v. 15a) to Elisha. Those images of material substance reappear ("he and all his company"), and Naaman once again stands before the prophet *(wayya'ămōd lěpānāyw).* For the first time in this narrative, distant formality devolves to face-to-face dialogue. Naaman is now a humble confessant; one might even say that at last he really fulfills the maiden's urging to stand "before the prophet" who is in Samaria (Cohn, 178). The writer suggests that Naaman's "turned about" flesh, and his "return" to Elisha has about it a "turning" to Elisha's God also. (See the similar use of *šûb,* "return," in Hos 6:1; Jer 3:7; 4:1.)

Naaman's first words (v. 15b) call up a type-scene in which a non-Israelite confesses belief in Yahweh because of some display of wondrous power (see Exod 18:1-12; Josh 2:9-13; 2 Macc 3:35-39; cf. 2 Chr 33:13; 1 Kgs 17:17-24; Dan 4:31-34 [*RSV* 34-37]; Gen 14:18-20; John 1:14-16; cf. Schult). The standard scene consists of two main elements: (1) a reference to an act of divine power which underlies confession (e.g., in a speech praising God, Exod 18:10; or simply a recitation of God's mighty acts, Josh 2:10; 2 Macc 3:36; or a narrative of miracle, 1 Kgs 17:17-23; 2 Kgs 5:14); (2) a confession of belief as new attainment (e.g., "Now I know . . ." [*'attâ yāda'tî*], as in Exod 18:11 or 1 Kgs 17:24 [about Elijah]) or as hymnic affirmation. Sometimes offerings are then given to the newly accepted deity (Exod 18:12; cf. 2 Chr 33:15-16).

While drawing upon this literary convention, the writer nonetheless develops a particularizing application. In this case, the words of confession, v. 15aβ, close a narrative loop on the level of narrator and reader. Naaman's awareness of Israel's God converges with that of author and reader, who at the outset knows of Yahweh's hand in forging this Aramean's successes (v. 1). Moreover, Naaman barely gets the pious words free before falling back into the habits of a commander used to dealing with practical matters. The broker of healing and faith must have his payment, entreats Naaman (v. 15b). When Elisha refuses, carefully stating his aversion to taking rewards for unwavering devotion to Yahweh's service, Naaman presses with newly discovered concerns (vv. 17-18). How can one worship Yahweh away from God's inheritance, away from the land of Israel (cf. Ps 137:4; 1 Sam 26:19)? And how may one worship this God while yet bound to serve Aram's king? Since the prophet refuses payment, Naaman apparently thinks that he is due at least some acknowledgment of his new situation. Naaman asks for a bit of Israelite soil, a scrip of holiness with which to worship Yahweh (or build an altar) in a foreign land. He will, after all, offer sacrifice to no God but Yahweh (v. 17). Yet, he still must serve his Aramean master as though a devotee of the Aramean god, Rimmon (see J. C. Greenfield, "The Aramean God *Rammān/Rimmōn*," *IEJ* 26 [1976] 195-98). Naaman vents this emotional conflict in a single phrase, "and he [the Aramean king] leaning on my arm," which he positions at the center of his stylized petition (v. 18; cf. Cohn, 179):

A   In this matter
  B   may the Lord pardon your servant
    C   when my master goes into the house of Rimmon to bow down there,
      D   and he leaning on my arm,
    C'   and I bow down in the house of Rimmon, when I bow down in the house of Rimmon,
  B'   may the Lord pardon your servant
A'   in this matter.

Thus Naaman seeks pardon in advance for these unavoidable semblances of his old self when his heart is newly, and really, wed to Yahweh. Elisha responds laconically with a simple formula of dismissal, "Go in peace," which suggests that he and God have heard and look favorably on these petitions (see Exod 4:18; Judg 18:6; 1 Sam 1:17; 2 Sam 5:19; cf. Gen 44:17; 1 Sam 25:35b).

Naaman's requests seem less important for their content than for their testimony about his spiritual transformation (see Cohn, 179). Formerly, he disdained the waters of Israel; now he wants a bit of Israel's earth to stay the tide of heathendom beyond Israel's borders. While standing outside Elisha's house, Naaman fumes in the disquiet of unmet expectations; now he turns back to offer a gift, not to the God whom he newly embraces, but to the prophet to whom he has just submitted. Formerly, Naaman seemed sure in his retinue of power, and now he appears anxious about the implications of his new-found piety. Yet he finds assurance apparently in Elisha's words, "Go in peace." They signify a pardon given in advance. The future is brought under the commanding aegis of this single moment of healing openness to God. (Cf. Solomon's dedicatory petitions which similarly put all future needs under the numinal power of the temple in Jerusalem; 1 Kgs 8:31-53; Long, *1 Kings,* 101-4.)

The current stirred by the unusually strong image of Naaman's arrogant, ignorant power (vv. 11-12) finds its rest in this transformation. Anger gives way to solicitous courtesy, arrogance to submission, and blindness to sight. And perhaps Elisha's desire for Naaman to learn that "there is a prophet in Israel" achieves, at least from Naaman's perspective, its fullest meaning. It is not that one finds a showy curative power in Israel, but that one encounters a prophet who confounds expectations, who is anchored in an oath to "stand before Yahweh," perhaps the better to prod someone else's turn to God.

In this intermediate resolution of narrative waves, the writer has created dramatic, contrasting reversals. He who was powerful in reputation, an *'îš gādôl* before his master (v. 1), now is humble, solicitous, grateful, worshipful, and submissive to the prophet he once arrogantly rejected. He even seems nervously respectful toward the God whose hand he once did not recognize. Elisha for his part is something of a mystery. He says little, but when he speaks, it is with succinct pointedness: instructions for healing, refusal of proffered payment, a word of dismissal. And yet one has a sure sense of his power. When the prophet's instructions are at last carried out, they yield the promised cure; Elisha firmly refuses reward and even turns away Naaman's insistent urgings; and he dismisses Naaman with the implication that somehow Elisha speaks for God to whom Naaman has after all addressed his plea for forgiveness (v. 18b).

These contrasting characterizations have their own generative power in the narrative, for Naaman's transformation and Elisha's stringent refusal of personal reward will prove to be the rule by which Gehazi, who has yet to appear, will be measured. Thus when Naaman departs, a new impulse in the drama is felt — the wave surges forward. He goes only a short distance from Elisha (*kibrat-'āreṣ,* v. 19b; cf. Gen 35:16; 48:7; Cohn, 179: "the author hints that the tale is not over").

The final wave in the narrative (III.B, vv. 20-27) builds a new theme out of three-way contrasts. Naaman is the humble and charitable healed one, who still, it develops, wishes to reward his benefactor. Gehazi, who suddenly appears and dominates this episode, is opportunistic and duplicitous, grasping at those outpourings of gratitude which a principled Elisha has refused. For his part, Elisha is now a preternaturally perceptive dispenser of punishment. As effortlessly as he heals and grants pardon, Elisha afflicts Gehazi, first to exact a consequence of dealing falsely with master prophet, and second, to punish him for profaning that power of cleansing which has been lavished upon Naaman. (For comparisons with other narratives in which transgression finds its punishment, see Culley, "Punishment Stories," 171.)

The writer introduces these archetypal avatars of morality by taking us into Gehazi's private thoughts, v. 20. As with other characters in the story, there can be no mistake about their social status. Naaman is "commander of the army . . . great man with his master," the Israelite "little maiden . . . waited upon Naaman's wife," and Elisha is "man of God" who addresses Naaman through a "messenger." Gehazi is "servant of Elisha, man of God." Yet the servant turns critical and insubordinate. It is unseemly that a cure be given out free of charge, Gehazi muses, and moreover, casting slight aspersion, given to such a man as Naaman, "this Aramean" (na'ămān hā'ărammî hazzeh). "I will run after him and get something from him," he thinks, and so is caught up in the narrator's key thematic word, lāqahtî, "I will take [get, accept]." When Naaman offers a reward he says, "accept now [qah-nā'] a gift" (v. 15b), and Elisha swears to take, accept, receive ('eqqāh) nothing (v. 16). Now Gehazi scorns that refusal: "my master spared Naaman, this Aramean, by not taking [accepting] from his hand [miqqahat mîyādô]," and the servant vows to do what the master has refused to do, to take or accept a gift from Naaman (lāqahtî). Gehazi's words hint that the delicate rituals of giving and receiving, offering and accepting, have already been or will be violated. Subsequent events leave no doubt.

Gehazi pursues Naaman. In reality, he hunts his quarry to prey on the convert's good intentions. Quickly putting aside Naaman's anxious query ("Is all well?"), Gehazi invents a situation, suggesting vaguely a need of material provisions, and directly requests some of the wealth he apparently knows Naaman to have brought with him: "Pray, give them a talent of silver and two festal garments" (cf. "what he brought," v. 20, and "silver . . . and festal garments," v. 5b). How clever to suggest a gift not for Elisha but for those (lāhem) who have unexpectedly joined Elisha! Gehazi plays perfectly upon the sentiments the reader knows to have been at work in Naaman's attitudinal transformation, vv. 15-19. He even artfully suggests that the whole matter comes from Elisha, to whom Naaman feels indebted ("my master has sent me to say . . ."), as though he were but a servant-messenger acting only on his lord's initiative.

Gehazi's duplicity now stands out in full relief against the direct, uncomplicated charity of Naaman. The Aramean alights from his chariot (contrast the images of arrogant aloofness in vv. 9, 11-12), having seen this running figure, and asks with anxious concern, "Is all well?" (see Gen 29:6; 2 Sam 18:32; 2 Kgs 4:26; 9:11). To Gehazi's request, Naaman responds without hesitation, and judging from the speech idiom, with urgent desire for goodwill: "Be pleased to accept . . ." (hô'ēl qah —the key word again; cf. 2 Sam 7:29; Judg 19:6; 2 Kgs 6:3). Apparently Naaman still assumes that the business is about giving and receiving, and the narrator has him "urge" the gifts upon Gehazi, as though expecting the same resistance he remembers of Elisha (cf. wayyipsar-bô, v. 16, and the same in v. 23, though with slight correction of spelling). The solicitous commander-turned-Yahwist even bundles, packages, and loads the gifts onto his own servants, v. 23b. (Cohn, 181, takes the servants as belonging to Gehazi, but in view of Gehazi's own status, and v. 24, where he sends the men away, this seems unlikely.) Then the narrator gives us one last image. The servants of Naaman "lift up" the wealth before his (Gehazi's) face (wayyiś'û lĕpānāyw, v. 23b). They hoist a standard to the heavens, the ambiguous emblem of Naaman's generosity and Gehazi's duplicity.

With a string of action verbs, we witness at last the depth of Gehazi's treachery, v. 24. Gehazi comes, takes (the ill-gotten gain), places (it) in the house, sends the men away, and they leave. Gehazi appears to have returned himself, and the reader, back to the place where everything began. But one sees clearly that he "has taken" fraudulently, and, the narrator suggests, quickly has stowed the goods and witnesses away from Elisha's gaze. The writer has shown a second major transformation: from "servant of Elisha, man of God," Gehazi is transformed into thief and victimizer.

In the final scene with Elisha, vv. 25-27, this dramatic irony builds to its climax and dénouement. What the reader has discovered about Gehazi's actions Elisha reveals himself to have known as well, and now Gehazi, entrapped, knows too. Here the relationship between prophet and servant is at issue, and its violation leads simply and unequivocally to punishment. Elisha is typically laconic. He snares Gehazi with a two-word question: *mēʾayin gēḥăzî,* "Where have you been, Gehazi?" Like Nathan's ploy when putting his innocent case to David (2 Sam 12:1-6, cf. 1 Kgs 20:39-40), Elisha really invites Gehazi to compound his string of deceptions, which he promptly does with the evasive, though properly courteous, answer, "Your servant went nowhere." His speech is polite, but the narrator notes that Gehazi stands "*next* to his lord" (*wayyaʿămōd ʾel-ʾădōnāyw,* v. 25a; cf. 2 Kgs 11:14) as though to contrast with Naaman's submissive "standing *before* Elisha" (*wayyaʿămōd lĕpānāyw,* v. 15; cf. v. 3). The relationship between prophet and "convert" is open, flowing with solicitous gratitude; between Elisha and this servant among the sons of prophets the channel is choked by secret greed, deception, and insubordination.

Elisha thus seizes upon Gehazi's evasion and heaps rhetorically exaggerated accusation and punishment upon him, v. 26. If he (Gehazi) has taken money and garments — and, Elisha adds with indignant hyperbole, olive orchards and vineyards, sheep, oxen, servants, amassing goods like some corrupt royal tyrant (Cohn, 182) — then he will also inherit Naaman's leprosy, as will his children. The essence of the offense is captured in two words: "Was [this] the [suitable] time to take . . . ?" *(haʿēt lāqaḥat).* This thematic verb now unambiguously carries a double meaning: "accept" something freely offered, as Naaman might think, and "steal" or "take illicitly," as Elisha, Gehazi, and the reader know to be the case (cf. 2 Sam 12:4, 10). Moreover, if miraculous cure is a "time" for spiritual transformation for which Elisha has refused reward, it ought not to have been profaned into an occasion for sordid opportunism and selfish personal gain (see Rofé, "Classification," 146; idem, *Prophetical Stories,* 108-12). Wounded, Gehazi departs a leper.

The narrator's final clipped remark (v. 27b) takes us back to Naaman's early affliction and makes this tale of reversals and contrasts into a wave doubling back on itself: Naaman — "now the man was a mighty man of valor, (but) leprous" (v. 1); Gehazi — "and he went out from his presence, leprous as snow" (v. 27b). Along the way successive waves of action, one subsiding while generating within itself another, show us Naaman the foreigner healed in body and spirit. Conversely, Gehazi the servant to Elisha, an insider, inherits Naaman's disease, and becomes, presumably, outcast. Through all of this, Elisha retains his authoritative position. People seek him out, and he dominates the cure which Naaman takes at the Jordan River. Even Gehazi's brief triumphant play Elisha trumps with preternatural insight and instantly realizable punishment. The author has shown us the consequences of dealing with Elisha, man of God, both in truth and deceit. Thus, the prophet whom the Israelite woman remembers, and whom Naaman discovers, stands at the "still point" to which two men come and go, each transformed by the encounter (Cohn, 184).

Genre

Leaving aside those generic identifications for subunits within this narrative (e.g., H.-Chr. Schmitt, 78, "Spottlegende" for vv. 1-14; Schult, 15, "conversion story" for vv. 1-19; Hentschel, 16, "miracle story" for vv. 1-19a), this narrative is a PROPHET LEGEND. It is a story especially concerned to portray the prophet as a worker of mighty, miraculous deeds, a conduit for divine power, and an exemplar of God-filled piety and morality. Rofé ("Classification," 145-47; idem, *Prophetical Stories*, 126-31), followed by Cohn (p. 183), speaks of "didactic" or "ethical" *legendum*, having been rightly impressed by the force of didacticism and ideology in this example of prophet legend (cf. von Rad, 55). That "didactic" or "ethical" legend grew out of more primitive and simple legends which simply projected awe without didacticism, as Rofé believes, may be doubted since, as may be shown from folklore studies, even the simplest legend is laden with values and ideology. De Vries (p. 54) also speaks of "legend," but in assigning it to a subcategory, "power-demonstration narrative," he unduly limits the scope of its literary play. The term "legend" makes more precise certain older descriptions such as "popular oral folktale" (Šanda, *Könige* II, 84-85) and German *Sage*, "tale" (Gressmann, *Geschichtsschreibung*, 298; cf. Gunkel, *Geschichten*, 45). Though this legend draws its narrative coloring from plausible historylike references to relations between Israel and Aram, the obvious emphases on miracle, pious confession, rewards, and punishment preclude our simply describing it as "historical narrative" or reading the text historically (against Gray, *Kings*, 468).

An important generic element in this legend is the type scene in which a foreigner comes to affirm belief in Israel's God. Typically a narrative reports a display of wondrous divine power, on the basis of which a person confesses allegiance to Yahweh, Israel's God. (See Exod 18:1-12; Josh 2:9-13; 2 Macc 3:35-39; and full discussion above; Schult.)

The functional equivalent to PROPHECY OF PUNISHMENT appears in vv. 26-27a. Citation of an offense (here in the form of rhetorical questions) leads to pronouncement of punishment (see 1 Kgs 13:21-22 and full discussion). This particular example differs formally from those prophecies which assume the style of divine word, with (→) messenger formula, (→) oracle formula (*nĕ'um yahweh*), and divine speech channeled through the prophet as, e.g., 1 Kgs 13:21-22. Compare this with other pronouncements by prophets on their own authority (e.g., the promise of a child, 2 Kgs 4:16, or disaster, 7:2b; instructions which lead to miraculous relief of distress, 4:3; 5:10; an oath which threatens punishment, 1 Kgs 17:1). In context, however, none of these prophetic declarations was likely to have been understood differently from those oracles which carry or presuppose a direct attribution to God (cf. 2 Kgs 4:41 and 4:43; 7:1 and 7:2b).

In addition to these stereotyped elements, we may note also: PETITION, vv. 17-18 (cf. v. 15b), which often appears in elevated style, as in v. 18 (cf. 2 Kgs 1:13b-14; 1 Sam 25:24-31; Josh 1:9-13), and OATH in vv. 16a, 20b; also DIS-

PENSATORY DISMISSAL FORMULA, "Go in peace," v. 19, which implies that one has granted a petitioner what has been asked (e.g., pardon, Gen 44:17; blessing, Judg 18:6; stay of revenge, 1 Sam 25:35b); also, the formulaic GREETING (hăšālôm, "Is all well?" v. 21b, and its simple answer, šālôm, "all is well"; cf. Gen 29:6; 2 Sam 18:32; 2 Kgs 4:26; 9:11). Finally, behind v. 6 may be a stylistic feature of LETTER, in which the body of the epistle typically begins with "and now" (wĕʿattâ). See Dennis Pardee, *Handbook of Ancient Hebrew Letters* (SBLSBS 15; Chico, CA: Scholars Press, 1982) 172; Hobbs, *2 Kings*, 62.

Setting

Belonging to the world of popular tale-telling, legends flourished in different societal situations. There is no evidence to suggest that legends about prophets were restricted to one particular social group in ancient society. Such stories would have been told by different people on various occasions depending on the circumstances and aims of the narrators. This particular example may have been at one time part of a separate collection of Elisha traditions. The more important issue has to do with its literary setting in the books of Kings. The story is presented by the Dtr writer as one of a series of incidents reputed to have occurred during Jehoram's reign. In this particular case, Elisha, for a second time, deals with a non-Israelite (see 4:8-37), but this time his actions take place amid a new sense of Aramean military pressures on the northern kingdom (see v. 2).

Intention

Legends aim to instruct and edify; they are told to inspire certain moral attitudes and inculcate religious values. Among other points, this particular example emphasizes the conversion of a foreign military man, unwittingly a prince of Yahweh (see v. 1), to belief in Israel's God. One can hardly miss the contrast with Israel's king, who in context must be Jehoram, and who next to Elisha appears ineffectual. The king nearly blocks the flow of prophetic power by misreading the meaning of Naaman's mission, and implicitly highlights the supernatural currents which move deep within events ("Am I God, to kill and make alive . . . ?," v. 7).

Like the military men, the prophetic characters are drawn contrastively. Elisha is a man of God in all his miraculous power — fully in control of the situation, determined to make an ethical and ideological point through his actions, and resolute in his ascetic disregard for rewards. There is indeed a prophet in Israel, v. 8, and his aims are congruent with those of the unnamed but dramatically important "little maid from . . . Israel" (v. 3; cf. chs. 2, 3, and 8). In contrast, Gehazi, the servant, always at Elisha's side, is protective of protocol with the intrusions of the Shunammite woman (4:27), but then is severely judged when he allows opportunism to sully the moment of Naaman's affirmation of Yahweh.

It is clear that the main characters in this legend are drawn primarily for their didactic value, and that the lessons are fairly conventional. In its particular context, however, the writer gives us a prophet who stands on firm ethical and religious principle and thus continues to act on those moral sensibilities first explored in ch. 4.

As for Jehoram, the legend is probably meant to contribute indirectly to an assessment of his reign. As in 3:4-27, he is portrayed unfavorably. Both instances suggest a character consistent with the historian's initial negative appraisal in 3:3.

Bibliography

See bibliographies at 2 Kgs 1:2-17a; 2:1-25. R. Cohn, "Form and Perspective in 2 Kings V," *VT* 33 (1983) 171-84; G. Hentschel, "Die Heilung Naamans durch das Wort des Gottesmannes (II Kön 5)," in *Künder des Wortes. Beiträge zur Theologie des Propheten* (*Fest.* J. Schreiner; ed. L. Ruppert et al.; Würzburg: Echter, 1982) 11-21; Rofé, "Classification" (→ 2 Kgs 2:1-18); H. Schult, "Naamans Übertritt zum Yahwismus (2 Kön 5,1-19a) und die biblischen Bekehrungsgeschichten," *Dielheimer Blätter zum Altes Testament* 9 (1975) 2-20; K. A. D. Smelik, "De betekenis van 2 Koningen 5. Een 'Amsterdamse' benadering," *Gereformeerd Theologisch Tijdschrift* 88 (1988) 98-115; C. Turiot, "La guérison de Naaman (2 Rois 5,1-27)," *Sémiotique et Bible* 16 (1979) 8-32; G. von Rad, *God at Work in Israel* (tr. J. H. Marks; Nashville: Abingdon, 1980) 47-57; Y. Zakovitch, *Every High Official Has a Higher One Set over Him: A Literary Analysis of 2 Kings 5* (Tel Aviv: Am Oved, 1985 [Hebr.]).

RECOVERY OF A SUNKEN AXE HEAD, 6:1-7

Structure

A. Elisha's instruction concerning axe head   7a
B. Instruction carried out   7b

At one time this unit may have been independent of its immediate context. Joined only to the resolute closure at 5:27 by a simple conjunction (*wāw,* "and" [*RSV* "now"]), it opens abruptly onto a scene of domestic ordinariness inhabited by prophet and followers, the "sons of prophets." The incident is quite removed from the grander scope of international relations in chs. 5 and 6:8-23. The tradition seems unified and self-contained, even if stylistically wooden and unimaginative. It is doubtful that literary developments which led to the present text may be reconstructed with any degree of confidence (cf. Cummings).

A simple plot determines narrative structure. Elisha and his followers decide to move to new quarters on the Jordan River (I, vv. 1-3), but while felling trees, one of the "sons of prophets" loses an axe head — its being borrowed was a moral dilemma — and upon crying for help, Elisha retrieves it miraculously from the stream (II-III, vv. 4-6). A concluding action restores former equilibrium (IV, v. 7). More abstractly seen, this unit consists of three constitutive elements: (1) a prophet is presented with a problem; (2) he responds with remedial action; (3) a miracle results and resolves the problem. Cf. Exod 15:22-27; 17:1-7; 2 Kgs 2:19-22; 4:38-41 (see Culley, *Narrative,* 81-83).

Writing with mimetic simplicity, the narrator-author creates the illusion of a perfectly ordinary world where miracle making is as commonplace as house building (see Licht, 24). Like flotsam, the wondrous drifts past on a flow of unrippled domesticity. Restraint governs the setting and the telling, with little indication of strong emotions or personalities. The central crisis — the loss of the axe head — receives only a slight emphasis with inverted word order in the Hebrew. The cry of distress is formulaic and conventional. In the end, austere economy of language suggests the routine resumption of house-building labors. The river's flow, flat to the eye, regains its command of place.

Genre

This narrative is a PROPHET LEGEND, a story which chiefly portrays a wondrous deed or ideal virtue of an exemplary holy man. (See discussion at 2:19-24; Rofé, "Classification," 430, speaks of "simple *legenda*"; see also his *Prophetical Stories,* 13-22; Licht, 24.) Close parallels in form and style may be found in 2:19-22; 4:38-41; Exod 15:22-27; 17:1-7. All these texts feature the miracle worker, helper, or solver-of-problems as the quiet manipulator of the ordinary (Culley, *Narrative,* 72-96).

Of interest is the formulaic CRY OF DISTRESS, v. 5b. A simple exclamation (*'ăhāh,* "Alas!") is usually followed by the name or title of the person addressed. Statements, questions, or protesting pleas which immediately follow may give the reason(s) for the distress and turn the cry into a PETITION addressed to one perceived as having the power to help (see 3:10; Judg 6:22; 11:35; Jer 1:6; 4:10; cf. 1 Sam 4:7-8). The cry-of-distress formula may often appear also as part of (→) dirge.

Setting

In oral tradition, simple prophet legends belong to many different social settings and would have been told on various occasions, depending on the circumstances and aims of the narrators. This particular example may have been associated with Elisha's followers (De Vries, 53-54; Gray, *Kings,* 466; Rofé, *Prophetical Stories,* 22), perhaps localized at Gilgal (Cummings). The absence of evidence on these matters makes it all the more important to consider carefully the literary setting of this legend in the Dtr-authored books of Kings, and specifically in the reign of Jehoram.

Intention

Without unduly restricting an author's or narrator's purposes, one primary aim of this legend would have been to demonstrate the hero's marvelous power, and to inculcate attitudes of awe and reverence toward him. (See the discussion at 2:19-24; see also Rofé, "Classification," 431; idem, *Prophetical Stories,* 13-22; Gray, *Kings,* 466; De Vries, 53.) In the present literary context, these purposes blend into others. The DtrH enhances our image of Elisha as powerful guide and helper, and — the ideology is implicit in the context here — a conduit for God's powers during the reign of Jehoram. (See the comments on the similarly brief legends at 4:39-42.)

Bibliography

See bibliography at 2 Kgs 1:2-17a. R. Culley, *Narrative* (→ 2 Kgs 2:19-24); J. Cummings, "The House of the Sons of the Prophets and the Tents of the Rechabites," in *Studia Biblica 1978: I. Papers on Old Testament and Related Themes* (JSOTSup 11; Sheffield: University of Sheffield, 1979) 119-26.

ELISHA AND THE ARAMEAN THREAT, 6:8-23

Text

The MT *taḥănōtî* at v. 8 is inexplicable as vocalized. The *RSV* "my camp" seems to assume Hebr. *mḥnty* in line with the Old Greek and the Hexapla, which gave *parembalō,* "I will encamp," apparently a verbal paraphrase of the noun. The problem of translation is related to v. 9, MT *nĕḥittîm,* which, according to conventions of repetition in biblical narrative, one would expect to involve the same idea as *taḥănōtî;* but as presently vocalized, this word, too, makes little sense. Ancient VSS simply add to the confusion, and have spawned modern emendations. For simplicity of solution and adherence to literary convention, it seems best to read *tinḥātû* in v. 8 and *nōḥātîm* in v. 9 from the root *nḥt,* meaning to "go down" in a military sense of "falling upon to commit hostile action," or, simply, "attack" (see Jer 21:13; Montgomery, *Kings,* 382; Schweizer, 213, n. 1; Schmitt, *Elisa,* 216, n. 128; Hentschel, *2 Könige,* 27). Thus, translate v. 8, "at such and such a place you shall attack," and v. 9, with the *RSV,* "the Arameans are attacking" (with Cogan and Tadmor, *II Kings,* 72).

Structure

Completely new subject matter begins with inverted word order in the Hebrew. This syntax is typical of new beginnings and openings to independent narratives (cf. 5:1; 4:38, 42), and distinguishes this unit from the preceding, vv. 1-7. The tradition seems to have ended in v. 23a with dismissal and departure, a standard motival device by which biblical narrators disengage their characters and bring action to its close (cf. 4:37; 1 Kgs 20:34; Gen 18:33; Judg 21:24).

Some scholars take v. 23b, "and the Syrians came no more on raids into the land of Israel," as a redactor's comment. Its simple conjunction with perfect tense breaks abruptly with the preceding *wāw*-conversive narrative style. And the narrative perspective is suddenly widened: the "great army" (v. 14) and recurring campaigns (v. 8a, the durative sense of *hāyâ nilhām*) involved nothing more than raiding parties (*gĕdûdîm*) of the sort associated earlier with Naaman's activities, 5:2a (v. 23b, *RSV* "Syrians" = *gĕdûdê 'ărām*, "bands of Aram"). Yet, v. 23b is understandable as a regular feature of Hebraic narrative style. The comment reverts to a level of narrating identical to that of v. 10, in which a simple perfect tense verb lends an iterative sense to the context. In both places, the narrator violates the temporal order of story events — v. 10 to portray recurring background incidents, and v. 23b to supply commentary on events. Similar anachronisms appear frequently, e.g., 1 Sam 18:30 (a comment), 2 Kgs 7:6 (a retrospective explanation); 6:32b (information given the reader to fill an ellipsis in story time). Read this way, v. 23b is a narrative closure which carries the reader back to the temporal perspective of vv. 8-10. Those recurring incursions into Israel that hang like canvas behind events simply vanish after Elisha's victory.

Attempts at finding major signs of disunity in this tradition have not been notably successful. H.-Chr. Schmitt (pp. 92-93), Schweizer (pp. 224-25), Würthwein (*Könige*, 304-5), and Hentschel (*2 Könige*, 27-28) suppose that vv. 15-17 are secondary additions (so Rofé, 62-63), but beyond that, they disagree substantially. Either the original story included vv. 18aβ-b and 20 (Schweizer) or excluded them (Schmitt, Würthwein, Hentschel). The impasse in opinion simply reflects the degree of arbitrariness in such judgments. It seems the wiser course to discuss the tradition as it stands (so Montgomery, *Kings,* 381; Gray, *Kings,* 468, 512-14; Šanda, *Könige* II, 49, 80; Hobbs, *2 Kings,* 73-74).

The narrative is built of a strong series of speech-plus-action sequences enclosed within an opening exposition of background (I, vv. 8-10) and closing statement (IV, v. 23b). Particularly uniform in construction are vv. 17, 18, 19, and 20, each of which consists of direct speech by Elisha (three times, a prayer) and its resulting action. Vv. 11-14 and 21-23a are similarly constructed of speech (dialogue) plus action. Vv. 15-16 simply reverse that sequence. Even though the nearly identical prayers in vv. 17 and 20 make different points, they provide a formal enclosure around the climactic center, vv. 18-19, in which Elisha successfully diverts the Aramean force from himself. We may visualize this formal structure of speech-action as follows:

```
Opening exposition   vv. 8-10
   Dialogue + action   vv. 11-14
   Action + dialogue   vv. 15-16
   Speech + action   v. 17 (= v. 20)
      Speech + action   v. 18
      Speech + action   v. 19
   Speech + action   vv. 20 (= v. 17)-23a
Closing statement   v. 23b
```

Taking into account the content and natural grouping of events, one sees that the writer really has depicted two major scenes in vv. 15-23 by means of pairs of speech-action sequences (cf. Schweizer, 246-47). After telling of the crisis posed for Elisha by the Aramean king (II, vv. 11-14), he shows at the center the prophet's efforts to deal with the threat (III.B.2, vv. 18-19). Around this thematic center are sequences of speech-action: one dramatizes the strength of Aram through the eyes of Elisha's servant (III.A, vv. 15-17), and the other illustrates the largesse with which a triumphant Elisha treats his opponents (III.B.3, vv. 20-23aα). Hence, one may refine the diagram of structure and relate it to the main outline as follows:

```
Opening exposition   I, vv. 8-10
   Dialogue + action   II, vv. 11-14 (crisis)
   Action + dialogue/Speech + action   III.A, vv. 15-17 (measure of crisis)
      Speech + action   III.B.2.a, v. 18 (disablement)
      Speech + action   III.B.2.b, v. 19 (deception)
   Speech + action   III.B.3, vv. 20-23a (Arameans spared)
Closing statement   IV, v. 23b
```

Onto this skeleton of speech-action sequences, the narrator suspended a plot, although it must be admitted that the sense of directionality is somewhat weak (see Schweizer, 229-30). His military campaigns continually frustrated (I, vv. 8-10) and having at last laid blame on Elisha, the Aramean king orders his forces to seize the prophet in Dothan (II, vv. 11-14). However, because Elisha has extraordinary powers and is wrapped in supernatural protection, the prophet captures the troops, turns aside the personal threat (III.B.2, vv. 18-19), and has the king of Israel send the enemy home, an event accompanied by great feasting (III.B.3, vv. 20-23a). The author-narrator sketches a status quo, the recurrent escapes by the Israelites, and a single act, the attempt to seize Elisha, which creates disequilibrium. Thus set in motion, events reach a turning point when Elisha captures the armies, and finally resolve themselves when the enemy troops

— reversing their movement of vv. 14 and 18aα — return to their master, v. 23aβ (note the repetition of *šlh,* "send," in vv. 14 and 23a). A closing comment which notes the cessation of raids into Israel takes the loop in the narrative onto another level. Even that originative and recurrent cloud on Israel's border (cf. v. 8a and 5:2) has been wondrously dissipated by Elisha's work.

At the beginning (I, vv. 8-10), the narrator sketches general background. A first statement unambiguously conveys frequentative action: "Now the king of Aram was [regularly] warring against Israel" (*hāyâ* + participle *nilhām* is an iterative construction; GKC, § 116r; *RSV* "once when . . ." obscures this nuance; cf. *NJPS* "while . . . waging war . . ."). A concluding statement, v. 10b, also suggests recurrence by use of the adverbial expression "more than once or twice" (*NJPS* "time and again," lit., "not once and not twice"). Even though Aram's military adventures and Elisha's warnings are expressed in the singulative, one-time-once-narrated style, vv. 9-10a, the narrator wraps these events in a frame of recurrence. (Cf. a similar literary structure in 1 Sam 1:3, 7, surrounding the singulative narration in vv. 4-6, which the *RSV* rightly translates as frequentative.) Aram's plans have been continuously frustrated by Elisha's disconcerting habit of alerting Israel to impending danger, time and again in place after place. (*pělōnî 'almōnî,* "such and such a place," is an iterative generalization; see A. Berlin, *Poetics and Interpretation of Biblical Narrative* [Bible and Literature Series; Sheffield: Almond, 1983] 99-101.) The whole exposition gains additional coherence in sonorous wordplays: Elisha warns the king, "Beware . . . [*hiššamer*] . . . for there Aram [*kî-šam 'ăram*] is going down. . . . And one was on guard there [*wěnišmar šām*]." (See LaBarbera, 640.)

The following section (II.A, vv. 11-14) converts that past recurrent energy into a fresh impulse and marks the beginning of narrative movement. The king of Aram, perhaps angry and agitated (Rofé, 61), meets with his advisors to identify the intelligence leak, and thus sets in motion those events which will directly threaten Elisha. A conventional *topos,* the scene recalls other occasions when a monarch seeks out or suppresses a prophet's advice (e.g., 1 Kgs 22:7-9, 27; 2 Kgs 1:9-16; 3:11-12; cf. Jeremiah 37-38). In this narrative, the Aramean king wants to seize Elisha and neutralize the powers of that "prophet who is in Israel" (cf. 5:8).

If the opening exposition sketches background and identifies the main protagonists, the next section, vv. 11-14, hints at the crisis which propels the drama and, by means of ironic play on two ideas, shapes the reader's perspective. First, the narrator plays on a twofold understanding of "sight." Aram commands his men, "Go and see . . ." (v. 13, employing the ordinary verb *r'h*), while the reader already realizes that Elisha is gifted with preternatural insight (v. 9). People other than Elisha and his servant are limited to ordinary senses. The Aramean king wants to be told the facts plainly: "Will you not show me?" (v. 11; the verb is from *haggîd,* "tell" or "show"). The same verb brings a report to the king: "it was told him" (v. 13); the Aramean messengers in fact describe Elisha's warnings to the Israelites on exactly that level of ordinary military intelligence ("the prophet . . . tells [*yaggîd*] the king of Israel," v. 12). Yet all these verbs of "telling" ring with ironic contrast. Elisha does divulge the Aramean's secrets, but out of some private reservoir from which the prophet alone drinks (cf. 2 Kgs

4:27; 1 Sam 15:16; Jer 42:3). Later in the narrative, this same ironic contrast depicts supernatural against natural perception, sight against blindness, vv. 17-20.

Second, the writer contrasts military forces. Aram sends "horses and chariots and a great army" (*sûsîm wĕrekeb wĕḥayil kābēd,* v. 14) to seize the prophet. This overwhelming horde (cf. 2 Kgs 1:9-12), it turns out, will face the mystical "horses and chariots of fire" *(sûsîm wĕrekeb 'ēš)* deployed around Elisha (v. 17). Thus in this scene, the writer carefully, but with well-practiced grace, manipulates those thematic oppositions which will determine the reader's "seeing" as the story proceeds.

The narrator turns from these Aramean actions, in which the potential threat to Elisha becomes clear, to Elisha's response (III, vv. 15-23a). Following literary convention, the pace slows to heighten the drama (cf. Josh 10:5-9; Num 21:33-35; Exod 14:9-25). The vast hordes are ranged against Dothan, poised for attack (Hiphil of *nqp,* "surround," appears also in Josh 6:3); the army will meet its quarry only in v. 18a (cf. Exod 14:9-10: Pharaoh's armies draw near, while active pursuit of the Israelites begins only at v. 23). In this pause between city surrounded and prophet confronted, the narrator-writer takes the reader inside the panicky despair of Elisha's attendant. One sees through his eyes: "the servant of the man of God . . . went out, and behold [*wĕhinnēh*], an army . . . round about the city." (Note the same device for focusing a narrative moment through a character's perspective in Exod 14:10.) The servant's distress is met with Elisha's assurances ("Fear not," v. 16; cf. Exod 14:13; Josh 10:8; Num 21:34). Then, as though to add conviction to exhortation, Elisha prays that his servant be given second sight into the hidden reaches of reality (see 2 Kgs 2:10; Num 24:3-4). Again, one looks with the servant's eyes: "he saw, and behold, the mountain was full of horses and chariots of fire round about Elisha" (v. 17) — an awesome ring *(sĕbîbōt)* of countervailing force to match the enemy round about *(sôbēb)* the city (v. 15; see LaBarbera, 641).

In this dramatic pause before the Aramean troops move with force against Elisha, the covert play of two levels of perception observed in vv. 8-14 becomes explicit. The scene dramatizes panic, focused in the servant's ordinary sighting of the enemy, and then quickly diffuses it through supernatural perception by prayer-induced vision. One sees the protective shield of Elisha — or perhaps a visionary rendering of the power of his honorific title (cf. 2 Kgs 2:12). The reader and both prophetic figures know, as the Arameans do not, that the *ḥayil* of Yahweh, his fighting force, is concentrated in Elisha.

When forward motion resumes, two deeds of power offer a turning point to the entire narrative (III.B.2, vv. 18-19). First, Elisha alters perceptions again, this time asking that blindness, or "dazzlement," strike the Arameans (cf. Gen 19:11). Second, he adds mental deception to physical sightlessness, and leads the confused army, so he tells them, to the one whom they seek (v. 19). Then, a third petition to God — but the second deed of power in this section — removes the blindness. Once again the narrator gives the reader a character's eyes: "and behold [*wĕhinnēh*], in the midst of Samaria!" One has moved through a see-scape, from blindness supernaturally sent, to ironic deception told, to natural sight supernaturally restored. The journey reveals the forces on Elisha's side and the ease with which he manipulates the world about him — with Yahweh's help, of course.

As if building on one's expectations that these duped captives will now be summarily disposed of, the narrator portrays a dialogue in which their fate is decided and the whole incident brought to its conclusion (III.B.3, vv. 20-23aα). Apparently looking to Elisha for guidance, the king of Israel asks, the words tumbling redundantly with excitement, "Shall I slay them? Shall I slay them?" (v. 21). Elisha's reply falsifies expectations: the prisoners are to be spared and sent away with food and drink (v. 22). The reason is not clear. Implied in Elisha's rhetorical question, v. 22aβ, seems to be a custom that prisoners of war are regularly spared, and thus in this case, as they have been captured without a fight, there is all the more reason to show mercy. (However, Ahab was censured precisely because he spared a prisoner, an enemy king, 1 Kgs 20:42.) In contrast, the Lucianic Greek VS casts Elisha's rhetorical question with a negative particle: "Would you slay those whom you have *not* taken captive?" This formulation may imply that prisoners were usually slain, but since these Arameans were not really captured in the normal way, they are to be spared (so Gray, *Kings,* 515; Würthwein, *Könige,* 304, accepting the Greek text as original). This custom, too, has its exception in other biblical narratives (e.g., 2 Sam 8:2; 12:30-31). In either case, the result of Elisha's argument is the same: when capture has been effected as a gift of the prophet's power-working manipulations, the victims are due their lives, perhaps just as they were so easily deprived of sight and given it again. Such, apparently, is the power (and high moral standards? cf. Rofé, 61) of this prophet who is in Israel, this man whom the army foolishly, and, the reader knows, without hope of success, seeks to restrain. Elisha clearly dominates the scene. His wishes are followed, and the troops are sent away (v. 23a). All tension drains away, the parties disengage, and one imagines once again the spring from which all has flowed, the troops at home with their commander.

The reader now sees differently, even if the Arameans do not. One has some sense of Elisha's preternatural powers of perception and his knack for producing miracle by prayer (v. 17). In retrospect, the Aramean's innocent report, "the prophet who is in Israel tells the king of Israel the words that you speak" (v. 12b), is heavy with implication and example. The narrator's concluding remark, v. 23b, adds yet another perspective. That awesome power by which personal danger is turned away also, as it happens, dissuades the Arameans from their habitual incursions into Israelite territory. Or is it that what the raiders may have seen as kindness following on strange blockage of sight, the reader understands as power rooted in unassailable divinity? In any case, as the narrative opens with a retrospective sketch of recurrence, so it reverts at the close to that same temporal period. That distant time, envisioned in a past well beyond the reach of this particular story, comes to its completion as well.

Genre

This unit is a PROPHET LEGEND, a narrative concerned primarily with the prophet as main character and exemplar of wondrous power, virtue, and divine favor (see Gressmann, *Geschichtsschreibung,* 300; seeking greater specificity, Rofé, 60, calls it a "political *legendum*"; and De Vries, 55, "supplicatory power story," for him a subtype of legend; cf. Schweizer, 261, who characterizes a hypothetical earlier version, vv. 8-14 + 18-23, as "anecdote," and H.-Chr. Schmitt, 93, as "miracle story"). General parallels may be seen in 1 Kgs 13:1-32; 17:2-24; 2 Kgs 4:8-37; 5:1-27. Less developed examples are 2 Kgs 4:1-7, 38-41, 42-44; 6:1-7.

Within this legend, the reader observes in v. 17b something close to VISION REPORT, with the characteristic root *r'h,* "to see," followed by *wĕhinnēh,* "and behold," a transitional particle preceding the visionary sight. Cf. the mention of a supranatural opening of one's eyes, v. 17a, with Num 24:3-4 (full discussion and parallels at 1 Kgs 22:1-38 in Long, *1 Kings,* 238). Other smaller generic elements worth noting are: (1) three examples of PRAYER OF PETITION, v. 17a, 18a, and 20, a PETITION directed to God and seeking some definite response (see 1 Kgs 18:36-37; 2 Kgs 19:15-19; 20:3); (2) a REASSURANCE FORMULA, v. 16, with the characteristic "Fear not" *('al-tîrā')* followed by a subordinating preposition, *kî,* "for" or "because," and the basis for reassurance (see Gen 35:17; 1 Sam 22:23; in 2 Kgs 6:16, the formula suffices for the entire speech, but it often occurs as an element in more extensive direct discourse, e.g., oracles [Isa 7:4-9; 10:24-27] and speeches [Josh 8:1]); (3) a CRY OF DISTRESS, v. 15b (see discussion at 6:5).

Setting

Prophet legends were used in a variety of societal situations. It is uncertain whether this particular example was created and transmitted originally by prophets or other admirers around Elisha (see De Vries, 55; Rofé, 60). The legend in its present context is one of several traditions which portray the reign of Jehoram in terms of Elisha's wondrous deeds. In the background are external troubles for Israel: the Moabite rebellion in chs. 1 and 3 have now given way to incursions from Aram. All this by implication redounds to the blame of Jehoram, as though Aram were the sign of Yahweh's judgment on Israel (Hobbs, *2 Kings,* 82).

Intention

In popular storytelling, one would have told prophet legends for various ends. With this particular example, an important aim probably would have been to show the wonders wrought by this powerful "man of God" who, against a record of successful early warnings for the king of Israel, easily turned aside the might of Aram and personal danger to himself (Hobbs, *2 Kings,* 74; contrast Gray's historicizing of Elisha's powers [*Kings,* 513], which is beside the literary point). Evidence for more specific original intentions is simply lacking (see Schweizer, 260). Rofé (p. 59) supposes that these "political" legends expressed and nurtured ideas differing from or even hostile toward the royal court; direct signs of polemics are not evident, however.

Elisha seems empowered and heroized by this legend and, in context, Jehoram seems weakened. Elisha is an object of admiration, religious awe, and devotion. Perhaps he is meant to be remembered as famed in the testimonies of people beyond the borders of Israel (Cogan and Tadmor, *II Kings,* 76). By contrast, without Elisha's power Jehoram can do little to counter Aram's military forays. De Vries (p. 59) sees in this story a conflict over who has authority to decide the Arameans' fate, but v. 21 implies that the question is not in dispute; LaBarbera's claim (p. 651) that this legend along with 6:24–7:20 is a social satire on the ruling elite is weakly argued and somewhat farfetched.

Bibliography

S. De Vries, *Prophet* (→ 2 Kgs 1:2-17a); R. LaBarbera, "The Man of War and the Man of God: Social Satire in 2 Kings 6:8–7:20," *CBQ* 46 (1984) 637-51; A. Rofé, *Prophetical Stories* (→ 2 Kgs 1:2-17a); H.-Chr. Schmitt, *Elisa* (→ 2 Kgs 2:1-25); H. Schweizer, *Elischa* (→ 2 Kgs 3:4-27).

A FAMINE RELIEVED, AN ORACLE FULFILLED, 6:24–7:20

Text

In 7:13b, after *min-hassûsîm hanniš'ārîm,* "the horses that remain," the MT is redundant, obscure, and perhaps corrupt. The situation has stimulated bold (e.g., Burncy, *Notes,* 292) and more moderate emendations (e.g., Gray, *Kings,* 520-21). By assuming a dittography in the text and, with most MSS, reading a simplified line, one comes close to the Hebrew that apparently underlies the RSV (see Montgomery, *Kings,* 390; Cogan and Tadmor, *II Kings,* 83). However, even if some original text could be recovered, there remains the ambiguity of *tammû,* which can mean "sound, in good condition" (Gray, *Kings,* 521; cf. Ps 19:14 [*RSV* 13]; Job 22:3).or the virtual opposite, "finished, expired" (*RSV* "perished"; see Gen 47:15, 18; Num 14:33, 35).

Structure

I. Exposition of crisis: Samaria under siege	24-25
A. General situation: gathering of forces	24
B. Specific situation: famine and siege in Samaria	25
II. Severity of crisis	26-31
A. Narrative setting	26a
B. Petition before the king	26b-29
1. Woman's call for help	26b
2. King's responses	27-28a
a. Indirect: statement of powerlessness	27

The vague connector "afterward" (*'aḥărê-kēn*) and the unclear logical transition between the cessation of Aramean raids (v. 23) and the beginning of a major military assault (v. 24) suggest that this unit be set apart from the tradition reflected in vv. 8-23. Its intended conclusion is not clear. Hobbs (*2 Kings*, 75) treats 6:24-31 and 7:1-20 separately, but the trajectory of plotted action initiated in 6:24 satisfactorily closes in 7:16 with the breaking of siege against Samaria and typical reference to prophecy having been fulfilled (cf. 2 Kgs 1:17a; 4:44; 1 Kgs 17:16). For these reasons, most critics who view the unit as extending into ch. 7 nevertheless take 7:18-20, often with the notice of prophecy fulfilled in v. 17bβ, as a late addition (H.-Chr. Schmitt, 37-38; De Vries, "Temporal Terms," 101; among the commentators see Würthwein, *Könige*, 309-10; Šanda, *Könige* II, 63; Montgomery, *Kings*, 388; Fricke, *2 Könige*, 96, n. 3; Hentschel, *2 Könige*, 30). Others express doubt (e.g., Schweizer, 218-25; Gray, *Kings*, 525; Gunkel, *Geschichten*, 46-66; Fohrer, *Erzählungen*, 105). In either case, the formal structure of the narrative is essentially the same. A completely new tradition begins in 8:1.

Those critics who have supplanted older notions of written sources with hypotheses about the history of redaction for this material have reached contradictory results. Würthwein's postulate of original tradition is similar to Schmitt's and Hentschel's, but substantially different from Schweizer's. Würthwein further disagrees with Schmitt and Schweizer in suggesting that 7:6-8a belongs to an entirely different layer of redaction. On the other hand, De Vries pursues a radically independent course and excludes, among other items, vv. 26-31; 7:3-5, 7b-13, from a hypothetical original narrative. Reiser (pp. 330-31) supposes that a prophetic saying, 7:1, generated or attracted a number of different narrative traditions which now make up the aggregate 6:24–7:20. Such widely divergent hypotheses arise from the ambiguity of evidence adduced and the arbitrary assumptions on which some judgments rest. (E.g., religious or theological motifs must be secondary additions to an earlier secular narrative [Würthwein, *Könige*; Schmitt]; or repetition is simple redundancy and a sign of editorial disruption [De Vries, "Temporal Terms," 101, and Würthwein, *Könige*, 308, on 7:5b-8]; for a contrary view, see discussion of repetition at 2 Kgs 4:8-37.)

In the light of such uncertainties, it seems the wiser course to treat the present unit as making structural and thematic sense, even if a history of gathering and editing lies behind it (cf. Gray, *Kings*, 517, and Fricke, *2 Könige*, 88, who see a general thematic and associational unity to the composite material). Indeed, most recently, Rofé (*Prophetical Stories*, 64-66) argues strongly a case for original unity.

One key to understanding the structure of this unit is to grasp the ironic interplay of various perspectives on two lines of plotted action: how the siege of Samaria was broken, and how Elisha's prophecies found their fulfillment in events. The trajectory of the first grows less distinct as the second becomes explicit (7:1-2, 16-17 [*RSV* 18-20]). Yet, explicitness is not the same as directness. The paths from crisis to resolution, and from prophecy to fulfillment, meander through four lepers' landscape of comic self-absorption; the crucial event, a miracle which befuddles leper and king alike, and which is the ultimate cause of Samaria's relief, is revealed to the reader alone — and then only as an indirect comment in retrospect, not as "watchable" primary narration (7:6-7). The writer seems less interested in reporting a miracle than in portraying how various people deal with its aftereffects. Yet the characters remain unenlightened; they bump into cryptic prophecies, discover strange events, and offer inadequate explanations for their experiences. Finally, it is the reader who must complete the sequence begun in 6:24-25 by inferring that the siege has been broken; the narrator notes only that Elisha's word, which was not directly related to the end of the military campaign, has found its fulfillment.

The "siege sequence" begins clearly enough in v. 24 with language that typically reports military assaults ("go up against" [ʿlh ʿl] and "besiege" [ṣwr ʿl]; cf. 1 Kgs 14:25; 20:1; 2 Kgs 16:5; 18:9, 13; 24:10; 25:1-2). Conventional motifs emphasize the gravity of the crisis: a famine of such severity descends upon the city that refuse items are sold for food at exorbitant prices; from a dispute brought to the king for judgment (II, vv. 26-31) one learns how desperate the situation has become: the king is in official mourning for the city (v. 30; cf. 1 Kgs 20:32; 21:27; 2 Kgs 19:1-2), and people devour their children. (Cf. Deut 28:52-57; Jer 19:9; Ezek 5:10. For parallels in other literary texts, see Gray, *Kings,* 522, the Atrahasis epic [*ANET,* 105b, lines 30ff.], and Ashurbanipal, "famine broke out among them, and they ate the flesh of their children to satisfy their hunger" [Streck, *Die Inschriften Assurbanipal* II (Leipzig: J. C. Hinrichs, 1916) 76]. From Neo-Babylonian Nippur [ca. 656-617 B.C.E.], similar references appear in records of legal transactions that took place during such times of distress; see A. L. Oppenheim, " 'Siege-Documents' from Nippur," *Iraq* 17 [1955] 69-89.)

In fact, the writer has used a stock scene — a petition before the king — to develop this picture of severe crisis in Samaria. The woman's initial cry is what one expects to initiate a juridical proceeding: "Help, my lord, O king!" (v. 26b; cf. 2 Sam 14:4b; 1 Kgs 3:17-27; 2 Kgs 8:5-6; Mabee). But the king's response violates literary convention. It is not encouragement to the petitioner that he offers initially (cf. 2 Sam 14:5), but in effect his own cry of futility and frustration: "Don't [ask]! Let the Lord help you. Where could I get help for you — from the threshing floor?" (v. 27; see Cogan and Tadmor, *II Kings,* 80). The first verb *(yôšîʿēk)* could be a jussive with *'al* as the negative particle in a hypothetical sentence (so *RSV* "If the Lord will not help you, whence shall I help you?"; *GKC,* § 109h; Burney, *Notes,* 289). In any case, the king ventilates his feeling of impotence. Then, as though recovering his sense of public propriety, Jehoram continues, this time in keeping with what the *topos* demands: "What is your trouble?" (v. 28; cf. 2 Sam 14:5). The woman states her complaint, including accusation of wrongdoing, and puts an implicit plea that the king provide a judgment in the matter (cf. 1 Kgs 3:28 where *mišpāṭ,* "judgment," is used in a similar situation). But instead of dealing with the complaint as one would expect (cf. 1 Kgs 3:24-25; 2 Sam 14:8), King Jehoram sinks back into his own, or rather his kingdom's, troubles. The woman's horrifying suit, that a neighbor has "unfairly" refused to give up her child for food, elicits a gesture of distress. The king "rent his clothes" (v. 30a), an act which the narrator — in a comment to the reader — associates with "sackcloth" and thereby suggests public lamentation and penitence in the midst of God-sent troubles (cf. 1 Kgs 21:27; 2 Kgs 19:1-2; Jer 48:37; Jonah 3:5). Furthermore, the narrator frames this scene of petition with a repeated circumstantial clause: "and he [the king] was passing by on the wall" (*hû' [melek] 'ōbēr 'al-haḥōmâ*, vv. 26, 30). The narrator tells of synchronous events: while the king mourns for his city, this little drama of extremity among the people is played out, mirrored in a woman's petition. To bring a complaint that is horrifying in itself, but even more, to bring one which is engulfed by the king's own despair, is to intensify all the more the reader's sense of the city's desperate plight.

Like this woman and her desperate suit, the king also seems little more than dramatic foil; his frustration sweeps aside the woman's claims, turns on Elisha in a death oath (v. 31), and reaches its climactic intensity in v. 33. Jehoram severs all links with the beneficent possibilities of Yahweh. The trouble is from God (cf. 3:10, 13b); why should he "wait for [hope in] the Lord," i.e., hope for divine deliverance? (See Ps 38:16 [*RSV* 15]; 42:6, 12 [*RSV* 5, 11]; 43:5; Mic 7:7; Lam 3:24.) In desperation, the king completely gives up. He hears the moral and perhaps legal claim of the woman, but is unable, or unwilling, to deal with it; he threatens Yahweh's prophet, as though Elisha somehow were behind the troubles of the realm, but nothing comes of it (cf. 1 Kings 17–18); and he refuses to hope in God (Isa 7:7-9).

Elisha's response to this unrelieved picture of powerless despair is a simple, and entirely typical, oracle (III.B, C, 7:1-2). The word is formulated in sonorous alliterative style: *kā'ēt māhār sĕ'â-sōlet bĕšeqel wĕsā'tayim šĕ'ōrîm bĕšeqel bĕ̌ša'ar šōmrôn*, "Tomorrow at this time a measure of meal [will be sold] for a shekel; and two measures of barley for a shekel in the gate of Samaria" (or perhaps "at the market price of Samaria"; so Cogan and Tadmor, *II Kings*, 81). Punishment awaits a royal attendant who dares to doubt this divine word (7:2). Subsequent events are explicitly noted as bearing him out (7:16, 17 [*RSV* 18-20]). This structural sequence is similar to that found in other narratives which stress the actualization of a prophet's word (cf. 8:7-15; 1 Kgs 13:20-25; 14:1-18; 17:8-16; De Vries, "Temporal Terms," 102, in fact postulated an original "word-fulfillment" narrative behind the present text).

Yet in this narrative, a simple oracle and the path to its fulfillment take on more complex shading, despite the emphasis and pedantic reiteration given it in the concluding reprise (7:18-20). Having grasped the severity of the crisis in the women's dispute as well as in the king's responses, Elisha's prophecies sound like improbable predictions given out by someone who plainly underestimates the situation. Indeed, the aide to King Jehoram takes just that view and suffers for it (7:2a). Yet, habits of reading lead one to expect that the divine word will have its actualization in some miraculous event, and directly, without delay or diversion (cf. 8:7-15; 1 Kgs 13:20-25; 20:35-36). This view, like that of the military aide, is mistaken, too. The narrator approaches the critical events obliquely, looks at miracle from a distance, and compromises even the reader's usually omniscient expectations.

A rather leisurely sequence reduces the larger crisis to comic dimensions. Four lepers, dim of wit and preoccupied with their own lives, stumble onto Samaria's deliverance (the abandoned siege camp); an uncomprehending king, no longer "waiting for the Lord," has his own plausible but entirely wrong explanation for what the lepers find. And the narrator tells of no miracle directly.

Doing so would draw a straight line to the prophecy's fulfillment. Instead, speaking with playful irony and satirizing humor, the writer shows various personages fumbling with the residue of some great, but unexplained, event (cf. Rofé, *Prophetical Stories*, 67-70).

A new scene, opening with inverted word order in the Hebrew, introduces the four lepers and their Pascal-like wager (IV.A.1, 2, 7:3-4). Perhaps the narrator intends a pun on their number, "four" (*'arbā'â*), and the "windows in heaven" (*'ărubbôt*) which the military aide had mentioned in v. 2 (LaBarbera, 648). Deciding that things could not be worse outside the city, they go to the camp of the Arameans. At the point at which the lepers gaze upon the abandoned siegeworks, the author breaks the flow of primary narrative time and directs to the reader a privileged explanation, in retrospect, of what the lepers see:

7:5b "they came to the edge of the camp"
    (wayyābō'û 'ad-qĕṣēh maḥănēh)

7:6 flashback explanation (Yahweh's deed)

7:8aα "and these lepers came to the edge of the camp"
    (wayyābō'û hamṣōrā'îm hā'ēlleh 'ad-qĕṣēh hammaḥăneh)

The repeated framing motif, v. 8aα, resumes the flow of time. One watches these lepers repeatedly plunder and hide the spoils. They are pictures of self-interest feasting on the unexpected bounty of mysterious grace. The reader now knows the city has been spared and why, but how will these comical figures rise to the larger demands of Samaria under siege? The answer comes in a twinge of conscience, at bottom still self-interest because the lepers fear punishment for withholding this "day of good news" (v. 9a). They make plans to report to the king, and relay their discovery with wide-eyed innocent objectivity to keepers of the city gate from whence they had departed (cf. v. 3). These messengers of good fortune have returned home, as it were, but remain outsiders to the city and the king's household.

Still there is no fulfillment of oracle. One overhears only talks of strategy between the king and his advisers (IV.C, vv. 12-15). The king suspects a ruse of some kind and seeks to confirm that the enemy camp really poses no danger to him. Jehoram looks to military intelligence rather than to a miracle for his explanation — hardly an improvement on the four lepers who sought no cause at all for the leavings they gathered up. The king's theory misses the depth in the situation. The reconnaissance party ("two horse chariots," v. 14a, reading *rekeb sûsîm* in a collective sense as in 6:17) report the littered trail of hasty flight, and the people go out to plunder the abandoned camp. Only then does the narrator comment at last that Elisha's oracles have been fulfilled (V, vv. 16b-20); the reader naturally closes the plot loop and assumes that the siege has been broken.

Prophecy is actualized, but the narrator has told the truth of it obliquely, as though it were equally important to convey competing perceptions amidst human folly. The narrator tells of the miracle through its effects, through the eyes of people removed from the event itself, like talking of snails while looking only at their silvery trails. The character of the narration depends upon this ironic vision of events. The narrator and his confidant, the reader (7:6-7), see one sequence from a point outside the narrative time (how the siege of Samaria is broken by a wondrously mysterious noise sent by Yahweh, and how, coincidentally, Elisha foresees the outcome). Constrained by their more limited perception, the people embedded in the narrative see another sequence (how a siege camp is abandoned, leaving provisions for the taking).

It is consistent with this controlled double vision of events that the writer aligns ignorance and knowledge with certain characters and their emotional states. Those who see only partially express despair and futility, and react comically to circumstances. In contrast, Elisha shows that resolute confidence of one who knows things that lie far beyond the capacities of others.

King Jehoram is preoccupied and impotent (6:26-30), and desperately strikes out at Elisha — as if he were God's surrogate, whom the king assumes to be behind the trouble (6:33), but, oddly, not responsible for rescue (7:12). The royal aide-de-camp believes the possible, and doubts the impossible, that the famine-siege will be broken (7:2a). Acting out of fatalistic desperation, the lepers take their chances with the Arameans and stumble unreflectively and greedily upon the salvation of Israel. Finally, the Aramean oppressors of Samaria are victimized not by Israelite armies, or by Yahweh-warrior himself, but by the *sound* of armies, or what they take to be menacing military clamor. Of course, it is only a deception sent by God — which turns out after all to be the only ruse in the whole story.

In contrast to these vignettes of blindness and distress, Elisha's calm pre-science seems not to dominate events (he is a minor character after all) so much as to determine one's perspective on them. He knows the king pursues him, 6:32; and he knows that by God's work the famine will end, 7:1, 2 (cf. 5:26; 6:9, 12). It is this power of insight into God's ways that the narrator generates in the reader's experience by imparting privileged information (7:6-7, 16-20).

From this point of view, one may appreciate a last finely tuned irony in the story. The social order has been severely disturbed, if not completely inverted — one mother devours her child and sees injustice only in another's attempt to spare her own offspring such horror; the king can save neither child nor city. Ironically, those whom custom relegates to the bottom fringe of society, the lepers "at the (city) gate," become the essential mediators of rescue and bring in their dim way knowledge that finally delivers from despair.

Genre

This narrative is a LEGEND, a story primarily concerned with the wondrous, miraculous, and exemplary. By avoiding a simplistic fixation on an exemplary character, miracle, or religious practice, the author-narrator achieves a literary sophistication comparable to 2 Kgs 4:8-37 and 5:1-27. (Rofé, *Prophetical Stories*, 63-70, specifies further with "political *legenda*," along with 6:8-23 and 13:13-17.)

Within this legend one finds other generic elements. In 7:1, Elisha offers a PROPHECY OF SALVATION which announces the health that will be restored to Samaria (cf. the doubts of Hobbs, *2 Kings*, 85). Formulas within this prophecy include: the CALL TO ATTENTION, "Hear the word of the Lord!" (see Isa 1:10; 2 Kgs 18:28) and a MESSENGER FORMULA, "Thus says the Lord!" which directly introduces the prophet's word. Near the end of the narrative there is a report of ORACLE FULFILLMENT, 7:16b, with its formulaic "according to the word of the Lord" (cf. 1 Kgs 16:34; 2 Kgs 1:17a; 4:44); vv. 17 and 20 function in the same way, but with less typical formulaic features. The king utters an OATH in 6:31 (cf. 1 Sam 3:17; 14:44; 1 Kgs 1:29-30; 2 Kgs 2:2a, 4a, 6a). Stereotyped expressions for reporting military assault appear in 6:24-25 ("go up against" and "besiege," sometimes with mention of gathering forces together; see 1 Kgs 14:25; 20:1; 2 Kgs 16:5; 18:9, 13; 24:1; 25:1-2).

Finally, one may note in 6:26-29 a stock scene which portrays a person petitioning a higher authority to grant a request or settle a dispute. (For possible background in the legal processes of ancient Israel, see H. J. Boecker, *Redeformen des Rechtslebens im Alten Testament* [WMANT 14; 2nd ed.; Neukirchen: Neukirchener, 1964], 63-66.) The petitioner may begin with a CRY FOR HELP (v. 26; cf. 2 Sam 14:4, "Help, O king!" or 1 Kgs 3:17a, "O, my lord"); then may follow a statement about the matter in question, which often accuses another party implicitly of wrongdoing. Despite its formulation as factual testimony, this statement serves in effect as the main petition addressed to the person in authority. The scene then depicts various responses to the petitioner in which the situation is resolved. This stereotyped scene typically involves kings and their subjects (see 1 Sam 25:24-35; 2 Sam 14:4-21; 1 Kgs 3:17-27; 2 Kgs 8:5-6; cf. 2 Sam 12:1-6 and 1 Kgs 20:39-40), but appeals come to prophets as well (2 Kgs 4:1-4; cf. 4:40-41; 6:5).

Setting

Legends belong to the world of folklore and would have originated with, and been preserved by, all manner of people in a given society. There is little evidence to support the assumption that this particular example took shape among prophets (against Schweizer, 394). Whatever its ultimate origin may have been, the legend now serves as part of the DtrH's recounting of the reign of Jehoram, with the help of Elisha as a main character operating in the political arena.

Intention

In a pre-literate context, legends would have served various purposes depending on the circumstances of the narrator and usage. A main point surely would have been to express awe and delight at Elisha's second sight. Perhaps his honor is even defended, as punishment awaits the scoffers (Cogan and Tadmor, *II Kings*, 84). Perhaps one can imagine a polemic against holders of temporal political power (Rofé, *Prophetical Stories*, 70), but the narrator seems to satirize many other elements of society as well, and even leads the reader astray. This array of targets for playful treatment warns us not to imagine too restrictive a connection between intentionality and genre.

In the context of the Dtr history, this example of legend indicates the continuing troubles and ineffectiveness of a king who already stands in the shadow of his transgressing forefathers and the negative appraisal of the historian (see 3:2-3, 14). Like the Aramean king in 6:8-23, the Israelite king (presumed in context to be Jehoram) really does not grasp what he is up against. But the reader understands that mysterious relief comes to Samaria, despite its king and his hostility to Yahweh's prophet. Miracle and a word of God that does not fail are still at the heart of events which count in some paradigmatic way for the DtrH's sense of meaningful past. God controls events — indeed, shapes them — through the word given to prophets. And he judges officialdom if it stands in opposition and transgression. Yet DtrH makes such claims with narrative color and humor. One takes delight in watching a miracle being uncovered but left unclaimed by human beings of only comic insight.

Bibliography

See bibliography at 2 Kgs 2:1-25. S. De Vries, "Temporal Terms as Structural Elements in the Holy-War Tradition," *VT* 25 (1975) 80-105; R. LaBarbera, "Man of War" (→ 2 Kgs 6:8-23); C. Mabee, "The Problem of Setting in Hebrew Royal Judicial Narratives" (Diss., Claremont Graduate School, 1977); A. Rofé, *Prophetical Stories* (→ 2 Kgs 1:2-17a); H. Schweizer, *Elischa* (→ 2 Kgs 3:4-27).

THE POWER OF ELISHA'S FAME, 8:1-6

Structure

I. Narrative background (Elisha and a woman)	1-3
A. Elisha's instructions	1
1. Narrative introduction	1a
2. Speech	1b
a. Instruction	1bα
b. Reason	1bβ
B. Instructions carried out	2
C. Woman's return to make appeal	3
II. The appeal at court	4-6
A. Circumstances (king and Gehazi)	4-5a
1. King's request for tales of Elisha	4
2. Gehazi's reports	5aα
3. Woman's appearance and appeal	5aβ
B. Gehazi's speech of recognition	5b
C. The appeal's outcome: royal decree	6

1. Investigation 6a
2. Decree of restitution 6b

This unit seems clearly separable from its immediate context, for in contrast to ch. 7, Elisha is not an active character; he exists for the reader only in a sketch of background (vv. 1-3) and in the memory of Gehazi (vv. 4-5). Further, the incident has nothing essential to do with the preceding legend of Samaria under siege. One might assume a tenuous link with the "famine" of 6:25, and one might suppose an audience with the king would have taken place most naturally in the capital city of Samaria. The end of the unit is marked by yet another shift in subject matter: Elisha suddenly strides onto an international stage in active pursuit of some new purpose in Damascus, far from Samaria and her kings (vv. 7-15).

The opening statement, which is cast in the inverted style of new narrative departures (subject plus perfect [qtl] verb) seems calculated to associate Elisha not with the Samaria of ch. 7, but with the "great woman" of Shunem (4:8-37), or as v. 1 has it, "the woman whose son he [Elisha] had restored to life." Whether this phrase justifies the assumption of some original literary connection with the Shunammite legend in 2 Kgs 4:8-37 is disputed; scholars offer conflicting hypotheses, but most take 8:1-6 in its present or reconstructed original form as independent of 4:8-37 (so, e.g., H.-Chr. Schmitt, 101; Gray, *Kings,* 525-26; Hentschel, *2 Könige,* 34-35; Rofé, "Classification," 434, n. 27; but see to the contrary Šanda, *Könige* II, 65; Gressmann, *Geschichtsschreibung,* 293-94; Robinson, *2 Kings,* 69). In context, however, the king's request, "Tell me all the great things that Elisha has done," naturally invites a reader to connect this episode with all of chs. 3–7. Such a perspective need not presuppose the death of Elisha (against Gray, *Kings,* 525).

Many scholars have taken this narrative to be essentially unified (e.g., Montgomery, *Kings,* 391; Fricke, *2 Könige,* 97; Hobbs, *2 Kings,* 96-97; H.-Chr. Schmitt, 90-91), although very recently Würthwein (*Könige,* 317) and Hentschel (*2 Könige,* 34) have argued that the Gehazi material, vv. 4-5, and other minor phrases are secondary accretions. The opinion seems arbitrary, or at least insufficiently argued (these scholars also eliminate Gehazi from 4:8-37 and 5:19-27).

As it now stands, the unit gains its structure from a weakly developed plot. The sense of a problem in need of resolution emerges from the background, vv. 1-3, which in context suggests a temporal sense like English past perfect: a woman who (had) fled famine at Elisha's behest (has) returned to find herself without house and land, and (has) set out to appeal to the king for its restoration. (Why she lost her property is taken to be either unimportant to the narrative action or self-evident — we have to guess that it somehow became crown property, perhaps after being abandoned for seven years, or that in the seventh year the real estate could have reverted to its original owner on the analogy of laws governing debts and slaves [see Exod 21:2; Deut 15:1-18].)

Now, having provided background to the main narrative action, the narrator sets time running forward. The woman's appeal breaks in on Gehazi's regaling the king with the exploits of Elisha. (Repeated mention of the woman "appealing," lit., "crying out," in vv. 3b and 5aβ surround Gehazi's and the king's discourse; this motival frame marks her action and the men's words as occurring simultaneously. See discussion of this chronological marker at 2 Kgs 4:8-37.) Moved by Gehazi's dramatic announcement, "This is the woman, and this her son whom Elisha restored to life" (v. 5b), the king inquires briefly (the narrator compresses this element to five words), and then decrees that the house and land be restored to her.

For the king, who is unnamed but presumed by context to be Jehoram, Elisha's power is embodied in someone else's story. The reader stands in a similar position, since Elisha is tucked into Gehazi's tale telling, which itself comes within a tale told by the writer of 1–2 Kings. Thus external and internal narrative voices fall together in momentary congruence. Similarly, two different narratees share one position relative to the events being told: Jehoram within the story hears of Elisha's great deeds, and the reader reads of them. Apparently what would have mattered most, the power of this "man of God," is refracted into the world of the main narrative, and into the reader's consciousness, through narrative recollection. Even the reflection of a flame may engender warmth. Just as those who see Samaria's rescue have only a tale and a batch of abandoned war materiel as tracings of God (7:7-10, 11-15), so the king and reader have only Gehazi's witness to Elisha's power.

Genre

This unit is a PROPHET LEGEND, a (→) story primarily concerned with the wondrous, miraculous, and exemplary powers and virtues of a prophet. (Cf. De Vries, *Prophet*, 53-54, "power demonstration narrative," for him a subtype of legend.) This example is unusual in that its dramatic energy flows from the prophet's reputation, not from the prophet himself. 2 Kgs 13:21 offers a similar portrayal of residual prophetic power, this time through contact with Elisha's bones (cf. 1 Kgs 13:31).

Setting

Prophet legends originated in various societal settings, and likely served narrators on different occasions, depending on particular circumstances. It is unwarranted to suppose, almost automatically, that they would have originated only or principally in "schools of prophets" (against De Vries, *Prophet*, 53). While it may plausibly be held that such groups might enshrine the exploits of their own heroes in legends (indeed, the narrator easily imagines Elisha's attendant telling such narratives), there is actually little evidence to support such a restrictive view of their origins. (See discussion at 1 Kgs 17:2-16 in Long, *1 Kings*, 182.) Far more crucial is the literary setting of the unit within the series of Elisha materials, and within the reign of Jehoram.

Intention

Prophet legend would have been told with various purposes, but perhaps primarily to inspire others to believe in the wondrous power of exemplary "men of God." In its present context, this particular legend clearly implies a narrator who meant to portray Elisha's wondrous power, even in the prophet's absence. Elisha goes on helping those in need through the power of his exploits being reported to the king; the Shunammite woman (perhaps in context the reader is meant to think of the woman of "great substance," 4:8) enjoys the benefits of this residual prophetic energy. This time Jehoram — unlike in most other materials selected for his reign — appears to be on the side of God's benevolent aid introduced into the world through Elisha. (Hobbs, *2 Kings,* 105, suggests without offering literary evidence that the woman's exile, loss, and restoration anticipates, and so introduces, the similar experiences of Joash [chs. 11–12] and Judah.)

Bibliography

S. De Vries, *Prophet* (→ 2 Kgs 1:2-17a); A. Rofé, "Classification" (→ 2 Kgs 2:1-17a); H.-Chr. Schmitt, *Elisa* (→ 2 Kgs 2:1-25).

ELISHA, BEN-HADAD, AND HAZAEL, 8:7-15

Text

In v. 10a the *RSV* "Go, say *to him*" *(lô)* is based on emendation of the MT *(lō')* in line with 18 Hebr. MSS and VSS. LXX[B] omits the word altogether. As it stands, one would translate the MT as "Go, say, 'You shall indeed *not* recover.' And Yahweh has shown me that he will surely die." Burney (*Notes*, 293) suggests that the negative *lō'* was a scribe's alteration from an original *lô* to remove the incongruity of Elisha's pronouncing both the recovery and death of Ben-hadad in one breath, or to eliminate the suggestion that the prophet lied (cf. v. 14). However, *l'* or *lw*, whichever might have been original, may have been read as optative *lû'* or *lû*, in which case one would understand Elisha to have commanded, "Go, say, 'May you indeed live [recover]!' But Yahweh has shown me . . ." (*GKC*, § 151e; Gray, *Kings*, 530; Fohrer, *Erzählungen*, 96). No solution to the difficulty is entirely satisfactory, and the resulting ambiguities are of some interest for literary interpretation. Most scholars support the emendation which underlies the *RSV* (but see commentary below).

Structure

I. Narrative setting 7-8
   A. Situation 7

This unit begins with an abrupt shift in characters, subject matter, and locale. Its end is marked by a royal succession formula, v. 15b, which is clearly separate from the introductory summary that opens the regnal period of Joram, son of Ahab, vv. 16-24.

Opinions differ as to whether vv. 7-15 as they stand are a unified narrative. With some minor differences, H.-Chr. Schmitt (*Elisa*, 82), Würthwein (*Könige*, 318), and Hentschel (*2 Könige*, 35) agree that vv. 11b-13 are secondary expansions to an original tradition which consisted mainly of vv. 7-10, 14-15. However, Hentschel and Würthwein envision the history of this supplemental editing and the motivations behind it in quite different ways. Other scholars take the narrative as a unity (see Šanda, *Könige* II, 85-86; Gressmann, *Geschichts-schreibung*, 304-5; Gray, *Kings*, 528; Ruprecht; De Vries, 64-65, 119; Hobbs,

2 Kings, 98-99). Indeed, the text shows little of the roughness that hypotheses about redaction are designed to explain. Even the supposed contradictions between vv. 10a, 10b, and 14 which have caused difficulties for scholars both ancient and modern and which both Würthwein and Hentschel use as anchor points for their reconstructions, are not viewed as problematic by Schmitt. Furthermore, vv. 10 and 14 have been read as some kind of intentional double talk (Labuschagne; Roth), or as a case of one oracle (v. 10a) being neutralized by a subsequent revelation (vv. 10b, 12-13; De Vries). Either explanation obviates the need for theories of redaction. In view of the clear impasse on these questions, it seems the wiser course to investigate the unit as it has reached us.

The literary structure of this unit may be easily grasped by noting a conventional literary *topos:* in a situation of distress, a person seeks and receives an oracle from a prophet and witnesses its fulfillment (cf. 1 Kings 14; 22; 2 Kings 3; Long). In 2 Kgs 8:7-15, this pattern is modified somewhat, and the expectations it arouses in the reader are shunted aside by dialogue and multiple prophecies (vv. 11-13) which seem to elaborate and explain an original oracle (v. 10). The logic of these new revelations presses to the surprising fulfillment of these revelations (vv. 14-15; Hobbs, *2 Kings,* 98, notes the motival correspondence between vv. 9-13 and 14-15). In the end, one has rafted along a diverted stream, arrived at a new place, and discovered the journey-initiating impulse ("Shall I recover from this sickness?") to have been partly suppressed and then transformed into an occasion for Hazael to become king in Damascus.

The structural outline tries to capture this mix of the typical, its modification, and the ambiguities which create interest and surprise. The narrator reports the king's (Ben-hadad's) illness and preparations for divining its outcome (I, vv. 7-8). In a subsequent audience with Elisha, Hazael (and the reader) meets a nearly unintelligible oracle concerning the sick monarch, and then, as if by force of unresolved questioning, dialogues tease out the new prophecy that Hazael will be king in Aram and inflict great suffering on Israel (II, vv. 9-14aα). The expected fulfillment of prophecy comes in III, vv. 14aβ-15, but in unexpected form. True, events make an end of sorts to the crisis in Damascus and at least partially fulfill Elisha's first oracle (v. 10). But more directly, events bear out what divine revelation had come to signify through the thrust and parry of inquiring dialogue. (Note the somewhat different structural analysis by De Vries, 64, who inappropriately draws upon the idea of a prophet's [→] symbolic action to explain vv. 11-13. Although Elisha's weeping does receive some explanation, his action is not treated as a symbolic form of proclamation, as, e.g., the tearing of garments for Jeroboam, 1 Kgs 11:30-31, or Ezekiel's acting out the siege of Jerusalem, Ezek 4:1-8. See G. Fohrer, *Die Symbolischen Handlungen der Propheten* [ATANT 54; 2nd ed.; Stuttgart: Zwingli, 1968].)

The narrative opens in medias res and offers only the barest essentials of background information. How one should construe matters in so compressed a style is hinted at by the Hebrew of v. 8, where the king orders Hazael, "Go to meet the man of God" *(wĕlēk liqra't 'îš hā'ĕlōhîm).* Since this idiom normally refers to meeting someone at a distance (see 2 Kgs 4:26), the sense of v. 7b, "The man of God has come here" *(bā' 'îš hā'ĕlōhîm 'ad-hēnnâ),* must be that Elisha is approaching, but not yet in Damascus (see *NJPS* "The man of God is on his way here"; cf. 2 Sam 20:16). Thus v. 7b matches 7aα in temporal referent (Elisha is on his way to Damascus; the verb *bô'* is repeated in both). Together they make a frame into which v. 7aβ, a circumstantial nominal clause, intrudes to inform us of a situation which antedates Elisha's arrival at court. Elisha has gone to Damascus, but has not yet arrived at his destination when a report of his journey reaches the Aramean king, who, by the way, has been ill. With these brief brush strokes, the narrator has sketched a typical situation calling for guidance from a giver of oracles (cf. 1 Kgs 14:1-3). Ben-hadad then initiates the preparations for inquiring of Yahweh. (Note the conventional vocabulary: "gift" [*minḥâ*]; "inquire of the Lord" [*dāraštā 'et-yahweh*]; cf. 1 Kgs 14:1-3; 22:4ff.; 2 Kgs 1:2.)

The main section of the narrative (II, vv. 9-14aα) is built of two dialogues framed by a meeting (v. 9a) and departure (v. 14aα). The narrator suggests extraordinary status for Elisha. The size of Ben-hadad's gift is emphasized ("took a present with him, that is, all the best of Damascus — forty camel loads"; see B. A. Mastin, "*Wāw Explicativum* in 2 Kings viii 9," *VT* 34 [1984] 353-55); Hazael presents himself as to a superior ("he came and stood before him"; cf. 2 Kgs 4:12; 5:15); and he adopts self-effacing, honorific language toward the prophet as part of his emissarial style ("your son Ben-hadad, king of Syria, has sent me to you"; cf. 2 Kgs 13:14; 2:12; on the messenger's self-introduction, "PN has sent me to you," see 2 Kgs 5:22; Exod 3:13, 14, 15; 7:16).

Elisha's response to Hazael's oracular inquiry is heavy with ambiguity. Assuming that the text of v. 10aα is to be read "And Elisha said *to him*" (see text note above), the oracle — which is structured as part of a charge for Hazael to deliver a message to his king — seems to have two parts. One word is for the king: "You [Ben-hadad] shall certainly recover"; another is meant as information, or perhaps suggestion, for Hazael: "but the Lord has shown me that he [Ben-hadad] shall surely die" (v. 10b). Alternatively, the word for Ben-hadad's ears may be a strong wish, with unstated implications: "And Elisha said, 'May you indeed recover!'" (vocalizing MT *l'* as *lû';* cf. Gray, *Kings,* 529-30; Fohrer, *Erzählungen,* 96). In any case, if the oracle is taken as direct speech, then the second-person form of the first clause, and the shift to third person in the second part, favor the understanding that Elisha addresses himself to two different people. (Cf. Labuschagne, who takes the oracle as *indirect* speech [grammatically possible, if somewhat strained]; in his view, the first part hints at a coronation speech, *yĕḥî hammelek,* "Long live the king," and is addressed to Hazael, while the second part refers to Ben-hadad.)

Even so, the meaning of what was spoken in this first oracle cannot be construed easily. First of all, its origins are veiled with the prophet's powers of supernatural sight. The expression "The Lord has shown me" (*wĕhir'anî yahweh*) suggests a vision (cf. Jer 38:21; Amos 7:1, 4, 7; 8:1; Ezek 11:25), or other means of private communication from God (cf. 1 Kgs 14:6b; 2 Kgs 4:27; 1 Sam 9:15). Second, the words are understandable, but their meaning is difficult to interpret. How can Elisha pronounce without further explanation that Ben-hadad will both live and die? Is there a contradiction? Or is the prophet deliberately lying, in the light of what he knows will be the case? The problem is further exacerbated a little later by unfulfilled reader expectations: the prophecy that Ben-hadad will recover has no realization — or is there simply a gap in the telling at v. 14, such that one must assume that the king recovers, only to be murdered the next day?

Ancient, medieval, and modern commentators have felt these difficulties and resorted to various artifices of interpretation to eliminate the incongruity. For example, Kimchi (cited from *Miqra'ôt Gedōlôt* [New York: Pardes Publishing House, 1951]), "he will not die unless he is killed"; or Montgomery (*Kings*, 393), "[there are] two distinct elements in the response: first the prophet's own spontaneous response, which is followed and contradicted by a supervening affect of second sight" (cf. De Vries, 64-65, for the notion of "superceding oracle"); alternatively, Fohrer (*Erzählungen*, 96) and Gray (*Kings*, 530-31) interpret v. 10a as a wish, "May you live!" and then suggest that it has a double edge by the subsequent revelation that the king will die. Even the Masoretes, if they shifted the vocable *lô* to the negative particle *lō'*, thereby reading, "You will surely *not* recover," sought to avoid contradiction and moral offense (see text note).

It is worth observing that all these impulses to determine meaning for an oracle which seems fundamentally cryptic already have their paradigm in the narrative itself. The writer relates that Elisha "fixed his gaze and stared at him [Hazael] until he [Hazael or Elisha?] was ashamed" (v. 11). One way of understanding this remark is that Elisha is probing in some mysterious (trancelike?) way the ambiguity of his own oracle. Moreover, the narrator's own language is opaque — if the text may be trusted: lit., "and he [Elisha] fixed his face, and he put [it] until he [Elisha or Hazael?] was ashamed. And the man of God wept." The first clause has no parallels; the phrase "until he was ashamed" (*'ad-bōš*) is idiomatic for "a long time" as in 2 Kgs 2:17 and Judg 3:15; cf. the Targum, "and he turned away his face and delayed a very long time," and the *NJPS*, "kept his face expressionless for a long time." Gray (*Kings*, 529) translates: "he stiffened his features and was appalled [emending *wayyāśem* to *wayyiššōm* after the Vulgate] until he [Hazael] was put out of countenance" (cf. Šanda, *Könige* II, 64; Würthwein, *Könige*, 318; Fohrer, *Erzählungen*, 95). If Elisha's first words seem cryptic, so too the description of his own further actions in v. 11 demands explanation. (Hobbs, *2 Kings*, 102 removes all the ambiguity without sufficient justification.)

Out of this ambiguity of the first oracular dialogue, vv. 9-11, springs a second exchange which is, by comparison, limpid and to the point (vv. 12-13). Hazael, maintaining his deference to the prophet, asks simply why Elisha ("my lord") is weeping. The answer amounts to a second prophecy, although in terms of literary form Elisha reports with stereotyped images his own peculiar foreknowledge of disaster, v. 12b (cf. Isa 13:16; Hos 14:1; Amos 1:13). Hazael's response is a rhetorical question put with courtly style (the opening *kî* is probably used for emphasis, meaning "truly," or "indeed," as in Gen 43:10; Ps 37:20): "What is your servant but a dog, that he should do this mighty thing?" (For this self-effacing rhetoric, cf. 2 Sam 9:8; 16:9; 1 Sam 24:15 [*RSV* 14].) Elisha hears the polite conventionality as a query for explanation, and he gives out a second prophecy (v. 13b), formed as the first to suggest a vision, but this time completely unambiguous: "The Lord has shown me you as king over Aram [Syria]."

Thus the reader has traveled a path of discovery with Elisha and Hazael, from cryptic revelation (vv. 9-11) to decoded prophecy (vv. 12-13), and along the way the images have blurred and reformed, like one oily color mixing and dissolving into another. A question about weeping, innocent on its face, blends into the presage of Hazael's gruesome oppression of Israel, and his self-abasing refusal to accept such a forecast finally elicits Elisha's disclosure that Hazael is destined to reign as king. This visionary image in retrospect appears to have been a hidden, or perhaps not clearly realized, premise in Elisha's half of the conversation. The dialogue has developed like a cross examination of discovery, and in the process a future has emerged, to one a prophecy, to the other — as events will show — a suggestion, an encouragement to shape his destiny.

The last section of the narrative (III, vv. 14aβ-15) quickly propels one through events which actualize Elisha's final clarifying prophecy. Hazael is clearly presented as devious, in contrast to his solicitous dealings with Elisha. He reports not what is discovered in probing Elisha's unfolding glimpses of the future — *his* future — but that first prophetic word, the minimal message which he has been charged to deliver to Ben-hadad (v. 10). What may have been simply cryptic in Elisha's first revelation now is wrenched and twisted into bold duplicity. Hazael reports that in his master's future is recovery, and on the next day hastens his own future by murdering Ben-hadad with some kind of netting (*makbēr, RSV* "coverlet"; cf. *kĕbîr* in 1 Sam 19:13, 16; *mikbār* in Exod 27:4). That at least seems a natural reading, although a few commentators argue that murder is not necessarily implied. (See, e.g., Gray, *Kings,* 531-32; cf. note by Montgomery, *Kings,* 394.) In any event, the narrative concludes with the matter-of-fact voice of a chronicler while retaining the cryptic ambiguity characteristic of the entire story. Obviously one important outcome is captured in the formulaic notice that Hazael "became king in his stead" (v. 15b). This accession formula fulfills a prophecy, concludes a narrative, and in the larger scheme of the history seals off one regnal period — a non-Israelite one — from another to open shortly in v. 16.

Genre

This narrative is a PROPHET LEGEND, a story involving a prophet as a central figure and portraying him as an exemplar of supernatural powers or edifying virtues. (Cf. Fohrer, *Erzählungen,* 96, who speaks of "miracle story" [*Wundererzählung*].) De Vries (pp. 63-65) agrees with the term "legend," but assigns this example to a subtype, "superceding oracle narrative," and cites 2 Kgs 20:1-11 and a hypothetical earlier version of 1 Kings 22 as parallel examples. A closer parallel to 8:7-15 may be seen in parts of 3:4-27, where Elisha delivers a cryptic oracle, v. 16b, and then gives it more determinate meanings through subsequent prophecies, vv. 17-19 (see discussion at 3:4-27).

An important element in both 2 Kings 3 and 8 is the conventional motival sequence ORACULAR INQUIRY, which typically recounts (1) the problem to be addressed by the prophet, followed by (2) preparations for inquiry (a payment is sometimes mentioned), (3) the audience with the prophet during which one requests an oracle (dāraš 'et-[dĕbar-] yahweh), (4) the oracle, and then (5) a report of its fulfillment. (See discussion at 1 Kgs 14:1-18 in Long, *1 Kings*, 156.) See also Long, "2 Kings iii," and other examples in 1 Kgs 22:4ff.; 2 Kgs 1:2 + 16; 3:4-25; 22:13-20.

Note also the formula of EMISSARIAL SELF-INTRODUCTION, "PN has sent me to you," in v. 9b. Biblical parallels may be seen in Gen 45:5; 2 Kgs 5:22; note its use to assert one's commission from God in Exod 3:13, 14, 15 (cf. Dan 10:11; Jer 26:12, 15). An indication of the formula's assumed appropriateness in the mouth of royal emissaries may be found in 2 Kgs 18:27 (= Isa 36:12). A similar expression is known among the oracle givers of Mari. See ARM xiii, 114:10-11 (*ANET*, 624a), "Dagan sent me." See also ARM iii, 40:13, and ARM ii, 90:19 (broken text; *ANET*, 624). See Ellermeier; Noort.

Finally, the legend closes with a SUCCESSION FORMULA, v. 15b, typically the last element in a Judean or Israelite king's concluding (→) regnal resumé. (See 1 Kgs 14:31b; 2 Kgs 1:17; Long, *1 Kings*, 161.) Though it is unusual to find such a formula applied to a foreign monarch (cf. reference to Babylonian kings in 2 Kgs 25:1, 8), it is not surprising in the light of other documents of ancient Near Eastern historiography. In Babylonian chronicles of the 8th-7th century B.C.E., scribes routinely employed standard Babylonian formulas to foreign rulers where their activities impinged on Babylon's affairs in some important way. In effect, while focusing on his own nation's monarchies, the chronicler sometimes maintained a synchronistic reckoning of the accessions and successions of foreigners in proper chronological sequence. See, e.g., Grayson, *Chronicles*, 1:i:1-2, 9-10, 23-25, 33-39; ii:35ff.; iii:9ff. See also 3:44-45, 50 (pp. 70-87, 90-96).

Setting

Generally speaking, prophet legends had their natural usage among prophetic groups and among other folk who related stories about their prophets (cf. 2 Kgs 8:4-5). Yet the conclusion in v. 15b shows already that this particular example has been given a particular setting in the Dtr history of the kings. The legend belongs to the coverage of Jehoram's reign, since no official end to this king's rule has yet been noted. At the same time, the legend marks the beginning of a new epoch, the first mention of Hazael, whose activities will form the backdrop for the waning years of Jehoram (8:28-29; 9:15) and of later kings in the north and south (2 Kgs 10:32 [Jehu of Israel]; 12:18-19 [Jehoash of Judah]; 13:22 [Jehoahaz, son of Jehu]). Formulaic notices of Hazael's death and of his successor appear in 2 Kgs 13:24. Thus, 8:7-15, together with 13:24, constitute a Hazael framework around 8:16–13:23. Or, on the analogy of synchronisms in the Babylonian chronicles, while focusing on Judah and Israel and reckoning their kings in relation to each other, the Dtr historian specifically correlated events with a foreigner whose impact was felt in both kingdoms for a considerable period of time. Although Hazael's predecessor Ben-hadad strides on and off the Hebrew stage (1 Kings 20; 2 Kgs 6:24), only Hazael's entrance and exit are so clearly noted with regnal formulas, and thus fully integrated with the compositional structure of the Dtr history.

Intention

A basic purpose of prophet legend would have been to edify and inculcate religious devotion to the ideals and power of the prophet. This particular example accordingly would have magnified Elisha's status by celebrating his astounding role in world events (he traveled to Damascus and dealt directly with the Syrian rulers; see H.-Chr. Schmitt, 108). Also one would have marveled at Elisha's power to foresee, at Yahweh's behest, a period of severe troubles for Israel from the hand of Hazael (see Steck, 98, n. 1). The legend describes Hazael's accession to the throne, and suggests the prophet's (and God's) mysterious involvement in the event. But it falls short of claiming that God had designated Hazael to be king (against Ruprecht, 321, n. 5; Fricke, 2 Könige, 102; cf. God's singling out of Jehu in 2 Kgs 9:6); and it seems only remotely related to more abstract claims about God's purposes in human history (against De Vries, 55). However, the legend certainly raises the question of God's relation to a kingdom which would prove so devastating for Israel (Würthwein, Könige, 321).

Already another tradition had viewed Hazael as an instrument by which God — through the agency of Elijah — would chastise his apostate people (1 Kgs 19:17). Regardless of how one might reconstruct the relationships, if any, which may have existed between this Elijah material and 2 Kgs 8:7-15 (see esp. Steck, 97-98), its importance here is that armed with the inner gaze of Elisha, man of God, the reader encounters Hazael forewarned about the implications of his rule for Israel and acquainted with his devious path to the throne. Integrated into the Dtr history in this way, this Aramean king will assume the role of external villain, a structural and thematic counterpart to the long-term internal evil, the Israelite Baalizers. From both, the historian's whole story will say, God protects (see 2 Kgs 9:1–10:28; 13:23).

Bibliography

See bibliographies at 2 Kgs 1:2-17a; 2:1-25. F. Ellermeier, Prophetie in Mari und Israel (Theologische und Orientalistische Arbeiten; Herzberg: Jungfer, 1968); A. K. Grayson, Assyrian and Babylonian Chronicles (Texts from Cuneiform Sources 5; Locust Valley, NY: Augustin, 1975); C. J. Labuschagne, "Did Elisha deliberately lie? — A note on II Kings 8:10," ZAW 77 (1965) 327-28; E. Noort, Untersuchungen zum Gottesbescheid in Mari. Die 'Mariprophetie' in der alttestamentlichen Forschung (AOAT 202; Kevelaer: Butzon & Bercker, 1977); Y. Roth, "The Intentional Double-Meaning Talk in Biblical Prose," Tarbiz 41 (1971-72) 245-54 (Hebr.); E. Ruprecht, "Entstehung und Zeitgeschichtlicher Bezug der Erzählung von der Designation Hasaels durch Elisa," VT 28 (1978) 73-82; O. H. Steck, Überlieferung und Zeitgeschichte in den Elia-Erzählungen (WMANT 26; Neukirchen: Neukirchener, 1968).

THE REIGN OF JEHORAM OF JUDAH, 8:16-24

Text

In v. 16 the MT reads after "Israel" an explanatory "now Jehoshaphat [was] king in Judah" *(wîhôšāpāṭ melek yĕhûdâ)*. The phrase is out of place in this conventional introduction to a new reign, and is missing in some Hebr. MSS and VSS. The *RSV* and most commentators consider it a secondary gloss. But it may have been original and necessitated by the long gap between Jehoram and the last reference to the regnal period of his father (1 Kgs 22:41-51 [*RSV* 41-50]).

In v. 19 the *RSV* "and to his sons" assumes an emendation of the awkwardly placed *lĕbānāyw* to *ûlĕbānāyw*. Some MSS and VSS support this change, and many commentators follow it (cf., however, Würthwein, *Könige*, 322, and Hentschel, *2 Könige*, 38, who read *lĕpānāyw*, "before him," on the analogy of 1 Kgs 11:36, but without any MS support). The translation of *nîr* as "lamp," which takes the word as a biform of *nēr* and which has been partially responsible for the felt awkwardness in the text, may be mistaken (but see the recent defense by Cogan and Tadmor, *II Kings*, 95). We follow P. Hanson ("The Song of Heshbon and David's *nîr*," *HTR* 61 [1968] 297-320, esp. 316) in translating, "since he promised to give dominion [*nîr*] to him [David] and to his sons forever."

Structure

This unit is clearly distinguishable from the preceding Hazael tradition (vv. 7-15) and the opening summary of Ahaziah's reign (vv. 25-27). Its structure conforms to the typical pattern used by the Dtr writer as he recounts in sequence the reigns of each monarch in Israel and Judah. Introductory (vv. 16-19) and concluding (vv. 23-24) summaries serve as a framework around two brief reports, possibly drawn from separate sources. One concerns rebellion against Jehoram's sovereignty over the Edomite territory to the east and the other the revolt of Libnah, a city probably located near the western border of Judah (see Josh 10:29-39; 12:15).

The frameworks consist of the usual formulaic elements in conventional sequence (see Long, *1 Kings*, 22, and full discussion at 1 Kgs 14:21-31, pp. 158-64). The introductory summary includes a somewhat unusual justification for the king's negative theological appraisal, v. 18b: Jehoram married a daughter of Ahab, son of Omri. (*bat-'aḥāb* may designate any female descendant, since 8:26 identifies her as "daughter of Omri" [*bat-'omrî*]. Whether or not the information is historically correct, the remark serves to connect Judah for the first time in the Dtr history with the notorious and maligned house of Omri; cf. 1 Kgs 16:29–22:40.) Immediately it seems necessary to administer an antidote to that poison. Although condemned for mimicking the ways of Ahab, this Judean king is not so apostate as to cause God to abrogate his special promise that David and his sons would have lasting "dominion" (*RSV* "lamp" [*nîr*]) in Judah. The same motif justifies Solomon's retention of sovereignty over Judah alone (1 Kgs 11:36) and Abijam's success in Jerusalem (1 Kgs 15:4-5). All three references draw out the implications of the grand text of Davidide legitimation found in 2 Sam 7:12-16.

Within the frameworks, the writer nests material on two rebellions which occur during Jehoram's rule. In typical reportorial style, vv. 20-22a recount the trouble in Edom and Jehoram's apparently unsuccessful attempt to suppress it (vv. 20-21; the Hebrew of v. 21 is somewhat ambiguous). The writer then steps free of the constraints of time to summarize in v. 22a: Edom has been in rebellion continuously down to his own day. (The imperfect verb "revolted" [*wayyipša'*] + "until this day" [*'ad hayyôm hazzeh*] yields a frequentative sense.) In this way, the author reaches the reader directly with a contemporizing comment (cf. 1 Kgs 12:18-19). Narrative past tense returns in v. 22b where one reads of Libnah's revolt. The notice is cast in reportorial style, and its content is only imprecisely related to the temporal context of the preceding material. The syntax of "then Libnah revolted" (*'āz* + imperfect tense, *tipša'*) requires that one take the new action to have occurred before, or during the course of, and not subsequent to, Edom's rebellion (Rabinowitz, 57).

Genre

This literary composition most likely originated with the Dtr writer-historian. It consists of (1) an introductory and concluding REGNAL RESUMÉ (vv. 16-19, 23-24); (2) a REPORT of rebellion (vv. 20-22a; cf. Montgomery, *Kings*, 35-36, "narrative of archival flavor"; Gray, *Kings*, 532, "extract from annals of Judah"); and (3) a NOTICE (v. 22b) of rebellion.

For a full description of regnal resumé, see 1 Kgs 14:21-31 (Long, *1 Kings*, 160-64). A close formal parallel to the brief report concerning Edom is 1 Kgs 12:18-19 (cf. 2 Kgs 1:1; 3:5). Such brief reports are regular features in late Babylonian and Assyrian chronicles and propagandistic historical works. For examples, see Grayson, I:iii, 6-11 (p. 79); 20A:11-13 (p. 153); 21:iii, 25-34 (p. 167); 22:i, 10-14 (p. 172). Of special interest is the CONTEMPORIZING SUMMARY, v. 22a, a concluding comment in the iterative or frequentative mode. The statement recapitulates the main action or its outcome, and with the (→) testimonial formula "until this day" (*'ad hayyôm hazzeh*) it affirms the continuance of effects into the time of the writer. Other examples may be seen in 1 Kgs 12:19 (= 2 Chr 10:19) — also a report of rebellion — and 1 Macc 13:30. Contemporizing summary belongs to the literary conventions of ancient historians, and so appears frequently in classic historiographical works, e.g., Herodotus *Histories* 2.154, 182; 4.11; 5.77; 6.14 (see Childs, 290-92). Compare other brief statements which similarly make claims about cultural or national facts of antiquity and, using the formula "until this day," assert continuity with, and relevance to, the narrator's time. (See, e.g., concerning territorial claims, Deut 2:22; 2 Kgs 16:6; 1 Chr 4:41, 43 [cf. 5:26]; or ethnic groups, Gen 19:37-38; Josh 16:10; 2 Sam 4:3; 1 Kgs 9:21 [= 2 Chr 8:8]; or evaluative remarks, 1 Kgs 10:12; 2 Kgs 10:27; 17:23, 34, 41; or custom, Gen 47:26; 1 Sam 30:25; or religious object, 1 Kgs 8:8 [→ etiology].)

Setting

This unit originated with the Dtr author-editor who drew upon various sources to arrange the recounting of Israel's and Judah's history. For general discussion, see Long, *1 Kings,* 164.

Intention

Clearly this text accounts for the reign of Jehoram of Judah in the Dtr writer's chronological presentation of all the kings of Judah and Israel. Two prominent features, however, suggest a more far-reaching purpose. The mention of Jehoram's marriage to a woman of Ahab's (Omri's) family is the first symptom that the debilitating poison associated with the house of Omri, Ahab/Jezebel, has now seeped into Judah's bloodstream. The poison was released in the events reported in 1 Kgs 16:29–22:40, was felt in the reproach of 2 Kgs 3:13 (with Jehoram of Israel, Ahab's son), and now that it has spread to Judah through Jehoram, the whole body politic is in need of purging — a process whose beginnings will be recounted during the reign of Jehoram's son, 8:25–9:29. At the same time, this poison in Judah has not yet become fatal, as the mitigating remark of v. 19 shows. (On the Dtr character of this note, see Weinfeld, 354.) In fact, despite lapses in Yahwistic devotion noted among various Judahite kings to this point, the promise that David would always have dominion in Jerusalem is invoked by the DtrH like a talisman to ward off the worst of punishments (1 Kgs 11:36, Solomon; 15:4-5, Abijam; and here in 2 Kgs 8:19 for a son-in-law to Ahab in Judah). Indeed, the spell will hold until the time of Manasseh, 2 Kgs 21:1-18. But Manasseh's deeds will prove so reprehensible, exacerbated by his infection through Ahab (21:3), that God will override his own promised Davidide privilege and execute the final purge of Judah (21:10-15; cf. 23:26-27).

Bibliography

B. S. Childs, "A Study of the Formula, 'Until this Day,'" *JBL* 82 (1963) 279-92, esp. 280-81, 290-92; A. K. Grayson, *Assyrian and Babylonian Chronicles* (→ 2 Kgs 8:7-15); Herodotus, *Histories* (see discussion and bibliography in Long, *1 Kings,* 19-20); I. Rabinowitz, "'*āz* followed by Imperfect Verb-form in Preterite Contexts: A Redactional Device in Biblical Hebrew," *VT* 34 (1984) 53-62; M. Weinfeld, *Deuteronomy and the Deuteronomic School* (Oxford: Clarendon, 1972).

THE REIGN OF AHAZIAH: CANONICAL FRAMEWORK, 8:25–9:29

Structure

This unit conforms to the typical plan of 1–2 Kings in which distinct regnal periods are presented to the reader as enclosed blocks of material. A summary of the usual regnal information, vv. 25-27, introduces Ahaziah's reign. After reporting his death and burial, the writer marks the frame with a notice of Ahaziah's accession, 9:29. The formula obviously is now out of place, since it normally appears as part of a monarch's introductory summary, and in any case repeats with a small correction the information already given in 8:25. While the notice may be a scribal adjustment to the chronology implied by 8:25 (Gray, *Kings*, 549), in the composite arrangement of the reigns it now serves as a closure to Ahaziah's time just where one would expect such to appear, and recapitulates, as the concluding summaries normally do, the main regnal period being recounted (cf., e.g., 8:23-24, which marks the close of the reign of Jehoram of Judah).

In any case, the ending to the unit, while clear enough, is unusual, and probably necessitated by the decision to show how events and personages impinged upon one another during these years. Jehu, arising out of the north with little more than a patronym (9:2, 14), brings two sitting kings to their violent ends. He murders Joram of Israel (whose reign has been ongoing since 3:1-3) and Ahaziah of Judah, whose short reign presents Jehu with his opportunity to seize the throne in Israel and dominate even the ruling house in Judah.

The literary structures accordingly reflect the disruptive violence of these events. The account of Jehu's rise to power eclipses any accomplishments which might have accrued to Ahaziah's importance, displaces Ahaziah's concluding summaries, and in general subverts the normal conventions of paratactic composition. The encroachment of Jehu's story on those of Ahaziah and Joram is reflected also in the synchronous arrangement of material in 8:28–9:28. While Joram lies wounded in Jezreel, and after his military ally Ahaziah has gone to be with him (8:28-29), Jehu receives his prophetic designation to be king over Israel (9:1-13) and conspires against Joram (9:14-15). He then travels to Jezreel, 9:16, at which point these three concurrent narrative sequences fall together as serial confrontations. First, Jehu kills Joram, and second, he kills Ahaziah (9:16-

111

28). When the next scene unfolds, 9:30-37, the narrator brings the reader beyond the limits of Ahaziah's regnal period, and into the midst of Jehu's rule, which will continue until the standard concluding summaries mark its end at 10:36 (see Reign of Jehu, 9:30–10:36).

One may recall only a few other instances of unusual circumstances which alter without fully negating the author's usual chainlike method of presenting the reigns. For example, Jeroboam's elevation to kingship in the north is announced while Solomon's kingdom is still intact (1 Kgs 11:29-39). Thus Jeroboam's accession to the throne is recorded in subsequent narrative, 1 Kgs 12:1-24, not in introductory summary. Similarly, Solomon becomes king in unusual circumstances while his father David is still in power (1 Kgs 1:1-48), and thus the customary opening summary is omitted for him, too. (See Long, *1 Kings*, 35-39, 131-36.) Yet the reports of all three kings, Solomon, Jeroboam, and Jehu, receive the typical closure (1 Kgs 11:41-43; 14:19-20; 2 Kgs 10:34-36), including information about the duration of their reigns, which would ordinarily be inserted into the introductory summary.

Genre

This unit is a literary composite whose genre cannot be specified with any precision. It offers an account of Ahaziah's reign and includes introductory REGNAL RESUMÉ, 8:25-27, and, at its end, a SYNCHRONISTIC ACCESSION FORMULA, 9:29. In between is a rather complex HISTORICAL STORY (see detailed analysis below).

Setting

This literary composition has its important setting in the work of the early exilic Dtr author-editor, who drew upon various sources to present an accounting of all the kings of Israel and Judah. For general discussion, see Long, *1 Kings*, 164.

Intention

Obviously, a first purpose of the writer would have been to account for the reign of Ahaziah in the history of Judah and Israel. Because the Dtr historian has an interest in vindicating exclusive worship of Yahweh (see 2 Kgs 10:18-28), it is important that he recount the prophetic warrant for Jehu's rebellion and show him implementing old words of judgment against the house of Ahab and Jezebel. It is during the reign of Ahaziah that ties among major parts of the book's thematic scaffolding will become explicit: the fulfillment of Elijah's prophecies against Ahab (1 Kings 21) in Jehu's rebellion, the oft-mentioned religious condemnation of the Omrides, and Jehu's cryptically prophesied role as Yahweh's avenging agent (1 Kgs 19:17).

JEHU BECOMES KING, 8:28–9:28

Structure

The beginning of this unit is clearly defined by the shift from theological appraisal, v. 27, to narrative-styled consecution, "And he [Ahaziah] went with Joram . . . to make war . . ." (v. 28a). The ending, v. 28, is a typical closure to narration about a king's death (cf. 1 Kgs 22:37; 2 Kgs 12:21-22; 14:19-22). The narrative with its chronological movement is nested within the atemporality of formulaic summary, 8:27 and 9:29 (see above, "The Reign of Ahaziah: Canonical Framework, 8:25–9:29").

Many critics agree that a pre-Dtr tradition about the rise of Jehu to the throne was taken over by the writer of Kings and integrated into the account of Ahaziah's reign. (Barré, 36-46, postulates an originally independent narrative substantially preserved in chs. 9–11, whose purpose was to justify Jehoiada's coup by favorably contrasting it with Jehu's bloody massacre. Campbell understands the Jehu material to have been part of a much longer pre-Dtr narrative now folded into 1 Samuel 1– 2 Kings 10.) Despite these recent studies, there is no consensus on what might have constituted an original written source or oral tradition, and on what is to be attributed to subsequent expansion. Many assume that an original tradition would have begun with something like 9:14b-15a, 16b. Accordingly, 8:28-29, which anticipate some of the information of 9:14-16, would have been derived from the original opening, and used to fold the material into the reign of Ahaziah (so, e.g., Benzinger, *Könige*, 148-49; Noth, *Deuteronomistic History*, 72; Montgomery, *Kings*, 396, 400; Steck, 32, nn. 1 and 2; Timm, 138; Gressmann, *Geschichtsschreibung*, 310; Campbell, 22; Peckham, 40, in defense of a two-version Dtr history). On the other hand, H.-Chr. Schmitt (p. 24) attributes 9:14-15a, 28-29 to an "annalistic redaction." Würthwein (*Könige*, 328-30) takes the original account to have begun at 8:28-29, and continued in 9:14a, 15b, 16aα; De Vries (pp. 67, 90, n. 58) begins the original tradition with 8:29b.

Similar disagreements undermine consensus about the history of the main tradition in ch. 9 (see recent discussions in Olyan, 654-59; Barré, 16-31). A widespread opinion holds that two different narratives lie behind the present text: a prophetic-theological and a political or secular tradition, vv. 1-13 and 14-24, respectively. Benzinger (*Könige*, 149) favors such; see also Würthwein, *Könige*, 330; Schüpphaus, 74-75; Gray (*Kings*, 537) also leans in this direction. Considering chs. 9 and 10 together, Rofé (*Prophetical Stories*, 79-88) thinks of a main historical narrative supplemented over time with two folkloristic anecdotes (10:1-10, 18-28) and further minor additions. Other scholars have long and persistently argued for one tradition having undergone various editings and interpolations, even multiple redactions, by members of a Dtr "school." Yet the critics who favor this option disagree on many details (e.g., Dietrich, 60; Hentschel, *2 Könige*, 39-40 [both arguing for multiple Dtr redactions]; Gressmann, *Geschichtsschreibung*, 306-10; Olyan; DeVries, 67-68; Gunkel, *Geschichten*, 67-94; H.-Chr. Schmitt, *Elisa*, 27-29; Timm, 137-38). A strong argument for unity, allowing for much less interpolation and glossing, was made early by Šanda (*Könige* II, 121-22) and followed by some recent critics (e.g., Noth, 72; Soleh; Hobbs, *2 Kings*, 110-13; Cogan and Tadmor, *II Kings*, 118).

Matters are clearly at an impasse. Barré (pp. 4-35) thoroughly documents this fact, while seeking to persuade readers of yet one more reconstruction. One may justly wonder whether further refinement of redactional hypotheses is likely to bring noticeable gains (see H.-Chr. Schmitt, 27-29). There are some obvious Dtr touches in vv. 7-10a, 25-26 (see Weinfeld, 20-21; Barré, 9-14). But whether these count as evidence of redactors or of the DtrH's shaping of sources is less clear. One may also doubt the assumed distinction between religious and secular versions of Jehu's rise to prominence, since these perspectives could well have been intermingled in one writer or tradent (against Würthwein; Gray; and others). Furthermore, a leitmotif captured in the repeated question *hăšālôm*, "Is it peace?" (with various nuances, vv. 11, 18, 19, 22; cf. v. 31), might suggest literary unity (Olyan), as would the ironic echo of a prophetic "madman" (v. 11, *mĕšuggāʿ*) in Jehu's "madly wild" rush to Jezreel (v. 20, *bĕšiggāʿôn*). Finally, the repetition in 8:28-29 and 9:14b-15a, 16b need not be the signature of a redactor. The framing device may indicate synchronous events — those going on in Jezreel (Joram with Ahaziah), while others (Jehu's designation) transpire at Ramoth-gilead (see discussion of this narrative technique at 2 Kgs 4:8-37; Long; Talmon).

In the light of these uncertainties, it seems reasonable to assume that the unit comprises traditions and sources worked into the Dtr history of Ahaziah through a process we can only dimly perceive. A somewhat neglected task is to investigate the literary form of the present text whatever its prior history might have been (see Soleh; Olyan; Hoffmann). After all, in the present arrangement 9:1-13 seems indispensable to the sense of 9:14-16, and especially v. 15b (see Campbell, 22, n. 8; note that Würthwein, 331, n. 18, translates v. 15b, *'im-yēš napšĕkem*, in line with his hypothesis of multiple redactions rather than according to its usual sense, "If you agree, i.e., if such is your wish [*NJPS*] . . ."; cf. Gen 23:8; see Gray, *Kings*, 544; Burney, *Notes*, 298).

The overall plot of the narrative is clear enough. The reader is gradually made aware that an old transgression, a breech of wholeness or well-being, *šālôm*, is in need of repair, and that Jehu has been chosen as the instrument by which Yahweh will make restitution (I, 8:28–9:16). The main action, therefore, portrays Jehu beginning to avenge the transgressions of Ahab and Jezebel in the murder of Ahab's descendant, King Joram of Israel (II, vv. 17-28; Olyan, 661-62). Ahaziah's death in vv. 27-28 is simply a by-product of the revolt and not explicitly interpreted as fulfillment of prophecy. (Putting aside Ahaziah's wrongs [8:27] will be presented later as the work of Jehoiada the priest [2 Kgs 11:17-20].)

Inverted word order in the Hebrew at 9:1, 11, 17, 24, 27 helps demarcate scenes, new turns in the plot, and shifts in temporal perspective. The last is important, since the sequence of events in the story world is not precisely the same as the order in which events are narrated. Gaining some clarity on the varied relationships between narrative (the story sequence) and narrating (the order of telling) helps one better grasp the literary structure of the unit.

The mainspring is set in v. 16, where the paths of Joram, Ahaziah, and Jehu coil together at Jezreel as if to contain momentarily the energy which drives the primary narrative, Jehu's murder of Joram and Ahaziah (II, vv. 17-28). The writer chooses to supply necessary background in 8:28–9:16. Earlier, Joram and Ahaziah had fought together, Joram was wounded, and both kings retired to Jezreel (I.A, 8:28-29). When this action is recapitulated at 9:14b-15a, 16b, one realizes that the narrator has stopped its forward movement, or at least left it unchronicled, while telling of an approximately concurrent sequence taking place at Ramoth-gilead (I.B, C, 9:1-13, 14-16). The inverted word order at 9:1 signals this new turn in the narration and, in context, a temporal shift to something like English pluperfect (see R. J. Williams, *Hebrew Syntax: An Outline* [2nd ed.; Toronto: University of Toronto, 1976] § 573). A prophet (had been) was sent out from Elisha, went to Ramoth-gilead, privately designated Jehu to be king in Israel, and charged him with exacting Yahweh's punishment on the house of Ahab. Jehu's fellow commanders subsequently offered him open acclamation (vv. 11-13; note another inversion of word order at v. 11).

Emboldened by their support, Jehu then took up the prophet's charge and began to claim his future in conspiracy (I.C, 9:14-16). This new departure is clearly marked with a formulaic statement, "And Jehu . . . conspired against

Joram" (v. 14a). (*RSV, "Thus . . . ,"* and critics who divide the scenes at v. 14b [e.g., Hentschel, *2 Könige,* 39; Gray, *Kings,* 541] mistakenly read v. 14a as a conclusion to vv. 1-13, rather than as a conventional introduction to the report of conspiracy which follows; see 1 Kgs 15:27-30; 16:9-13; 2 Kgs 15:10, 14, 25, 30; 21:23.)

Having supplied all this background information and set Jehu on his course, the writer loads the mainspring, v. 16, and merges the synchronous Jezreel and Ramoth-gilead sequences into one. The action at Jezreel resumes, with Jehu now in a position to transform his private conspiracy into open rebellion (II, vv. 17-28). Events then run their natural course, and are reported sequentially. Narrative tension builds around the question of when and how Jehu's intent will become known to Joram and Ahaziah, and, for the reader, what the outcome of Jehu's private conspiracy will be. A series of reconnaissance missions leads into and defines the climax: Joram discovers the truth and is murdered, vv. 23-24. Like an inexorable corollary, Ahaziah's death follows shortly thereafter. Yet it is presented less graphically, like a dispassionate report, as though the writer-editor were dissipating the energies already released and bringing events to a resting point. This is not simply dénouement in the story world of Jehu and the kings, however. It simultaneously touches the historian's more encompassing literary horizon and closes out the regnal period of Ahaziah. The writer is now poised to continue his account, but fully within the regnal period of Jehu (9:30-37; see below).

The entire unit begins with a summary of background circumstances (I.A, vv. 28-29). In straightforward reportorial style, one learns of the war with the vicious and aggressive Hazael (he had been introduced into the immediate surroundings at 8:7-15 but into the larger Dtr history at 1 Kgs 19:15-18). A wounded Joram withdraws to Jezreel where he is joined by Ahaziah, his comrade in the battle. Presumably the hostilities continue, for one learns later that the field commanders remain at Ramoth-gilead (9:4), and that eventually Aram will reclaim some Israelite territory (see 10:32-33). For now it is sufficient to realize that a military crisis has brought Ahaziah and Joram fatefully together.

The scene abruptly shifts in ch. 9 (note inversion at v. 1a, subject + perfect verb). Either before Joram's withdrawal to Jezreel, or contemporaneous with it, Elisha commissions one of his band ("one of the sons of prophets," cf. 6:1; 4:1) to find Jehu in Ramoth-gilead and designate him "king over Israel." Elisha's speech is full of secret directives, as though his emissary requires detailed instructions for an unfamiliar (or seditious) task. But designations of a king-to-be, and the theology of displacement by divine selection that underlies such action, are anything but unfamiliar to the reader. Saul (1 Sam 9:1–10:16), David (1 Sam 16:1-13), and Jeroboam (1 Kgs 11:29-38) each are singled out by a prophet whose eye — in the cases of Saul and David — has been set by a commissioning from God, and whose speech at the moment of designation — in the cases of Saul and Jeroboam, and now Jehu — is delivered as divine oracle (1 Sam 10:1; 1 Kgs 11:31; cf. 2 Sam 5:2; 6:21; 7:8; 1 Kgs 19:15, 16).

Notable in Elisha's commission to the "son of prophet" (he is called a "youth" [na'ar] or young male "aide" in v. 4; cf. 5:20) is the atmosphere of urgency and mystery which surrounds the mission. Elisha's motivations are not clearly stated (Barré, 68-69, probably infers too much about these matters). However, like the private oracle about David's selection, 1 Sam 16:1-2, the secret charge undermines Joram's rule in the name of Yahweh's purposes, which of course are hidden from ordinary perception. Jehu is fully identified by lineage, and bears a name which is perhaps symbolic of his historic role ("Jehu" means "Yah[weh] is [God]" or perhaps "Yah[weh] [it is] he"; cf. 1 Kgs 18:39). But how is he to be found? The young prophet must somehow single him out "from among his fellows" (lit., "his brothers") and subject him to ritual anointing *in camera* but without the leisure of state-sanctioned ceremony. An oracle of anointing is even specified, v. 3bα. Its presence here in contrast to its absence in the scenes of commissioning around Saul's and David's election, and its subsequent delivery in a much expanded form during the actual designation, vv. 6-10, invite special attention (see below).

Quickly the prophet carries out his charge (I.B.2, vv. 4-10). Arriving at Ramoth-gilead, and, so it seems, confronting a group of look-alikes, all described as *śārê hahayil yōšĕbîm*, "army commanders sitting [in council?]," he parries and thrusts to identify Jehu "from among his fellows." Perhaps gazing at all of them, or at one in particular, the prophet announces, "I have a message for you" (s. pronoun object). But Jehu seeks clarification, "For which of us?" and the emissary immediately singles him out from all the rest, "For you, O commander" (v. 5).

This exchange suggests something of the egalitarian ethos of the military group, at least from Jehu's perspective, while indicating just what is meant by Elisha's charge, "bid him rise from among his fellows" (lit., "cause him to stand up from among his brothers," v. 2b). The king-designate is known only by the elitism of mysterious election — the prophet's inner seeing and hearing (e.g., 1 Sam 9:17; 16:12). The patina of camaraderie attempts, or pretends, to protect the royal institution from hardening into the personal elitism of social privilege, or worse, becoming a foreigner's right (Deut 17:15; cf. the Deuteronomic expression *miqqereb 'aḥêkā*, "from among your brothers," with *mittôk 'eḥāyw,* "from among his brothers," in the prophet's charge, v. 2).

Jehu is then anointed with oil and ceremonially set apart from his peers. An accompanying prophetic oracle empowers him with the energy and legitimacy of divine mission (cf. 1 Sam 10:1-2 LXX). As directed, the prophet then flees, having discharged his duty.

The young prophet's oracle is greatly expanded over that which the reader might have expected from v. 3. Beginning with a word of anointing-designation (cf. 1 Sam 10:1), the prophet — speaking as if God speaks — defines Jehu's duty (v. 7a) as well as divine intent, "[so] that I may avenge on Jezebel the blood of my servants the prophets . . . [and so] that the whole house of Ahab may perish" (vv. 7b-8a). Then the oracle takes up two announcements of punishment: first on the house of Ahab whose male heirs will perish (lit., "those who urinate against the wall," or in the upper royal chamber [Talmon and Fields, "Collocation"]; cf. 1 Kgs 14:10; 21:21); second, and with emphasis, punishment for Jezebel (her body will suffer the curse of nonburial, ignobly eaten by dogs; cf. 1 Kgs 14:11; 16:4; 21:23-24; note similar language in ancient Near Eastern treaty curses, e.g., *ANET,* 538, § 47; D. Hillers, *Treaty-Curses and the Old Testament Prophets* [BibOr 16; Rome: Pontifical Biblical Institute, 1964]).

Both the expansion of the oracle's form and content, as compared with v. 3, and the appearance of stereotyped motifs which are used elsewhere for different situations (cf. v. 10 with 1 Kgs 14:11; 16:4; 21:24), justify the view that within the story world prophets creatively applied their inspirations to changing circumstances (Ackroyd). Yet the author has the speaker and his words in vv. 6b-10a transcend their immediate context: they transform the simple word of anointing-designation, "I anoint you king over Israel," into an elaborate announcement of judgment and, at the same time, evoke much of the connective tissue belonging to the larger story of the northern monarchs. The first charge to Jehu, v. 7a, most naturally recalls the tradition reflected in 1 Kgs 18:4 where Jezebel is associated with "cutting off" the prophets of Yahweh. Then vv. 8-9, 10a virtually duplicate the wording and order of the punishments promised Ahab and Jezebel after the murder of Naboth (1 Kgs 21:21-22, 23). This association will surface again when Jehu casts Joram's body onto the plot of ground belonging to Naboth, v. 26 (cf. v. 21b). Thus the young prophet's oracle achieves paradigmatic status: Ahab's crime, and Jezebel's opposition to Yahweh's "servants" the prophets, both of which are emblematic of the northern kingdom's apostasy, will find their retribution at last in Jehu's God-given mission of destruction (cf. the slightly variant tradition in 1 Kgs 19:16, which has not been totally harmonized by the DtrH). Furthermore, if prophecy is to have its usual fulfillment, Ahab will shortly join Jeroboam (1 Kgs 14:10-11 + 15:29) and Baasha (1 Kgs 16:1-3 + 11-13), to complete a string of prophesied destructions, the inevitable tit for tat of transgression and punishment which runs through the northern kingdom.

Having set this note of expectation and left it in the privacy of Jehu's inner chamber, the narrator quickly moves events into the open. The king-designate returns to his fellow commanders, whom the narrator now calls "servants of his [Jehu's] master" (v. 11). With this phrase, the writer subtly persuades us that Jehu has abandoned, or that God has relieved him of, the feudal allegiance that still defines his compatriots as servants to Joram (contrast Barré, 70). At the same time, Jehu seems somewhat coy (as he may have been at v. 5b). His fellows ask why the "madman" (cf. Jer 29:26) has intruded into their company, "Is all well?" (the first use of *hăšālôm*). Jehu demurs; the commanders apply direct pressure: "A lie! Tell us now." (In their frankness, the men still assume a parity in status which the writer has already undermined.) Finally Jehu yields and reports the oracle which has come to him.

One may assume that he has told all. The summarizing phrase "Thus and so he spoke to me" (v. 12) is conventional to avoid repeating what is already, or shortly to be, known by a reader (against Hobbs, *2 Kings*, 111, who sees evasive generalities here; see, e.g., 2 Sam 17:15 [cf. v. 21]; 2 Kgs 5:4; 1 Kgs 14:5). It is not so clear, therefore, that the agreement between vv. 12b and 3bα against the longer vv. 7-10a gives reason to affirm the latter as secondary expansion on some pristine original (see, e.g., Dietrich, 48; Olyan, 656; Barré, 9-10). The writer presupposes the fullness of the matter, but repeats only the word of anointing, "I anoint you king over Israel," which by now has been given three times (vv. 3, 6b, 12b). The oracle amounts to a coded shorthand — decipherable to Jehu, his fellows, and the reader — for a momentous task yet to be undertaken. Hence, "in haste" the men openly acclaim Jehu as king with a rebel ceremony that mimics state-sanctioned coronations (v. 13; see 2 Sam 15:10; cf. 1 Kgs 1:11, 18; for ceremonies of legitimate dynastic accession, see 1 Kgs 1:34, 38-40; 2 Kgs 11:12).

Following this show of political support, Jehu begins to move against the crown (I.C, vv. 14-16; v. 14 opens a typical report of conspiracy, against the *RSV* and many critics who read the verse as the conclusion to vv. 1-13; see 2 Kgs 15:10, 14, 25, 30; 21:23; 1 Kgs 15:27-30; 16:9-13). Jehu demands a show of allegiance, v. 15b (there is no question now that he is first among equals), and then makes his way to Jezreel. At this point, the background has been filled in, the synchronous sequences of action have come together (the narrator resumes the action left off at 8:28-29), and Jehu stands ready to challenge royal authority openly. Only Joram and Ahaziah do not yet know the truth.

The perspective on events shifts in II.A, vv. 17-20. A circumstantial clause in v. 17aα situates the reader with Joram in Jezreel, and the writer contrives to describe Jehu's approach to Jezreel largely through the words of a watchman who calls out what he sees in the distance. (See a similar generation of visuality from direct speech in 2 Sam 18:24-27.) The first report sounds mildly ominous: "I see a company" ("a multitude" or "crowd"; cf. Isa 60:6; Ezek 26:10), but the writer offers no hint as to the king's attitude toward the information. Instead, Joram acts, sending out the first of two reconnaissance missions. Each is built of the same elements, and consists mainly of dialogue (vv. 17b-18; 19-20). A messenger-horseman is sent out by the king; he inquires of Jehu ("Is it peace [*hăšālôm*]?"); Jehu answers ("What have you to do with peace [*šālôm*]? Turn round and ride behind me!"); the watchman reports to Joram how matters appear from the tower. Irony, however, enriches the simplicity of repetition. The reader, of course, knows that Jehu is on his way to remove Joram from the throne, but the king may or may not suspect. His actions betray no inkling that a man freshly anointed by Yahweh's prophet approaches a king already out of favor with God (cf. 1 Sam 16:1-18 + 19-23). Yet, Joram's question, "Is it peace?" *(hăšālôm),* is quite ambiguous; it could mean that Joram inquires about the military situation in Ramoth-gilead, or about the intentions of the approaching rider, or that — suspecting trouble — he maneuvers for political negotiation (cf. Wiseman; 1 Sam 25:5; Deut 20:10-14). However, Jehu's reply — which the king does not hear — suggests that the messenger has nothing to do with a God-sanctioned, healthy *(šālôm)* kingdom, and that he ought rather to associate himself with right order, i.e., with Jehu's bloody restoration of *šālôm* (Olyan, 664). At the same time, the reader gathers that Jehu approaches Joram's camp with invective, having already dissociated himself in secret from this regime.

At v. 20b, the end of the second reconnaissance mission, the watchman reports: "the driving is like the driving of Jehu . . . for he drives wildly" *(běšiggāʿôn,* "madly" or "wildly," from the same root as "madman" used of the prophetic emissary in v. 11). In retrospect, one now senses a contrast between the madly dashing entourage and the narrator's deliberateness of patterned repetition. The dissonance seems calculated to create narrative tension and ironic distance. Joram sees only what the watchman reports, and perhaps is unable to evaluate it fully. We have no certain clue as to Joram's attitudes toward events. Yet the reader knows of Jehu's resolve, naturally infers hostile intent, and thus reads these signals (the riders who do not return, and the wild rush of a man like Jehu) far less ambiguously. Joram faces a gathering epiphany of judgment.

Suddenly, with decisive resolution, Joram acts on the watchman's last word (II.B.1, vv. 21-24). The pattern of reconnaissance lingers, but with even more significant alterations. Joram and Ahaziah, like the horsemen before, go out to meet Jehu. But now a place is mentioned: they encounter him at the property of Naboth (a motival anticipation of v. 25). The question put to Jehu, "Is it peace, Jehu?," differs a little from the messengers' earlier queries. Joram now knows with whom he deals, and he apparently suspects trouble; or perhaps he wants to achieve some negotiated outcome (Wiseman, 321; cf. 1 Kgs 20:33, where kings meet personally and bargain for terms). Jehu's reply also breaks with the earlier pattern. He confronts Joram with bold and impertinent rhetoric, invokes the specter of Jezebel, and smears the king with the tar of his mother's "harlotries" and "sorceries," i.e., religious failings (v. 22b; cf. 3:13; this seems to be another motival anticipation, this time of 9:30-37). Joram's fate is tied to the actions of Jezebel, just as it is in the oracle designating Jehu as king. As in the earlier Naboth incident (1 Kings 21), the writer-narrator pronounces the house of Ahab guilty by association with Jezebel.

Jehu's challenge to Joram, v. 22b, gains emphasis from its position at the end of a series of repeated reconnaissance missions. One may visualize the basic sequence as follows:

Vv. 17-18a
    a. Watchman's report
    b. Horseman approaches Jehu
    c. Query: "Is it peace?" *(hăšālôm)*
    d. Jehu's reply

This sequence repeats in vv. 18b-19, thus yielding an ABCD/ABCD structure. When the pattern emerges a third time, v. 20, modifications are evident. There is new information in the watchman's report, v. 20b; the kings themselves now go out; the *šālôm* query addresses Jehu by name. Finally, Jehu's reply is entirely different from that given the earlier messengers, and perhaps to Joram it seems utterly startling and unambiguously hostile. This decisive break in the pattern coincides with the climax of vv. 17-22 and marks the turning point of the entire narrative (cf. Parunak, 166). Here Jehu openly takes up his prophetically empowered mission, and speaks like some avatar of Elijah or Elisha, both of whom had zealously hurled accusatory barbs at monarchs (1 Kgs 18:18; 21:19, 20; 2 Kgs 1:3; 3:13). Jehu will soon lay aside mere talk and act forcefully like Elijah, that severest of prophets, who mercilessly cut down the prophets of Baal beside the brook Kishon (1 Kgs 18:40).

An epiphany of self-realization breaks over Joram in v. 23. He reins about and cries out to Ahaziah, "Treachery!" *(mirmâ)*. The word perhaps connotes a state of deceit and broken relations, the very opposite of *šālôm* (so Olyan, 667; see Ps 35:20). The narrator's perspective is ironic. To Joram, Jehu threatens to destroy peace in the kingdom. But the restoration of God's *šālôm*, the righting of a wrong, is at hand.

Thereafter, it is a matter of quickly reporting Joram's death (v. 24). This time visual imagery assaults the reader directly, without the artifice of watchmen on a tower. Inversion in the Hebrew word order at v. 24aα, which marks the turn in the narrative, perhaps should be read as English pluperfect: "Jehu [had] drawn his bow . . . [at the moment in which Joram reined about], and he shot Joram between his shoulders so that the arrow came out from his heart, and he collapsed in his chariot." (Cf. *RSV* "pierced his heart," and *NJPS* "issued from his heart"; cf. the similarly stark images of Judg 4:21; 5:26-27). The conspiracy that had been noted in a characterizing introduction, 9:14a, has now achieved its first aim, the murder and overthrow of the king (see 1 Kgs 15:27-30; 16:9-13; 2 Kgs 15:10, 14, 25, 30).

Jehu then orders Joram's body to be dumped onto Naboth's plot of land to inflict the further indignity of dishonorable, even ritually unclean, abandonment (vv. 25-26; cf. Deut 21:22-23; 2 Sam 21:10-14; Num 19:11-14). Obviously, conveying the content of the order is more important to the narrator than reporting its execution, which must be assumed by the reader. Typical of artfully turned speech in biblical narrative, the writer has Jehu frame the important point — the prophetic oracle, v. 26a — with repeated orders to dispose of Joram's body (vv. 25a and 26b). The oracle takes the form of a truncated oath, "As surely as I saw" (*'im-lō' . . . rā'îtî;* cf. 1 Kgs 17:1), and makes a second direct allusion (along with 9:8-10) to the tradition reflected in 1 Kings 21, wherein Jezebel engineers Naboth's execution with Ahab's acquiescence. Clearly, the narrator means Jehu to justify his actions beyond the reasons given in vv. 22b and 6b-10a. Jehu improvises. He has avenged Yahweh, presumably, in the mere killing of Joram. Now he intends that this last act should fulfill a prophecy against Ahab and his dynasty. Hence, when Jehu concludes with a reprise of his order to Bidkar, he adds piously "in accordance with the word of the Lord" (*kidbar yahweh,* v. 26b), as though to actualize divine retribution on his own initiative. So it is not just the "harlotries" of a mother with which a son may be condemned, but the transgressions of a father as well. Both disturbances in the order of *šālôm* may be overcome by one connected assault: piercing the body and defiling the corpse of Joram, son of Ahab.

The dramatic energy seems spent now. Events move in a new direction (marked by word-order inversion, v. 27aα), and the writer assumes a flatter, reportorial voice (II.C, vv. 27-28). The narrator recounts in a series of statements the wounding, death, and burial of Joram's ally, Ahaziah. The fatal wound of this Judahite king seems merely a by-product, or an afterthought, to the ideologically charged murder of Joram. And its telling is fully consistent with formulaic closings of regnal periods (cf., e.g., 2 Kgs 12:21-22; 14:19-20; 1 Kgs 22:37). Although brought down at the command of Jehu-avenger-of-Yahweh's-honor, and perhaps in the author's view justly punished (see 8:27), Ahaziah at least seems to have been honored in burial (v. 28). With this tiny hold on dignity, he is at least accorded some respect that was denied to Joram. One finds no prophetic legitimation for the king's death, no grand theological purpose in the common lot of kings and ordinary folk. It appears that Ahaziah's main importance to the Dtr writer's larger story is that he came and went while God effected the first stirrings of a momentous purge in the rebellious northern kingdom (see 1 Kgs 19:17; 2 Kgs 9:30-37; 10:1-35). At the same time, Ahaziah's death creates a problem for Judah and the continuity within David's household (see 11:1).

Genre

This unit is a HISTORICAL STORY, a narrative that recounts events of the past largely according to canons of ordinary, realistic human experience (see Gunkel, 67; H.-Chr. Schmitt, 29; Plein, 15; Steck, 32, n. 2). However, since the writer- narrator has given such an important role to a prophet, and attached so much of the story's religious and cultural outlook to prophetic oracles and their fulfillment, one might be justified in refining the designation to PROPHET STORY, a special type of historical narrative. (Cf. Gray, *Kings*, 538, "prophetic adaption of historical narrative." Rofé, 79-88, classifies the story as "prophetic historiography," whose essential characteristic — other than historical trustworthiness, a feature I am less sure about — is that it locates causality in a divine word spoken by a prophet.) Historical narrative does not exclude the tendentious and imaginative qualities inherent in the Bible's recounting of history (cf. Ahlström, 61, "history as it should have been"; Campbell, 105, "theologically inspired history"; perhaps Montgomery, *Kings*, 399, "objective and highly dramatic political history"; Barré, 51-52, prefers "political novella" for the reconstructed pre-Dtr story preserved in chs. 9–11 to emphasize the imaginative and apologetic elements in this historical story). Thus one may affirm the substance of De Vries's understanding that this narrative extols ideals and paradigmatic values while rejecting his term (→) "prophetic legend" (pp. 56, 65-69) since the writer in this instance does not give center place to a prophet's exemplary power and virtue.

A conventional schema used to build a part of this story depicts a prophet anointing someone as king-designate, 9:1-13 (see Campbell, 17-32). Other examples may be seen in 1 Sam 9:1–10:16 (Saul), 1 Sam 16:1-13 (David), and 1 Kgs 11:29-38 (Jeroboam). First, a prophet receives a COMMISSION to search out God's choice for king (so 1 Sam 9:15-16; 16:1-3 [both charges come from God directly]; 2 Kgs 9:1-3 [from Elisha]). Then the prophet carries out his commission by privately anointing someone with oil, or otherwise indicating (e.g., with symbolic action, as in 1 Kgs 11:30-31) that Yahweh has designated the person as "king" *(melek),* or "king-designate" *(nāgîd).* Finally, the prophet empowers God's choice with a mission or special "signs." In all cases, the authority for these actions is clearly attributed to God himself. In the case of 2 Kgs 9:1-13, Elisha clearly empowers an aide to deliver an oracle of anointing as part of the designating act, and so makes the unnamed prophet both agent and spokesman. There are numerous OT examples of one prophet commissioning another, e.g., 1 Kgs 14:7-11; 2 Kgs 22:15-20; Jer 21:4-7 (Schmidt). Elements of the larger schema for designating a king-to-be are reflected in 2 Sam 5:2 and 1 Kgs 19:15, 16. (Cf. the official rites of coronation ordered by David, 1 Kgs 1:32-40 [see also 2 Kgs 11:12]. For the historical reference of this schema and its cultural significance see T. N. D. Mettinger, *King and Messiah: The Civil and Sacral Legitimation of the Israelite Kings* [ConB, OT Series 8; Lund: Gleerup, 1976]; K. Seybold, *TWAT* VI, 46-59; Campbell, 47-61.)

As minor generic elements, one may note (1) features indigenous to reports of THRONE CONSPIRACY in 9:14-15, which together with the actual scene of slaying the reigning king, vv. 23-24, constitute a kind of skeleton for much of the larger narrative in vv. 14-28. Examples of the typical report may be seen in 1 Kgs 15:27-30; 16:9-13; 2 Kgs 12:21-22 [*RSV* 20-21]; 14:19-20; 15:10, 14, 25, 30; and 21:23; (2) announcements of judgment, vv. 8-9 and 10a, which are elements belonging to PROPHETIC JUDGMENT SPEECH (see Wallace); vv. 8-9, the stereotyped judgment on Ahab, appears also in 1 Kgs 21:21-22; for the comparison with Jeroboam's house, see 1 Kgs 13:33-34; 14:10-11; the motif of dogs eating a desecrated and abandoned corpse, v. 10 (also 1 Kgs 14:11; 16:4; 21:24), is found regularly in the maledictory sanctions attached to international treaties, primarily Assyrian, from the ancient Near East; see Weinfeld, 131-38; Margalith; (3) an ORACULAR REPORT, which cites a prophetic word of judgment formulated as divine OATH, v. 26 (cf. 1 Kgs 17:1); (4) the declaration upon anointing a king-designate, v. 6bβ, may be a stereotyped bit of speech drawn from actual rituals of king making, official and unofficial, but the one close parallel at 2 Sam 15:10 hardly proves the supposition (cf. also 1 Sam 10:1, 24).

Setting

Historical story implies a class of scribes at work in royal courts or religious institutions. This particular example may very well have come from the written sources used by the Dtr writer who composed 1–2 Kings from the vantage point of early exile. But the evidence one would like to possess in support of such a conjecture, or indeed to define more precisely the context in which such a narrative may have been preserved, is simply not available. Nevertheless, some critics have thought of prophetic groups as a likely societal origin and setting for this unit (De Vries, 56; Šanda, *Könige* II, 121; Campbell, 106, situates it as part of a longer, and hypothetical, "prophetic record" promulgated by disciples of Elisha). Alternatively, H.-Chr. Schmitt (p. 30) surmises that the narrative stems from circles favorable to Jehu; Barré (pp. 52-54) argues that ch. 9 was part of a pre-Dtr account (chs. 9*–11*) commissioned by Jehoiada to legitimate his own coup in contrast to that of Jehu.

The plain fact is that we lack good evidence for such specific assertions about the story prior to its being placed in the books of Kings. More to the point, the narrative constitutes the entire picture of Ahaziah's reign, while in effect concluding the reign of Joram first reported in 2 Kgs 3:1.

Intention

The literary intentions most accessible to us have to do with the Dtr writer's implied purposes in using this historical story at this place in 1–2 Kings. Clearly, one aim would have been to represent the reign of Ahaziah as that of a Davidide king in league with Joram of the house of Omri (Ahab), the archetypal despiser of Yahweh. Joram (and thus the Omride dynasty) goes the way of Jeroboam, the aboriginal apostate in the north (1 Kings 12–13), and Ahaziah's murder has probably also been assimilated to the same theological justification. It is sufficient for the DtrH's condemnation of Ahaziah that the tainted blood of Omri has passed to him from Ahab and Jezebel (8:26-27); how much more that Ahaziah put himself in league with Joram against the Aramean Hazael, whose rise Elisha has foretold?

Yet, Joram and Jehu seem more important than Ahaziah to the writer. Jehu emerges suddenly as the divinely authorized agent of Yahweh's avenging judgment upon the Baalizing northern kings. In Elijah's time the struggle to preserve an exclusive and stringent devotion to Yahweh alone is depicted in the idealized and paradigmatic oppositions between Elijah on the one hand and the Baalists — Ahab, Jezebel, and the prophets — on the other. In that moment, a proleptic glimpse of an eventual resolution to this struggle is linked to Jehu (1 Kgs 19:17-18). Although the events during Ahaziah's rule are not remarked as connecting precisely with that moment in 1 Kings, the author-narrator does allude to Elijah's confrontations with Ahab and Jezebel through repetition of prophecy (2 Kgs 9:7-10; 1 Kgs 21:21-24). There seems little doubt that to the Dtr author, Jehu's stirrings in Jezreel constitute the beginning of Yahweh's long foretold judgment against the house of Omri. An implicit protest against Jehu (Uffenheimer) or a moral revulsion against his actions that delegitimates his rule (Barré) is difficult to maintain.

The slaying of Joram and Ahaziah would have been understood as only the first in a series of actions taken by Jehu. He will in time kill Jezebel (9:30-37), the rest of Ahab's sons (10:1-11), the kinsmen of Ahaziah (10:12-14), and all the devotees of Baal he can find (10:15-27). He is an agent of God, and, by analogy, extends Elijah's paradigmatic opposition to Ahab and Baalism into this later day. Jehu's actions also threaten continuity in the southern kingdom (9:27-28; see 10:13-14; 11:1). The Judahite Dtr writer, who champions the Davidide house throughout 1–2 Kings, will face this problem in ch. 11 (see discussion below).

Bibliography

See bibliographies at 2 Kgs 1:2-17a; 2:1-25; 4:8-37. P. Ackroyd, "The Vitality of the Word of God," *ASTI* 1 (1962) 7-23; G. W. Ahlström, "King Jehu — a Prophet's Mistake," in *Scripture in History and Theology: Essays in Honor of J. Coert Rylaarsdam* (ed. A. Merrill and T. Overholt; PTMS 17; Pittsburgh: Pickwick, 1977) 47-69; L. Barré, *The Rhetoric of Political Persuasion* (CBQMS 20; Washington: Catholic Biblical Association, 1988); A. F. Campbell, *Of Prophets and Kings: A Late Ninth-Century Document (1 Samuel 1–2 Kings 10)* (CBQMS 17; Washington: Catholic Biblical Association, 1986); W. Dietrich, *Prophetie und Geschichte* (FRLANT 108; Göttingen: Vandenhoeck & Ruprecht, 1972); H. D. Hoffmann, *Reform* (→ 2 Kgs 3:1-3); O. Margalith, "The *Kĕlābīm* of Ahab," *VT* 34 (1984) 228-31; M. Noth, *The Deuteronomistic History* (tr. J. Douall, et al.; JSOTSup 15; Sheffield: University of Sheffield, 1981); S. Olyan, *"Hāšālôm:* Some Literary Considerations of 2 Kings 9," *CBQ* 46 (1984) 652-68; H. Van Dyke Parunak, "Oral Typesetting: Some Uses of Biblical Structure," *Bib* 62 (1981) 153-68; B. Peckham, *The Composition of the Deuteronomistic History* (HSM 35; Atlanta: Scholars Press, 1985); I. Plein, "Erwägungen zur Überlieferung von 1 Reg. 11:26–14:20," *ZAW* 78 (1966) 8-24; K. W. Schmidt, "Prophetic Delegation: A Form-Critical Inquiry," *Bib* 63 (1982) 206-18; J. Schüpphaus, "Richter- und Prophetengeschichten als Glieder der Geschichtsdarstellung der Richter- und Königszeit" (Diss., Bonn, 1967); A. S. Soleh, "The Artistic Structure of the Narrative of the Crowning of Jehu," *BethM* 92 (1982) 64-71 (Hebr.); O. H. Steck, *Überlieferung und Zeitgeschichte* (→ 2 Kgs 8:7-15); S. Talmon and W. Fields, "The Collocation *mštyn bqyr sʿṣwr wʿzwb* and its Meaning," *ZAW* 101 (1989) 85-112; S. Timm, *Die Dynastie Omri* (FRLANT 124; Göttingen: Vandenhoeck & Ruprecht, 1982); B. Uffenheimer, "The Meaning of the Story of Jehu," *Oz Le-David. Studies Presented to D. Ben-Gurion* (Jerusalem: Kiryath Sepher, 1964) 291-311 (Hebr.); H. N. Wallace, "The Oracles Against the Israelite Dynasties in 1 and 2 Kings," *Bib* 67 (1987) 21- 40; M. Weinfeld, *Deuteronomy* (→ 2 Kgs 8:16-24); D. J. Wiseman, " 'Is it Peace?' — Covenant and Diplomacy," *VT* 32 (1982) 311-26.

THE CONSOLIDATION OF JEHU'S RULE: CANONICAL FRAMEWORK, 9:30–10:36

Structure

I. Report concerning the death of Jezebel	9:30-37
II. Account of purging Baal from the kingdom	10:1-27
A. Concerning the house of Ahab	1-11
B. Concerning the house of Ahaziah	12-14
C. Concerning the worshipers of Baal	15-27
III. Regnal summaries	28-36
A. Theological appraisal	28-31
B. Notice of defeat by Hazael	32-33
C. Concluding regnal resumé	34-36

This unit describes the consolidation of Jehu's political power in Israel and Judah as a religious campaign to eliminate Baalism in the kingdoms. In effect, this material marks the regnal period of Jehu, but it is accorded no opening summary. His rise to power is presented as the main event during Ahaziah's reign, and the material gathered together within 9:30–10:36 essentially continues that account, hardly taking notice of the weakly marked closing of Ahaziah's rule (9:28-29; see discussion at 8:25–9:29, Canonical Framework). By means of this concluding summary and the introductory one at 8:25-27, a connected narrative centered on Jehu's deeds running from 8:28 through 10:27 has been inserted into the reign-by-reign organization of 1–2 Kings.

The structure of this unit in which Jehu takes full control of events is straightforward. The Dtr writer covers and surrounds raw political aggression with zealous defense of Yahwism. First, Jehu eliminates Jezebel, who is possibly a political rival; for the Dtr writer, the queen mother is also a symbol of apostasy in the north, and conversely her death marks the beginning of Jehu's holy revenge on unfaithfulness (I, 9:30-37; cf. 9:7-10). His Yahwistic loyalties established, Jehu next destroys the families of Joram and Ahaziah and secures the throne of both kingdoms for himself (II.A, B, 10:1-11, 12-14). Last, he moves to fulfill his prophetic commission by annihilating the Baalists and their temple in Samaria (II.C, vv. 15-27). His reign closes with evaluations and the usual regnal summaries, including qualified approval (10:29-31) and the ominous note (10:32-33) that Hazael began to inflict losses on the kingdom during Jehu's days (III, vv. 28-36).

Genre

The genre of this composition cannot be specified with any precision, but its components follow recognizable literary types. There is a REPORT concerning the death of Jezebel (9:30-37), and a longer ACCOUNT dealing with Jehu's consolidation of power and purge of the Baalists (10:1-27). Regnal summaries at the end include a PROMISE (10:30) and two literary elements usually associated with (→) introductory resumé: THEOLOGICAL REVIEW (10:29, 31) and the STATEMENT on length of reign (10:36). Their position at the end of a report of a regnal period is unusual, although not without parallel. Both David's and Jeroboam's rules conclude on remarks about the duration of their reigns; in both instances, as with Jehu, the Dtr writer foregoes the usual introductory summaries for extensive accounts of how the kings came to power. As part of this closure to Jehu's reign, the writer includes a NOTICE concerning military incursions into Jehu's kingdom (10:32-33), and the typical concluding REGNAL RESUMÉ (10:34-35).

Setting

This literary composition has its setting in the work of the Dtr writer, who from his vantage point in the Judean exile drew upon various sources to write the story of the Israelite and Judean kings. See the general discussion at 1 Kgs 14:21-31 in Long, *1 Kings,* 164.

Intention

Clearly the main intention of the writer was to present the consolidation of Jehu's political power as a religious reformation in Israel. Jehu moves against Jezebel, the archetypal symbol of Baalist opposition to Yahweh (1 Kgs 18:19; 19:1-3; 21:1-16); in so doing he fulfills earlier prophecy (1 Kgs 19:17; 21: 21-26; 2 Kgs 9:7-10). Jehu cleans out the nest of Baal worshipers in Samaria, and thus embodies the fierce attachment to Yahweh so well displayed by Elijah (cf. 10:16,

127

17, 25 with 1 Kgs 19:10, 14 and 18:19-20, 40). Indeed, the king- reformer seems a kind of latter-day embodiment of that prophetic severity of spirit which guarded the Dtr writer's idea of true religion during the Omride period. Jehu, who is presented as usurper king, leader of reformed worship, and prophetlike zealot, completes Elijah's struggle against Baalism by undoing precisely what Ahab, son of Omri, had put in place (cf. 2 Kgs 10:26-27 with 1 Kgs 16:32-33).

Yet, the Dtr writer is of two minds about Jehu. His heroic place in the narrative derives from carrying out God's wishes (10:30), but the loss of territory mentioned at the close seems to be a consequence of Jehu's religious shortcomings (10:29-33). While limited approval is reported as God's speech in 10:30, it will be taken as prophecy to be expressly fulfilled in 2 Kgs 15:12. This motival connection between disparate parts of the larger story is a familiar mark of the writer's claim that God's unseen purpose shapes events which in this case, to ordinary sight, appear to be merely vicious and opportunistic assaults on established political power.

THE DEATH OF JEZEBEL, 9:30-37

Structure

I. Narrative setting	30
A. Jehu's travel to Jezreel	30a
B. Jezebel's preparations to meet Jehu	30b
II. Meeting of Jehu and Jezebel	31-33
A. Jezebel's greeting	31
B. Jehu's reply (call for loyalty)	32
C. Result: Jezebel killed	33
III. Aftermath	34-37
A. Jehu's instructions for burial	34
B. Instructions carried out	35-36aα
1. Remains discovered	35
2. Report to Jehu	36aα
C. Jehu's response: recognition of oracle fulfillment	36aβ-37

This unit is easily distinguished from the foregoing formulaic remark (9:29) and the opening of completely new tradition at 10:1.

Some scholars argue that the narrative was originally independent and that the Dtr writer integrated it into the present context chiefly by means of the fulfillment motif, vv. 36-37 (cf. 1 Kgs 21:23; so Dietrich, 26; H.-Chr. Schmitt, 21; Weinfeld, 20-21; Barré, 15-16, takes part of v. 36 as post-Dtr redaction). Würthwein (*Könige*, 334) and Hentschel (*2 Könige*, 45) go on to reconstruct an original form of vv. 30-35, but with a good deal of arbitrariness. Other critics imply that the essential part of the tradition about Jezebel's death was always a part of the larger story of Jehu's rise to power (e.g., recently, Olyan, on the connective force of *šlm*, 9:18, 19, 22, 26, 31; DeVries, 56, reconstructs an original narrative consisting of 9:1-8a, 10-14a, 15b-16a, 17-25a, 27, 30-36a; cf. Campbell, 103; Barré, 29).

Whatever one's judgments might be about such attempts at picturing redactional history, this tradition about Jezebel's death now is clearly continuous in style and theme with the foregoing account in which Jehu gathers political power to himself by murdering the sitting monarchs (8:28–9:28; see Olyan and discussion above). It seems reasonable, therefore, to treat vv. 30-37 as an episode within this larger narrative.

The structure is straightforward. When Jehu returns to Jezreel from his exploits at the property of Naboth (see 9:21), he is met by Jezebel who presents herself to him as a proper queen, gazing from a window, but also with ambiguous sarcasm and irony, v. 30. The painted eyes and "adorned head" may suggest only royal affluence instead of lurid sexuality. (Parker sees her as intent on seducing Jehu; Jer 4:30 and Ezek 23:40 associate painted eyes with harlots.) The motif of a woman looking from a window may have been entirely traditional, even in the decorative arts (see J. W. and G. W. Crowfoot, *Early Ivories from Samaria* [Samaria-Sebaste 2; London: Palestine Exploration Fund, 1938] pl. XIII, fig. 2; *ANEP*, no. 131, as cited in Cogan and Tadmor, *II Kings*, 111).

Jezebel greets Jehu with an insulting allusion to Zimri, who earlier had usurped royal authority (see 1 Kgs 16:9-20). Parker denies this nuance, and proposes that "Zimri" be taken to mean "hero" or "champion," in which case Jezebel would continue to press her self-serving and flattering attentions on a man who newly holds the kingdom's power. Olyan ("Jehu as Zimri") reads the name as *zāmîr*, "vineyard pruning," from another root *zmr* and suggests an allusion to Naboth's vineyard (1 Kings 21). Whatever Jezebel's or the narrator's intentions, Jehu apparently takes her words as a challenge to his newly won position. He demands allegiance ("Who is on my side?"), commands two eunuchs to cast Jezebel from her window, and presumably looks on as she plummets to her death (vv. 31-33; on *sārîs*, "eunuch," see the recent discussion by Cogan and Tadmor, *II Kings*, 112). In the aftermath, amid Jehu's callous eating and drinking, we are told that honorable burial as ordered by Jehu (but for unstated reasons) is impossible. Too little remains of the queen's body. In this circumstance, the narrator has Jehu recognize a fulfillment of prophecy and so bring the tawdry episode to its theologically sanctioned closure (vv. 36-37; cf. 1 Kgs 21:23; 2 Kgs 9:10 with v. 36b; v. 37 does not correspond to a specific oracle in the Bible, although it may have alluded originally to a tradition now lost to us).

Within the compressed simplicity of this narrative, the writer nevertheless achieves some measure of sophistication in the words which Jezebel flings at Jehu: "Is it peace, you Zimri, murderer of his master?" (v. 31). They push the action forward in the story world (Jehu takes them as a challenge and responds accordingly), but on the level of the reader, the words suggest wider interpretative allusions.

First, the formulaic greeting, "Is it peace?" *(hăšālôm)* or "how goes everything?," is hardly innocent (as it probably was on Gehazi's lips, 4:26); nor is it the greeting of one blinded by circumstance (as with Joram's messenger, 9:18-19), unless one may assume that Jezebel knows nothing of events. Is she being sarcastic, playing with *šālôm* in its connotation of "peace"?

Second, her allusion to "Zimri" is doubly ambiguous. If the word relates to √*zmr* II and means "strong one, hero" (Parker), Jezebel may be engaging in political or self-protective flattery. If the former "king" Zimri is meant (1 Kgs 16:9-20), then the queen mother may be reproaching Jehu with memories of failure and violent end. Like Zimri, Jehu is a military man who has "conspired against" and assassinated his king (2 Kgs 9:17-26; cf. 1 Kgs 16:9-10). As did Zimri, Jehu moves — fully justified by prophecy — to eliminate all opposition to his rule (9:27-28; 10:1-14; cf. 1 Kgs 16:11-13). But despite this prophetic mission, Zimri came to his end after only seven days on the throne, and failed finally to win the Dtr writer's approval (1 Kgs 16:15-19). Nor will Jehu escape the DtrH's condemnation, despite his view that the military coup serves God's purposes (2 Kgs 10:29-31).

Thus, within the story world, the exchange between Jezebel and Jehu is fraught with multiple suggestions. He takes her as a threat and her words as a challenge; she may manipulate by flattery, or she may taunt with derisive allusion. At the same time, her words presage the writer's own mixed attitude toward Jehu: he is not only prophetically empowered to restore the wholeness (*šālôm*) fractured by faithlessness (Olyan), but he is also in the process of failing, like Zimri, that most orthodox of litmus tests, whether or not his ways are those of Jeroboam (see 10:29-31). In this sense Jezebel not only epitomizes evil for the Dtr writer but also is a kind of unwitting prophetess, seeing through Jehu's prophetic warrant to the further truth of his ultimate failure.

Genre

This unit is a REPORT which forms an episode within a (→) historical narrative. Note the formula of GREETING ("Is it peace?") in v. 31 and the prophetic ANNOUNCEMENT OF JUDGMENT (vv. 36b-37) quoted as part of Jehu's speech, in which he recognizes that events conform to a previously uttered (→) prophetic judgment speech (cf. 1 Kgs 13:26, 32). The speech therefore functions in the mouth of a character like the well-attested report of ORACLE FULFILLMENT, which usually appears as a comment from the writer-narrator (see, e.g., 1 Kgs 14:17-18; 16:34; 17:16; 2 Kgs 1:17a).

Setting

Because this report presupposes events narrated in 8:28–9:28 and continues the leitmotif *šālôm*, it is doubtful that the tradition existed independently of its present context. In any case, the most important "setting" which lends significance to the unit is the present literary context. The death of Jezebel at the wish, if not the hand, of Jehu is one stage of several through which Jehu consolidates his power and moves to fulfill his religious mission, to purge the kingdom of its Baalist worshipers. Prophecy-fulfillment binds this episode to the larger Dtr history.

Intention

From what has been said, it is clear that a main intention of the Dtr writer was to account for Jehu's doubly significant actions — a political coup and a religiously sanctioned reformation — by means of this encounter with both a plausible "historical" character, i.e., a political rival, and a religious archetype, the symbol of anti-Yahwistic, pro-Baal fervor. Jezebel meets her death at the wish of an agent of Yahweh, and in fulfillment of the prophecy which commissioned him (9:7-10) and more generally of those earlier oracles that foreshadow his role in fostering the victory of Yahwism (1 Kgs 21:23; 19:17). Contrast this picture of Jehu with Hos 1:4-5, where he is given no theological sanction at all. In this system of cross reference by prophecy-fulfillment, the DtrH suggests repeatedly that events of history have their shaping power in God's purposes, enunciated by his prophets and recorded by his writers of history.

Bibliography

See bibliography at 2 Kgs 8:28–9:28. S. De Vries, *Prophet* (→ 2 Kgs 1:2-17a); S. Olyan, "2 Kings 9:31 — Jehu as Zimri," *HTR* 78 (1985) 203-7; S. Parker, "Jezebel's Reception of Jehu," *Maarav* 1 (1978) 67-78; H.-Chr. Schmitt, *Elisa* (→ 2 Kgs 2:1-25); Weinfeld, *Deuteronomy* (→ 2 Kgs 8:16-24).

JEHU'S PURGE OF THE BAALISTS, 10:1-27

Structure

I. Murder of Ahab's descendants and supporters	1-11
A. Slayings in Samaria (Jehu in Jezreel)	1-7
1. Preparations	1-6
a. Circumstances (70 descendants)	1a
b. Jehu's letter to leaders	1b-3
1) Narrative introduction	1b
2) Body of letter: challenge	2-3
c. Response from leaders	4-5
1) Concerning the leaders' fear	4
2) Letter to Jehu	5
a) Narrative introduction	5a
b) Body of letter: declarations of loyalty	5b
d. Jehu's reply	6a
1) Narrative introduction	6aα
2) Body of letter: instructions	6aβ
e. Circumstances (70 descendants)	6b
2. Killing of the seventy	7
B. Slayings in Jezreel	8-11

b. Cultic assembly   23-24a
    1) Jehu and Jehonadab enter temple   23a
    2) Jehu's order concerning exclusions   23b
    3) Beginning of cultic sacrifices   24a
B. Springing the trap   24b-25
   1. Circumstances: Jehu's warning to guards   24b
   2. Slaying of Baal worshipers   25
    a. Narrative setting   25aα
    b. Jehu's death order   25aβ
    c. Execution of order: slaughter   25b
C. Enumeration of further reform actions   26-27
   1. Pillar (asherah?) burned   26
   2. Destruction of pillar and temple   27a-bα
   3. Narrator's comment: temple a latrine   27bβ

This unit opens with a nominal clause which abruptly begins a new turn in the larger narrative. Jehu is still in Jezreel, and having disposed of the queen mother, Jezebel (9:30-37), he turns his attention to eliminating any authority the descendants and supporters of Ahab may possess in Israel. The material may have originally been part of a connected narrative telling of Jehu's rise to power (10:4 clearly seems to allude to the events of 9:21-28; De Vries, 119, calls chs. 9–10 an "accession narrative"); but like many other elements in that larger account, this tradition about the final purge of Baalists from Israel stands as a self-contained episode within the whole. The end is most probably in v. 27, a familiar closure to narrative units in the books of Kings (cf. 2 Kgs 17:23, 41). With v. 28, the author-editor presents evaluative statements typical of the regnal summaries (cf. 2 Kgs 3:2-3).

Many critics see in this unit an old tradition, or compilation of shorter traditions, joined to ch. 9 with editorial touches, or — following Noth — drawn into the Dtr history with only minor editorial additions (e.g., Sanda, Könige II, 121-22; Gressmann, Geschichtsschreibung, 308-10; Montgomery, Kings, 407; Noth, Deuteronomistic History, 69; Fricke, 2 Könige, 112-13; Gray, Kings, 537-38; Hobbs, 2 Kings, 123-26; De Vries, 119; Barré, 16-23; Rofé, Prophetical Stories, 79-86). Hoffmann (pp. 99-100) emphasizes the important role that Jehu's cultic measures (vv. 25b-27) play in the integrated vision of the Dtr writer. See especially the Dtr touches in vv. 10, 16-17, 26-27.

Würthwein (Könige, 326-27) carries through a theory of multiple editions of the Dtr history (see Dietrich; Veijola), and reconstructs two originally separate traditions, vv. 1-17 and 18-27, each of which passed through a complicated history of redaction. The oldest material is to be found in vv. 1b-6a, 7-9, 12a, 17aα. All the rest, including vv. 18-27 (also a composite of two versions), stems from various editors and glossators. (Cf. the less radical application of multiple-edition theory in Hentschel, 2 Könige, 45-49.)

Würthwein offers little evidence for his conclusions, and two items which he mentions, e.g., twice-reported actions at vv. 21b/24a (the Baal worshipers enter the temple) and 24b/25a (Jehu's order to kill the Baalists), admit of other explanations. If v. 24a, wayyābō'û la'ăśôt, means "they entered [the temple] to offer [sacrifice]," then the sentence would simply repeat v. 21b. Yet, Hebrew syntax allows another possibility. The expression can indicate incipient, purposeful action, and hence be translated, "they [Jehu and Jehonadab] started to offer [sacrifice]." See Gen 23:2, *wayyābō' 'abrāhām lispōd lĕśārâ*, "and Abraham began to mourn for Sarah" (cf. *NJPS* "proceeded to mourn . . ."). Also, against Würthwein, v. 24b does not simply duplicate v. 25a, Jehu's direct order to kill the assembled Baal worshipers. Rather, the sentence seems to report an event anterior to the main action (note the inversion of word order, subject + perfect verb, a syntactical order which often signals a pluperfect sense [R. J. Williams, *Hebrew Syntax* (2nd ed.; Toronto: University of Toronto, 1976), § 162]). In other words, before the cultic rites began, v. 24a, Jehu (had) warned his guards of the penalty for their allowing anybody to escape, v. 24b. His command in v. 25a, therefore, falls on receptive ears.

Yet, one must admit to certain remaining problems in the narrative. What is the relation between "eighty men" (v. 24b) and the "guard and the officers" who carry out Jehu's orders (vv. 25b-27)? Why does the narrator repeatedly mention "pillar" in vv. 26-27, or indicate so little connection between vv. 12-14 and 15-17 and the whole? It is reasonable to assume that diverse materials lie behind the present text, even if critics cannot agree on its redactional history.

As presently constituted, the narrative consists of a series of self-contained episodes that describe both a geographic and thematic progression. Jehu moves from Jezreel to Samaria while serially eliminating political rivals to himself. Jehu acts first in Jezreel (I, vv. 1-11), and at the last in Samaria (IV, vv. 18-27). Two reports situated "on-the-way" to Samaria (II, III, vv. 12-14, 15-17) trace out the move from one place to the other. With similarly configured sequences (itinerary note, meeting, dialogue, resulting action), these transitional reports relate ancillary "mopping-up" steps which Jehu takes toward realizing his political goals. The writer also provides a bit of alchemy. A ruthless rebel turns into king-zealot-for-Yahweh.

In addition, vv. 15-17 form a kind of motival hinge within the larger unit. On the one hand, the report completes a series of three episodes in which Jehu utterly annihilates his opponents, and its closure recalls those images of slaughter without survival which are part of the earlier episodes (cf. v. 17 with vv. 11 and 14b). On the other hand, the encounter with Jehonadab, son of Rechab, vv. 15-16, anticipates the last section of the narrative, in which this Rechabite, whose presence is otherwise unexplained, looks on (v. 23) while Jehu's men offer up the remaining vestige of Baalism to utter destruction.

Although resembling enumeration more than artistically conceived literature, this narrative unit recounts the steps taken by Jehu to consolidate his political power — first from a base at Jezreel (9:30-37 is a part of this progression), and then in the Omride city, Samaria. As is usually the case in the books of Kings, politics are infused with theological justification. Just as Jehonadab is bidden to watch Jehu's "zeal for the Lord" (v. 16), the reader is asked to view serial slaughter, the license of political power, as single-minded religious devotion and fulfillment of prophecy (vv. 10, 17).

The first phase (I, vv. 1-11) is set in Jezreel. Jehu's primary design, achieving unrivaled position in Samaria, is circumscribed by a massive circumstance, Ahab's "seventy sons." The expression is traditional, and refers in round numbers both to biological sons and, more generally, to "descendants"; see Exod 1:5, "all the offspring [*nepeš*, 'soul(s)'] of Jacob were seventy"; Judg 8:30, "now Gideon had seventy sons"; cf. the "seventy relatives" of the Aramean king, Panammuwa (*KAI*, no. 215, 3). The narrator has incorporated this motif as a framework around vv. 1b-6a, and thereby suggests the pressing importance of the "seventy" as background to, and object of, Jehu's first calculations.

The narrator reports an exchange of letters which, in the telling, shades into direct dialogic speech: demand, reply, and response (vv. 2-3, 5, 6a). Jehu sends a cleverly worded challenge to the leaders in Samaria, including those who have responsibility for rearing the royal children (*'ōmnîm*, v. 1; cf. v. 6b). He commands them to do their duty: set the fittest of Ahab's sons on Joram's vacant throne, amass their forces, and fight for the kingdom. Assessing their situation, and fearing the same end as befell the "two kings" (v. 4; cf. 9:21-28), the leaders capitulate. Perhaps to convey their strategic importance and the officially binding nature of their actions, the writer now mentions specific royal officeholders — "he who was over the palace" (cf. 1 Kgs 4:6; Isa 22:15) and "he who was over the city," presumably the commandant of those "commanders" (*śārê*) mentioned in v. 1. These two officials, along with the others, extract from Jehu's command an implied alternative. They quickly abandon the house of Ahab and declare their fealty to Jehu (v. 5). In a second letter, Jehu acknowledges their reply and demands that they demonstrate their allegiance by delivering to him in Jezreel the heads of Ahab's "seventy sons" (v. 6a). Complying immediately, Samaria's leaders remove a major obstacle to Jehu's consolidation of political power (v. 7).

This exchange of letters represents the substance of a mutually declared and negotiated agreement between parties. The stylized declarations made to Jehu (v. 5b) imply the conventions of individual or international covenants (Kalluveettil, 139-64, esp. 152-64). "We are your servants" is often a declaration of vassalage (Josh 9:8 [cf. v. 6]; 2 Kgs 16:7; 1 Kgs 20:31-34); "all that you say we will do" appears where one addresses a superior treaty partner (Neh 5:12; Exod 19:8; 24:3, 7 — the last two imply a covenant between God and Israel); "do whatever is good in your eyes" denotes the loyal attitude of a vassal (Kalluveettil, 118-19, 151, n. 137); "we will not make anyone king" alludes to a treaty obligation which guarantees that a king's son will accede to the throne (cf. v. 3; Kalluveettil, 150; cf. 2 Kgs 14:2; 21:24; 23:30, 2 Chr 22.1). Of course, Jehu now gathers this obligation to his own benefit.

Given these motival associations, one realizes that the leaders in Samaria declare themselves to be loyal subjects of Jehu and obligated to him by mutual covenant (although the word "covenant" is not used here). Jehu in turn seals the compact in v. 6aβ by acknowledging the new relationship. His words, "If you are on my side, and if you are ready to obey me" (*RSV*), refer less to some future circumstance than to affirmation and corroboration (cf. 9:15b, "If this is in your mind"). One might better translate: "Since [indeed], as you are with me, [then] take the heads of your master's sons" (Kalluveettil, 160-61; see a similar use of subordinate clause with *'im*, "if," in the concluding of contracts in Gen 23:8, 13). It is on the basis of such agreements that the superior party may order his "servants" (the word often means "vassal") to take action in accord with the pact's obligations. The descendants of Ahab (Joram) die, and their murderers deliver in effect a vassal's tribute to their new overlord (v. 7), without Jehu ever having to leave Jezreel or directly wield the sword.

Then Jehu turns to the supporters of Ahab who remain close at hand in Jezreel (I.B, vv. 8-11). The scene is understated, but grandly dramatic. Jehu takes the grim reminders of death — which are, privately, tokens of newly won political support — and turns them into a public object lesson. Ordering the Omride heads to be massed in heaps at the city gate, like the Assyrian kings who sought with similar measures to deter rebellion (*ANET*, 276a, 277b; cf. *ANEP*, no. 236), Jehu addresses a crowd of onlookers (defined only as "the people," presumably Jezreelites). In a curious blend of juridical and theological pronouncement, he declares the people free of guilt ("You are innocent" [*saddiqîm*], v. 9bα; cf. Prov. 24:24; Exod 9:27; 1 Sam 24:18; Neh 9:33), confesses his own guilt in striking down Joram (v. 9bβ$_1$), and finally asks, rather obscurely, "But who struck down all these?" (v. 9bβ$_2$). Does he imply that the executions were done with divine connivance (Montgomery, *Kings,* 409)? Or that he knows nothing of the affair in Samaria, and fair-minded people (reading "you are impartial" [*saddiqîm*]) will see that these decapitations in no way implicate him? (So Burney, *Notes,* 303; Šanda, *Könige* II, 107.) Or does Jehu appeal to a people "right" (*saddîq*) with God to act as witness to the Lord's work? (So Gray, *Kings,* 555, who translates: "and whoever has slain all these, know now that there shall not fall to the ground a single word of Yahweh.") Or perhaps Jehu wants the Jezreelites to conclude that his actions against Joram have the support of leaders in Samaria (Barré, 83).

Whatever the precise implications of v. 9bβ$_2$, it is clear that Jehu's speech is weighted toward a theological remark about the inevitable fulfillment of the Lord's promises as spoken through Elijah (v. 10; cf. 1 Sam 3:19). The perspective is double-edged, as though he is drawing a lesson from what had happened in Samaria and also announcing an interpretative code for what is about to happen. One may translate, "The Lord has done what he said" (taking '*āśâ* as simple perfect for completed action in the past), i.e., the Lord has wiped out the house of Ahab (cf. 1 Kgs 21:21, 29). Alternatively, the verb may be taken to express certainty that a future circumstance is as good as accomplished (see Num 17:27 [*RSV* 12]; Isa 5:13; *GKC,* § 106n). In this case, Jehu alludes to an imminent blow, like the triumphant cry of the warrior about to finish off his victim.

It comes as no surprise, then, that Jehu immediately slays all those who remain attached by office or sentiment to the house of Ahab in Jezreel — his "great men" (or perhaps, with the LXX, his "kinsmen"; cf. 1 Kgs 16:11), his intimate associates (cf. Job 19:14; Ps 55:14 [*RSV* 13]), and his "priests" (cf. 1 Kgs 4:4, 5; 2 Sam 8:17, 18). Emboldened and assured with the ideology of holy crusade, Jehu (and the narrator) show the Lord's word being fulfilled in this second terrifying massacre (see Josh 8:22; 10:33; 11:8; Num 21:35).

The next two scenes (II, III, vv. 12-14, 15-17) depict Jehu moving with purpose and determination toward Samaria. The writer casts each phase of travel in similar molds (cf. Hobbs, *2 Kings,* 125):

(1) an itinerarylike transition ("he went [*wayyēlek*] to Samaria," v. 12a; or "he went [*wayyēlek*] from there" [*RSV* "when he departed from there"], v. 15aα);

(2) a meeting ("and Jehu found [*māṣā'*; *RSV* 'met'] the kinsmen of Ahaziah," v. 13; or "and he found [*wayyimṣā'*; *RSV* 'met'] Jehonadab," v. 15aα);

(3) dialogue, vv. 13b-14a and 15b-16;

(4) resulting action: massacre, with none remaining, vv. 14b and 17a.

The obscurities inherent in these two incidents are due largely to the lack of narrative connections to their wider context, owing to the episodic structure given the whole. First, vv. 12-14: How can Ahaziah's kinsmen not know of the king's death? (The leaders in Samaria seem to know, v. 4.) Or have they learned of the murders, and so are on their way to "pay their respects" (*NJPS*) to a grieving family (*nēred lišlôm*, v. 13; *RSV* "visit")? Or perhaps they were going to "avenge" Ahaziah's death (revocalizing *lišlôm* to *lĕšallēm* [Hobbs, *2 Kings*, 128])? Moreover, why would the kinsmen of Ahaziah, on their way to the Judean capital (if they intend a visit with the royal princes), find themselves somewhere (the exact location is unknown) in the north on an approach to Samaria? Or if they plan revenge, why reveal it to Jehu, presumably the object of their anger? Whatever one may answer to these questions, the main point seems clear enough. After murdering the reigning son of Ahab, King Joram (9:21-26), Jehu strikes at the Judean kingdom and slays Ahaziah (9:27). So, in this place, following the attack on those attached to Joram (house of Ahab) in Samaria and Jezreel, Jehu now attacks Judean royalty, killing forty-two of them (the number is traditional; cf. 2 Kgs 2:24). And as in ch. 9, the narrator offers no explicit theological justification. It is enough, given his interest in recounting the purge of Baalists from the north, to associate the murder of these Judeans with the general prospective pronouncements of v. 10b. Here at Beth-eked, Jehu continues his zealous march to Samaria, solidifying his credentials as religious reformer, while establishing himself without any possible political rivals in either kingdom.

The second scene "on the way," vv. 15-17, abruptly introduces an unknown figure into the narrative. Who is Jehonadab, son of Rechab, and why should he be given a privileged status as witness to the religious purge? Elsewhere, the Rechabites are mentioned only in Jeremiah 35. Even if both texts refer to the same family, one may hardly conclude on this account that the Rechabites, either actually or in the view of narrator, were "enthusiasts for the primitive religion of Yahweh and simple life of the desert" (Montgomery, *Kings*, 409; see the doubts of Würthwein, *Könige*, 339; and F. S. Frick, *IDBSup*, 726-28, esp. 727).

If Jehonadab were a nobleman associated with chariotry in some way ("son of *rkb*," a verbal root associated with riding and chariots), then an alliance with him might be advantageous to depict Jehu's growing power (F. S. Frick, "The Rechabites Reconsidered," *JBL* 90 [1971] 279-87; also idem, *IDBSup*, 727). In fact, the compressed dialogue between Jehu and Jehonadab (v. 15b) suggests that they, as in the earlier case of the Omride officials and Jehu, are concluding a pact. Jehu asks, "Is it straight [true] with your heart as my heart is with your heart?" (The syntax is difficult, but the sense seems clear enough.) When Jehonadab replies in the affirmative, Jehu then asks for a sign of that solidarity, one with the other: "If so, give me your hand." The narrator then reports closure, "So he gave him his hand."

That final gesture suggests that an oath accompanies and symbolizes Jehonadab's pledge. In like manner, the Chronicler renders a scene in which military commanders, militiamen, and "sons of David" offer their devotion to Solomon at his enthronement ceremony (1 Chr 29:24, "All the leaders . . . pledged their allegiance to King Solomon" [lit. "gave (their) hand under *(tahat)* Solomon"]). Cf. Gen 24:2; 47:29, "place the hand under [*taḥat*] the loins" as symbolic, perhaps empowering of, an oath. Similar language applies to a vassal king who, despite having taken a covenant oath of loyalty to his master, has nevertheless rebelled: "he despised the oath and broke the covenant . . . he gave his hand [to the overlord] yet did all these [rebellious] things" (Ezek 17:18). Cogan and Tadmor (*II Kings,* 115) cite an artistic representation of this procedure from a palace at Nimrud (see D. Oates, "The Excavations at Nimrud [Kalḫu]," *Iraq* 25 [1963] 6-37, esp. 20-22, pl. 7c).

Other details also allude to covenant making. When Jehu "took him [Jehonadab] up . . . into the chariot," v. 15b, the image is precisely that which a narrator uses when Ahab "caused [Ben-hadad] to come up into the chariot" on the occasion of concluding a covenant (1 Kgs 20:33; cf. v. 34b and Long, *1 Kings,* 215). Moreover, Jehu's question of Jehonadab about the oneness of the "heart," v. 15bα₁, may be compared to a similar figure, "my heart will be knit to you" or be "one with yours" (*hāyâ lēbāb lĕyāḥad;* 1 Chr 12:18 [*RSV* 17]). In this text David expresses loyalty to the approaching Benjamites and Judahites, to whom he offers a mutual covenant (Kalluveettil, 53-56, 163). The narrative continues with the inspired poetry of fealty: "The spirit came upon Amasai . . . and he said, 'We are yours, O David/and with you, O son of Jesse'" (v. 19 [*RSV* 18]).

Yet for all the suggestion of political alliance in this scene, the narrator also sounds a theological note. Having concluded their pact, and sealed it with "giving the hand," Jehu invites this newly bound subject to witness Jehu's "zeal for the Lord" (v. 16). The expression recalls Elijah's self-description in the aftermath of his fanatically single-minded defense of Yahwism (1 Kgs 19:10, 14; the root *qn'* appears in both Elijah's and Jehu's idiom). Whatever Jehonadab's political importance to Jehu may have signified, his presence in the narrative at just this moment is a harbinger of harsh religious reform. As Jehu has been shaded earlier in Elijah's colors as a severe prophet-destroyer (9:22-23), so now, with Jehonadab as witness, one expects Jehu to show that same passionate devotion to achieving a kingdom exclusively attached to Yahweh.

Immediately, the writer reports a third-in-series slaughter, this time of "all who remained [loyal] to Ahab in Samaria," v. 17a. Now the memory, the name, of Elijah floats visibly to the surface. Events happen just as the prophet had predicted (v. 17b; see 1 Kgs 21:21, 29), and just as Jehu himself had announced proleptically to the people of Jezreel, v. 10b. The way to the throne in Samaria, Omri's city on a hill (1 Kgs 16:24), has been traversed and left littered with Baalist (and politically adversarial) corpses. It remains now to cleanse the hill itself, to clear away the temple and citadel of royal service to the Baals.

The final episode (IV, vv. 18-27) is built essentially of four sequences, each of which depicts an order and its execution: vv. 19a-20a + 20b-21; 22a + 22b; 23b (carrying out of order assumed); 25aβ + 25b. The writer adopts a reportorial style approaching simple enumeration, and in the urge to itemize Jehu's purge of the cult from Samaria, abandons most of the subtler features of imaginative literary creation (see esp. vv. 25b-27; cf. the styles of 2 Kgs 23:4-20; 1 Kings 6–7). One watches and listens as Jehu, feigning devotion, calls together all the worshipers of Baal, amasses them in the temple, and then gives the order to slay them liked trapped animals. Concluding reports briefly recount the destruction of Baal's sacred "pillar" *(maṣṣēbâ)* and the temple itself.

Certain features of the narration, however, display touches of imagination and flare. The narrator explicitly contrives double channels of communication: one between characters in the narrative itself, and one between narrator and reader, who is addressed directly at two places, v. 19b ("But Jehu did it with cunning") and v. 27b ("to this day," i.e., the time of the reader). This obviously encourages one to uncover irony at almost every stage of the action.

Jehu sets and springs his trap with grandly elaborate style. His speech in v. 18 seems calculated to appear self-serving in a way that the people in Samaria would have most approved. The king will care for the kingdom's god with more devotion and extravagance than his predecessor displayed. (For similar ideological claims outside Israelite literature, see the numerous Assyrian royal inscriptions which glorify a monarch by recording his fantastic building projects, including splendid repairs to the cultic places left in desuetude by other kings; e.g., *ARI* II, § 437 [p. 92]: "the ancient temple of the goddess Gula, my mistress, which previously Tukulti-Ninurta [I] my forefather, vice regent of Ashur, had built — that temple had become dilapidated . . . I greatly enlarged that temple beyond previous extent. I completed it from top to bottom and deposited my steles" [Adad-nerari II, ca. 911-891 B.C.E.]).

In short, Jehu assumes the expected role as royal patron and titular head of the cult (cf. 1 Kgs 8:1-66 [Solomon]; 2 Kgs 23:1-3 [Josiah]; 1 Chr 29:10-22 [David]). He calls for a great cultic celebration, vv. 19-20 (cf. Joel 1:14), insisting on a full house ("Let none be missing," v. 19), and proper vestments for the worshipers (v. 22). The gathered company must not be diluted by nonbelievers (v. 23), and the king himself — with Jehonadab at his side — lifts up the burnt offerings (vv. 24a, 25a).

Of course, Jehu cleverly builds a stageplay. He announces, "I have a great sacrifice [*zebaḥ*] to offer to Baal" (v. 19), but the reader recalls that the Dtr historian had used that same word to describe King Josiah's offering-slaughter of Baal priests (1 Kgs 13:2; 2 Kgs 23:20; Hobbs, *2 Kings,* 129). Moreover, Jehu's declaration to the people, "Jehu will serve [*'bd*] him [Baal] much," may contain a pun. With a slight change in the sound of the first guttural consonant in the verb, Jehu can be heard to say that he will *destroy* Baal (*'bd,* "destroy," cf. v. 19b; Robinson, *2 Kings,* 100). And obviously, a kind of ironic play shapes Jehu's demand that no "servant of the Lord" be among the worshipers. Disbelievers according to the people's scale of values are believers to writer and reader.

One is fully persuaded, presumably, to enjoy Jehu's triumph despite its calculated ruthlessness. Jehu starts to offer the sacrifices (v. 24a; *bô'* + infinitive

= incipient action, "he proceeded to offer sacrifices"). A digression — really delayed exposition — tells us that he has already stationed guardsmen outside, v. 24b. It is worship in progress, but also a deadly trap. When finished, Jehu drops the illusion of Baalist devotion and orders his men to slay everyone inside the temple. The soldiers actually go quite a bit further than commanded (at least we do not hear any subsequent orders). The ruling literary pattern of command-execution breaks down in the narrator's rush to tell of reformation, or in the report of Jehu's hot zealotry. The guards slaughter the helpless and unsuspecting, cast the corpses outside, and enter the inner reaches of the temple. (The word *ʿîr*, usually translated as "city," here translated as "inner room," means a temple's interior holy chamber in a Ugaritic text [Gray, *Kings*, 562].) The guardsmen then bring religious objects outside and, like high priests of desecration, offer a second sacrifice by destruction. They utterly destroy the "pillars of the Baal temple" (some MSS read the singular; cf. Gen 35:14; 2 Kgs 3:2; 17:10; 23:14); they burn the wooden Asherah — the symbol of a goddess and consort to Baal (following Šanda, *Könige* II, 117, and others, who take the second mention of "pillar" [*maṣṣēbâ*] as an error for *ʾăšērâ*); they destroy the temple of Baal. Finally, the writer closes the account by collapsing the distinction between the past of narrative and the present of narration, attesting to the reader that the destroyed temple became a "latrine until the present day" (v. 27).

In this climactic episode Jehu leaves no political or religious adversary standing. Generally speaking, he lives up to the expectations given to Elijah (1 Kgs 19:17), and he specifically fulfills those execrations which Elijah hurled at the house of Ahab (1 Kgs 21:21-29). Indeed, Jehu embodies that same prophetic severity of spirit. Like Elijah, he slays the prophets of Baal (they are mentioned only at v. 19; cf. 1 Kgs 18:19-20, 40); and like the prophet, Jehu lets no one escape the sweeping massacre (cf. 1 Kgs 18:40). For the author of this account, Jehu takes on the roles of king, cult leader, prophet-like zealot. He finishes Elijah's struggle by undoing precisely what Ahab had put in place (cf. vv. 26-27 and 1 Kgs 16:32-33; see Hoffmann, 100-101). Whether the DtrH approved of Jehu's actions strongly enough to override any possible scruples he may have felt toward the appalling ruthlessness of the reformer's actions must remain a matter of conjecture. (See Barré, 81-86, who argues that an original, pre-DtrH version of this account was quite negative toward Jehu.)

Genre

This unit is an ACCOUNT consisting of four REPORTS arranged as episodes by which Jehu wins political supremacy for himself and religious supremacy for Yahweh. (I do not follow Rofé, *Prophetical Stories*, 80-86, who elides matters of historicity with those of literary genre, and defines most of ch. 10 as "folkloristic anecdote.") To the former, one may compare the account of Solomon's "establishing the kingdom" (1 Kgs 2:12b-46; see Long, *1 Kings*, 47-49); to the latter, the cultic reforms of Josiah (2 Kgs 23:1-20). Although the narrative shows some features typically associated with (→) story, the writer does not sustain a dramatic plot from beginning to end or significantly develop characters.

Some important generic elements now reflected in this account are: (1) LETTER, vv. 2-3; typical epistolary greetings can be recognized at v. 1b, although in narrative style; transition to the letter's contents is still reflected by the phrase "and now" *(wĕ'attâ)* in v. 2; even the opening line, "as soon as this letter comes to you," is conventional in many actual examples of ancient Near Eastern letters; cf. 2 Kgs 5:6 and parallels cited by Pardee (p. 173); (2) stock scene of covenant making, vv. 2-6 (the pact is concluded through the exchange of letters) and v. 15b (concluded in direct dialogue); see discussion above, and parallels in 1 Kgs 20:31-34; Josh 9:6-15 (Kalluveettil, 139-65); (3) juridical language, v. 9, which reflects the STATEMENT OF ACQUITTAL, "You are innocent" (cf. Prov 24:24; Exod 9:27; Neh 9:33) and the CONFESSION OF GUILT, "I conspired against my master" (cf. 2 Kgs 18:14; Josh 7:20-21; 1 Sam 15:24; Boecker, *Redeformen*, 125-26).

Setting

There is no evidence on which to base an estimate of the original settings of this account or the self-contained reports that constitute it. The most important matter is the literary context which the Dtr writer has created for the unit. It is a major element of the longer composition which tells of the reign of Jehu — in effect the actions by which he consolidates his grip on the northern kingdom and carries out a prophetically commissioned reformation.

Intention

The writer clearly meant to recount Jehu's ruthless and calculating elimination of political rivals to himself and religious competition to Yahweh. The tale unfolds methodically. It develops on two levels: the geographical, from Jezreel to Samaria, and the characterological, from prophet-charged rebel to king-Yahwist-zealot. Jehonadab witnesses Jehu's reforming "zeal for the Lord," and thus guides the reader to view Jehu as an Elijah-like defender of true religion. Just as Jehonadab is bidden to admire Jehu's final act, the utter destruction of the Baalists and their temple in Samaria, so the reader is asked to take Jehu's ruthless actions as direct fulfillment of prophecy (vv. 10, 17) and — as in the case of Elijah — single-minded devotion to Yahweh.

Jehu lives up to his advance billing (1 Kgs 19:17) and fulfills those execrations which Elijah hurled at the house of Ahab (1 Kgs 21:21-29). He dismantles precisely what Ahab (and the Omrides) had put in place (cf. vv. 26-27 with 1 Kgs 16:32-33). And he concludes the struggle initiated a generation earlier with Elijah.

The writer implied by the canonical text seems to overlook Jehu's brutality in admiration for his zeal. Yet the DtrH will immediately draw back from this narrational endorsement to suggest that Jehu will be judged in the end by the standard applied to all other northern rulers. Even though he embodies the prophetic impulse and burns with a reformer's zeal for Yahweh alone, the curse of Jeroboam still hovers over him, and will account for his final place in the DtrH's reckoning (see below, 10:28-31).

Bibliography

See bibliographies at 2 Kgs 1:2-17a; 2:1-25; 8:28–9:28. H. J. Boecker, *Redeformen des Rechtsleben im Alten Testament* (WMANT 14; Neukirchen: Neukirchener, 1964); O. Eissfeldt, "Die Komposition von I Reg. 16:29–II Reg. 13:25," in *Das ferne und nahe Wort* (*Fest.* L. Rost; ed. F. Maass; BZAW 105; Berlin: de Gruyter, 1967) 49-58; H.-D. Hoffmann, *Reform* (→ 2 Kgs 3:1-3); P. Kalluveettil, *Declaration and Covenant: A Comprehensive Review of Covenant Formulae from the Old Testament and the Ancient Near East* (AnBib 88; Rome: Biblical Institute, 1982); A. Kuyt and J. Wesselius, "A Ugaritic Parallel for the Feast for Ba'al in 2 Kings X:18-25," *VT* 35 (1985) 109-11; J. M. Miller, "The Fall of the House of Ahab," *VT* 17 (1967) 307-24; D. Pardee, *Handbook of Ancient Hebrew Letters* (SBLSBS 15; Chico, CA: Scholars Press, 1982); O. H. Steck, *Überlieferung und Zeitgeschichte* (→ 2 Kgs 8:7-15); T. Veijola, *Die ewige Dynastie: David und die Entstehung seiner Dynastie nach der deuteronomistischen Darstellung* (Annales Acadameiae Scientiarum Fennicae B/193; Helsinki: Suomalainen Tiedeakatemia, 1975).

THE END OF JEHU'S RULE, 10:28-36

Structure

I. Statement of summary/transition		28
II. Theological review		29-31
III. Notice of defeat		32-33
IV. Concluding regnal resumé		34-35
V. Statement of length of reign		36

This unit closes out the regnal period of Jehu with typical formulaic material surrounding a simple note about Hazael cutting away parts of the Israelite kingdom. The opening, v. 28, is best seen as both summary and transition. It reads like an epitomizing conclusion to the preceding account (10:18-27; so *RSV* "thus," which interprets the simple Hebrew conjunction; Hobbs, *2 Kings*, 125). The restrictive adverb which follows in v. 29 (*raq,* "but," "only"), while depending on what precedes, also leads directly to the writer's evaluation of Jehu's reign, vv. 29-31. To the typical concluding summary, vv. 34-35, the narrator has added a statement about the duration of Jehu's reign, normally a part of the material which introduces a ruler for the first time (cf. a similar inclusion at the close of David's and Jeroboam's reigns, 1 Kgs 2:11; 14:20).

Scholars concerned with reconstructing a history of redaction naturally find reason to detect the traces of multiple editors within this unit. For example, Gray (*Kings,* 562) posits at least two redactors, one each for vv. 28-29 and 30-32; Würthwein (*Könige,* 343) attributes vv. 28-31 to an editorial hand later than the final redaction of the Dtr history and involving a number of secondary glosses (cf. Dietrich, 34); Barré (pp. 22-23) understands v. 29 alone to be an expansion on a DtrH composition.

As usual, the disagreements among scholars indicate the problematic grounds for such hypotheses. In any case, the chiastic form of vv. 29-31 points to authorial integrity and puts in question such evidence of disunity as may be adduced. Theological evaluations (vv. 29 and 31) repeat reference to the "sins of Jeroboam" and neatly frame a centered Yahweh speech (v. 30):

A   "sins of Jeroboam . . . which he made Israel to commit"
     (ḥāṭāʾê yārobʿām . . . ʾăšer heḥĕṭîʾ ʾet-yiśrāʾēl), v. 29a

B   Yahweh speech (v. 30)

A'   "sins of Jeroboam which he caused Israel to commit"
     (ḥaṭṭōʾwt yārobʿām ʾăšer heḥĕṭîʾ ʾet-yiśrāʾēl), v. 31b

This section is alive to a larger context. As already mentioned, v. 28 epitomizes the writer's view of Jehu's significance to the history of the kings (note a leitmotif, "wiped out" [*wayyašmēd*], v. 28 and 10:17). The concrete detail added to the conventional references to the sins of Jeroboam (vv. 29a, 31b) creates an even wider conceptual horizon. First, Jeroboam's transgression centers on those "golden calves that were in Bethel and Dan" (see 1 Kgs 12:25-33). Even though the Dtr writer undoubtedly has this matter in mind whenever he invokes Jeroboam's sin as a measure of subsequent kings' failures (as frequently happens in introductory summaries, e.g., 1 Kgs 15:26, 34; 16:26; 2 Kgs 13:2, 11), the actual phrase "golden calves" occurs only at 1 Kgs 12:28 (cf. v. 32) and 2 Kgs 10:29 in the books of Kings (cf. 2 Chr 13:8). Second, Jeroboam's "sin" is singularly characterized as being "not careful to walk in the law of the Lord [*tôrat-yahweh*]." The phrase occurs nowhere else in the Dtr history, but finds a close analogue, "law of Moses" *(tôrat-mōšeh)*, in three places: 1 Kgs 2:3, the admonition that David gives the impending ruler Solomon; 2 Kgs 14:6, a comment in praise of Amaziah; 23:25, a lavish reference to Josiah's probity. Thus, in characterizing Jehu, the writer points us back to the symbols of Jeroboam's misdeeds and the real standard of kingship under God (the conditions inherent in David's rule, which for the Dtr writer is a paradigm for all kings). And he looks to the future, to that same standard being invoked on behalf of two Judean kings of whom the Dtr writer will express approval.

With v. 30, the writer looks to the future as well. God announces to Jehu (the narrator does not specify the circumstances, just as in 1 Kgs 6:11) that his reward for carrying out God's judgment on the house of Ahab will be dynastic security, i.e., sons on the throne until the fourth generation. This promise recalls, first, Yahweh's unconditional word to David which still obtains in Judah (2 Sam 7:12-16; 2 Kgs 8:19) and, second, the conditional grant of rule that God offers Jeroboam and then rescinds when Jeroboam fails in his obligations (1 Kgs 11:37-38; 13:34). The remark in 2 Kgs 15:12 that this promise to Jehu receives its fulfillment brings disparate material under the meta-historical rubric of God's overlord-vassal relations with Israel's kings and his purposeful intentions for human events (see Mullen).

Finally, vv. 32-33 recall the Aramean ruler Hazael and his relentless threat against Israel. Introduced at 8:7-15, he looms in the reader's memory of Elisha's introspection (8:11-12), moves into range of peripheral vision on the margins of Jehu's successes (8:28; 9:15), and now confronts the reader directly with the first substantive military victory. It will not be the last (see 2 Kgs 12:18 [*RSV* 17]; 13:3-7, 14-19, 22-24).

Genre

This unit is a literary composition of the Dtr writer who offers a series of statements to conclude the regnal period of Jehu. Important generic elements are: (1) THEOLOGICAL REVIEW (vv. 29-31); see full discussion at 1 Kgs 11:1-13, in Long, *1 Kings*, 122-25; cf. 2 Kgs 17:7-18; 21:2-15; (2) concluding REGNAL RESUMÉ (vv. 34-35); see full discussion at 1 Kgs 14:21-31, in Long, *1 Kings*, 158-65; (3) a historical NOTICE (vv. 32-33), and (4) a typical LENGTH OF REIGN formula (v. 36). Of special interest is the PROMISE of dynastic rule (v. 30). In the background may be the widespread ancient Near Eastern form of "royal grant," by which a superior monarch bequeaths a reward to his vassal, usually a gift of land or dynastic right of rule (see Mullen; Weinfeld, "Covenant of Grant"; idem, *TDOT* II, 270-72). In the summarizing context at the end of Jehu's reign, however, this divine word is less a formal grant than a promise which functions in the Dtr history as a fully quoted prophecy whose fulfillment is noted at 15:12. Cf. the similarly styled prophecy of punishment in the midst of a theological review at 1 Kgs 11:11-13 and 2 Kgs 21:10-15.

Setting

This unit has its origin in the work of the Dtr writer who composed the history of the monarchy from the vantage point of exile after 587 B.C.E. The immediate literary context marks an important point in the ongoing story of the kings. Jehu's regnal period is over. With his rise to power and religious zealotry, the long dominance of the Omrides in the writer's telling of Israel's and Judah's history has also come to an end. From this point forward, the story of the divided kingdom will emphasize Judahite affairs, except for the extensive comment on the destruction of the northern kingdom (2 Kgs 17:7-41).

Intention

It is clear that the main purpose of the Dtr writer was to conclude the regnal epoch of Jehu. Yet, he brings a network of associations to bear on the occasion so that one recalls specifically the symbol of Israel's failure, the "sins of Jeroboam," and its opposite, the conditional, *tôrâ*-centered principles on which faithful kingship rests. On this basis, the DtrH explains the longevity and stability of Jehu's dynasty, which lasted, by the historian's reckoning, some 102 ½ years (see 2 Kgs 15:9-12; Mullen). At the same time, it is clear that the writer is of two minds about Jehu. The loss of territory to Hazael seems associated with Jehu's religious shortcomings (vv. 30-31 + 32-33), and like every other Israelite king, he persists in following Jeroboam's ways (vv. 29, 31b). His heroic place in the narrative derives from carrying out God's wishes, from being an instrument of God's judgment on a dynasty gone astray (v. 30). However, approval is qualified, and Jehu's reward is limited to four generations of ruling sons. In the end, nothing will derail the northern kingdom from its rush toward self-destruction (2 Kings 17).

Bibliography

L. Barré, *Political Persuasion* (→ 2 Kgs 8:28– 9:28); W. Dietrich, *Prophetie* (→ 2 Kgs 8:28–9:28); E. Theodore Mullen, "The Royal Dynastic Grant to Jehu and the Structure of the Books of Kings," *JBL* 107 (1988) 193-206; M. Weinfeld, "The Covenant of Grant in the Old Testament and in the Ancient Near East," *JAOS* 90 (1970) 184-203.

J(EH)OASH IS KING (REVOLT AGAINST ATHALIAH), 11:1-20

Text

In vv. 5b-7, 11, obscurities, possible corruptions, and a completely unknown word *(massāh)* at the end of v. 6 have made for variants and confusions in the MT and VSS. Attempts at solutions inevitably involve v. 11, which one would expect to report the execution of Jehoiada's orders in a way that is consistent with vv. 5b-7. The former focuses on the temple guard, the latter, as presently given in the MT, appears to order duty stations at both temple and palace. All translations reflect a certain amount of reconstruction and conjecture about internal consistency (see discussion below; also Cogan and Tadmor, *II Kings*, 127). The phrase "to [for] the king" (*'el-hammelek*), v. 7, omitted by the *RSV* and many critics but supported by the VSS, should be retained as part of the point that Jehoiada's plan is ultimately aimed at protecting the young prince (cf. vv. 8, 11; cf. *NJPS*).

Structure

I. Athaliah's seizure of the Judean throne		1-3
A. Purge of royal sons		1
1. Circumstance: King Ahaziah's death		1a
2. Athaliah's massacre of princes		1b
B. Continuing results		2-3

Formulaic regnal summaries define the outer limits of this section, which covers a six-year span of time presumably during the early years of Jehu's reign. In effect, Athaliah abruptly enters the Dtr story line as a flashback after the close of Jehu's reign (10:34-36), and leaves it before one encounters the typical introduction to the reign of Jehu's successor (12:1-4 [*RSV* 11:21–12:3]). Her story in important ways presupposes the final form of the Jehu traditions in chs. 9–10 (Hoffmann, 104).

Many critics see evidence in this material that at least two sources, now reflected in vv. 4-12 + 18b-20 and vv. 13-18a, were merged to make a composite document (e.g., see Gray, *Kings,* 566-67, resting largely on Stade; and Würthwein, *Könige,* 344; Hoffmann, 106-7, summarizes the history of critical research). Barré (pp. 7-56) posits a simpler picture — this text reflects an original narrative that took on minor editorial additions in two stages. Recently, Levin finely tuned this line of research and argued that an early narrative, still visible in vv. 1-2, 3b, 5-6, 8a, 12b, 13a, 14b, 16, 17b, 19b, 20a, underwent three successive redactions to arrive at its present canonical form.

As evidence for such hypotheses, critics often cite (1) the double mention of Athaliah's death (vv. 16, 20); (2) variant spellings of Athaliah's name (vv. 2, 20 [the long form] and vv. 13-14 [short form]); (3) the important roles given priests and military leaders (vv. 4-12, 18b-20) in contrast to the general populace (vv. 13-18a, esp. vv. 17-18); (4) the differing ideological perspectives — one is mostly official and political (vv. 4-12, 19-20), the other popular and theological (vv. 17-18a).

As Gray admits, and as Hoffmann argues (cf. Hobbs, *2 Kings*, 135-36), these literary features are neither wholly convincing nor consistent with divisions into sources (see Rudolph). Obviously, vv. 13-16, part of a reputed second source, depend entirely upon vv. 4-12 for their intelligibility and could hardly have stood alone. The mention of Athaliah's death in v. 20 seems less a second report than a summarizing statement of circumstances to conclude the narrative (Rudolph, 476). Variant spellings of Athaliah's name have no known significance, since both forms are interchangeable in vv. 1-4; Jehoiada the priest is fully in command of events in vv. 13-16, reputedly the more populist version of events; the introduction of "the people" in the scene at vv. 12, 13-14 may stem from the use of a stock scene wherein supportive "people" typically acclaim a new king (cf. 1 Kgs 1:38-40). Finally, the modern division between political (official) and religious (popular) perspectives seems contrary to the narrator's most basic assumption that a political coup has been initiated by a high priest and directed from the temple. Moreover, the writer's implicit justification for Jehoiada's action is both political and theological, since Athaliah is not of the house of David but belongs to the theologically suspect and discredited Omride family (cf. 11:1 and 8:26-27).

In the light of these considerations, it seems a reasonable alternative to treat this narrative as a formal and thematic unity (so also Cogan and Tadmor, *II Kings*, 132). Whatever its prior history may have been, the material is now presented with a clear structure and plot. Beginning the story with the massacre of royal princes, the narrator suggests a crisis and its partly successful avoidance as background for the main action (I, vv. 1-3). We must assume that, knowing of the successful rescue of a single prince, Jehoiada then sets out to insure that a Judean take his rightful place on the throne. The priest moves methodically. He builds a loyalist entourage around the young prince — Jehoiada presents him to potential supporters as the "son of the king," v. 4b; he orchestrates a coronation; and he summarily orders Athaliah's execution (II.A, B, vv. 4-16). Having rid the kingdom of this "daughter of Omri" (8:26), Jehoiada quickly purges it of Omride-like Baalism as well (II.C.1, vv. 17-18). Finally, in an act reminiscent of triumphal procession (cf. 1 Kgs 1:38-40; 2 Sam 6:15; 1 Kgs 8:1-13), the newly crowned king takes his seat in the Davidide palace (II.C.2, v. 19). The closing sections (vv. 19 and 20) in fact draw together all major actors and events into a final statement of equilibrium: the sounds of popular rejoicing fade to city-quiet. In the very same place where Athaliah was slain sits the Judean monarch, his kingdom at rest and sanctioned by God's priestly representative (III, v. 20).

In all this action, we are urged implicitly to support Jehoiada as he restores legitimate kingship and exclusive Yahwistic religion. Like the DtrH, Jehoiada seems to carry the model of David in his mind (cf. 1 Kgs 2:3-4; 11:38; 2 Kgs 18:3; 22:2). The writer catches these twin aspects of political and theological restoration in a metaphor of space: a fouled and profaned Judah/Jerusalem/royal palace is reclaimed for Davidide Yahwism as priest and temple come to dominate events and kingdom.

Section I (vv. 1-3) begins and ends with formally parallel nominal clauses that situate Athaliah as a powerful character and contribute important information about her. She enters onstage as the "mother of Ahaziah" and strides off, objectives accomplished, "ruling over the land" (vv. 1aα and 3bβ). (The *RSV* does not adequately convey the durative aspect to *mōleket* in v. 3b.) Tucked inside this line of action is another sequence that depicts successful opposition to her designs. On realizing that King Ahaziah is dead (for the reader, this is a flashback to 8:27-28), Athaliah "began to destroy all the royal family" (reading the conjoined verbs, "she arose and destroyed," as incipient action, v. 1b). Meanwhile, Jehosheba, a sister to Ahaziah and daughter of King Joram (who also is dead, 8:24), interposes herself between Athaliah's massacre-in-progress and Joash, a young son of Ahaziah, and succeeds in protecting him from Athaliah's grasp (v. 2). In the end, the writer depicts an ongoing state of tense equilibrium. The young prince Joash is continually hidden away during six years, while Athaliah rules over the kingdom (*hāyâ* + participle *mithabbē'* yields this durative sense, v. 3a). Implicit are two value-laden images of space that will be mapped against each other as the narration progresses. Within the temple's bounds, the scion of David survives; outside these protective courts, in the palace, Athaliah presides over Judah.

With brilliantly economic prose, the writer provides a scene of coup d'état and countercoup. In structure and plot this first episode, vv. 1-3, is a diminutive version of the whole narrative, whose grand political sweep is here reduced to a more immediate human scale. The matter, of course, has to do with a ruthless reach for the throne by a person of apostate origins (Athaliah is queen mother to Ahaziah and a [grand]daughter of the much maligned Omride house [see 8:26-27]). Such a reference provides a hint of color to the scene, just enough to move the reader's sympathies toward the writer's Yahwistic loyalties. The brighter shade simply depicts two women thrown into conflict. One gives in to ambition and denies the biological urge to nurture the young; the other surrenders to the opposite — Jehosheba selflessly offers protection to the child, in fact her nephew, whom the writer takes to be a helpless infant (see v. 4 and 12:1 [*RSV* 11:21]).

In the seventh year of this status quo, Jehoiada sets in motion a plan to deny Athaliah her victory (II, vv. 4-19). In private, then public, stages Jehoiada takes command and acts entirely from within the boundaries of holy space. He brings guards into the temple of Yahweh and builds a loyalist cadre by means of an oath (the word "covenant" in v. 4 seems to mean something like a sworn agreement [to secrecy or loyalty?] rather than the religio-political idea of v. 17). Then he ceremoniously presents "the king's son" to them. (In this designation, here and in v. 12 the writer acknowledges his own sympathies; Jehoiada himself will voice the same view in v. 8, "Be with the king"; cf. 1 Sam 10:24.)

The high priest immediately orders a protective shield of men placed around the king, just as the temple itself has sheltered him for six years from Athaliah's murderous ambition. The direct correspondence between the order (vv. 5b-8) and its execution (vv. 9-11) is typical of biblical narrative and mightily reinforces our sense of Jehoiada's dominance. However, clarity on the details of his instructions eludes us. If one assumes that the giving of orders and their execution are ordinarily reported consistently with each other, then the text appears to reflect a contradiction, for vv. 5-8 suggest a split guard — one at the temple, one at the palace (cf. *RSV* vv. 5-6 with v. 7) — while vv. 9-11 report that all the guardsmen took up duty inside the temple around Prince Joash. Moreover, a few textual corruptions may have crept into the MSS, and the word at the end of v. 6, *massāh*, is unintelligible. Some critics remove most of the inconsistency by dropping v. 6; others resort to various textual emendations and reordering. Some amount of reconstruction is inescapable.

Jehoiada's instructions take the following syntactical form:

A Recipient of order: designation and descriptive appositional phrase
B Order: simple *wāw* + *qtl* (perfect) verb clause

Verses 5b-6, without any emendations, follow this form exactly:

A One third of you, those who come on duty on the sabbath and [who] stand guard [in] the house of Yahweh — now the third in the Gate of Sur, and a third in the gate behind the palace guards —
B you shall stand guard [*ûšĕmartem 'et-mišmeret*] [in/over] the house *massāh* [on every side? *NJPS*] (vv. 5b-6).

The formal pattern repeats in v. 7:

A and two divisions of you, all those who go off duty on the sabbath,
B they shall stand guard [*wĕšāmĕrû 'et-mišmeret*] [in] the house of Yahweh for [to, on behalf of] the king (v. 7).

A third command follows, this time presumably intended for all those guardsmen previously mentioned:

And you shall surround the king, each man with his weapons in his hand; and whoever approaches the ranks is to be slain. Be with the king in his coming and going (v. 8).

Some obscurities and awkwardness remain, of course. And the term *massāh* we have left untranslated. (See full discussion of the various suggestions, which have not been improved upon since 1951, in Montgomery, *Kings*, 424; Cogan and Tadmor, *II Kings*, 127, drop *msh* as a copyist's error.) If one assumes simply that *habbayit massāh* in v. 6 refers in some way not to the royal palace, as most translators have it, but to the temple (*bêt-yahweh;* cf. vv. 4, 7b and *NJPS*), then a fairly intelligible picture emerges. Jehoiada assembles two groups of guardsmen — those who go off duty on the sabbath (or perhaps "weekly") and those who come on duty at that same time — and orders them all to take up duty stations in or near the temple. In short, he constructs a protective ring around the temple and the prince at the changing of the guard (cf. v. 11). The language is priestly and encompassing, as though the men take up their watch around a holy object to have charge of it and to protect it at all times from profanation (cf. Num 1:53; 3:38; 4:32). The guards who "come" and "go" *(bô' and yāṣā')* are to be with Joash as he "comes and goes" *(bĕṣē' tô ûbĕbō' ô)*. From within the sacred space of the "house of Yahweh," they are to mirror completely the comprehensive possibilities of privileged royal movement and rule (cf. 1 Sam 18:16; 1 Kgs 3:7; 2 Chr 1:10; Jer 17:19; 37:4; for a different elucidation of the passage, see Montgomery, *Kings*, 419, followed by Cogan and Tadmor, *II Kings*, 127).

Indeed, their duty is so charged with the emotions of sacrality and dynasty that upon reporting for duty to Jehoiada, the guardsmen receive certain public symbols of David's Yahweh-blessed rule, the "spears and quivers . . . which were kept in the temple" (on the implements, cf. 1 Kgs 14:26; 1 Sam 21:10 [*RSV* 9]; 2 Sam 8:7; Cogan and Tadmor, *II Kings*, 128). Thereupon the guards take up their stations — again the language is all-encompassing — every man, weapon at the ready, "from the south side of the temple to the north side of the temple, at the altar and the temple, for the king's sake all around" (v. 11; cf. *NJPS;* the *RSV* needlessly drops reference to the king).

Not only does the writer accord to Jehoiada the commanding presence in these scenes, but he defines the temple as the dominant space within which the really significant actions gain their authority and power. The priest orders the guards — he converts them, as though by specially vested powers, into a kind of Levitical circle around the sacral center (v. 11; cf. Num 1:53); he provides a protective barrier between king and potential assailant (v. 8), or between holy and profane, such that whoever shall infringe upon the sacred sphere faces death (cf. Exod 19:12). He sets the ring of guards around the temple, and moving inward, it seems, around the altar itself (v. 11b), thereby converts the secret refuge (v. 3a) into a public, royal, and sacralized sanctuary (cf. 1 Kgs 1:50-51). Of course, as we shall see, these actions amount to preparing for a coup d'état. But they also assemble the forces of sacrality to distinguish on some ideological map the legitimate from the illegitimate. Bulking large over this narrative and conceptual landscape, the temple and its sanctified priest mark out the inviolate zone of energy from which politico-religious action will gain the authority and power of ultimacy. Joash's claim to the throne carries a priestly, God-sanctioned, temple-blessed authority with the added weight of Davidide tradition behind it.

Within this shield of protection, and still physically within the temple bounds, Joash receives the investitures of office (v. 12). What has been a private conspiracy now becomes public through the tumultuous acclamations reverberating around the young king. Jehoiada's (and the writer's) earlier designation of Joash as "king" and "son of the king" is now ratified as the loyalists transform their secret oaths into public, committed action. Inevitably, the conspirators' actions challenge Athaliah and imply that she had been granted neither authority nor legitimacy when she took the throne. The palace wherein she rules sits outside the bounds of temple, beyond sacral space, and thus is without ultimate political authority. Even the guardians of the royal residence have apparently been secretly reassigned, inducted into the holiness of Jehoiada's band (v. 5b).

That same holiness will now demand its purgative, as the next scene shows (II.B.2, vv. 13-16). The writer shifts our vantage point: Athaliah hears the commotion, goes to the temple, and — now the narrator draws us into her point of view — observes the coronation in progress (v. 14). The idiomatic phrase, "she looked, and behold . . . ," followed by a string of participles in the Hebrew, lends vivid intensity to the scene. We (and Athaliah) observe the king (the writer's designation, not Athaliah's) "standing by the pillar according to the custom . . . rejoicing and blowing trumpets." (*kammišpāṭ*, "according to custom," carries the writer's suggestion of established habit, if not legality, or perhaps simply allusion to Davidide tradition, that hovers over the scene, 1 Kgs 1:38-40.)

Indeed, the formal solemnity and special vocabulary used for the occasion hint at the traditional association of royal and priestly authority which invests state occasions with transcendent authority. For the investiture of Solomon, see 1 Kgs 1:39-40; for Aaron's investiture, see Exod 29:5-8; Lev 8:6-12. If the exact meaning of the phrase rendered by the *RSV* as "[he] put the crown upon him, and gave him the testimony" is uncertain, its royal/priestly associations are not. The MT translates more exactly, "and he [Jehoiada] set the *nēzer* and the *'ēdût* upon him" (*NJPS* "placed upon him the crown and the insignia"). Ps 132:12 associates *'ēdût* with *běrît* ("covenant") as something that can be taught and kept, like *tôrâ*, though the word is not used (cf. Gen 17:9-10). In the case of Joash, the *'ēdût* seems to be a royal insignia, perhaps "jewels" (Cogan and Tadmor, *II Kings*, 128) or a medallion inscribed with official protocol or "testimony" of some kind (G. von Rad, 225-29; Falk). Ps 89:40 (*RSV* 39) reads, "You [God] have renounced the *běrît* of your servant, you have utterly desecrated his *nēzer*." The Aaronide passages suggest that *nēzer haqqōdeš* (*NJPS* "holy diadem") is positioned on top of the priest's official headdress (Exod 29:6), which is explained in Lev 8:9 as a golden shiny thing *(sîṣ hazzāhāb)*. So Joash is invested with the badges of office (cf. Ps 132:18), a diadem and royal insignia, both heavy with symbolism of regnal authority, covenant with God, and priestly *tôrâ*. He begins his rule clothed in garments of divinely ordained legitimacy (see further details in Widengren).

Naturally, Athaliah views the proceedings as seditious, but she discovers what we already know, that her power has flowed to others. Jehoiada, not the queen mother, commands, and the temple dominates narrative space. The priest orders the "captains in charge of the army" (are these separate from the temple guard set up in vv. 5-7?) to remove Athaliah from the temple and to fend off any rescue attempts (v. 15a). The command is an indirect order for Athaliah's execution, as the writer's explanation in v. 15b shows, for the priest had said (or "thought" — the verb *'āmar* allows both translations): "Let her not be slain in the house of the Lord." Jehoiada thus continues to enforce the ritual separation between sacred (temple, priest, Joash, Davidide house) and profane (criminal execution, Athaliah, the granddaughter to Omri, Baal worshiper). There is something entirely fitting, therefore, in the fact that the queen mother dies in the "king's house," not in "Yahweh's house" (v. 16). The royal palace is one bit of space which lies as yet beyond the reach of a priest and his powers of ordering the world into sacred and profane.

Jehoiada's coup d'état would seem to be complete with the death of Athaliah. However, the consummation of the conspiracy against the queen mother actually comes only when Joash triumphantly reclaims the royal palace as his own, thus altering its status from illegitimate to legitimate seat of royal authority (II.C, vv. 17-19). Again, priestly ideology seems to be the key to our understanding. As though to rid the land and kingdom of Athaliah's unholy influences, Jehoiada presides over a ceremony of covenant making, followed by a general purge of Baalism and its temple from the kingdom. The scene anticipates a similar sequence of action that will mark Josiah's reign (23:1-24), and it recalls Jehu's destruction of Baal worshipers (10:18-27). However, covenant making and religious reform are rooted in the logic of the Athaliah narrative itself. By these acts, Jehoiada extends the reach of the temple's sacred power carefully placed around the young king. Protective holiness, that priestly way of ordering reality into categories of sacred and profane, will now achieve its furthest limit, the entire kingdom, and overcome its virulent opponent, the spiritual force of Baalism.

Jehoiada begins by making a covenant (v. 17; for a summary of current discussion, see Cogan and Tadmor, *II Kings*, 132-33). The narrator has finely honed the details. It is *"the* covenant." Perhaps the writer has in mind a covenant regularly affirmed on state occasions and conceived of as the theological foundation for the Judean kingdom, a multifaceted set of obligations with the objective "that [they] should be the people of the Lord." First, Jehoiada renews the bonds between Yahweh and the Davidic dynasty (see discussion above for *'ēdût,* "testimony"; see Gray, *Kings,* 573-74; Widengren; for God's promissory covenant with David in the Dtr history, see 2 Sam 7:11-16; 23:5-7; 1 Kgs 8:15-16, 25-26; 11:36-38). Second, Jehoiada's covenant alludes to the notion of *tôrâ*-centered relationship with Yahweh as given in the Mosaic traditions, and through which the people become a "people of God." See especially the Dtr formulation: "Keep silence and hear, O Israel: this day you have become the people of the Lord your God. You shall therefore obey the voice of the Lord your God, keeping his commandments and his statutes, which I command you this day" (Deut 27:1-10; cf. Exodus 19–20). Third, Jehoiada mediates a covenant "between the king and the people" (the phrase is absent from 2 Chr 23:16), which possibly alludes to mutual obligations assumed by a king and his supporters in order to achieve some political stability for the monarchy (cf. 2 Sam 5:3; 1 Kings 12). The narrator gives little if any sociopolitical information about this "people of the land" who are party to events (vv. 14, 18, 19, 20; for a convenient summary of the historical question, see B. Oded, "Judah and the Exile," in *Israelite and Judaean History* [ed. J. H. Hayes and J. M. Miller; OTL; Philadelphia: Westminster, 1977] 435-88, esp. 456-58; an update in Cogan and Tadmor, *II Kings,* 129-30). Rather, in literary terms, the phrase suggests the comprehensiveness of support for Joash, to whom both God and people who constitute theologically defined Israel are attached.

These three aspects of Jehoiada's covenant — mutual obligations between God and Davidic king, between God and people, and between people and king — all seem in the narrator's view to constitute a theocratic entity, a "people of the Lord," which Jehoiada reclaims for Judah. (We note a certain irony in reading this within the larger narrative. In reclaiming this theocratic definition for Judah, Jehoiada in effect supplants a similar designation which the prophet had given to the northern kingdom as the reconstituted Israel of God by Jehu's coup d'état, 2 Kgs 9:6.)

Having made new commitments to this theologically expressed identity, the people rush to the "house of Baal," tear it down, destroy its altars and statuary, and murder the officiating priest. Then Jehoiada sets guards "over the house of Yahweh" (v. 18). The writer implies that the last vestige of Athaliah's influence, her Baalistic tendencies arising from kinship to the house of Omri, are at last cleared away. Is the temple to Baal assumed to be inside the Yahwistic Jerusalem temple? Or in the royal palace? Or somewhere outside these precincts of monarchical power, or even in the countryside? (See Y. Yadin, "The 'House of Ba'al' of Ahab and Jezebel in Samaria, and That of Athalia in Judah," in *Archaeology in the Levant. Essays for Kathleen Kenyon* [ed. R. Moorey and P. Parr; Warminster: Aris & Phillips, 1978] 127-35.) In any case, the symbolic point seems to be that the priest's reshaping the geography of holiness reaches its completion in a violent purge of Baalism. The temple in Jerusalem is now ringed with guards and the alien element removed, banished forever from the garden. And Judah is purified, ritually prepared, to receive her newly consecrated monarch.

There remains only for Joash to assume his place on David's throne after a triumphal procession to the palace. The writer parades across our field of vision all the major characters from previous action: the "captains" (*śārê hummē'ôt*, lit., "captains of hundreds," cf. vv. 4, 9, 10), the Carites (cf. v. 4), the "guards" (*rāṣîm*, vv. 4, 6, 11), and the "people of the land" (vv. 14, 18a). All these loyalists usher Joash into the royal palace ("house of the king") where he takes his seat — the language becomes majestic here — "on the throne of the kings" (cf. 1 Kgs 1:46, "throne of the kingdom"). Ascension is an apt figure: we meet Joash first as an infant hidden away inside the temple; he then rises to the status of youthful king whom the priest protects from harm and unholy influence (cf. 12:3 [*RSV* 2]); finally Joash takes possession of palace and throne, both of which, like those ceremonial spears and shields (v. 10), are redolent of David. As Jehoiada surrounded the king with protection, and temple sacrality spread outward to purge the kingdom of its Baalism, so now the new and always legitimate king takes up the garments of the Yahweh-blessed Davidic dynasty. The writer's concluding note, v. 20, suggests a relieved finality to the ascent of Joash. The people rejoice, the city grows quiet as in rest after turmoil (Halpern, 41), and Athaliah is dead, slain in the very same place that now, ironically, represents the completed induction of Joash into Davidic blessing.

Genre

This unit is a HISTORICAL STORY, a narrative that recounts events of the past largely according to the norms of ordinary human experience, although often using apologetic and fictional elements that run contrary to a modern sense of objectivity. (For this reason Barré, 51-52, prefers the term "political novella." See discussion at 2 Kgs 8:28–9:28.) The propagandistic flavor to the story is evident in many other biblical narratives (cf. 1 Kgs 1:1-53; 12:1-20; 2 Kgs 8:28–9:28) as well as in other ancient Near Eastern texts.

An inscription carved on a statue of Idrimi of Alalakh (Syria, 15th century B.C.E.) tells the story of Idrimi's youth, rise to the throne, and regnal achievements (*ANET,* 557-58). On the basis of this text and a few others somewhat similar in style and form, Liverani defines a distinct literary genre, "political propaganda story," includes the Joash narrative among the examples, and even speculates that the biblical account derives from a statue dedicated to Joash. The argument is strained and flawed by a rather loose analysis of literary form (see discussion by Hobbs, *2 Kings,* 156-58). Hardly more may be claimed than the existence of a few motival similarities between the biblical story and Idrimi's inscription, and this only with the reservation that the Akkadian text remains problematic in very basic ways, and may not yet be correctly restored and translated.

Setting

The setting for historical story would probably have been among scribes employed by royal courts or religious institutions. Accordingly, Barré (pp. 88-90) attributes this particular example in its original form to scribes who wrote this apology for Jehoiada's coup during the reign of Joash. However, there is really no evidence for the claim, and one cannot exclude the possibility that some examples of historical story may have originated with, and been preserved by, less literate storytellers in ancient Israel.

Lacking firm evidence, it is prudent to give fullest attention to the literary setting of this particular narrative. The Dtr writer has placed it between the more typically ordered regnal materials of Jehu and Joash (chs. 9–10 and 12), after the death of Jehu and before the reign of Joash. Unlike the stories which record the rise of Solomon and Jeroboam I (1 Kgs 1:1-53; 12:1-20), the account of Joash's coronation does not supplant his introductory summary. Moreover, the narrative presupposes the events of Jehu's reformation, and even transports us back in time to the point at which Jehu murders Ahaziah. These structural cues effectively urge a reader to glance back into the reign of Jehu, rather than forward into that of Joash. Thematic links between Jehu's coup d'état in the north and Jehoiada's overthrow of Athaliah in the south are thereby given somewhat more significance than links with the official regnal periods of Joash (ch. 12) or later kings (see Barré).

Indeed, the story presupposes the murderous work of Jehu, and demands that it be read in close proximity, even parallel, to the narrative of Jehu's rise to the throne in the north (see Hoffmann, 104-6). Both are narratives about political revolution that culminate in the murder of the reigning monarch; both connect a purge of Baal from the body politic with placing the legitimate king on the throne; both Jehu and Athaliah try to exterminate all members of the royal family who have an immediate claim to the kingship (10:12-14; 11:1). Of course, the story of Joash's rise also introduces him and his high priest mentor to us, and thereby prepares us in part for the Dtr writer's evaluation of this king and his accomplishments (12:3, 5-17 [*RSV* 2, 4-16]). We shall also notice an important anticipation of Josiah's reign of covenant making and reform (chs. 22–23). In sum, we must view the story of Joash's rise and Athaliah's fall as a kind of pivotal piece in the larger Dtr history.

Intention

One basic intention of the writer is to represent Joash's accession to the throne as fully legitimated by priestly authority, even as Jehu's coup d'état against Jehoram had been sanctioned by prophetic oracle and divine choice. Barré's thesis (pp. 97-98), that in some original form of the narrative Jehu was compared unfavorably to Jehoiada in the interest of claiming the latter's heroic and righteous loyalty to the Davidic house, is somewhat strained and unconvincing. In any case, as now assembled by the Dtr writer, both conspiracies are presented as fully approved by God. In Jehu, Yahweh finds a zealot patterned somewhat after Elijah to cut off the apostate Omride line and ruthlessly annihilate offensive worship of Baal (see discussion above, chs. 8–10). In the case of Joash, God's implicit approval is carried in a geographical metaphor. Jehoiada extends sacral space, priestly authority, from temple to Joash and then to the royal palace — all while presiding over a massive purge of Baal worship from the entire kingdom. (Cf. a similar metaphor for the temple's influence in Ezekiel 47, the spread of life-giving waters from inside the temple to the Arabah desert.)

Conversely, the narrative delegitimates Athaliah, like Jehoram in the north, because each is related to the Omride dynasty (cf. 8:18, 26-27). It is a question of the foreigner and foreign influence, particularly in religious practice, that dominates the writer's concerns. In this sense, the Dtr writer pursues the theme of outright war between the forces of Yahweh and Baal, so much a part of his recounting the monarchical story of the northern kingdom, into Judah. The disease enters the body politic through marriage (8:18, 26-27; Solomon, too, is faulted by this same measure, 1 Kgs 11:1-5); it will persist in Judah, even beyond the demise of the north (2 Kings 17), and reach its terrifying result in Manasseh's reign (21:2-3). It is probably no accident, then, that the reformative actions of Jehoiada (and of Joash's revision of temple procedures under the priest's "instruction," 12:5-17 [RSV 4-16]) anticipate in important ways the actions of Josiah. For we will learn that Josiah also struggles against these same errant ways of apostasy, and seeks without success to reverse the power of the Omrides (alluded to variously by mentioning Omri, Ahab, or the kings of Israel), which has worked itself into Judah. The Dtr writer, from his vantage point in exile, begins with Ahaziah/Jehu/Joash/Athaliah to build his narrative explanation for Judah's ultimate demise.

Bibliography

L. Barré, *Political Persuasion* (→ 2 Kgs 8:28– 9:28); Z. W. Falk, "Forms of Testimony," *VT* 11 (1961) 88-91; B. Halpern, "Sacred History and Ideology: Chronicles' Thematic Structure — Indications of an Earlier Source," in *The Creation of Sacred Literature* (ed. R. E. Friedman; Near Eastern Studies 22; Berkeley: University of California, 1981) 35-54; H.-D. Hoffmann, *Reform*, 104-13 (→ 2 Kgs 3:1-3); C. Levin, *Der Sturz der Königin Atalja: Ein Kapitel zur Geschichte Judas im 9. Jahrhundert v. Chr.* (SBS 105; Stuttgart: Katholisches Bibelwerk, 1982); M. Liverani, "L'Histoire de Joas," *VT* 24 (1974) 438-53; G. Robinson, "Is 2 Kings XI 6 a Gloss?" *VT* 27 (1977) 56-61; W. Rudolph, "Die

Einheitlichkeit der Erzählung vom Sturz der Atalja (2 Kön 11)," in *Festschrift Bertholet* (ed. W. Baumgartner, et al.; Tübingen: Mohr, 1950) 473-78; B. Stade, "Anmerkungen zu 2 Kö. 10-14," *ZAW* 5 (1885) 275-97, esp. 280-88; J. Trebolle Barrera, "La coronación de Joás (2 Re 11). Texto, narración e historia," *EstBib* 41 (1983) 5-16; idem, "Glosas en 2 Re 11,6-10. De la crítica textual a la crítica literaria e histórica," *EstBib* 41 (1983) 375-80; T. Veijola, " 'Jäljestäpäin lisätty laki.' Crux Interpretum 2 Kun 11:12 ("Das hinzugefügte Gesetz." Crux interpretum 2 Kön 11,12)," *TAik* 84/2 (1979) 91-104; G. von Rad, "The Royal Ritual in Judah," in *The Problem of the Hexateuch and Other Essays* (tr. E. W. Trueman Dicken; New York: McGraw-Hill, 1966) 222-31; G. Widengren, "King and Covenant," *JSS* 2 (1957) 1-32.

THE REIGN OF J(EH)OASH, 12:1-22 (*RSV* 11:21-12:21)

Text

In v. 5 (*RSV* 4) the meaning of the phrase "the money for which each man is assessed . . . assessment of persons" is uncertain. *RSV* "is assessed" evidently presupposes the LXX[BL] reading of ʿ*erek* for MT ʿ*ôbēr* in the phrase *kesep* ʿ*ôbēr* ʾ*îš*. Many critics accept the Greek rendering as the better text (e.g., Šanda, *Könige* II, 139; Gray, *Kings,* 584). On the basis of Gen 23:16, ʿ*ōbēr lassōḥēr,* "at the current merchant's price," however, the MT can stand, but not trouble free, as referring to current rates of value exchange or taxation (Burney, *Notes,* 313). Hobbs (*2 Kings,* 146) offers a plausible "the money reckoned against each person currently" (cf. *NJPS*). Cogan and Tadmor (*II Kings,* 137) take the expression to be priestly shorthand for an entrance levy, "silver for entering, per person." Hurowitz (p. 290, n. 3) draws upon Akkadian mercantile expressions to suggest "silver which travels [overland to merchants]."

 In v. 6 (*RSV* 5) *makkār* is unknown (see Cogan and Tadmor, *II Kings,* 137). *RSV* "from his acquaintance" (also in v. 8 [*RSV* 7]) accepts the MT pointing of *makkārô* (from √*nkr*), which in late Hebrew came to mean "acquaintance"; despite a long tradition of acceptance, this translation ill fits the context. LXX[B] read √*mkr* ("sell"), hence, "from his trade"; accepting this, Hobbs (*2 Kings,* 147) proposes "from his income." However, this runs into difficulties at v. 8, *mēʾēt makkārêkem,* which Hobbs translates as "from your incomes," because the preposition *mēʾēt* is not normally associated with inanimate objects (see BDB, 86). From Ugarit, *mkrm* appears in lists of various occupations, sometimes with temple officials such as *khnm* (priests) and *qdšm* (dedicated ones). See *Ras Shamra Parallels* II (Rome: Pontifical Biblical Institute, 1975) § ii:23. Rather than "acquaintance," we perhaps should think of a functionary who receives and values offerings given to the priests (see E. Lipiński, "*mkr,*" *TWAT* IV, 869-75, esp. 873-74; Robinson, *2 Kings,* 117; Gray, *Kings,* 586; Fricke, *2 Könige,* 160).

Structure

Stereotypical opening and concluding summaries distinguish this unit from its immediate context as a typically composed regnal epoch. Within these outer frames, the writer addresses two main subjects: the royal plan (and pious deed) for financing temple repairs (II.A, vv. 5-17), and J(eh)oash's success at removing Hazael's threat to Jerusalem (II.B, vv. 18-19).

Most critics see little evidence of redactional history in this material prior to the DtrH's work in representing the reign of Joash (e.g., Gray, *Kings,* 582-83; Šanda, *Könige* II, 148-49). It is possible that the DtrH drew vv. 5-17 and 18-19 from different sources (their character and provenance is disputed) and connected them by means of the vague "then" (*'āz; RSV* "at that time"). From similar records, the Dtr writer may have inserted the notice of conspiracy into the concluding summary, vv. 21-22a. Würthwein (*Könige,* 354) supposes only parts of vv. 18-19 rest on pre-Dtr materials; for him vv. 5-13 are post-Dtr additions, and to this a still later redactor added vv. 14-17 (so, similarly, Rendtorff, 54). However, as Hoffmann (*Reform,* 120-21) notes, not all explanatory, appendixlike statements, such as vv. 14-17, necessarily imply a second editorial hand. It seems adequate to assume that a Dtr writer assembled the present chapter from existing sources to create a unified impression of Joash's reign. There are no compelling reasons to suspect literary disunity within the major blocks of material, vv. 5-17 and 18-19.

The report concerning a system to finance repairs to the temple (II.A, vv. 5-17) emphasizes royal initiative, in contrast to the failure or negligence of the priests. The driving actions are direct orders from the king, vv. 5-6, 8, who exercises unquestioned authority over the temple and its priesthood. In the end, the narrator creates an image of King Jehoash as patron of the state's official deity and temple in the mold of Solomon and royal counterparts in other ancient Near Eastern kingdoms. It will be a role that Josiah will continue, 22:3-7. (See A. L. Oppenheim, *Ancient Mesopotamia* [Chicago: University of Chicago, 1964] 106-9.)

In an uncomplicated narrative sequence, the writer presents Joash's definitive decree at the center of the account (v. 8) and against the background of an earlier plan which failed (vv. 5-7; cf. the structural outline by Hoffmann, 119-20, who fails to capture adequately the narrative sequentiality). The reasons for failure are left ambiguous. Does the king's rhetorical question at v. 8bα imply an accusation or at least mild reprimand of the priests? And if so, what exactly is their offense, other than failing to carry out the responsibility laid upon them to repair the temple? In any event, the narrative runs rapidly toward specifying a revised procedure. Jehoash relieves the priests of their responsibilities (v. 8b) and the writer asserts that the priests agreed to this diminishment, without telling us what the new plan entails (v. 9).

Jehoiada, in command of events at the behest of the king, seems to know, however. He sets about immediately to prepare a "chest." Gradually, we learn that the priests who guard the "threshold," probably gatekeepers (cf. 22:4; 25:19; Jer 29:25), collect valuables as they are brought into the temple and deposit them in this special coffer (the word '*ărôn*, "chest," is the same as the "box" that holds the tables of *tôrâ*, 1 Kgs 8:5-6). A royal secretary and the high priest (is Jehoiada in mind?) together share responsibility for weighing out the silver (*RSV* "money" should not imply for us "coins") and paying for repairs, possibly after smelting the metal (vv. 11-13; on smelting works in the temple, see Montgomery, *Kings*, 430). The writer's language is emphatic in its comprehensiveness. All the artisans — carpenters and builders, masons and stonecutters — are to be paid from these collections; supplies should be purchased for "making repairs on the temple," and, moreover, the very same collections are to be used "for all expenditures necessary to repair the temple" (v. 13).

In line with a similar fiscal procedure in Assyria (Hurowitz; Oppenheim, "Fiscal Practice"), the Jerusalemite priests collect "silver" at the temple gates but now have only limited authority over the funds and expenditures. The king's representative, as indeed the new system's exclusive basis in the king's decree, provides royal sanction for shared responsibility, but fundamentally for royal control.

Almost imperceptibly, in vv. 11-12 the writer weakens the sense of consecutive sequence that governs vv. 5-10 so as to describe the continual workings of this new procedure. Although the Hebrew shows no particular linguistic markers for this change, the *RSV* (vv. 10-11; MT 11-12) and most translators catch the nuance. It is the case that "whenever" the coffer was full, the royal secretary and high priest "would" disburse the silver, i.e., regularly and systematically as a matter of ongoing procedure.

The explanatory remarks, vv. 14-17, continue this iterative mode of speech, as though now the narrator were addressing the reader and specifying with priestly thoroughness certain limits and qualifications to the system. Cultic implements are not made from this silver (v. 14; the list is probably stereotypical; cf. 1 Kgs 7:50; 2 Kgs 25:14-15); rather (MT *kî* at v. 15) this wealth is given directly to the supervisors of workmen, and no accounting is asked of them because they "dealt honestly." (Since the entire passage is imbued with the concerns and language of priests, it seems unlikely that the writer now implies an invidious contrast between the workers' honesty and the priests' dishonesty [against Hobbs, *2 Kings*, 155; cf. esp. the excessively anticlerical reading by Montgomery, *Kings*, 428].) Finally, we learn that Joash's new procedure does not endanger the livelihood of the priests; the "guilt offerings" and the "sin offerings," which belong to the priests, are excluded from the silver dedicated for repairs to the temple.

In sum, Jehoash establishes a method of ensuring ongoing repairs under the joint authority of crown and priesthood. The system works because it is agreed to by the priests, whose livelihood is protected, and because the workmen deal honestly. Moreover, money for repairs does not interfere with the temple's priceless cultic vessels, which are apparently of special interest to the DtrH (cf. 1 Kgs 7:50, where they are first fashioned; 2 Kgs 25:14-15, where Nebuchadnezzar takes them as booty). The writer thinks of Joash as a good and pious king, not only instructed by Jehoiada (v. 3; cf. ch. 11) but attentive to the needs of the priests and supportive of Judah's Yahwistic religion.

Nevertheless, by immediately associating this praiseworthy king with payoffs to stave off a military threat (II.B, vv. 18-19), the DtrH suggests a qualification to Jehoash's high marks. This little unit of tradition shows only the vaguest link to vv. 5-17 (the editorial connector '*āz*, "then," is not a precise temporal marker, and does not allow us to infer [against Rabinowitz, 62] that money allocated for repair of the temple is paid to Hazael before any work is undertaken). In simple reportorial style with normal *wyqtl* sequence, we are told that Hazael, last encountered at 10:32, invades the coastal plain of Judah (Gath) and turns with determination ("set his face"; cf. Gen 31:21; Jer 42:15, 17; Dan 11:17) toward Jerusalem. Joash responds to this threat with payments from the royal treasuries that induce Hazael to withdraw.

The price for peace is high, and it is stated in comprehensive fashion. Joash depleted the treasuries of "*all* the sacred objects [*haqqŏdāšîm*]" which he and his ancestors had dedicated to Yahweh, and "*all* the gold" to be found in both the temple and the royal palace. Yet the cost may not be simply reckoned in monetary terms, since these valuables are the outward signs of a king's status among kings, his prosperity, and his attentiveness to the state religion. The treasure is a kind of holy estate given to the cult and to God by the royal family.

The Dtr writer keeps the accounts for us, or at least systematically includes in his story of monarchy those sources that do so. We are told that Solomon deposited David's votive objects in the temple (1 Kgs 7:51), and that Rehoboam his son lost them to Shishak (1 Kgs 14:26). Asa built the treasuries up again, bringing his and his father's "dedicated things, silver and gold, and vessels" into the house of Yahweh (1 Kgs 15:15). Shortly thereafter Asa came under military threat and had to deplete the storehouses of their "silver and gold" (1 Kgs 15:18). Now, some four generations later, Jehoash pays out the votive objects and the gold that had presumably been deposited by each of his ancestors since Asa, specifically the dedicated objects of Jehoshaphat, Jehoram, and Ahaziah (v. 19a). Later we will learn about the loss of treasure under Ahaz (2 Kgs 16:8) and Hezekiah (18:15; cf. 20:13), and finally, the catastrophic pillage by Nebuchadnezzar (24:13; 25:13-17).

Read in this broader context, it is no light thing that Joash is pressed to such an extent that he takes everything from the store of holy objects. It is not a question of strict fiscal accounting, for monetary values are never mentioned and each of the various notices creates the impression of a near total depletion of the treasury. Rather, these riches are conventional signs of a king's piety and of his kingdom's favor with God. Despite Jehoash's provision for regular repairs to the temple, a grave question mark hangs over his reign. Just as the Dtr writer qualifies the king's uprightness by noting the continuing religious activity at non-Jerusalemite "high places" (12:3-4), so the approbation due him because of his care for the temple's maintenance seems muted by this report of payment to Hazael.

Genre

Like all materials that cover a particular reign in the books of Kings, this unit is an editorial composition whose genre may not be specified with precision. We may define smaller generic units with more success. The outer frame consists of the typical introductory and concluding REGNAL RESUMÉ (see discussion at 1 Kings 14:21-31, in Long, *1 Kings,* 158-64). The introductory summary reverses the typical order of two of its elements, the (→) synchronistic accession formula and the (→) accession age formula. Perhaps the reason is to effect a smoother transition from ch. 11, which tells of how a young prince finally comes to sit on the throne. The concluding resumé carries within it a NOTICE of conspiracy against the king (vv. 21-22a) in a place fairly often reserved for isolated particulars relevant to a monarch (cf. 1 Kgs 15:23; 22:47-50 [*RSV* 46-49]; 2 Kgs 23:29-30a). On notices and reports of throne conspiracy, cf. 1 Kgs 15:27-30; 16:9-13; 2 Kgs 15:10, 14, 25, 30; 21:23. See fuller discussion in Long, *1 Kings,* 168-69.

Most of the material in the reign of Jehoash is an ACCOUNT of the king's attention to temple repairs (vv. 5-17); a brief REPORT tells of a foreign military threat to Jerusalem (vv. 18-19). The latter draws upon a stock scene of diplomatic exchange that has its parallels in the Bible (e.g., 1 Kgs 15:18-19 [see Long, *1 Kings,* 169]; 2 Kgs 16:5-9; 18:13-16) and analogues in a few ancient Near Eastern treaty documents (see fuller discussion at 2 Kgs 16:5-9).

160

Setting

Aside from the regnal resumé, which most critics take to have its setting and origin with the Dtr writer, many scholars suggest that most of the materials that make up this unit derive from royal records (so, e.g., Noth, *Deuteronomistic History,* 66, thinking of a literary history of Judean kings; see Šanda, *Könige* II, 149; Montgomery, *Kings,* 36; Hobbs, *2 Kings,* 150, seems to imagine something less comprehensive: "the record is an official one, taken from royal archives"). An older view supposes that a history of the temple lies behind the Kings account (e.g., Burney, *Notes,* 307-8). The question of literary source turns on how one evaluates the obvious priestly language and concerns in the passage. Gray (*Kings,* 582-83) compromises with the notion of a priestly author writing a history of the Judean kings.

Because the evidence is insufficient, such issues cannot be settled decisively. More to the point is the literary setting given to this regnal unit by the Dtr writer from his vantage point in exile. Despite the formal enclosures provided by the regnal resumé, the account of Jehoash's reign is to be read as continuous with the story of how he came to sit on the throne in the first place (ch. 11; Šanda, *Könige* II, 149; Montgomery, *Kings,* 426). The events in Judah run concurrently with Jehu in the north (12:2), and proximity of literary setting has left its mark in parallel themes and organization (see discussion at 2 Kings 11). Later, it will become clear that the procedures for repairing the Jerusalem temple are still in force during Josiah's reign and that the language of ch. 12 has been effectively duplicated in 22:3-7. Thus Jehoash must be seen in tandem with Jehu, and as anticipating in some important ways the time of Josiah.

Intention

The main intent of this unit is obviously to present the reign of Joash in an approving light. Joash is one of the few Judean kings whom the DtrH evaluates positively, though with a major reservation (12:2-3). His rule is characterized by a happy convergence of priestly and royal interests; earlier the young king is helped to reclaim his rightful throne by Jehoiada, and that event, imagined through priestly eyes, is likened to an expansion of holy space and power beyond the confines of the temple (ch. 11). Here, we are told that this same Jehoiada instructs Jehoash, and that this accounts for his positive evaluation (12:3). But more importantly, Jehoash cares for the temple, assures that it will remain in good repair, and so takes on a conventional duty of royal piety for Judean kings (cf. Solomon, 1 Kings 7–9).

Such deeds were expected of other ancient Near Eastern monarchs as well (see, e.g., an inscription of the Assyrian Adad-Nerari II [ca. 911-891 B.C.E.]: "At that time the ancient temple of the goddess Gula, my mistress, which previously Tukulti-Ninurta, my forefather, vice-regent of Ashur, had built — that temple had become dilapidated and I removed its debris down to the bottom of the foundation pit. I greatly enlarged that temple beyond previous extent. I completed it from top to bottom and deposited my steles" [Grayson, *ARI* 2, § 437,

p. 92; cf. ibid., § 480, p. 105]). The point of such inscriptions is revealed in the last lines of yet another monumental text (ibid., § 666, p. 170; Ashur-nasir-apli II [883-859 B.C.E.]): "O later prince among the kings my sons whom Ashur will name for the shepherdship of Assyria: [restore] the weakened (portions) of that temple; [write] your name with mine (and) return (my inscriptions) to their places so that Ashur the great lord (and) the goddess Ishtar, mistress of battle and conflict, [in wars] with kings on the battlefield will cause him to achieve success."

Against the background of this prevalent ideology, the Dtr writer shaped his sources to present the reign of Joash as godly and, we may say on the basis of the incident with Hazael, blessed with success as well. In this sense, Jehoash stands as an approved counterpart to Jehu. For a time, Yahwism seems on the ascendancy; in this sense, Jehoash prepares the way for Josiah (see Hoffmann, 124). But as Jehu's accomplishment is flawed not by ruthlessness but by his refusal to "walk in the *tôrâ* of Yahweh . . . with all his heart" (10:31), so Joash's good rating suffers more from the continuance of "high places" (12:4) than from his taking devoted objects from the temple (12:18-19).

From his vantage point in the exile, the Dtr writer is showing goodness in the kingdom, but always with an eye to the ultimate insufficiency in stemming the disaster that was his own experience, and the goal toward which the larger story moves. In this sense, too, the mixed evaluation of Jehoash anticipates a similarly ambiguous view of Josiah, whose goodness cannot undo the wrongs of others.

Bibliography

H.-D. Hoffmann, *Reform* (→ 2 Kgs 3:1-3); V. Hurowitz, "Another Fiscal Practice in the Ancient Near East: 2 Kings 12:5-17 and a Letter to Esarhaddon (LAS 277)," *JNES* 45 (1986) 289-94; M. Noth, *Deuteronomistic History* (→ 2 Kgs 8:28–9:28); A. Oppenheim, "A Fiscal Practice of the Ancient Near East," *JNES* 6 (1947) 116-20; I. Rabinowitz, "ʿāz followed by Imperfect Verb-Form" (→ 2 Kgs 8:16-24); R. Rendtorff, *Studien zur Geschichte des Opfers im Alten Israel* (WMANT 24; Neukirchen-Vluyn: Neukirchener, 1967).

ISRAEL AND JUDAH UNDER ARAM'S DOMINATION: CANONICAL FRAMEWORK, 13:1–14:29

Text

In 13:21 MT *wayyēlek,* "and he left," probably should be plur., "they left," the pluralizing *wāw* having dropped out by haplography. The *RSV* omits the verb entirely. Cf. *NJPS* "and [they] made off."

In 14:28 MT "for Judah in Israel" *(lîhûdâ bĕyiśrā'ēl)* is senseless. *RSV* "for Israel . . . which had belonged to Judah" is barely possible grammatically but raises difficult historical problems. Montgomery (*Kings,* 446) acknowledges that the "text remains a conundrum, and all correction is arbitrary"; with Cogan and Tadmor (*II Kings,* 161-62) and some ancient support, drop *lîhûdâ.*

Structure

I. Reign of Jehoahaz of Israel	13:1-9
A. Introductory resumé	1-2
B. Theological review (events during reign)	3-7
1. Yahweh's anger over "sin"/Aram's victories	3
2. Rescue by God's deliverer	4-5
3. Continuing "sins"/Aram's victories	6-7
C. Concluding resumé	8-9
II. Reign of Jehoash of Israel	10-25
A. Regnal resumé	10-13
B. Epilogue: Elisha and the victory over Aram	14-25
1. Elisha's symbolic action (prophecy of victory)	14-19
2. The miracle of life from death	20-21
3. Fulfillment of prophecy (victory over Aram)	22-25
a. Theological comment on Aram's oppression	22-23
b. Report of victory	24-25
III. Reign of Amaziah of Judah	14:1-22
A. Introductory resumé	1-4
B. Events during the reign	5-17
1. Concerning revenge for Judean Jehoash's murder	5-6
2. Conquest of Edom	7
3. The Israelite-Judahite war	8-14
4. Concluding summary for Joash of Israel	15-16
5. Note on Amaziah's length of reign	17
C. Concluding resumé for Amaziah	18-21
D. Postscript: the recovery of Elath	22
IV. Reign of Jeroboam (II) of Israel	23-29
A. Introductory regnal resumé	23-24
B. Theological review	25-27
1. Report of oracle fulfillment (recovery of territory)	25
2. Commentary	26-27
C. Concluding regnal resumé	28-29

This canonical unit is bounded by the closing summary for Joash, king of Judah (12:20-22 [*RSV* 19-21]), and the opening resumé of Azariah (15:1-4). It covers the regnal epochs of four kings, two each in Israel and Judah, whose reigns are reckoned synchronistically with one another and demarcated by the usual Dtr regnal summaries. The material is arranged in such a way that the motif of "deliverer" and "delivering" (*môšîaʿ, lĕhôšîaʿ*), which is linked to the claim of Yahweh's graciousness toward Israel (13:4, 23; 14:26-27), appears at beginning, middle, and end. Thus, 14:26-27 refers back to 13:5, 23, and provides a sense of thematic closure. We may observe other internal connections as well. The writer explicitly anticipates the encounter between Jehoash and Amaziah (13:12; 14:8-14); 13:14-25 carries the reader back into the time of Joash, even though his reign has been closed out; 14:17 connects with the preceding material that reports the death of Jehoash; 14:22, in connection with the death of Amaziah, remarks on the expansion of Judah in advance of the same topic for Israel, 14:25. Behind all these various materials loom the armies of Aram (*RSV* "Syria"), who are noted as a continual menace to Israel (13:3, 7; cf. 10:32-33) and are finally defeated (13:14-25; 14:25).

These signs of motival and structural linkage across the borders of self-contained regnal epochs make this canonical unit somewhat unusual (but cf. 1 Kgs 15:1–16:28, in Long, *1 Kings*, 165-68). Whether by design or accident, or a combination of both, the cross-references work against the dominant mode of composition found elsewhere in the books of Kings. (For a description, see Long, *1 Kings*, 22-23.) One finds here the usual self-contained blocks of regnal material, but arranged in partial disarray, and with motival connections that violate the literary borders between reigns. These links transcend the system of simple parataxis, define this particular canonical unit over against, for example, the more regularly composed ch. 15, and help to account for those places where the more usual form of presentation has been altered (e.g., 14:15-16 repeats 13:10-13; 13:14-24 appears outside the enclosures around reports concerning the reign of Joash, the reign to which events belong).

Of course, some of these same features suggest to many scholars that the material in this unit may have resulted from a complex process of composition, editing, and perhaps glossing. A concluding summary for Jehoash, 14:15-16, virtually repeats the resumé in 13:12-13, and seems misplaced in its present location. Yet 13:12-13, which reports the death of Jehoash in the expected way, does not in fact close off the story of his reign, since in vv. 14-25 Jehoash is very much alive and ruling his kingdom. It is, therefore, not clear which concluding summary is the more original.

Chapter 13 reflects additional compositional problems. First, many critics cite difficulties in vv. 1-7, all of which are usually attributed to one or more Dtr writers (Würthwein, *Könige*, 359-60, takes v. 7 to be pre-Dtr). Some see vv. 4-6 as secondary (e.g., Montgomery, *Kings*, 433; Gray, *Kings*, 591; Robinson, *2 Kings*, 121; McCarthy, 409-10; cf. De Vries, 119-20, who envisions the editorial history quite differently). Hentschel (*2 Könige*, 58) suggests that the intrusion begins with v. 3. Repeated motifs at vv. 2 and 6, the so-called resumptive repetition, could indicate that only vv. 3-5 were spliced into the regnal summary (see Kuhl); the pattern in Judges to which these verses conform might support such a hypothesis (cf. Judg 3:7-9, 12-15; 4:1-3; 10:6-10). However, the same observation convinces Hoffmann (*Reform*, 114-16) that a single Dtr author integrated this Judges-like comment into the regnal summary of Jehoahaz. Second, the two Elisha narratives, vv. 14-19 and 20-21, seem rather independent of their present context; furthermore, vv. 20-21 impede the narrative flow from v. 19 to v. 24 and awkwardly separate Elisha's prophecy (vv. 17-19) from its fulfillment (v. 25). Third, vv. 22-23 seem to offer secondary commentary on the whole historical period (Gray, *Kings*, 592, calls v. 23 an "editorial gloss").

While most critics recognize these and other difficulties, no comprehensive explanation as yet commands wide support. It seems inadequate to make a virtue of textual confusion by asserting that whatever its origins, disorder "reflects in a literary way the breakdown of the institutions and structures of national life which these chapters report" (Nelson, *Kings*, 216). Nevertheless, there is some point to exploring thoroughly the elements of structure, motif, and theme which can make the rough edges and broken literary patterns in the canonical text more understandable (cf. Hobbs, *2 Kings*, 164-65).

In its final form, the Dtr writer's text presents us with reports of two reigns that are defined by extensive narrative (II and III, Jehoash and Amaziah, 13:10-25; 14:1-22). Enclosing this material on either side are reports of regnal periods of kings whose rules are characterized largely by theological commentary (I and IV, Jehoahaz and Jeroboam II, 13:1-9; 14:23-29). A third explicit theological remark emerges at a middle point, 13:22-23. In terms of structure, this third comment marks analepsis in the larger Dtr history. That is to say, narrative chronology is interrupted, and the narrator fills the resulting time lapse between the reigns of Jehoash and Amaziah with new information (on this notion of "pausal moment," see Long, *1 Kings*, 26-27). The writer illuminates the background for this portion of the larger story (Aram's continual military threat to Israel) while reiterating the theological claim stated in the outer frames, 13:5 and 14:26-27 (Yahweh protects and delivers Israel). Against the ever-present incursions by Aram, who threatens Israel's very life, and in the light of God's promise to Jehu (10:30), Yahweh delivers Israel and maintains dynastic stability, at least until the fourth generation (see 15:12). Within the constraints of synchronistically arranged regnal blocks, the writer manages to concentrate on the fortunes of the northern kingdom and explain its stability (see Mullen).

The first section (I, 13:1-9) covers the reign of Jehoahaz but sets the larger background and theological theme. Breaking into the typical formulaic evaluation of the king (v. 2), the writer builds iterative summary on the pattern of similar material in the Dtr frameworks within the book of Judges. The typical schema is as follows: responding to the people's unfaithfulness, Yahweh's "anger burns hot" against them (*yhr 'p bĕ-*) and he sends punishment (he "sells/gives [*mkr/ntn*] them into the hand" of an enemy); the oppressed people then "cry out" (*z'q*) to God, who sends a ruler (*šôpēṭ;* RSV "judge") to rescue or "deliver" (*lĕhôšîaʿ*) them to their former state of peace. (See Judg 3:7-11; 3:12-15 [16-29], 30; 4:1-3 [4-22], 23; 10:6-10; see also Richter; for application to 2 Kings, see Hentschel, *2 Könige*, 58; Hoffmann, 114-16.)

With some modification toward the images of Mosaic-styled prophets (see Hobbs, *2 Kings*, 167), the Dtr writer uses this pattern to iterate a trio of punishment, petition, and deliverance within the claim of generalized apostasy that characterizes Jehoahaz's reign. We are told that Israel is given "continually" into the hand of enemies, and not only during Jehoahaz's time, since the two Syrian kings mentioned extend into his successor's reign. Jehoahaz "besought the Lord," presumably over and over again. (Piel of *ḥlh*, "besought," recalls the Dtr image of Moses as "prophet-ruler" more than "judge" [*šôpēṭ*]; cf. Exod 32:11; 1 Kgs 13:6; Jer 26:19, where Hezekiah is cast in this role). Yahweh "heard" the plea, for "he saw the oppression of Israel" (*laḥaṣ,* "oppression," echoes Mosaic traditions, e.g., Deut 26:7; Exod 3:9). Yahweh then sends Israel a "deliverer" (*môšîaʿ;* is there a wordplay on "Moses" [*mōšeh*]?), and the people of Israel escape.

Fundamentally, however, the situation remains static. Despite the (repeated) rescue from continual consignment to Aram's power — here the writer reverts to the generalizing evaluation disrupted at v. 2 — the people do not give up the ways of Jeroboam, and moreover, the cultic symbol of Canaan's fertility goddess, the Asherah, remains in Samaria (v. 6). This is the object built by Ahab (1 Kgs 16:33), to be imitated in Judah by Manasseh (2 Kgs 21:3) and to be destroyed by both Hezekiah (18:4) and Josiah (23:4, 6, 15). The result is a trampling that leaves to Jehoahaz only a decimated remnant of national pride (v. 7) which survives nonetheless because of Yahweh's "deliverer." (It is pointless to speculate on the identity of the "deliverer," but the writer's temporal horizon, which takes in two regnal epochs [v. 3], might suggest Jeroboam II [cf. 14:27].) Implicitly, we must see here the outworking of God's promise of four generations to Jehu's house (10:30; see discussion at 10:28-31).

The next section (II, 13:10-25) represents in formulaic summary the entire regnal period of Jehoahaz's son Jehoash, from accession to death, with a brief allusion that anticipates the account of war with Amaziah (vv. 10-13; see 14:8-14). The principal theological theme of vv. 1-7 is sounded again in an epilogue (II.B, vv. 14-25).

With the barest of narrative detail, the writer thrusts us back into the time of Jehoash, suggesting at once Elisha's last days and cordial relations between king and prophet (the words "My father! My father" seem to be honorific; cf. 2:12; 6:21; J. Williams, "The Prophetic 'Father,'" *JBL* 85 [1966] 344-48). Quickly we come onto a carefully managed double series of divination-like actions (note how the narrator has action track command with a regularity that suggests punctilious ritual, vv. 15-17a, 18). Each series issues in a prophecy (vv. 17b, 19); the first foretells total victory over Aram, and the second snatches away victory's glow — with blame laid at Jehoash's door. So the problem of Aramean oppression, the conditions set forth in vv. 3-7, continues to haunt Israel. These seemingly innocent acts, shooting arrows and striking the earth, take on the powers of revelation and make of Elisha's last words a prophecy of "yes, but not quite." The "man of God" foretells a limited triumph without a sense of finality — indeed, just the opposite, since the writer has earlier described deliverance at the cost of dissolution and destruction (v. 7).

Perhaps as a foretaste of that lease on life, or perhaps simply to confirm the power and authority of Elisha's last message, the writer immediately presents us with the somewhat obscure anecdote about Elisha's bones transferring life to a corpse (II.B.2, vv. 20-21). It is the prophet's final appearance in the Dtr history. As he was a man of power in life (chs. 2–7), moving and persuasive even in stories told about him (8:1-6), so now his awesome powers continue working in death, confirming the prophet and foreshadowing the victory to come. (Cf. a similar arrangement of traditions in 13:2-5: a "sign" is announced, and before it is noted as realized, v. 5, a sudden wonder intervenes. See Long, *1 Kings,* 147.)

Elisha's prophecy finds its exact fulfillment in vv. 22-25. But first, a reprise of the chapter's opening themes intervenes. The specter of Aram returns: Hazael "oppressed Israel all the days of Jehoahaz" (v. 22; cf. v. 5). Then, an evaluative comment restates the opening theme of Yahweh's attentive protection of Israel (cf. vv. 4-5). God turns toward this wayward nation because of his covenant with the ancestors, v. 23. The comment chronicles a deepening of the stream from which Israel lives in these particular times of Aramean oppression. For the Dtr writer, God's promise to David is a key element in Judah's longevity, and Jeroboam's violation of that same trust is the reason that God (or the DtrH) condemns Israel as unfaithful (cf. 1 Kgs 11:37-38). Now we must understand that apostate Israel's protection rests on Yahweh's obligations to Abraham, Isaac, and Jacob, to whom he promised a homeland (Deut 6:10; Josh 24:3-13). From this attachment comes Israel's victory, even if qualified and limited, and even if — in hindsight, from the perspective of the exile — the writer and reader know that eventually the northern kingdom collapsed (v. 23b, "nor has he cast them from his presence until now"; cf. 2 Kgs 17:23).

Shifting from the atemporal mood of commentary, the Dtr writer provides a succession formula for Hazael, as though concurring with v. 5 that his oppression of Israel is unremittingly carried by father to son. With strikingly exact diction, the narrator brings Israel and Aram in familial relation: son regains from son what father had lost to father (v. 25a). The final words offer epitomizing closure and indicate the less than total, as-prophesied dimensions of fulfillment: "*three times* Joash defeated him" (v. 25b).

Forward motion in the larger narrative resumes immediately with the opening summaries of Amaziah's reign (III, 14:1-22). The typical frameworks (vv. 1-4, 18-21) provide a thoroughly Judean frame of reference, and the events recorded have to do with Amaziah. The king avenges his father's death, but within the limits of *tôrâ* (vv. 5-6; cf. 12:21-22 [*RSV* 20-21] and Deut 24:16). He also takes Edomite territory for Judahistic expansion (v. 7). Nevertheless, the writer's emphasis actually falls on the good military fortunes of Israel at the expense of Judah (vv. 8-14; even the reference to the Edomite campaign is subordinate to this war narrative [cf. v. 10]).

Amaziah starts the trouble between sibling states (v. 8; the expression "let us look one another in the face" [*nitrā'eh pānîm*] is not necessarily indicative of hostile intent, but Jehoash surely interprets matters thus, and v. 11 leaves no doubt in the matter). Events prove the correctness of Jehoash's perception, communicated in a brief fable, that Amaziah has delusively inflated his military strength (vv. 9-10). Amaziah not only loses face — he loses the war. The cataloguing of details suggests subjugation by a foreign power. Jehoash "captures" *(tpś)* Amaziah (the word order in the Hebrew gives emphasis to Amaziah's name); he breaks through *(prṣ)* a large section of Jerusalem's defensive wall, seizes *(lqh)* treasures from temple and palace, and takes hostages (vv. 13-14; cf. 12:17-18; 17:4-6; 25:1-7; 1 Kgs 14:25-26; the word "hostages" [*běnê hattaʿărūbôt*] appears only here and in the parallel 2 Chr 25:24, and possibly mimics the Assyrian practice of taking members of the royal family as hostages to assure the good behavior of a conquered ruler [Cogan and Tadmor, *II Kings*, 157]). In short, this account highlights the success of Jehoash and shows the notable weakness of Amaziah. Judah can lay some claim to strength perhaps, but only in Amaziah's successor and as an afterthought outside the usual regnal framework (v. 22). What is very clear is that Israel, who is regularly faulted for following the ways of Jeroboam, enjoys remarkable success as though she is charmed or especially protected (cf. 13:23).

In this context of strength, the writer presents the reign of Jeroboam II of Israel (IV, 14:23-29). He notes yet another military success, presumably against Aram (v. 25a; cf. v. 28, where the borders of Israel return to their Solomonic ideal), but remarkably folds the incident into a theological comment. The reader is required to reconstruct a line of thought that might have issued in this compressed commentary. Jeroboam's victory comes as fulfillment of prophecy, as though guaranteed by Yahweh (v. 25b); moreover (calling again upon the language of the Mosaic exodus tradition as at 13:4-5), this oracle comes as God's response to Israel's severe plight (v. 26). But why would God give victory to unfaithful Israel and her king who, like all the rest, has been condemned (v. 24)? Because God has not decreed total annihilation (v. 27a; cf. Deut 9:14; 29:19; more distant, Exod 32:32-33). Thus — now the writer invokes the motif of 13:5, and brings closure to the canonical unit — God "saved" the people through Jeroboam (v. 27b).

Judah is apparently not held in much favor during this period of the Dtr history, despite the routine positive evaluations given Jehoash (12:2) and Amaziah (14:3). At least, Judah is weak and unstable (12:21-22 [*RSV* 20-21]; 14:13-14; cf. ch. 11) when evaluated in the light of the northern kingdom and Jehu's dynasty. And Yahweh especially looks after Israel, comments the Dtr writer while maintaining absolute silence with regard to Judah. (Later, in 15:5, the narrator will express only a negative attitude toward the Davidides, reporting that "the Lord smote the king [Azariah]," presumably as punishment.) Israel, unfaithful Israel no less, endures and succeeds. This is the outworking of a promise to Jehu (10:30) and the covenant with the ancestors (13:23; see Mullen). Victory comes to Israel as God's gift, defeat as his punishment (see 13:2-3, 6). This dialectical theme is presented in the knowledge of the final disaster that befalls both kingdoms (13:23; 17:20). It is further complicated by the implication that God's reasons for victory and defeat are qualified — Jehu's winning sons are recorded as following the "sins of Jeroboam" (13:2, 11; 14:24) and Judah's kings, weak and defeated, are nonetheless pronounced "good" in the eyes of Yahweh (14:3; see 12:3 [*RSV* 2]; 15:3).

Genre

Since this unit is an editorial composition, we may not specify a genre for the whole with any precision. However, certain traditions that the writer used conform to recognizable literary types and patterns. There is the introductory and concluding REGNAL RESUMÉ (13:10-13; 14:1-4, 17-21; 14:23-24, 28-29), which is modified by a THEOLOGICAL REVIEW (13:3-7; 14:25-27). The information on war between Judah and Israel is developed in a HISTORICAL STORY (14:8-14). Included within this is an attenuated political FABLE (14:9b), a short (→) tale that renders plants or animals as talking characters and expresses a moral principle or judgment (see Solomon, 115, 126-32; cf. Judg 9:8-15). Jehoash's and Elisha's last meeting is styled as a somewhat atypical SYMBOLIC ACTION REPORT (13:14-19) that includes two prophetic sayings functioning in context like an oracle, but suggestive of magical (→) incantation (Schmitt, 175; see 1 Kgs 11:29-39 and full discussion of symbolic action in Long, *1 Kings*, 129; Fohrer, 23-25).

Smaller generic elements include: (1) report of ORACLE FULFILLMENT (14:25), which somewhat atypically conveys information independently of extensive narrative (cf. 1 Kgs 16:34; 17:16; 2 Kgs 1:17); (2) various REPORTS or NOTICES of military campaigns (13:25; 14:7), royal construction (14:22), length of reign (14:17), consolidation of royal power (14:5-6), and miracle (13:20-21). Finally we may note the ACCESSION FORMULA (14:24), which in this case coordinates events in the Hebrew kingdoms with royal succession in Aram. Taking this note along with Hazael's (→) succession formula in 8:15b, we note a significant and unusual broadening of the literary and chronological reference points for the DtrH's presentation of the Jehu dynasty. A similar intercalation of native with foreign kingdoms may be found in a few examples of Babylonian (→) chronicles (see discussion in Long, *1 Kings*, 163).

Setting

This text is shaped by the Dtr writer, who draws upon diverse sources to compose this account of the kingdoms from his vantage point in the Judean exile, after 587 B.C.E. Insofar as some of the material conforms to recognizable literary types, one may perhaps suggest pre-Dtr settings. For example, reports of symbolic action may have evolved from accounts of magical actions among the prophets (Fohrer, 19); the report of miracle (13:20-21) would have been at home among legends preserved by followers and admirers of the prophets; the fable (14:9), although embedded in a politically oriented story, may draw upon folkloristic literary stock and social custom; reports and notices of royal affairs (13:25; 14:5-6, 7, 22) have their original setting in court records or royal inscriptions, none of which we possess.

Intention

Since we enjoy full access to the written work of the Dtr historian, the most accessible intentions are those implied by the literary form of the canonical unit. An obvious purpose of the writer is to narrate the succession of kings, north and south, during a time of Aramean military encroachment, and to explain the strength and stability of the Jehu dynasty while holding to the routinized condemnation of these northern regimes. Although given its due space in the composition, Judah recedes into a kind of byplay relative to the main action. A reader gleans that Jehu's sons achieve remarkable success, however qualified, in surviving the Aramean pressures. We knew already that longevity for Jehu's household is a reward for his role in avenging God against the Omride house and the forces of Baalism (10:30). Now one reads that Yahweh attends to the pleas of Jehoahaz (13:4), shows compassion toward the northern kingdom because of his covenant with the ancestors (13:23), and decrees a restoration of Israelite territory (14:25-26) — all this while the generally approved-of Judah is weak, even defeated by Israel (14:8-14). It is a moment of remarkable openness toward the north, and one that perhaps shows the DtrH fitting the realities of history to a schematic theological evaluation. Success of Israel is admitted, but offset by a general condemnation of her kings (13:2, 11; 14:24); likewise, weakness and unimpressive achievement in Judah correspond here, as elsewhere in the Dtr history, to a limping praise of her kings (14:3; cf. 12:3-4 [*RSV* 2-3] and 15:3-4). From the exile, having known the defeat of national ambition, north and south (cf. 13:23), the Dtr writer seeks to explain interim success and failure along the road to final destruction as part of Yahweh's (the historian's) judgment on the religious practice of king and subject alike (cf. Nelson, *Kings,* 165, 177).

Bibliography

B. Couroyer, "À propos de II Rois XIII,14-19," *SBFLA* 30 (1980) 177-96; S. De Vries, *Prophet* (→ 2 Kgs 1:2-17a); G. Fohrer, *Die Symbolischen Handlungen der Propheten* (2nd ed.; ATANT 54; Zürich: Zwingli, 1968); H.-D. Hoffmann, *Reform,* 113-18 (→ 2 Kgs 3:1-3); C. Kuhl, "Die 'Wiederaufnahme' — ein literarkritisches Prinzip?" *ZAW* 64 (1952) 1-11; D. McCarthy, "2 Kings 13,4-6," *Bib* 54 (1973) 409-10; E. Mullen, "Dynastic Grant" (→ 2 Kgs 10:28-36); W. Richter, *Traditionsgeschichtliche Untersuchungen zum Richterbuch* (BBB 18; Bonn: Hanstein, 1966); H.-Chr. Schmitt, *Elisa* (→ 2 Kgs 2:1-25); A. Solomon, "Jehoash's Fable of the Thistle and the Cedar," in *Saga, Legend, Tale, Novella, Fable. Narrative Forms in OT Literature* (ed. G. Coats; JSOTSup 35; Sheffield: University of Sheffield, 1985) 114-32; S. Yeivin, " 'To Judah in Israel' (2 Kings 14:28)," *Eretz Israel* 10 (1971) 150-51 (Hebr.).

ISRAEL IN DECLINE DURING THE REIGNS OF AZARIAH AND JOTHAM, 15:1-38

Structure

The typical sequence of synchronistically reckoned regnal epochs, each marked by opening and concluding formulaic summaries, defines this canonical unit. (Compared with other places in 1–2 Kings, the space devoted to "events" within each reign is severely attenuated, and the concluding formulas are abbreviated at those points where a particular ruler comes to a violent end, vv. 11, 15, 26, 31.) According to the DtrH's selective presentation, five Israelite kings pass in rapid, tumultuous succession, while in the south Azariah and Jotham preside over a 62-year span of dynastic stability.

In terms of literary structure, five Israelite epochs are enclosed by two in Judah, a kind of ABA construction. Within the limits of this mode of composition, the Dtr writer manages to suggest an ongoing plot. Following its earlier successes (ch. 14), the protected and "saved" dynasty of Jehu (see 13:5, 23; 14:26-27) now crumbles under waves of assassinations, coups d'état, and foreign intervention. The end of Jehu's house is marked by a comment that submits chaotic closure on the family's rule to the reassuring order of divine word that finds fulfillment (v. 12; cf. 10:30). Thereafter, one gains the impression of rapid decay leading to catastrophic collapse. Shallum, who murders Zechariah (v. 10), is himself murdered after six months (v. 14); a short-lived stability under Menahem and his son Pekahiah, though under pressure from Assyria (vv. 19-20), ends in another murderous coup d'état (v. 25). And this latest usurper to the throne gives up territory to Assyrian invasion (v. 29) and loses his own life at the hands of yet a third assassin (v. 30). Read in a larger context, these events, especially those of v. 29, anticipate a violent conclusion yet to be told, Assyria's murder of Israel by conquest and exile (17:4-6).

Against this rush to tragedy, Judah lives in a serenity marred only by a less-than-full approval by God (vv. 3-4, 34-35) and the suggestion of compensatory divine punishment (v. 5a, 37). In a word, the coloring and pattern in the picture of chs. 13–14 is exactly reversed by ch. 15. Victorious Israel, heretofore sharply foregrounded against the weakness of Judah, is now characterized as a confused and weak figure, framed on both sides by the stable strength of Judah. Yet matters are not quite so simple. It is hinted toward the end of the unit that Judah also begins to feel the effects of Assyria's incursions (v. 37; the note anticipates and leads into ch. 16). Indeed, one might say that the whole era, in the north and the south, is characterized by incursion and threat, as though a monstrous beast approaches the borders of both kingdoms.

Genre

This unit is a composition of the Dtr historian, who assembled his materials from the vantage point of exile, post-587 B.C.E.

Important generic building blocks include (1) introductory and concluding REGNAL RESUMÉ (vv. 1-4, 6-7; 8-9; 17-18, 21-22; 23-24; 27-28; 32-35a, 36-38) or formulas usually associated with resumé, i.e., ACCESSION FORMULA, v. 13; CITATION FORMULA, vv. 11, 15, 26, 31 (see full discussion at 1 Kgs 14:21-31, in Long, *1 Kings*, 158-64); (2) REPORTS of (→) throne conspiracy (vv. 10, 14, 25, and 30; see 1 Kgs 15:27-30; 16:9-13, and Long, *1 Kings*, 168-69), invasions (vv. 19-20, 29), and construction (v. 35b). The narrator's comment at v. 12 functions like a notice of (→) oracle fulfillment, and is formally similar to the speech of recognition put into the mouth of the Bethelite prophet at 1 Kgs 13:26a.

Setting

This unit was shaped by the Dtr writer who composed his history of monarchy from the vantage point of exile, after 587 B.C.E. Some of the material may have derived from official records or earlier historiographical writings (e.g., the reports of throne conspiracy, or the note about Pekah's construction of a gate for the temple; Cogan and Tadmor suggest that the notice of Assyrian invasion, v. 29, derives from the "royal chancelleries of Israel and Judah"). However, we have no direct evidence for such matters. The most important consideration, therefore, is the literary setting. Following upon the picture of Israel's good fortune in chs. 13–14, this account serves as a kind of bridge to ch. 17, a harbinger of catastrophe yet to be narrated. It represents a narrowing of focus to the worsening political health of the northern kingdom, which has been consistently castigated for its apostate ways. The simultaneous story of Judah remains essentially without such clear definition, except that the goodness of her kings is always in formulaic evaluation counterweighted with a lapse among the people, and Judah's stability appears striking by contrast to the chaos in Israel. Yet, at v. 37 the writer provides an important lead-in to ch. 16, as though to suggest that even Judah cannot withstand the steady incursions from foreign powers for very long.

Intention

It is clear that the most important intention of the Dtr writer is to present the story of the twin monarchies in such a way as to emphasize the fast-approaching collapse of the northern kingdom. Implicit in this presentation, of course, is that events are taking place according to the purposes of Yahweh. Jehu's dynasty persisted, indeed survived, because of God's gracious concern (see discussion at chs. 13–14), and now that it has come to an end — as promised by God — Israel's fate seems sealed because of the apostasy of her kings. In v. 29, the writer offers an anticipatory glimpse of that final destiny. Yahweh moves events in Judah, too. He "strikes" Azariah with leprosy (v. 5) and begins to "send Rezin . . . and Pekah against Judah" (v. 37). In both north and south, a system of reward for the faithful and punishment for the unfaithful is assumed, and this lends a particular thematic focus to the material. Both Israel's decline into chaos and eventually Judah's feeling the shock waves of Assyrian invasion stem from the power of God to move events.

Bibliography

M. Cogan and H. Tadmor, "Ahaz and Tiglath-Pileser in the Book of Kings: Historiographic Considerations," *Bib* 60 (1979) 491-508.

THE REIGN OF AHAZ, 16:1-20

Text

In v. 6 the MT reads as follows: "Rezin, king of Aram [Syria], recovered Elath for Aram, and he drove Judeans from Elath, and the Arameans came to Elath, and they dwell there to this day." The *RSV* and most commentators understand all references to Aram and Arameans as a mistake for the similarly spelled "Edom." This understanding reflects 2 Chr 28:17, in which Edom is reported to be an aggressor against Judah, and the lack of other evidence that Aram was ever involved in Judah's troubles with Edom (cf. 14:7; Cogan and Tadmor, *II Kings,* 184). However, the received text is problematic only at one place, where some Hebr. MSS and early VSS read "Edomites" in v. 6b and thus introduce a possible inconsistency into the verse. (Cf. *NJPS,* which refuses emendation and accepts the reading "Edom" in v. 6b.) Deciding the textual question on what we know of Judah's history ignores entirely the question of whether the text as given makes dramatic or literary sense. Even if historically incorrect, as Hobbs (*2 Kings,* 213) seems to acknowledge, the MT seems to state that Aram assaults both Jerusalem (v. 5) and Elath (v. 6), displacing Judahites from Elath, and that this twin threat powerfully motivates Ahaz to seek help (vv. 7-8). If Edom were the focus of v. 6, as many scholars claim, then the verse would lack a clear relation to this larger literary context.

In v. 18 the *RSV* "covered way for the sabbath" (MT *myysk*, Qere *mûsak*) is dubious, but any other alternatives are equally tentative. Cogan and Tadmor (*II Kings,* 189-90) suggest an awninglike "sabbath covering."

Structure

This unit is clearly defined by the typical Dtr summaries (vv. 1-4, 19-20) enclosing the reign of Ahaz and distinguishing it from the regnal periods which precede (15:32-38) and follow (17:1-2).

Most scholars agree that the writer composed the presentation of Ahaz's reign from a variety of sources which are now reflected in vv. 5-9, 10-16, and 17-18. However, the nature and extent of those sources and the degree to which a final literary unity has been achieved remain in dispute. Against a line of argument that assumes incoherence in vv. 5-9 (see, e.g., Hentschel, *2 Könige*, 73-74), Cogan and Tadmor cite stylistic features of Assyrian royal inscriptions to argue that (1) the words "then" (*'āz*, v. 5) and "at that time" (*bāʿēt hahî*, v. 6) have no chronological significance but are scribal signatures for excerpted source material; (2) the word "gift" or "present" (*šōḥad*, v. 8) is to be understood pejoratively as "bribe." This evidence implies for Cogan and Tadmor that a Dtr author quoted from source material (here most scholars agree), but made of it a "critique of Ahaz based upon sources from both court and temple, rewritten so as to be consonant with the Deuteronomistic historical outlook," i.e., with a negative presentation of Ahaz ("Ahaz and Tiglath-Pileser," 506-7; see Cogan and Tadmor, *II Kings*, 192).

Regarding vv. 10-18, all commentators notice the priestly language and technical interest in cultic affairs; virtually all suggest that the writer's sources are different from those used in vv. 5-9, identified variously as an independent history of Ahaz (Šanda, *II Könige*, 207-8), temple record (Hobbs, *2 Kings*, 210), or history of the temple (cf. Burney, *Notes*, 325). Consensus breaks down on the question of literary unity. With only minor disagreement, Würthwein (*Könige*, 389-90), Hentschel (*2 Könige*, 73-74), and Rendtorff (pp. 46-50) posit a continuous tradition, vv. 10-11, (14) 15-16, that was supplemented over time with accretions in vv. 12-13 and 17-18. Rendtorff is unsure whether the redaction is pre- or post-DtrH in date. Hoffmann (pp. 142-43) argues for a unified text written by a post-DtrH author whose comments on cultic and priestly matters are at variance with the interests of the DtrH. Yet, it is difficult to rule out the DtrH's interest in these topics, since elsewhere it is abundantly attested (see 1 Kings 6-8; 2 Kgs 12:4-16; 22:3-23:25; 25:13-17; esp. see the view that Jeroboam leads an illegitimate cult, 1 Kings 12).

The evidence for identifying such literary breaks is equivocal and heavily dependent on a priori theories of composition that rule out alternatives. For example, the various references to Ahaz ("King Ahaz," vv. 10-11, 15-16; "the king," v. 12; and simply "Ahaz," vv. 5-9) may indicate different editors, as some critics have alleged, or, on another view of compositional practice, they may be natural stylistic variants that any author might choose. (Note that variations in references to Tiglath-pileser and Rezin in vv. 5, 7-9 are not invoked as reason to suspect redactional layers in this material.) Vv. 17-18 treat a subject different from vv. 10-16, and may imply the work of a supplementing editor or of an author who gathered diverse materials into a loose relationship. Moreover, if material in vv. 5-9 was arranged by a single writer without regard to strict chronology, as Cogan and Tadmor believe, then perhaps one might also understand vv. 10-18 without recourse to temporal sequentiality, thus removing a major difficulty in connecting vv. 17-18 with the preceding vv. 10-16 (see below). M. Cogan ("Ahaz Altar") argues for literary unity by proposing that vv. 17-18 revert to the subject matter of v. 8 and describe in detail what was involved in robbing the temple to pay a bribe to Tiglath-pileser.

These comments do not establish any particular claim. They simply indicate that the discussion of redaction is at something of an impasse, in part because of the conflicting assumptions held by various critics. However one might view the source and redactional questions, we might still look to implicit principles by which the canonical text now hangs together.

First, the form of the material is entirely typical of the DtrH's presentation: regnal summaries (I, III, vv. 1-4 and 19-20) surround "events" that represent Ahaz's rule: his defense of Jerusalem (II.A, vv. 5-9) and his cultic activities (II.B, vv. 10-16). A material connection to the king of Assyria links the various parts: II.A, vv. 5-9, with II.B.1, vv. 10-13, and II.C, vv. 17-18. Second, vv. 5-9 and 10-13 seem tied internally through repeated references to "Damascus" (vv. 9, 10, 11, 12). Third, vv. 17-18 appear to resume the subject left in v. 8, and supply added detail about how Ahaz robbed the temple of its treasures (Cogan, "Ahaz Altar"). In that case, the great altar of Ahaz, vv. 10-16, which may in another context have been read positively, now takes on the negative tone associated with the writer's attitude toward Ahaz's bribery of Aram (Cogan and Tadmor). This reading also meets the usual expectations that whatever is selected for the "events" section of the reign would have illustrated the summarizing judgment given at the beginning, vv. 3-4.

The first major section nested within the regnal framework (II.A, vv. 5-9) reports a successful strategy to protect Jerusalem from attack and to preserve Ahaz's rule. Assaulted by Israelite and Aramean forces in Jerusalem (v. 5), and by Aram on his Edomite border (v. 6), Ahaz concludes an alliance with Tiglath-pileser, who then defeats Aram and removes, by implication, any threat which Pekah of Israel poses to Judah. The report follows a stereotyped pattern (see Kalluveettil, 93-101, 122-39):

I. Military crisis
II. Report of defensive alliance
    A. Besieged party approaches another for help
        1. Sending of envoys
        2. Alliance
            a. Declaration (proposal) of alliance
            b. Petition (for removal of threat)
        3. Mention of payment
    B. Results
        1. The helper heeds the appeal
        2. Threat removed

This stock scene appears in 1 Kgs 15:16-22; 2 Kgs 16:5-9 (2 Chr 16:1-6; 28:16-21); and 2 Kgs 18:13-16. 2 Kgs 12:18-19 follows the same pattern, but without elaborate dialogue. Typically the crisis occurs when a foreign king "goes up against" (ʿlh ʿl) a land or city to "fight against it" or "lay siege to it" (nlḥm or ṣûr). Then through his envoys (malʾākîm), the threatened king makes a representation to a third party, declaring an existing alliance still in force, or, in effect, proposing a new treaty (e.g., "a treaty [exists] between me and you" [běrît bênî ûbênekā, 1 Kgs 15:19; "your vassal and your son [am] I" [ʿabděkā ûbinkā ʾānî], 2 Kgs 16:7; in 2 Kgs 18:14, a similar declaration seeks to repair a broken relationship). The petition that follows specifically asks for one ally to come to the other's defense and so stave off disaster (e.g., Ahaz says simply, "Help me,"

v. 7b; in Hezekiah's case, the king pleads directly to Sennacherib, "Withdraw from me . . . ," 2 Kgs 18:14; cf. 1 Kgs 15:19b, where King Asa of Judah urges Ben-hadad to break his alliance with Israel and thus weaken the threat to Judah; cf. 2 Kgs 12:18-19 [RSV 17-18]). There is usually mention of payment: gold and silver taken from the temple treasury. The writer then typically notes that the foreign king "heeded" the request, implying that a treaty is upheld or consummated, and Jerusalem saved from destruction (see 1 Kgs 15:20-21; 2 Kgs 12:19 [RSV 18]; 16:9; for Hezekiah, the ploy does not work; see discussion at 2 Kgs 18:13–19:37).

The declaration that Ahaz's envoys convey to Tiglath-pileser (v. 7a, "I am your servant and your son") is unique in the Bible, although some relationship to the language of international treaty making, especially the use of ʿebed ("vassal" or "servant"), seems hardly in doubt (Kalluveettil, 129-30; Cogan and Tadmor, 504-5; see also M. Cogan, *Imperialism and Religion* [SBLMS 19; Missoula, MT: Scholars Press, 1974] 66, n. 4). The writer suggests that Ahaz's appeal to Tiglath-pileser, while saving Jerusalem, nevertheless marks the beginning of Judah's servitude to Assyria. By invoking the word "bribe" (šōḥad) as the price Ahaz willingly pays, the Dtr writer shapes a reader's negative attitude toward events, and especially toward Ahaz's cavalier appropriation of temple resources (cf. 1 Kgs 15:18-19; Cogan and Tadmor, 499-502; idem, *II Kings,* 187-88).

This sequence of events is interrupted by vv. 10-16 (the repetition of "king of Assyria" in vv. 9 and 18 signals the hiatus). Inside this pausal space, the writer presents King Ahaz's cultic innovations as following directly from his orders and his dealings with the king of Assyria (II.B, vv. 10-16; see v. 18, "because of the king of Assyria"). The unit consists of three distinct scenes, each of which emphasizes the king's actions (vv. 10-11, 12-14, 15-16) and a less dramatically rendered report of his further actions.

The first and third scenes follow a structure of command-execution (see Hoffman, 142). The king "saw" the altar at Damascus, "sent" a model to the priest (implying a command to build it), and the priest acts accordingly. The full and repetitious style of v. 11 reinforces a strict correspondence between royal order and its execution. Similarly, in v. 15, Ahaz "commanded" (wayĕsawweh) that new cultic practices be put in place: the new altar, now called "great altar," is to supplant a smaller "bronze altar," presumably the one that was already too small for Solomon's use (1 Kgs 8:64), as the focal point for major cultic activities. The bronze altar is to be devoted to the king's private use (Cogan and Tadmor, *II Kings,* 189; the uncertain meaning of lĕbaqqēr [RSV "inquire by"] in this context has inspired a tradition of ill-justified translation that associates Ahaz with divinatory rites; see Gray, *Kings,* 637; Würthwein, *Könige,* 386; Montgomery, *Kings,* 461). The Dtr writer notes, again emphasizing correspondence between decree and its execution, that "Uriah the priest acted according to everything which King Ahaz [had] commanded [siwwāh]."

Enclosed within these outer scenes, King Ahaz presides over the inaugural (dedicatory?) rites at the new Assyrian-styled altar in Jerusalem, vv. 12-14. The writer invokes priestly language to portray Ahaz as a royal priest, head of the state religion, like David and Solomon before him (cf. 2 Sam 6:17-18; 1 Kgs 8:63), or, given the DtrH's negative attitude, like Jeroboam (1 Kgs 12:32-33).

The king "drew near . . . went up" and offered a typical Judahite series of offerings (cf. 2 Sam 6:17-18; 1 Kgs 8:63; Lev 7:14; 23:18; Num 6:15; on the technical vocabulary, see Rendtorff, 49).

The result of this envelope construction, a scene of Ahaz officiating as royal priest enclosed within scenes in which he commands to build and to reorganize, is that one views the king as cultic innovator in Judah. He is curiously aligned in function, if not in stature, with other royal "priests" such as David, Solomon, and Jeroboam. Yet unlike these forerunners, Ahaz operates in the shadow of vassalage to a foreign nation (vv. 6-9) and is captivated by Syria (or Assyria, since the text is ambiguous) through a Damascene high altar (note how the word "Damascus," repeated in vv. 9 and 10, conceptually and visually ties vv. 5-9 to vv. 10-16).

Having established this representation, the writer reverts to discussing the bribe given Tiglath-pileser (vv. 17-18). In simple reportorial style, the writer mentions decorative materials that were presumably stripped from the temple to make payments for the defense of Jerusalem (cf. v. 8). All this was done "because of the King of Assyria" (v. 18b), a phrase which not only brings closure to the report of Ahaz's innovations, vv. 10-16, but also serves as an epithet to his whole rule in the shadow of Tiglath-pileser.

Genre

Since the larger literary unit is an editorial compilation, its genre may not be specified. However, smaller generic elements define some of the material used by the Dtr writer to represent Ahaz's reign. There is the usual introductory and concluding REGNAL RESUMÉ, vv. 1-4 and 19-20; and REPORT, one of which deals with cultic innovation, vv. 10-16, and the other with making a defensive alliance.

The latter is of particular interest because its basic narrative pattern or *topos,* making a defensive alliance for self-defense, has parallels in both the Dtr history (see 1 Kgs 15:16-22; 2 Kgs 12:18-19 [*RSV* 17-18]; 16:5-9; 18:13-16; and discussion above) and ancient Near Eastern inscriptions. Two remarkable examples appear in treaty documents from Ugarit (see above all Kalluveettil, 122-24). One text (RS 17.340 [= Nougayrol, *PRU* IV, 48-52]), in rehearsing past relations between vassal (Niqmaddu of Ugarit) and overlord (Šuppiluliuma of Hatti), reports a menacing situation in which Niqmaddu approaches his protector for aid. The text continues:

> "May the Sun, the Great King, my Lord deliver me from the hand of my enemies. I am the Servant of My Sun, the Great King, my Lord. Against an enemy of my Lord I am enemy-like, with an ally of my Lord, I am allied. The kings press me." The Great King heard these words of Niqmaddu. Šuppiluliuma, the Great King, sent princes . . . with foot troopers . . . to Ugarit.

(Kalluveettil, 123, provides a partial translation; a more complete translation into German is to be found in *TUAT* I [1983], 131-32, from which the foregoing is adapted.) For a second example, see the treaty between Šuppiluliuma and

Tette of Nikhash (portions of the text and commentary in Kalluveettil, 96-97; full German translation in E. Weidner, *Politische Dokumente aus Kleinasien* [Boghazköi-Studien 8-9; Leipzig: J. C. Hinrichs, 1923] 58-59).

Setting

It is likely that some of the material now included by the Dtr writer in this representation of Ahaz's reign had its original setting in royal archival records. But since we have no way of verifying the hypothesis, it is more important to remind ourselves that the unit's primary setting is with the exilic Dtr writer, who compiled this picture of Ahaz's reign from selected sources, shaping it into a comment on Judah's impending downfall and illustration of the judgment against Ahaz's religious orthodoxy.

Intention

It is clear that the primary purpose is to present Ahaz's reign in the monarchical history and to render a negative verdict on it (for a somewhat more positive reading, see Nelson, *Kings,* 226-28). With him Judah's subservience to Assyria begins; with him comes a lessening of the Solomonic temple's splendor (some of its finery and riches had been used for foreign alliances, albeit to save Jerusalem); he legitimates Israel's orthodox sacrificial practices on a foreign-style altar. Ahaz, and only two other Judahite monarchs, walk in the ways of the much maligned northern "kings of Israel" (v. 3).

If the transgressions of Jeroboam had been introduced in chs. 14–15 as the cause of Israel's eventual downfall (to be narrated in ch. 17), then Ahaz in Judah falls heir to that same legacy of apostasy, just as Jehoram (8:18) and Ahaziah (8:27), father and son, previously had done. And down the road of years, Manasseh, the most egregious Judahite miscreant in the DtrH's eyes, will echo and magnify that summarial judgment against Ahaz (cf. 16:3b with 21:2b). Thus on the side of apostasy, Ahaz and Manasseh make up a cross-referenced pair. In between these reigns stand their opposites, the archetypes of pious obedience in the late kingdom: Hezekiah, son of Ahaz (chs. 18–20), and Josiah, grandson of Ahaz (chs. 22–23).

Bibliography

P. Ackroyd, "Historian and Prophets," *SEÅ* 33 (1968) 18-54; M. Cogan, "The Ahaz Altar," in *Proceedings of the Sixth World Congress of Jewish Studies* (vol. 1; Jerusalem: World Union of Jewish Studies, 1977) 119-24; M. Cogan and H. Tadmor, "Ahaz and Tiglath-Pileser" (→ 2 Kgs 15:1-38); Hoffman, *Reform* (→ 2 Kgs 3:1-3); P. Kalluveettil, *Declaration and Covenant* (→ 2 Kgs 10:1-27); R. Rendtorff, *Geschichte des Opfers* (→ 2 Kgs 12:1-22); M. Thompson, *Situation and Theology: Old Testament Interpretations of the Syro-Ephraimite War* (Prophets and Historians 1; Sheffield: Almond, 1982).

THE REIGN OF HOSHEA:
CANONICAL FRAMEWORK, 17:1-41

Text

In vv. 26-27 *RSV* "law of the god of the land" *(mišpaṭ 'ĕlōhê hā'āreṣ)* apparently follows the Lucianic Greek MS (LXX[L]) for the translation of *mišpaṭ* as "law." The sense is better conveyed by "religious customs" (Hobbs, *2 Kings,* 221) or "rules" *(NJPS)* or "rites" (Cogan and Tadmor, *II Kings,* 208) "of the god of the land."

In v. 29 *RSV* "Samaritans" is misleading. The Hebrew gentilic form *šō-mĕrōnîm,* which occurs only here in the OT, means simply "inhabitants of Samaria" or "Samarians." They most probably should be distinguished from the Samaritans known from the second temple period and mentioned in the NT.

Structure

I. Introductory regnal summary	1-2
II. Reflection on the fall of Samaria	3-41
A. Report of Samaria's exile	3-6
B. First comment: reasons for the exile	7-23
C. Report of aftermath: resettlement of Samaria and syncretistic religion	24-33
D. Second comment: persistence of syncretism in Samaria	34-41

This unit is defined at its outer limits by the typical Dtr regnal formulas which set off the reign of Hoshea from Judah's King Ahaz (16:19-20) and his successor, Hezekiah (18:1-3). After the conventional introductory summary for Hoshea (I, vv. 1-2), the writer reports briefly on Israel's troubles with Assyria and the consequent demise of the northern kingdom (II.A, vv. 3-6). On this base the writer interrupts forward movement in the narrative, and fills this pausal moment with a sustained reflection on the religious failings that led to the catastrophe and the persistence of those misdeeds even in the aftermath of disaster (II.B-D, vv. 7-41; on "pausal moment" as a compositional technique of the Dtr writer, see Long, *1 Kings,* 26-28). There is no concluding summary for Hoshea's reign. In effect his time constitutes catastrophic loss and didactic reflection.

Most critics assume that to create this picture of Hoshea's reign, the DtrH drew in part upon previously extant royal records (vv. 3-6 and 24) and legendary material (vv. 25-28). The rest of the chapter is attributed variously to the original historian or later redactors who expressed similar religious commitments in unmistakably Dtr language and style (see Weinfeld, 320-65). Not surprisingly, major disagreements arise over the details, depending on one's theory of composition and redaction. Indeed, vv. 7-41 have become a well-worn proving ground for conflicting hypotheses about the literary history of 1–2 Kings as well as the larger Dtr history. (Convenient summaries of the debate may be found in Macdonald; Mayes; Nelson.)

Virtually every hypothesis has been controverted. Most agreement centers on the unity of vv. 3-6, but recently this has been disputed by Trebolle Barrera, who reconstructs two independent sources behind the text). Hardly anyone, not even Noth and Hoffman, who believe in a single author for the Dtr history, denies that vv. 34-40 belong to the latest, and post-DtrH, material in the chapter. Yet, M. Cogan questions even that consensus, and argues to the contrary that vv. 34-40 originally continued the account of exile broken off at v. 23, and belong to a preexilic writing from Josianic times. Similar disagreements swirl around vv. 7-23, with most scholars seeking to fit three segments of the text, vv. 7-17(18), 19-20, and 21-23, into varying theories of redactional history. It is fair to say that no single view commands a near consensus, except that vv. 7- 41 are in some sense supplementary to the mere record of Israel's demise reported in vv. 3-6.

Whatever its prior history, the canonical text is clearly now broadly coherent. Following the usual introductory regnal summary, the writer reports the exile of Israel to Assyria as the first and only event in Hoshea's reign. This is the base upon which to build a moralizing reflection (II.B-D, vv. 7-41). Not only has repeated apostasy in the manner of all the kings of the northern kingdom led to this disaster, but even Judah will in time go the way of Israel (vv. 19-20). Moreover, the religious problem persists in the north even after the exile down to the writer's own day (vv. 24-41).

Recently, certain scholars have investigated this sense of surface coherence more rigorously. Hoffman (pp. 133-37) finds original literary unity in vv. 7-33, and incorporates this conclusion into his thesis that the Dtr history was composed by one person and is basically a unified story of actions that the kings took to reform or corrupt the state religion. Viviano ("Literary Study") admits to a complicated background for the chapter, but sidesteps the redactional and source-critical questions altogether so as to argue that ch. 17 is a carefully structured unit whose rhetorical intent goes beyond that of simply accounting for the fall of the northern kingdom (cf. Nelson, *1–2 Kings,* 228-33).

In view of the lack of consensus on redactional and source-critical matters, there is much to be said for concentrating our formal analysis on the received text as Viviano has done. Indeed, a few signs of literary linkage cut across the boundaries of alleged independent units. If one adopts a different theoretical posture, imagining a writer composing, rather than a number of redactors modifying, a document, then some of the factors in the text that give rise to diachronic explanations may also be understood in terms of an author's technique.

Many critics assume that the concern to mark Judah's fate at vv. 19-20, and thus the mere mention of Judah in vv. 13 and 18b, is secondary to vv. 7-17. Yet the word *ḥuqqôt,* with the somewhat unusual sense of firmly established habits or "customs" (cf. Mic 6:16; Jer 10:3), appears in vv. 8 and 19 in a similar phrase: "customs which the kings of Israel engaged in ['*śh, RSV* 'introduced']." Moreover, both Judah and Israel are implicitly linked in the recital of offenses, vv. 14-17. Most of the misdeeds are precisely those attributed to Judah throughout the books of Kings (Viviano, "Rhetorical Analysis," 552; in particular v. 17 recalls the Judean kings Ahaz, 16:3, and Manasseh, 21:6). Yet mention of the "golden calves," v. 16, invokes the stigma of Manasseh's opposite number in the north, Jeroboam. This in turn provides a context for Jeroboam to return explicitly in vv. 21-22. (The beginning of v. 21 is awkward in the Hebrew. Although often taken as a rough edge left by editing hands, the first word [*kî*] may mark an author's own supplement [cf. 1 Kgs 11:16; 2 Kgs 18:4; 24:20; Gen 43:10], or an emphatic particle, "Indeed, he [Yahweh] tore Israel from the house of David.")

This sort of sustained comparison of both kingdoms, side by side, is not unheard-of in Dtr-styled material (e.g., Jer 3:6-12; cf. Ezek 23:1-21). If one assumes that the DtrH wrote from the perspective of the exile, knowing the fates of both kingdoms, then it is understandable that anticipatory glimpses of Judah's end would be offered a reader, and sometimes under the rubric of prophecy-fulfillment (besides 2 Kgs 17:19-20, see 21:12; 23:26-27 [Judah] and 13:23 [Israel]).

A second mark of literary unity may be seen in motival repetitions. The vocabulary of "sin" or "transgression" *(ḥṭ')*, like a thematic *Leitwort*, opens and closes the lengthy recitation on the reasons for Israel's fate (vv. 7 and 21-22). Moreover, the statement of general offenses, vv. 8-9a, mentions three deeds: (1) the Israelites "feared other gods" (the word *yr'* means to worship or hold in awe-filled reverence); (2) "walked in the customs *(ḥuqqôt)* of the nations" whom Yahweh had displaced for Israel's sake; (3) and walked in the customs that the kings of Israel had practiced. (The last phrase in v. 8b, *ûmalkê yiśrā'ēl 'ăšer 'āśû*, is elliptical, which demands that we supply "they walked in the customs that. . . ." The syntactical awkwardness is reflected in MS variants and textual critics' debates about originality, but the MT is perfectly clear as it stands.) This threefold charge in effect offers a thematic overview of vv. 7-41. Worshiping foreign gods, or conversely, *not* worshiping Yahweh (*wayyîrě'û 'elōhîm 'ăhērîm* or *lō' yārě'û 'et- yahweh* or the like) is the umbrella motif for the whole passage. The offense is illustrated in the details of vv. 9-17 (see esp. vv. 15-17) and comes back with explicit obsession in vv. 24-41 (note that the exact vocabulary occurs repeatedly in vv. 25, 28, 32-35, 37-39, 41). The phrase "customs of the nations" *(ḥuqqôt haggôyim)* similarly has its illustration in vv. 9-18 (see esp. mention of "nations" in vv. 11 and 15) and becomes an explicit preoccupation in vv. 24-41, where foreign "nations" who "are carried away to" Samaria — it is a mirror image of Israel's exile — perpetuate the wrong modes of worship. Finally, the third thematic element, "the customs of the kings of Israel," is precisely what led the people astray in vv. 9-17, including Judah (v. 19), and one king in particular, Jeroboam I, is implicated by allusion (v. 16, "golden calves") and explicit condemnation (vv. 21-22). Ironically, these are the customs which were taught the foreigners who were forcibly settled in Samaria after Israel's exile, vv. 24-28. For the DtrH, the religious perversity of Bethel in the north, including the mimicking of Jeroboam's ways, simply was replicated under new social circumstances (vv. 29-41; cf. v. 32 and vv. 9-10 and 1 Kgs 12:29, 31).

Beyond these general thematic concerns that impose a substantial conceptual unity on the whole, we may consider the effect of so-called resumptive repetitions (Kuhl) in vv. 6 and 23, "he carried the Israelites away to Assyria" *(wayyegel 'et-yiśrā'ēl 'aššûrāh)* and vv. 34, 40-41, "to this day they act according to the former manner" *('ad hayyôm hazzeh hēm 'ōśîm kammišpāṭîm hāri' šōnîm).*

Such repetitions do not always signal an editor's insertion of material into an earlier narrative (against Kuhl and others). Often they mark a purposeful pause in forward temporal movement, to varied effect (e.g., 1 Kgs 1:1, 4, 15b; 2 Kgs 4:8aα, 11aα; 7:5b, 8a; 1 Sam 1:3a, 7a; 18:5, 14, 30; for details, see Long, "Framing Repetitions"). Within such frames, a writer ranges freely over time relative to narrative chronology, and may invoke moments long past or far into the future, or simply an enduring condition (e.g., Saul's brooding madness has no beginning or foreseeable end within the framework marked out by 1 Sam 18:5, 30).

Thus in Hoshea's reign, the text may be read as implying a writer who paused at the moment of exile to create an elaborate commentary on the demise of the northern kingdom. (Talmon's use of resumptive repetition as a clue to the activity of many editors rather than a single author falters in this case in asserting that the narration at 17:4 was broken and then resumed at 18:9-11. This ignores the shaping force of the reign-by-reign pattern in ordering the books of Kings; and Talmon needs to explain why an original narrative in reference to Hoshea [17:4] would have continued, or been resumed, by an editor in 18:9 in a way that is totally subordinate to an interest in Hezekiah.)

However, reading the space between 17:6 and 18:1 as the more natural pause in narrating, the temporal reach of the interruption extends far back beyond the parameters of Israel's first king (vv. 7-8) and covers an indefinite time span during the monarchy itself, but still anterior to this moment in Hoshea's reign. The writer's horizon even moves out toward the demise of the southern kingdom, vv. 19-20, and thus completely runs ahead of the moment at which the primary narrative sequence had been suspended. Having glimpsed Judah's fate, one moves back in time to recall that decisive moment in which the people of the northern kingdom went astray (vv. 21-22). Finally, at v. 23, the writer leads us back to the primary narrative present, the moment of Israel's exile, and just as quickly — the distance between the past of narration and a reader's present is now collapsed — addresses us directly with the testimony formula "as at this day." What one sees in vv. 7-23, therefore, may be explained as a literary technique that expresses the omnitemporal freedom of the remembering consciousness. Similar observations may be made about vv. 34-41 in which the writer gazes far beyond the time frame of vv. 24-33 to condemn the syncretistic religion that persists into the aftermath of exile, even "until this [a reader's] day."

In all these ways, the canonical text offers a formal and thematic literary unit whose rhetoric of persuasion deserves closer analysis (cf. esp. Viviano; Hoffman). One discovers a style of discourse that depends for its rhetorical effect upon systematic ordering, upon repetition and elaboration, on a substratum of concept which is continually particularized and recalled, spun out and closed in on itself. Although cast as description, the text acts to apply a lesson to the reader's time, "as at this day." Through this device, among others, the writer seeks to win ideological commitment.

The first major subsection declares the reasons for Israel's exile (II.B, vv. 7-23). Its structure may be visualized as follows (cf. Viviano, "Rhetorical Analysis," 556; idem, "Literary Study," 99-103):

This section is constructed as much in the style of recitation as rhetorical argument. The writer makes one basic claim, that exile occurred because the Israelites transgressed (*RSV* "sinned") against Yahweh (v. 7), and then provides evidence in an elaborate survey of Israel's behavior (vv. 8-18). Judah is also in mind, but in the background, as v. 13a shows. The observation in v. 18b that Judah alone was left after Samaria's demise brings the southern kingdom to full consciousness: even Judah (*RSV* "also" misses somewhat the emphatic Hebrew construction) spurns the commandments of God, follows the customs of Israel, and meets a similar end (vv. 19-20). Then the transgressions of Israel return to view (vv. 21-22). Focus on Jeroboam I, the archetypal figure of evil in the Dtr history, allows the writer to recapitulate his basic claim and frame the whole argument with the opening (cf. v. 7) thematic idea, "transgress/transgression" *(√ḥṭ'):* "Jeroboam . . . made them commit a great transgression [*heḥĕṭê'ām ḥăṭā'â gĕdôlâ*]. The people of Israel walked in all the transgressions [*ḥaṭṭō'wt*] which Jeroboam committed." Finally, having completed the argument, the Dtr writer rejoins narrative time and reminds us that Israel has been sent into exile (v. 23b; cf. v. 6).

The heart of the rhetorical argument consists of two similarly constructed series of statements that catalogue specific misdeeds (vv. 8-12 and 16-17). Herein lies the particularization of the general claim that Israel (and Judah) followed the habits of the "nations" (*gôyim,* vv. 8 and 15). These particularities enclose a generalized picture of an ongoing process: *every* prophet and seer, all of them, acted alike to bring Yahweh's admonition to the Israelites: "Turn from your evil ways and keep my commandments and my laws, in accordance with all the teaching which I commanded your ancestors and which I sent to you by my servants the prophets" (v. 13b; cf. *NJPS*). This characteristically Dtr language is associated with the obligations of covenant (the word actually appears in v. 15) and thereby provides a specific point of view on Israel's actions. She transgressed the special relationship between God and his people that had been defined in concrete obligations (commandments, laws, teaching [*miṣwōt, ḥuqqôt, tôrâ*]), and transmitted by prophets among whom the DtrH reckoned Moses to be the greatest (Deut 34:10). These obligations are encapsulated in the mention of "commandments" *(miṣwōt)* in the second series of misdeeds, v. 16a. The same covenant terms will assume prominence again, vv. 34, 37. In this way, the themes enunciated here in prophetic teachings and warnings provide an important inner coherence to the whole of ch. 17: the breaking of covenant obligations that condemn Israel of the north to exile will persist among those who settle Samaria later on and who are taught those same obligations (v. 28).

It seems natural, then, that when the writer resumes the forward movement of the narrative in v. 24, the moralizing reflection is not abandoned. Story telling, vv. 24-33, like simple report earlier, serves as the basis for religious explanation and condemnation, vv. 34-41. The structure may be envisioned as follows (cf. Viviano, "Rhetorical Analysis," 556; idem, "Literary Study," 114-49):

I. Report of resettlement of Samaria	24
II. Cultic affairs in Samaria	25-33
A. The problem	25
1. No worship of Yahweh ("fear" of the Lord)	25a
2. Yahweh's punishment	25b
B. The proposed solution	26-27
1. Report to the king of Assyria	26
2. Response: royal orders for Yahweh priest	27
C. Orders carried out: priest to teach how to "fear" Yahweh	28
D. Results	29-33
1. Concerning non-Yahwistic worship	29-31
2. Concerning Yahweh worship ("fear" the Lord)	32
3. Epitomizing summary: syncretism ("fear" Yahweh while serving other gods)	33
III. Comment: persistence of syncretism in Samaria	34-41
A. Thematic framework	34a
1. Attestation formula ("as at this day")	34aα

This section falls naturally into three closely connected divisions: vv. 24, 25-33, and 34-41. Although edging toward folk narrative in vv. 25-28, the style of vv. 24-33 is basically reportorial, and vv. 34-41 are theological commentary. Thus, the text is a structural and functional twin of vv. 3-6 + 7-23. In both, a report of an event occasions extensive commentary.

In vv. 24-28 a simply plotted report about settlement of Samaria in the aftermath of Israel's exile sets a leitmotif, "fear" (or worship) of the gods in Samaria, and a theme, that cultic affairs in Samaria perpetuate a familiar and perverse syncretism. This moralistic judgment is expressed explicitly only at v. 33, but the tone of the writer throughout is polemical, and the language is typical of the DtrH (see Hoffman, 136-37). The religious situation, even without the Israelites, if that is what is intended, is fundamentally unaltered after Israel's exile, and therefore reprehensible to the DtrH. Not only the Samarians but the land itself is polluted by alien ways, for the settlers do not know the "religion proper to the god[s] of the land." And what is worse, the people do not learn, even when taught by a priest of Israel (v. 28), how to revere Yahweh properly (v. 33). The names of the foreign gods worshiped on Israel's soil have changed, but the loose rather than exclusive devotion to Yahweh continues as before. (The listlike enumeration of deities in vv. 30-31, some of whose names are badly garbled, perhaps parodies their powers. On the various gods mentioned, see R. Zadok, "Geographical and Onomastic Notes," *JANESCU* 8 [1976] 113-26; Cogan and Tadmor, *II Kings,* 211-12; on the parody, see Hobbs, *2 Kings,* 239.) The willful appointment of "all sorts of people as priests" who continue to officiate at the hill shrines *(bāmôt)* alludes to and perpetuates Jeroboam's actions of an earlier day (see 1 Kgs 13:33; 12:31). These are practices, of course, which the DtrH regularly condemns and which will be definitively eradicated by Josiah in 2 Kgs 23:15-20.

Thus, this report of cultic affairs in Samaria is a structural piece of the larger Dtr story (Hoffman, 134). The narrative situation is realistic (Paul), with perhaps a touch of legendary embellishment (i.e., the lions in v. 25b), but the writer's point of view is heavily ideological. The legacy of apostasy bequeathed to the northern kingdom by Jeroboam I (1 Kgs 12:31) is not annulled. There may even be some irony in the writer's suggestion that a priest of Yahweh was sent from exile to teach the non-Israelite Samarians how to revere Yahweh at Bethel (v. 28). Of all places in the DtrH's geography of sacred ground, this cultic center was antipodal to Jerusalem (see 1 Kgs 12:29-32). Rather, Samaria's residual cultic waywardness demands the purifying ardor of a reformer, and the writer will assign this role to King Josiah of Judah (see discussion of 2 Kings 22–23).

Having reported this situation, the writer offers extensive commentary in typical Dtr language and style (III, vv. 34-41). Repeated motifs create an enclosing picture of ongoing (the Hebrew construction suggests continual activity) divided allegiances. "To this day" (*'ad hayyôm hazzeh*, vv. 34aα and 41bβ) the Samarians continue to act "according to their former manner" (*hēm 'ōśîm kammišpāṭîm hāri'šōnîm*, vv. 34aβ and 40), which is to say — the writer slides directly into the specifics of the case — the people (repeatedly) "do not [properly] revere Yahweh" (*yěrē'îm 'et-yahweh*, v. 34a), for after all is said and done, "they [continually] revere Yahweh [*yěrē'îm 'et-yahweh*] but also their graven images" (v. 41).

Within this frame of condemnation, the writer elaborates the charge (III.B, vv. 34b-40) in terms of those standard covenant obligations mentioned earlier which ought to have gone hand in hand with learning how one should worship the God of Samaria (v. 28). The settlers failed the lesson, however, and continually acted without regard to the "statutes or the ordinances or the teaching or the commandment" (*ḥuqqôt, mišpaṭîm, tôrâ, miṣwâ*; cf. vv. 13 and 15) that had been given to the Israelites who preceded them as inhabitants of the land. (Much confusion about this passage in its present context can be avoided by noting that vv. 34a and 40-41 refer to the foreigners brought into Samaria [see vv. 24-33], while vv. 34b-39 supply, with a sense of the English pluperfect, a sketch of the religion which had been set forth as proper to the God of Samaria [cf. vv. 26-28].) Against this standard the author measures those who settled the land after Israel's exile.

This glance back to the covenant and its admonitions to the "children of Jacob" is the heart of the writer's argument (III.B.2, vv. 35-39). Two series of commands, each with a strongly reversing positive and negative component, amplify the concept that obligations of exclusive devotion went along with this relationship to Yahweh. At the time of covenant making God delivered twin exhortations to Israel:

(1) do *not* revere other gods, or bow down, serve, sacrifice to them,
     but *(kî 'im)*
     Yahweh *do* revere, and bow down, and sacrifice (vv. 35b-36)

(2)   do *not* forget the covenant; do *not* revere other gods,
but *(kî 'im)*
do revere Yahweh, and he will deliver you (vv. 38-39)

Nested within this double series of covenantal admonitions is the string of terms so frequently used by the DtrH to summarize covenant obligation: to perform the "statutes, ordinances, teaching, commandment" (*ḥuqqôt, mišpāṭîm, tôrâ, miṣwâ;* v. 37). The writer focuses once again on the main issue, while circling back to the beginning of his commentary (v. 34b) and recalling the same idea and terms in vv. 13, 15. As Israel before had failed (vv. 7-23), so the new settlers in Samaria, Israelites by instruction, failed the test, and moreover, down to the writer's and readers' own day (v. 41).

Genre

Since the DtrH created the picture of Hoshea's reign out of various materials, we may not designate a single genre for the whole composition. Viviano ("Rhetorical Analysis," 557) characterizes all of ch. 17 as (→) parenesis (cf. Hobbs, *2 Kings,* 224: the chapter purports to be an account of Israel's downfall, but is "more nearly a theological commentary" on the event). While accepting that this chapter may have been taken, and perhaps was intended, as admonition and exhortation, the form is not the direct address of parenesis, but reflective, didactic description in third-person style. Hobbs is closer to the mark, although "commentary" does not describe vv. 1-6 very well.

However, certain portions may be more precisely identified: (1) an introductory REGNAL RESUMÉ in vv. 1-2 (see discussion at 1 Kgs 14:21-31, in Long, *1 Kings,* 159-63); (2) REPORT, the first of which itemizes Hoshea's vassalage to Shalmaneser, his violation of that imposed arrangement, and the resulting crushing defeat by Shalmaneser, vv. 3-6 (these events are simply enumerated; by translating the simple conjunction variously as "but," "therefore," and "then," the *RSV* suggests more explicit causal and temporal connectivity than does the Hebrew text); a second report in vv. 24-33 deals with Samaria's resettlement and blends elements of (→) story (esp. in vv. 25-28) with (→) theological review (esp. in vv. 29-33); (3) THEOLOGICAL REVIEW in vv. 7-23a and 34-41 (see discussion at 1 Kgs 11:1-13, in Long, *1 Kings,* 122-23; cf. Noth, 6, who calls these verses "retrospective reflection").

Setting

We are not in a very good position to know much about the extent of, and settings for, the various materials the writer used to compose this unit. The reports in vv. 3-6 and 24 possibly derive from royal records of some kind, and vv. 25-28 perhaps from popular narrative. In view of the uncertainty, the most important consideration is that an exilic DtrH composed this representation of Hoshea's reign as part of the longer account of the failed monarchy. The chapter contains one of several extensive retrospective reviews that are positioned at critical junctures in the Dtr history (Noth, 5-6). As elsewhere in 1–2 Kings, most of this material constitutes an interruption in the forward progress of the larger narrative, a pausal moment between reigns. In this particular case, we linger between the demise of the northern kingdom and resumption of the Judahite story (ch. 18). Hoshea's reign is largely a moment filled with thematic material of special importance to the writer's particular theological interests.

Intention

From a vantage point in the exile, the DtrH represents the reign of Hoshea as a time of disaster, and explains the catastrophe as the result of repeated moral and religious failure by the Israelites and their kings. The theological reflection draws to an end the outworking of Jeroboam's transgression in the political life of the northern kingdom (cf. the allusions to Jeroboam in vv. 16, 21-23 with 1 Kgs 12:26-32; 13:33-34), while looking ahead to the disaster which would overtake Judah because she would walk "in the customs which Israel had introduced" (vv. 19-20).

Throughout the Dtr history, the fate of Judah is never very far from consciousness because both writer and reader suffered the final breakdown of Judah's kingdom, live among its ruins, and now recall their past experience in order to understand their present circumstances. Nowhere is this perspective clearer than in ch. 17. Judah, too, was warned unceasingly by prophets and seers (v. 13); the catalogue of "sins" attributed to the Israelites are mostly transgressions that are elsewhere laid at the feet of Judean kings (vv. 15-17; Viviano, "Rhetorical Analysis," 552); sacrifice of sons and daughters to the gods of nations roundabout (v. 17) is a religious failing associated explicitly with Ahaz and Manasseh of Judah (16:3; 21:6; on inner links between ch. 17 and other sections of Kings, see above all Hoffman, 132-33; Dietrich, 45).

So it is not at all surprising that these covert allusions come to the surface in vv. 19-20 when Judah's demise is explicitly mentioned. In hindsight, the writer suggests that the apostasy in the north spread into the south like a systemic disease: by intermarriage within royal houses (8:18, 26-27) or simply by doing as Israel had done (16:3, 17:19; 21:3). Perhaps the writer intends that the remnants of Judah in exile learn from these mistakes of the past and purge themselves of the contamination, especially in the light of the continued virulence of the infection in Israel's capital district, Samaria, long after her exile (vv. 34-41).

Bibliography

G. Baena, "Carácter literario de Reyes 17,7-23," *EstBib* 33 (1974) 5-29; B. Becking, "Theologie na de Ondergang. Enkele Opmerkingen bij 2 Koningen 17," *Beiträge zur Förderung christlicher Theologie* 49 (1988) 150-74; M. Cogan, "Israel in Exile — The View of a Josianic Historian," *JBL* 97 (1978) 40-44; W. Dietrich, *Prophetie*, 41-46 (→ 2 Kgs 8:28–9:28); H.-D. Hoffman, *Reform*, 127-39 (→ 2 Kgs 3:1-3); A. van der Kooij, "Zur Exegese von II Reg 17:2," *ZAW* 96 (1984) 109-12; C. Kuhl, "Wiederaufnahme" (→ 2 Kgs 13:1–14:29, Canonical Framework); B. Long, "Framing Repetitions" (→ 2 Kgs 4:8-37); J. Macdonald, "The Structure of 2 Kings 17," *Glasgow Oriental Society Transactions* 23 (1969) 29-41; A. D. H. Mayes, *Story of Israel between Settlement and Exile* (London: SCM, 1983); R. D. Nelson, *Double Redaction of the Deuteronomistic History* (JSOTSup 18; Sheffield: University of Sheffield, 1981); M. Noth, *Deuteronomistic History* (→ 2 Kgs 8:28–9:28); S. M. Paul, "Sargon's Administrative Diction in II Kings 17:27," *JBL* 88 (1969) 73-74; S. Talmon, "Polemics and Apology in Biblical Historiography: 2 Kings 17:24-41," in *The Creation of Sacred Literature: Composition and Redaction of the Biblical Text* (ed. Richard Friedman; Near Eastern Studies 22; Berkeley: University of California, 1981) 57-68; J. Trebolle Barrera, "La caida de Samaría. Crítica textual, literaria e histórica de 2 Re 17,3-6," in *Escritos de Biblia y Oriente* (ed. R. Aguirre and F. García López; Bibliotheca Salmanticensis 38; Salamanca: Universidad Pontificia, 1981) 137-52; P. A. Viviano, "A Literary Study of 2 Kings 17:7-41" (Diss., St. Louis, 1981); idem, "2 Kings 17: A Rhetorical and Form-Critical Analysis," *CBQ* 49 (1987) 548-59; M. Weinfeld, *Deuteronomy* (→ 2 Kgs 8:16-24).

THE REIGN OF HEZEKIAH: CANONICAL FRAMEWORK, 18:1–20:21

Structure

I. Introduction to Hezekiah's reign — 18:1-8
   A. Introductory resumé — 1-6
   B. Summary of successes — 7-8
II. Events during the reign — 18:9–20:19
   A. Fourth to sixth years: Assyria's campaign against Samaria — 18:9-12
     1. Fourth year: siege — 9-10
     2. Sixth year: capture — 11-12
   B. Fourteenth year: Sennacherib's campaign against Judah — 18:13– 20:19
     1. Invasion of Judean cities — 18:13-16
     2. Siege and deliverance of Jerusalem — 18:17–19:37
     3. Healing of Hezekiah — 20:1-11
     4. Hezekiah and the Babylonian delegation — 20:12-19
III. Concluding regnal resumé — 20:20-21

Reflecting the usual method of composition, the DtrH opens and concludes Hezekiah's rule with stereotyped regnal summaries (I, III, 18:1-8 and 20:20-21).

Within this framework, the writer arranges material of diverse kind and origin to represent the king's accomplishments and to further the aims of the entire book of Kings (see Long, *1 Kings,* 22; cf. other large blocks of tradition in 1 Kgs 16:29–22:40; 2 Kings 22–23).

The chronistic structure given to the recounting of events is somewhat unusual in 1–2 Kings. The writer dates incidents to the fourth, sixth, and fourteenth years of Hezekiah's rule and creates an effect of chroniclelike sequence (cf. only 1 Kgs 14:25; 2 Kgs 12:7 [*RSV* 6]; 17:6; 25:1-30). Several items, some of which may have existed independently of one another, are now joined together with minimal connective phrases and placed within the fourteenth year: (1) 18:13-16; (2) 18:17–19:37 (which may derive from two traditions); (3) 20:1-11; (4) 20:12-19. This compilation is a good example of the DtrH's use of a paratactic style of composition, i.e., arranging items in a series without strongly indicating how we are to understand relationships among individual elements.

By supplying temporal connections where indicators are lacking, one may make out a tolerably clear plot sequence. During Hezekiah's first years, the Assyrian forces overrun Samaria (II.A, 18:9-12), and now in the fourteenth year, they threaten Judah. Hezekiah tries to purchase peace (II.B.1, 18:13-16), but Sennacherib presses for Jerusalem's surrender anyway, once from his camp at Lachish (18:17–19:7) and again from Libnah (19:8-13). During this crisis, Hezekiah turns directly to Yahweh and receives assurances from God through Isaiah that Jerusalem will not be taken — indeed, Yahweh himself will bring about the downfall of Sennacherib and save the city (19:7, 21-34), a promise that finds its fulfillment in 19:35-37. Having finished this basic account, the DtrH interrupts the narrative sequence and reports two further incidents that supposedly occurred during Jerusalem's siege. "In those days" and "at that time" (20:1, 12), before Assyria had been defeated by God (20:6) and perhaps even before the kingdom's treasuries had been depleted (20:13, cf. 18:15-16), Hezekiah fell ill and recovered through God's (and Isaiah's) intervention (20:1-11), and concluded a pact with the Babylonians for which he was criticized (20:12-19).

Yet in this paratactic mode of composition, implied temporal relationships seem finally less important than thematic and motival analogies (see Long, *1 Kings,* 22-24). In terms of literary analysis, the DtrH manipulates sequentiality within his narrative world to express thematic concerns all the more forcefully. For example, Sennacherib's deputation from Libnah (19:8ff.) appears to be a *second* effort on his part. But in the telling, the narrator reduces the conflict to a theological point — Sennacherib mocks and reviles Israel's God (19:10, 16, 22, 28) — and shifts the locus of the drama from the earthly stage where military emissaries shuttle their messages back and forth to a cosmic stage on which God himself confronts Sennacherib (19:21-28). Moreover, this reading of events confirms exactly both Hezekiah's and Isaiah's perspectives expressed during Sennacherib's *first* deputation (19:4, 6). Our sympathies are won to Yahwistic theology and to Hezekiah not by sequential presentation of this siege against Jerusalem but by the gradual making known of the coincidence between God's view of events and those of Hezekiah and Isaiah. In this respect, the portrayal of Hezekiah takes on importance as a key element in the narrative's continuity.

The king does only the properly religious thing — he turns to God in prayer (19:3-4, 15-19) — but he is spared any personal rebuke for his dealings with the Babylonians and Assyrians (20:12-19; 18:13-16). Thus one receives through the confusions of war the sure image of a king assuredly cleaving to Yahweh; we see another king who just as clearly dismisses such allegiances (18:33; 19:11-12). The former picture, of course, is given its caption by the DtrH in Hezekiah's regnal summary (18:5-6; cf. 18:19-25).

Similarly, when the DtrH introduces the illness of Hezekiah and his concordat with the Babylonians as two narrative flashbacks (ch. 20), we look to thematic analogy and structural continuities as explanatory principles. As Yahweh defends Jerusalem for the sake of his own honor and his steadfast attachment to David's house (the reader already has this information from 19:34), so in that same dark hour of Assyria's threat God also grants personal recovery and longevity to Hezekiah, and for the same God-specific reasons (20:6). As Jerusalem faces Sennacherib and peers into a future of defeat — the situation recalls Samaria's demise (18:9-12; cf. 17:7-23) — Isaiah's comment on Hezekiah's dealings with the Babylonian Merodach-baladan hints that judgment on this city and its king, even in the midst of their rescue, materializes like a vision from afar (20:12-19). Particularly from the DtrH's exilic point of view, the Davidic ideal of kingship and dynasty has been upheld — herein lies a hope that can nurture Judah's remnant — and yet the fact of exile is legitimated in prophetic judgment, even before the transgressions of Manasseh (21:10-15) and before Jerusalem has been spared humiliation by Assyria.

Genre

Like all regnal epochs in the Dtr history, this unit is an editorial composite made up of several different literary genres. The REGNAL RESUMÉ provides the outer boundaries (18:1-6; 20:20-21; see discussion below; on regnal resumé, see Long, *1 Kings,* 158-64). Within, we find LEGENDS (18:17–19:37; 20:1-11) and various kinds of REPORT (18:7-8, 9-12, 13-16; 20:12-19). For detailed analysis, see below.

Setting

The unit stems from the DtrH, who compiled materials and wrote this history out of the situation of exile. He presents the success of Hezekiah and Judah immediately after commenting extensively on Israel's failure (ch. 17) and before providing a condemnatory summary of Manasseh (ch. 21). Hezekiah's regnal epoch, therefore, emerges against, and is framed by, the chaos of apostasy.

Intention

Obviously, a main intention of the Dtr writer would have been to represent the reign of Hezekiah as a paradigm of David-like obedience. When Jeroboam cast aside the Davidide standard (1 Kgs 11:38; 12:25-33), the light grew weak in the north and was finally extinguished. In the south, not since David himself ruled over the kingdom had the filament burned so brightly as it did in Hezekiah's time. Yet, its very intensity, like the burst of brightness that signals burnout, already announced Judah's ultimate failure as well (20:17-18). To an exilic remnant, these traditions may have been taken as part of the Dtr history's implied message of hope and exhortation: Jerusalem had been saved once, destroyed once, and might be delivered again if the flame of David-like obedience to covenant obligation and people of God were to be lit.

Bibliography

P. R. Ackroyd, "The Biblical Interpretation of the Reigns of Ahaz and Hezekiah," in *In the Shelter of Elyon. Essays on Ancient Palestinian Life and Literature (Fest.* G. Ahlström; ed. W. B. Barrick and J. R. Spencer; JSOTSup 31; Sheffield: University of Sheffield, 1984) 247-59; R. Deutsch, "Die Hiskiaerzählungen. Eine formgeschichtliche Untersuchung der Texte Js 36–39 und 2R 18–20" (diss., Basel: Basileia, 1969); G. Gerbrandt, *Kingship According to the Deuteronomistic History* (SBLDS 87; Atlanta: Scholars Press, 1986) 68-89; I. Provan, *Hezekiah and the Books of Kings* (BZAW 172; Berlin: de Gruyter, 1988); K. Smelik, " 'Zegt toch tot Hízkia': een voorbeeld van profetische geschiedenisschrijving (2 Kgs 18–20; Isa 36–39)," *AmstCah* 2 (1981) 50-67.

INTRODUCTION TO HEZEKIAH'S REIGN, 18:1-8

Structure

I. Introductory resumé	1-6
A. General information	1-2
1. Synchronistic accession formula	1
2. Accession age, length of reign, name of queen mother	2
B. Theological appraisal	3-6
1. General statement	3
2. Illustrative details	4
3. General statements	5-6
II. Summary of military successes	7-8

This unit begins with a typical regnal summary, vv. 1-6, and continues less typically with brief reports in vv. 7-8. The latter verses appear at first glance to move beyond the bounds of conventional introduction and to enumerate the first events that occurred during Hezekiah's rule (cf. the usual pattern at 1 Kgs 14:21-24, 25; 2 Kgs 8:16-19, 20). The Dtr writer appears to have expanded the theological appraisal of Hezekiah by binding these summarial notices to evaluative motifs: "the Lord was with him; wherever he went forth, he prospered" (cf. 1 Sam 18:14-15; 2 Sam 8:13-14; 1 Kgs 2:3). Moreover, the writer depicts rebellion against Assyria, v. 7b, with a verb that is both rare in the Dtr history and firmly attached to the tradition about Sennacherib's threat to Jerusalem in Hezekiah's time (*wayyimrōd*, "and he rebelled"; cf. 18:20; elsewhere only 2 Kgs 24:1, 20; Josh 22:18, 19). This unusual word choice suggests that vv. 7-8, while dealing with specific events, also introduce a main contour in the sculptured impression of Hezekiah's rule. A new topic with its own synchronistic date formula in v. 9 demarcates a move away from this general introduction to more detailed narrative.

Most critics assume that this material derives from the DtrH, who perhaps drew upon older sources for information about the king, especially for the exploits mentioned in vv. 7-8. Representative of scholars who envision multiple stages of redaction for the Dtr history, Würthwein (*Könige*, 407) supposes that an original Dtr text (vv. 1-3a, 7b; he actually considers vv. 13b-16 as part of the original unit) was supplemented by younger Dtr writers (vv. 3b, 5-7a) and expanded still later by unknown glossators (vv. 4, 5* [the phrase "nor among those who were before him"], and 8). The criteria for such reconstructions are inevitably somewhat arbitrary. (Note the impasse reached by Würthwein [411, n. 15] and Hoffmann [215-17] about whether the use of emphatic third person pronoun "he" [*hû'*] followed by simple *wāw* + perfect [*qātal*] verb, reliably indicates younger additions to the text, i.e., in vv. 4 and 8.)

Regardless of such controversies, the unit as it stands gives evidence of structural and thematic coherence. The conventional opening resumé, vv. 1-4 (only *wayĕhî* in v. 1 is atypical), leads into an unusually intensive theological appraisal in vv. 5-6. Here, the writer emphasizes Hezekiah's "trust" (*bṭḥ, bṭḥwn*) in God (v. 5) and his "clinging to God" (*dbq*) in keeping the Mosaic commandments (v. 6). These are precisely those aspects of Hezekiah's "good" behavior that come to prominence in the narratives of 18:17–20:11 (see esp. 18:19-35; 19:14-19; 20:3). Then vv. 7-8 enumerate the successes that flow from this exemplary devotion while alluding to the king's rebellion against Assyria. It is that act, of course, which the following narratives, 18:13–20:11, presuppose (see 18:20; cf. Deutsch, 56; Hobbs, *2 Kings*, 246-47).

While using standard literary formulas to evaluate Hezekiah positively (vv. 3-4), the author-editor subtly varies convention to construct a nearly unparalleled monument to this king. At the same time, the writer makes thematic and motival bridges to other biblical figures and to the narrative about Sennacherib's threat to Jerusalem.

Hezekiah "removed the high places and broke the pillars and cut down the Asherah" (v. 4a). These acts are the first examples of the writer's general claim that Hezekiah "did what was right in the eyes of the Lord according to all that David his father had done" (v. 3). More than mere illustration, however, Hezekiah's dismantling of cultic apparatus fits into a network of wider literary associations. The language of breaking and cutting down (*šibbar* and *kārat*) belongs to the Dtr picture of Moses, the zealous reformer, and of Yahweh, "whose name is Jealous" (Exod 34:14; cf. Gideon, equally zealous for undivided devotion to Yahweh, Judg 6:25-27, 30; cf. Deut 7:5; 12:3). Perhaps even surpassing Moses' zeal, Hezekiah "crushed fine [*kittat; RSV* 'broke in pieces'] the bronze serpent" that Moses himself had made (v. 4b; the verb *ktt* is also used of Moses destroying the golden calf, Deut 9:21). This cultic object was apparently a fertility symbol associated with the mother goddess Asherah at Ras Shamra and pre-Israelite Beth-shan, and thus a Canaanite legacy in the Israelite-Judahite religion (Gray, *Kings*, 670; see K. R. Joines, "The Bronze Serpent in the Israelite Cult," *JBL* 87 [1968] 245-56). For the Dtr writer, however, its destruction — whatever the real historical situation may have been — underscores Hezekiah's role as reformer. Since Moses, this bit of cultic apparatus signified that the first and second commandments had not been perfectly kept at least until the time of Hezekiah (Hoffmann, 148-49).

If destroying the gods suggests the past of reformer Moses, abolishing the "high places" (*bāmôt*, illegitimate shrines outside the Jerusalem temple's authority) connects Hezekiah with a reforming future — his grandson Josiah (23:19), who will rid the northern territories of their rural shrines, presumably those left in use after the demise of Israel (23:15, 19; see 17:29-33). At the same time, this deed disassociates Hezekiah from his father Ahaz (16:4), who was singled out for worshiping at the "high places," and from his son Manasseh, who will undo Hezekiah's work (21:3) and thereby earn the DtrH's reproof for Judah's downfall (21:10-15; 23:26-27). The same action exempts both Hezekiah and Josiah from the depreciation levied against a few otherwise righteous Judahite kings, who "did *not* remove the high places" (1 Kgs 22:44 [*RSV* 43]; 2 Kgs 12:4 [*RSV* 3]; 14:4; cf. 1 Kgs 11:7). It is this act, moreover, which Sennacherib's envoy will link to the centralization of worship in Jerusalem (18:22).

Through these associations, the Dtr writer suggests that the reader imagine Hezekiah as a consummate reformer who forged a new epoch in Judah's history. (For proposals about the historical substance of Hezekiah's reforms in relation to Josiah, and based upon hypotheses of two editions of the Dtr history, see Rosenbaum.) This king even surpassed all monarchs before and after in putting his "trust" in Yahweh (v. 5), although Josiah exceeded all rulers in his act of repentance, of "turning to the Lord" (23:25). One may find similar hyperbolic qualifiers, evidently a matter of scribal convention, in Assyrian and Neo-Babylonian royal inscriptions. See, e.g., in praise of an idealized king's prodigal offerings to the gods, "What no one had done like this from time immemorial, they [the gods] received from his pure hands for eternity and constantly blessed his kingship" (W. G. Lambert, "Nebuchadnezzar King of Justice," *Iraq* 27 [1965] 9-10); see also for Tiglath-Pileser I (ca. 1114-1076 B.C.E.): "I constructed it [the royal palace] from top to bottom [and] decorated [it] in a fashion more splendid than ever" [Grayson, *ARI*, 2, § 126, p. 33]; see also ibid., § 480, p. 105 [Tukulti-Ninurta II, ca. 890-884 B.C.E.). The aim of such exaggeration, of course, is to aggrandize the particular accomplishment being claimed for the king.

In the case of Hezekiah, the lavish praise of v. 5 introduces an interpretative key into the account, for the matter of "trust" in God (*bittāhôn*) will be met as a structural and thematic leitmotif in the dramatic deputation from Sennacherib to Hezekiah (18:19, 20, 21, 22, 24, 30; see full discussion below). Thus, one will read that story in the light of the Dtr writer's introductory appraisal, and see in the Rabshakeh's insistent rhetoric an ironic antithesis of Hezekiah's piety.

Genre

This composition consists of two main genres: (→) introductory REGNAL RE-SUMÉ, vv. 1-6, and two (→) REPORTS, vv. 7-8. See the full discussion of regnal resumé at 1 Kgs 14:21-31 (Long, *1 Kings*, 158-64).

Setting

Most critics take this sort of introductory material to have originated with the exilic DtrH who composed this story of the Israelite kings. See full discussion at 1 Kgs 14:21-31 (Long, *1 Kings*, 164).

Intention

The author's main intention is to introduce and to characterize the reign of Hezekiah. This king's time is marked by religious reform and fervent devotion, even in the midst of rebellion. Indeed, the implied successes in rebellion against Assyria (v. 7b) and in prevailing over former vassals of Assyria (v. 8) come as blessings from a God who rewards the good king (v. 7a), just as he had done with David (2 Sam 8:1-14). Against this interpretative grid, the DtrH presents those events which epitomize Hezekiah's rule. The hint of legendary stature for this king (vv. 5-6) will grow to full characterization in 19:1–20:11.

Bibliography

R. Deutsch, "Hiskiaerzählungen" (→ 2 Kings 18:1–20:21, Canonical Framework); H.-D. Hoffmann, *Reform* (→ 2 Kgs 3:1-3); J. Rosenbaum, "Hezekiah's Reform and the Deuteronomistic Tradition," *HTR* 72 (1979) 23-43.

ASSYRIA'S CAMPAIGN AGAINST SAMARIA, 18:9-12

Structure

I. Report of military campaign	9-11
A. Opening formula	9
B. Campaign results: defeat of Samaria	10-11
II. Explanatory comment	12

The outer limits of this unit may be seen in the chronistic reckoning of dates: v. 9 marks its beginning and v. 13 its end with a shift to new subject matter. Beginning with a synchronistic date and a formulaic mention of invasion ("Shalmaneser . . . came up against [ʿlh ʿl] Samaria"), the writer recounts three events in standard reportorial style: Samaria's siege, its capture, and the exile of its inhabitants. Only the explanatory comment at v. 12 relieves the rhetorical semblance of factuality.

The writer's style of chronistic reporting, especially with synchronisms, is fairly unusual in the books of Kings but not unknown (see 1 Kgs 14:25-26; 2 Kgs 18:13; 25:1, 3, 8, 25, 27 [the last with synchronism]; cf. 12:7 [*RSV* 6]). The concern to relate an event to so precise a chronology seems characteristic of royal record keeping (see discussion at 1 Kgs 14:21-31, in Long, *1 Kings*, 159-60), but mere archival impulse has been directed in v. 12 toward establishing the cause of Samaria's defeat in her willful transgression of the covenant with God (cf. other Dtr-styled brief explanatory comments in 1 Kgs 9:9; 15:30; 2 Kgs 22:13; Deut 32:51; a longer digression in 2 Kgs 17:7-23).

The report amounts to a recapitulation of information already given in ch. 17, although cast from the viewpoint of Judean royal chronology. Vv. 9-11 are a close paraphrase of 17:5-6; v. 12 summarizes a main point from the longer comment of 17:7-23, while omitting reference to Jeroboam's special place in the kingdom's religious and political failure (see 17:21-22). These similarities between 18:9-12 and 17:7-23 hint at a redactional or authorial relationship whose exact nature and history must of necessity remain obscure and open to speculation. (See Talmon, 58-59, who argues that 17:5-6 and 18:9-11 [+ v. 12 as redactional linkage] formed a framework around 17:7-41, when the latter was inserted into the ongoing account of the kings.)

Genre

This unit is a chronistic (→) INVASION REPORT. Such a report characteristically opens with a formula, with or without date: "RN came up against [*ʿlh ʿal* or *bĕ*] XY [royal or place name]." It continues variously with mention of besieging a fortress (*ṣûr*) or fighting against it (*nilḥam*). The report then usually recounts the simple result of the invasion (e.g., *wayyilkĕdāh*, "he took it," i.e., the city or territory). Sometimes the writer will include mention of capture and taking of prisoners, or even of bargaining and treaty making to save a city from defeat (e.g., 2 Kgs 16:7-9; 18:14-16; cf. Vuk, who limits his analysis unnecessarily to only those reports which mention tribute being given to ward off an invasion).

Good examples of invasion reports may be found in 1 Kgs 14:25-28; 2 Kgs 12:18-19 (*RSV* 17-18); 17:3-6; 18:13-16; 24:10-17. Cf. 2 Chr 20:22; 32:1; see also 1 Kgs 20:1, where elements of the typical invasion report appear in a highly dramatic account of battle (see Long, *1 Kings*, 209-18). Note Mesopotamian parallels in A. K. Grayson, "Königslisten und Chroniken," *RLA* VI, 105-6, 111, 113. Because of its explicit and precise date, the report of Samaria's defeat during Hezekiah's reign takes the form of (→) chronistic report (see discussion at 1 Kgs 14:21-31, in Long, *1 Kings*, 159).

Setting

Originally, invasion reports may have been a regular feature of chronicles, annals, or even king lists, all of which would have been constructed by scribes out of various kinds of royal records (see Long, *1 Kings*, 164). The more important setting, however, is the literary context within the Dtr history. The report comes as the first full-scale "event" during the regnal period of Hezekiah, and it recapitulates an Assyrian assault on Judah's sister kingdom. The fuller version of that event in 17:3-6 shows interesting similarities to that which Hezekiah had to face, as reported in vv. 13-16. Shalmaneser invades Samaria, and the vanquished Hoshea pays tribute as a vassal to Assyria. Later he offends his overlord because he sends "messengers to So, king of Egypt" (to make an alliance?) and stops his annual payments (17:4). Assyria's retaliation brings imprisonment for the king and loss of Samaria's independence. The Dtr writer attaches religious significance to these events (v. 12), and follows their reiteration with a report of Hezekiah's own confrontation with a later Assyrian king, 18:13-16.

Intention

A main intention of this invasion report is to offer a kind of admonitory background to Hezekiah's reign and actions. As one reads further into the DtrH's account, it will become clear that Hezekiah and Judah confront a fate like that of Samaria. However, forewarned by vv. 5-6, which report Hezekiah's exceptional devotion, a reader expects that the Davidide monarch and Jerusalem will survive. Recapitulation of Samaria's defeat reinforces a contrastive lesson: the north failed because of its transgression of covenant (v. 12), but Judah will live on because of Hezekiah's "trust" in Yahweh (see Würthwein, *Könige*, 410; Hobbs, *2 Kings*, 246-47).

Bibliography

S. Talmon, "Polemics and Apology" (→ 2 Kgs 17:1-41); T. Vuk, "Wiedererkaufte Freiheit; der Feldzug Sanheribs gegen Juda nach dem Invasionsbericht 2 Kön 18,13-16" (diss., Jerusalem, 1979; summary in *SBFLA* 30 [1980] 485-87).

SENNACHERIB'S CAMPAIGN AGAINST JUDAH: CANONICAL FRAMEWORK, 18:13–19:37

Structure

I. Report of invasion	18:13-16
A. Invasion of Judean cities	13
B. Hezekiah's response: deputation and tribute	14-16

In addition to a distinctive, yet parallel, version in 2 Chronicles 32, this block of tradition appears in Isaiah 36–37, although in somewhat shortened form (e.g., 2 Kgs 18:14-16 is missing from Isaiah). Moreover, the siege of Jerusalem has an independent witness in the inscriptions of Sennacherib himself (see *ANET*, 287-88). The compositional and redactional relationships among the various texts and the difficulties in reconstructing the sequence of historical events to which all the writings relate have occasioned extensive research and much debate. Scholars have posited multiple versions of one invasion by Sennacherib, or two separate invasions refracted in several traditions. Notions about whether there were one or two Assyrian campaigns have inevitably affected judgments about the textual traditions, and hypotheses about sources and redaction have guided in turn the reconstruction of history (see Childs; Clements; Gonçalves). Although it is not entirely possible to isolate literary issues from questions of historical reference (what really happened in what sequence), it is prudent to attempt such. At least in the light of recent research (see esp. Gonçalves), we may reject any explanation of the literary facts that resorts to the unsubstantiated idea of a double Assyrian invasion (so, most recently, Cogan and Tadmor, *II Kings*, 249-50; but cf. Shea).

On the surface the narrative falls into four main divisions: (1) 18:13-16, a report about Hezekiah's strategy to save Jerusalem in the face of Sennacherib's conquest of coastal Judean cities; (2) 18:17–19:7, the Rabshakeh demands that Jerusalem surrender, Hezekiah appeals to Isaiah, and the prophet responds with an oracle of deliverance; (3) 19:8-34, a second demand for surrender moves Hezekiah to appeal directly to God for rescue, and this in turn elicits a series of divine speeches through Isaiah, all promising the defeat of Sennacherib and the deliverance of Jerusalem; (4) as though fulfilling those prophecies, wholesale destruction of the Assyrian army induces Sennacherib to return home, where he dies by the hand of his own sons, 19:35-37.

There is widespread agreement that 18:13-16 (the so-called A account) is followed by material from a different source, 18:17–19:37 (the B account). The former is compressed and cool, chronistic in style (note the precise date formula), while the latter expands into extensive and dramatic narrative without a single allusion to the events recounted in vv. 13-16. Moreover, since Stade, a majority of scholars, with only minor disagreements, identify two parallel versions within the B account: B_1 = 18:17–19:9a, 36-37, and B_2 = 19:9b-35 (B_2 is usually taken as a separate version or an expansion of the first); there is also some disagreement over where B_1 ended (the transition in ch. 18 from v. 9a to 9b is a bit rough, with resulting textual variants) and over how to assign parts of vv. 35-37 to the two accounts. Beyond this, many critics assume that B_2 is not entirely unified, with 19:20-34 consisting of at least three originally independent pieces: a poem against a foreign nation, vv. 21b-28; a prophetic announcement of sign, vv. 29-31; and a promise of deliverance, vv. 32-34. Among the earlier commentators, Šanda mostly stood alone in opposing these source divisions (see his *Könige* II, 289-91). A summary of these issues will be found in Childs (pp. 70-103); see most recently Gonçalves (and further, Burney, *Notes*, 338; Clements, 52-71; Deutsch; Rofé, 88-91; Vogt; Fricke, *2 Könige*, 258; Cogan and Tadmor, *II Kings*, 240-43; Gray, *Kings*, 659; Hentschel, *2 Könige*, 87-88, 92; Montgomery, *Kings*, 514-15; Würthwein, *Könige*, 414-19 [although postulating multiple Dtr redactions within the accounts]). Criticism of the parallel Isaiah narrative tends to follow similar lines (see H. Wildberger, *Jesaja*, 1384-91).

Such an impressive consensus rests primarily on duplications observed within the narrative: (1) doubled diplomatic negotiations, 18:17-35 and 19:9-13; (2) a twice narrated end to Sennacherib's threat, 19:8 + 35 and 19:7 + 36-37; (3) repeated accounts of Hezekiah's seeking help and assurance in the temple, 19:3-7 and 19:15-34. As noted elsewhere in this commentary, however, repetitions in themselves do not necessarily signify different authors or editors, or even clumsy composition.

For example, the deputation to Hezekiah is represented much more fully and dramatically in 18:17-35 than in 19:9-13. The effect of the latter text is to distill the outcome of the Rabshakeh's earlier rhetoric into a new thematic essence. The Assyrian emissaries had hitherto attacked only Hezekiah's and the people's misplaced confidence in Yahweh, vv. 22, 25, 34-35. In 19:10, however, Sennacherib's messengers raise the bid and accuse God himself: (to Hezekiah) "Do not let *your God . . .* deceive you." Only here is the challenge to God uttered so directly, and yet so clearly built of materials at the heart of the first deputation (cf. the wording of vv. 10-11 with 18:29-30, 33-35). One might doubt that an independent source would have shown so close a relation to 18:17- 35 (cf. Šanda, *Könige* II, 291). Moreover, two prayers of Hezekiah, 19:3-4, 15b-19, label Sennacherib's actions as hubristic blasphemy. In their framing position the prayers guide the reader to encompass the image of Sennacherib's direct challenge to God (19:10) within this particular ideological perspective (the verb is *lĕhārēp*, 19:4, 16, *RSV* "to mock"). Isaiah uses a similar characterization (*giddĕpû . . . 'ōtî*, "reviled me," in v. 6), and the text of 19:22 has Yahweh himself adopt the same view, using both key words in his answer to Hezekiah: "Whom have you mocked [*hēraptā*] and reviled [*giddaptā*]?"

This sort of thematic linkage cuts across the lines of B₁ and B₂ and suggests coherent intentionality in the final text, however one might think of its origins. Such observations do not decisively rule out the traditional consensus on sources so much as point to the fruitfulness of asking how the text, whatever its prior literary history, implies authorial presence (see Hobbs, *2 Kings,* 246-49, and esp. Fewell, 79).

In terms of plot, the narrative in its canonical form moves through four stages. Sennacherib invades Judah (I, 18:13-16). Despite Hezekiah's payment of tribute, the Assyrian armies still threaten Jerusalem while their king remains at Lachish (II, 18:17–19:7) and even later when he moves to Libnah (III, 19:8-34). Finally, without letting loose a single arrow, but faced with unexplainable carnage, Sennacherib departs Judah as though in fulfillment of Isaiah's prophecy (IV, 19:35-37; cf. v. 7).

One key to understanding the structure of this narrative lies in grasping how scenes of dialogue characterize invisible, opposing forces (for some of what follows, cf. Fewell, 81-83). Within the confines of the story, the Rabshakeh confronts Hezekiah and his people, and Hezekiah in turn deals with the prophet Isaiah. For the reader, however, the action implies another set of relationships. Sennacherib and Yahweh, each as kingly warriors, belligerently confront one another through envoys and their boastful taunts (cf. 1 Kgs 20:1-12; 1 Sam 17:41-47). Sennacherib's ominous potentiality for destruction (made present through the words of the Rabshakeh and unspecified "messengers," 19:9) eventually draws forth the same potentiality in Yahweh (expressed through his prophet Isaiah). Hezekiah is a kind of mediating figure: each time he responds to the rhetorical assaults of Sennacherib, Yahweh replies through prophecy, but in words that focus less on Hezekiah than on Sennacherib's offenses against God.

Accordingly, the narrative consists largely of dialogues arranged as challenge and response (II, III, 18:19–19:7 + 19:10-34). These scenes are framed and connected by minimal descriptive prose, such that Sennacherib's military action against Judah leads to his verbal offense against God, which in turn leads to Hezekiah's responses, which finally elicit Yahweh's decisive reply and military action against Sennacherib (Fewell, 89).

Divine protagonist and earthly antagonist confront one another in a drama of words. Sennacherib's speech dominates the first part of the narrative (18:19-25, 28-35), and Yahweh's words the second part (19:20-34). Yahweh mimics the tone and disputational style of Sennacherib's (the Rabshakeh's) verbal assault in 18:19-35. Yahweh's words narrow the focus to Sennacherib's verbal actions, now defined as offense against God: "mocking" *(hrp)*, "reviling" *(gdp)*, "raging" (Hithpael of *rgz*), and arrogant "raising of the voice" (19:22-24, 28). They snatch the supports from Sennacherib's ridicule of Hezekiah's "trust" (18:19-25) and expectation of "deliverance" (18:29-35; 19:10-13). As the speeches progress, one realizes (but Sennacherib does not know it) that a transposition in power takes place. Hezekiah moves from a certain reticence to act to appealing directly for God's help, while Sennacherib tumbles from his self-assigned dominance, even divine commission (18:25), to become an enemy of God. In Yahweh's view (19:21-28), Sennacherib has been manipulated (v. 25), and now will be defeated (vv. 28, 32-34), not for threatening Judah, which is where the prose narrative began (18:13), but for raising an arrogant voice against God, which is where the speech-drama ends (19:27-28). The outcome, 19:35-37, amounts to a simple reversal of the Assyrian's position and rhetorical strategy: Hezekiah's "trust" is indeed not misplaced, "deliverance" is imminent, and Sennacherib's posture of military superiority is an illusion (Fewell, 86).

Genre

Some elements within this canonical unit conform to the form and style of historical reporting (e.g., 18:13-16, 17-18; 19:36-37). Other features, such as the Assyrian terms for military officers and the similarity between incidents reported in Assyrian letters and the speeches of the Rabshakeh, also suggest a closeness to historically based narrative (see esp. Childs). Yet, for the most part Hezekiah is presented as an ideal and exemplary king, who will have nothing to do with the arrogant Assyrian and who looks only for God's help. Like a prophet or a priest, Hezekiah defines the situation as a struggle between Yahweh and the mocking Sennacherib, and defines the substantive issue as faith opposed by apostasy. Deliverance finally comes as a result of Yahweh's direct involvement as military commander (19:35).

On balance, the narrative seems closest to a LEGEND, a story which is concerned primarily with the wondrous and exemplary. The plot is rudimentary, and the writer devotes most of his efforts toward building an impression of two ideological oppositions: (1) the boisterous persona of Sennacherib contrasted with the direct, guileless piety of Hezekiah (18:19-35; 19:10-13 + 19:1-7, 14-19); and (2) the confrontation between Sennacherib and Yahweh, in which the bluster of a blasphemer is matched by the rhetoric and power of the one true God of Israel.

Major generic elements within this legend are (1) DISPUTATION, 18:19-25, 29b-35; 19:10b-13; (2) Prayer of PETITION, 19:15-19; (3) PROPHECY OF SALVATION, 19:32-34; PROPHECY OF PUNISHMENT, 19:21-28; PROPHETIC ANNOUNCEMENT OF SIGN, 19:29-31; (4) REPORTS: of invasion (18:13-16), of military defeat (19:35-36), and of Sennacherib's death, including a SUCCESSION FORMULA (19:37). For detailed analysis of these genres and other more minor speech forms, see below.

Setting

This unit derives from the compositional activity of the Dtr historian, who selected it as the centerpiece of Hezekiah's reign. The historian's story leads into this high moment (18:9-12 reiterates the substance of ch. 17), all events are set within its time span (including 20:1-19), and nothing save perhaps the brief construction notice at 20:20 is left outside its reach.

Intention

Clearly a main intention of this legend is to account for the wondrous deliverance of Jerusalem in the aftermath of Assyria's successful assaults on both the northern kingdom and the cities of Judah. Perhaps of equal importance to the writer is the portrayal of Hezekiah as a paradigmatic faithful king who depends on God alone for his strength (18:5-6; cf. a similar notion in the warning to Ahaz in Isa 7:7-9; in later rabbinic tradition Hezekiah will be identified with the person spoken of in the Isaianic "immanuel prophecy" [Isa 7:14], as in, e.g., *Exod. Rab.* 18:5; *Num. Rab.* 14:2; see Laato-Åbo, 67). In contrast, Sennacherib is merely a presence in the drama through the words of the Rabshakeh, and seems a comic figure. He is ridiculously arrogant and thus oblivious to the forces of faith and divine power that oppose and finally overwhelm him, word for word and man for man (19:21-28, 32-34, 35; cf. 1 Kgs 20:23-30). For the DtrH's exilic audience, such an account of Jerusalem's deliverance may have been aimed at explanation and exhortation. The city eventually fell, the historian will claim, because of impious action (see ch. 21), and its reconstitution may depend on a reversal of such behavior.

Bibliography

See bibliography at 2 Kgs 18:1–20:21, Canonical Framework. J. Briend, "Comment fut sauvée Jerusalem; le second livre des Rois et l'invasion assyrienne de 701," *Le Monde de la Bible* 49 (1987) 21-24; B. S. Childs, *Isaiah and the Assyrian Crisis* (SBT 2/3; London: SCM, 1967); R. E. Clements, *Isaiah and the Deliverance of Jerusalem: A Study of the Interpretation of Prophecy in the Old Testament* (JSOTSup 13; Sheffield: University of Sheffield, 1980); D. N. Fewell, "Sennacherib's Defeat: Words at War in 2 Kings 18:13–19:37," *JSOT* 34 (1986) 79-90; F. J. Gonçalves, *L'Expédition de Sennachérib en Palestine dans la Littérature Hébraïque Ancienne* (EBib 7; Paris: Gabalda, 1986); L. Honor, *Sennacherib's Invasion of Palestine. A Critical Source Study* (New York: Columbia University, 1926); M. Hutter, *Hiskija, König von Juda; ein Beitrag zur judäischen Geschichte in assyrischer Zeit* (Grazer theologische Studien 6; Graz: Die Universität Graz, 1982); S. de Jong, "Hizkia en Zedekia; over de verbouding van 2 Kon. 18:17–19:37/Jes. 36–37 tot Jer. 37:1-10," *AmstCah* 5 (1984) 135-46; A. Laato-Åbo, "Hezekiah and the Assyrian Crisis in 701 B.C.," *Scandinavian Journal of the Old Testament* 2 (1987) 49-68; R. Liwak, "Die Rettung Jerusalems im Jahr 701 v. Chr.," *ZTK* 83 (1986) 137-66; A. Rofé, *Prophetical Stories* (→ 2 Kgs 1:2-17a); H. Rowley, "Hezekiah's Reform and Rebellion," *BJRL* 44 (1961) 395-431; W. Shea, "Sennacherib's Second Palestinian Campaign," *JBL* 104 (1985) 401-18; B. Stade, "Anmerkungen zu 2 Kö. 15–21," *ZAW* 6 (1886) 156-89; H. Tadmor, "Sennacherib's Campaign to Judah: Historical and Historiographical Considerations," *Zion* 50 (1985) 65-80; E. Vogt, *Der Aufstand*

Hiskias und die Belagerung Jerusalems 701 v. Chr. (AnBib 106; Rome: Biblical Institute Press, 1986); H. Wildberger, *Jesaja* (BKAT X; Neukirchen: Neukirchener, 1965-82).

CAMPAIGN AGAINST JUDAH AND HEZEKIAH: INVASION OF JUDEAN CITIES, 18:13-16

Structure

I. Invasion of Judah 13
   A. Opening formula 13a-bα
   B. Invasion results: defeat of cities 13bβ
II. Hezekiah's response 14-16
   A. Deputation to Sennacherib 14a
     1. Narrative introduction 14aα
     2. Message to Sennacherib 14aβ
       a. Confession of rebellion 14aβ₁
       b. Petition 14aβ₂
       c. Pledge 14aβ₃
   B. Report of outcome 14b-16
     1. Concerning payment required 14b
     2. Concerning payments made 15-16
       a. Silver from temple and palace 15
       b. Additional: gold from temple doors 16

This account apparently refers to events of 701 B.C.E. that are also mentioned in Sennacherib's own inscriptions. (See *ANET,* 287-88; and M. Görg, "Ein Keilschriftfragment des Berichtes vom dritten Feldzug des Sanherib mit dem Namen des Hiskija," *Biblische Notizen* 24 [1984] 16-17; on the lack of consistency with the biblical report, despite many proffered opinions to the contrary, note J. B. Geyer, "2 Kings xviii 14-16 and the Annals of Sennacherib," *VT* 21 [1971] 604-6; see the summary of historical problems by B. Oded, "Judah and the Exile," in *Israelite and Judaean History,* ed. J. H. Hayes and J. M. Miller [OTL; Philadelphia: Westminster, 1977] 435-88, esp. 441-51.)

In its literary setting (note the parallels in Isa 36:1 and 2 Chr 32:1), the biblical unit opens an extensive section that deals with events and subjects set against the background of Sennacherib's campaign against Judah (18:13–20:19; on the problem of reconstructing the actual historical sequence, see Clements; Ackroyd; standard histories). The new subject matter and synchronistic date formula in v. 13a set vv. 13-16 apart from the preceding report about Samaria's demise. The unit's ending is demarcated in two ways: (1) in the Hebrew of vv. 15 and 16, repetition of a simple statement, "and he [Hezekiah] gave . . ." *(wayyittēn/wayyittĕnēm),* precisely frames the report of Hezekiah's tribute payments to Sennacherib and brings the episode to rest like a formal coda; (2) v. 17 begins a new scene, fuller characterization and drama, and use of a longer form of Hezekiah's name, *ḥizqîyāhû.*

Many critics assume that originally v. 13a introduced v. 17, and that vv. 14-16 were inserted at some stage in the history of redaction (the verses are absent from Isaiah 36 and 2 Chronicles 32). The evidence is weak and ambiguous, and the fabric of the text shows no obvious sutures (see Childs, 70; Deutsch, 99). However, the phrase "at that time" suggests to some scholars that v. 16 was originally an independent item. Whether drawn from a second source by the author-editor of Kings or a later glossator remains a matter of dispute (see Würthwein, *Könige,* 409; Deutsch, 31; and the doubts by Childs, 70-71). Since recent study of Assyriological parallels shows that writers of inscriptions used similar indeterminate adverbial phrases to mark their use of a second source, one need not infer more from the biblical examples (cf. Montgomery, *Kings,* 485, "an independent item apparently culled from temple archives"; H. Tadmor and M. Cogan, "Ahaz and Tiglath-Pileser in the Book of Kings," *Bib* 60 [1979] 491-508, esp. 493-97). In any case, the shaped closure of vv. 15-16 suggests coherent intentionality and probably not haphazard composition or editing.

These disputes aside, the structure of the unit is rather clear. Faced with an invasion and loss of key cities (I, v. 13), King Hezekiah sends to Sennacherib and pledges to accept any imposition Sennacherib might require in return for his withdrawal from Jerusalem (II.A, v. 14a; the idiom "So-and-So sent" can mean dispatching a message by personal envoy, letter, or both; cf. 1 Kgs 5:15ff. [*RSV* 1ff.]; 20:2-3; 2 Kgs 19:9-13, 14). Hezekiah in fact confesses his disloyalty as a vassal ("I have done wrong"; cf. Gen 40:1; 1 Sam 24:12 [*RSV* 11]; 26:21), pleads for relief ("withdraw from me"; cf. 1 Sam 26:21), and pledges to accept whatever terms Sennacherib dictates (the verb *nāśā'* relates to the imposition and assumption of a burden; Gray, *Kings,* 674). The writer then simply reports the results of Hezekiah's negotiation: the amount of tribute demanded by Sennacherib and Hezekiah's payments (II.B, vv. 14b-16). This stereotyped closure emphasizes and probably exaggerates the depletion of palace and temple riches (cf. 1 Kgs 14:25-26; 2 Kgs 12:18-19 [*RSV* 17-18]).

The report follows a conventional *topos.* To turn away a military threat against Judah or Jerusalem, the king draws from the royal treasuries, including the temple, and pays tribute to the invading enemy (1 Kgs 14:25-28; 2 Kgs 12:18-19 [*RSV* 17-18] [2 Chr 24:23-24]; 18:14-16). Sometimes the king uses these same riches to purchase a defensive alliance with a second foreign king who then counteracts the might of the threatening armies (1 Kgs 15:16-22 [2 Chr 16:1-6]; 2 Kgs 16:5-9 [2 Chr 28:16-21]). Typically, the writer ends by noting that the strategy was successful (1 Kgs 15:20-21; 2 Kgs 12:19 [*RSV* 18]; 16:9).

It is quite wrong to describe these events as Hezekiah's "capitulation," as is often done by scholars who see an inherent contradiction between the position taken by Hezekiah in vv. 14-16 and vv. 17-36 (see, e.g., Gray, *Kings,* 685: v. 14 depicts a "final surrender"). Rather, the *topos* describes a strategy to relieve military pressure on Jerusalem and to preserve Judah's independence. Pointedly missing from the Hezekian example is a statement of success. Sennacherib receives the payment, actually the price of a treaty (cf. discussion at 2 Kgs 16:7; 1 Kgs 15:18-19), but — contrary to reader expectations — we are not told that Assyria reduced in any way her menacing thrust toward Jerusalem. In context, this variant on convention suggests that vv. 17-35 be understood as dramatizing

Sennacherib's continued pressure on Jerusalem. Assyria will not be bound by any alliance-sealing gifts, and by implication, Hezekiah's attempt at foreign alliance has failed.

Genre

This unit is an example of an (→) INVASION REPORT. Terms such as "historical digest" (Gray, *Kings*, 672) or "excerpt from annals" (Montgomery, *Kings*, 334) embody some judgment as to the historical credibility of such reports and are best avoided as inadequate for literary description. See Vuk for a special study of invasion reports, although he limits himself unnecessarily to those examples that describe payment of tribute. See full discussion and parallels at 2 Kgs 18:9-12.

In fact, Vuk concentrates on a stock scene often found as part of invasion reports in which a Judean king sues for peace by paying tribute to an invading enemy (1 Kgs 14:25-28; 2 Kgs 12:18-19 [*RSV* 17-18] [2 Chr 24:23-24]; 18:14-16; cf. 2 Kgs 14:8-14) or negotiates a defensive alliance with a foreign king (1 Kgs 15:16-22 [2 Chr 16:1-6]; 2 Kgs 16:5-9 [2 Chr 28:16-21]). A similar literary convention sometimes appears in the prologues to Hittite treaties. In one example, a vassal king, having suffered military defeat, sends a message to the king of Hatti: "Servant of the king of the land of Hatti [am] I; save me!" The Hittite king then reports that he sent a fighting force and drove off the invaders (E. Weidner, *Politische Dokumente aus Kleinasien* [Boghazköi Studien 8-9; Leipzig: J. C. Hinrich, 1923] #3, col. i, pp. 58-59). Another treaty prologue narrates how Niqmaddu, under pressure from invaders, sent a message to his master, Šuppiluliuma. In a stylized speech, he declares his vassal status, alludes to the severity of a military crisis, and pleads, "Deliver me!" The writer then states that "The great king [of Hatti] heard the words of Niqmaddu" and rescued his vassal (J. Nougayrol, *PRU* IV (= *Mission de Ras Shamra* IX; Paris: Klincksieck, 1956; RS 17.340, pp. 48-52).

All the biblical examples of this *topos* fix on Judah or Jerusalem and show a special concern for the palace and temple treasures. The language is formulaic and highly generalized, e.g., 1 Kgs 15:18, "all the silver and the gold that was left in the treasure houses," or 2 Kgs 12:19 (*RSV* 18), "all the votive offerings [of all the kings of Judah], and all the gold to be found in the treasuries of the temple," or 2 Kgs 18:15, "all the silver that was found in the temple of Yahweh and in the treasuries of the palace." The Judean kings singled out in this fashion are Rehoboam (1 Kgs 14:26), Asa (1 Kgs 15:18), Jehoash (2 Kgs 12:19 [*RSV* 18]), Ahaz (2 Kgs 16:8), and Hezekiah (2 Kgs 18:15). What, if any, special significance the Dtr writer may have attached to these incidents is difficult to determine. At the very least, they indicate an interest in recording the efforts of various kings to defend a city which — in Hezekiah's time — God himself will protect.

The speech attributed to Hezekiah, 2 Kgs 18:14b, is analogous to confessional statements in legal proceedings in which a guilty party admits wrongdoing and pledges to correct the infraction (see Boecker, 111-17). The (→)

A shift in subject matter and style marks the beginning of this unit. The immediately preceding verse brought measured closure to a commentarial description of Hezekiah's payments to Sennacherib. In 18:17, narrative time resumes its forward progress as the writer describes the deputation sent from Lachish to Jerusalem. A certain ambiguity in the Hebrew and the possibility that two independent sources may have been joined at 19:8-9 make it difficult to decide where the scene ends — with the last words of Isaiah's prophecy (19:7) or with the departure of the Rabshakeh (19:8-9). If source-critical hypotheses about B_1 and B_2 narratives are correct, then 19:8-9a would have originally concluded one account of Sennacherib's deputation to Hezekiah (→ 18:13–19:37, Canonical Framework). As presently situated, however, vv. 8-9a constitute a transition to, and narrative setting for, a second mission from Sennacherib. Parenthetical details clearly look ahead to new activity at a different location (→ full discussion 19:8-34; Gray, *Kings,* 663, views vv. 8-9 as "editorial bridges between the two versions of the same delegation"). In any case, vv. 8-9 abruptly shift the attention of the reader from private dealings between Hezekiah and Isaiah back to the Rabshakeh who was last heard from at 18:35. On these grounds alone, one may consider the unit for analysis to conclude with Isaiah's prophecy, 19:7, without making any claims for redactional history.

Certain features of this narrative pose the question of literary and logical coherence. The Rabshakeh's speeches to Hezekiah's servants, vv. 19-25, 28-35, open with traditional formulas which lead one to expect that a message is simply being transmitted, first to Hezekiah, then to the Jerusalemites (cf. v. 19a with 1 Kgs 20:2-3, 5-6; 2 Kgs 1:2). Yet the "message" in both instances gives the impression of sprawling improvisation as the speaker mixes quotes, threats, taunts, and blustery argumentation into a rolling assault on his listeners' self-confidence. Moreover, the indications of addressee and addresser shift in unusual ways. At various points the Rabshakeh takes the role of messenger; he quotes Sennacherib directly (vv. 19b-20, 31-32), refers to his master as message giver (vv. 19a, 28), and refers to Hezekiah or the people as recipients (vv. 19a, 29-31). But sometimes the distinctions blur, as in v. 25, or the Rabshakeh seems to invent statements of his own, referring in such cases to the king in the third person (vv. 23-24, 33; see Gevaryahu for a study of these distinctions). Also, the second person singular forms of address in vv. 19b-21 shift suddenly to a plural in v. 22, and back to singular in vv. 23-24, while the second plural suffixes remain consistent throughout vv. 29-32. Further, the separated references to Yahweh's help, vv. 22 and 25, and a similar dislocation of the motif of Hezekiah's "deception," vv. 29-30, 32b, suggest a certain illogic in the arrangement of material (Rudolph; cf. Wildberger on the parallel text in Isaiah 36).

While recognizing that some material in this section probably derives from oral tradition and may have undergone complex literary development (e.g., are vv. 32b-35 an addition under the influence of 19:10?), many scholars view the present text, despite its tensions, as sufficiently unified to discourage confident reconstructions of its precanonical history. Childs (pp. 78-93) argues that the various problems cannot be solved with recourse to traditional methods of source and redaction criticism. Instead, he attributes many of the stylistic and motival peculiarities to historically attested patterns of diplomatic speech or to developments in theological reflection.

Würthwein (*Könige,* 415-19) proposes that before its Dtr rendering, this section of the B_1 narrative already combined two independent traditions, the earlier one a speech to the people (18:28-29, 31aβ-bα, 32aβ, 36aα), and the other an address to the king (18:18-21, 23-24, 36*-37). Vv. 26-27 joined the two together. Later elaborations from the DtrH in 18:22, 25, 30, 31b-35, and

19:1-7 brought the traditions to their present form (cf. Hentschel, *2 Könige*, 87-88). In support, Würthwein mentions the criteria of "resumptive repetition" (Kuhl). The verb "and he stood up" *(wayya'āmōd)*, resumed in v. 28 from v. 17, suggests to him that vv. 18-25 were inserted between vv. 17 and 28ff., and that vv. 26-27 were consequently created as a transition (*Könige*, 418).

One may doubt the adequacy of Würthwein's view in particular, and of the various analyses that find source or redactional explanations for unusual stylistic features in the narrative. Würthwein applies a general theory of multiple redaction throughout his commentary on 1–2 Kings, but in this instance he makes the repetition of a single verb carry too much weight.

Beyond this, some features that are so often found to be troublesome may be explained with reference to rhetorical style and function. Childs argues, for example, that if the typical features of rhetorical argument are taken seriously, one should not be surprised to find a speaker freely switching ground between quotes, questions, statements, imperatives, threats, accusations, and hypothetical cases (Childs, 82; cf. Jer 27:16-22; Mic 2:6-11). This need not imply a tolerable disorder, as Child's suggests, for implicit claims and counterclaims hidden in the rhetoric actually delineate lines of structural and logical coherence.

The Rabshakeh's address consists of two separate arguments — one aimed at Hezekiah and his men, and the other delivered to the defenders on the city's walls (vv. 19-25; 28-35). The first deals with "confidence" or "trust" *(bātaḥ, biṭṭāḥôn)*, a leitmotif of Hezekiah's reign (cf. 18:5); the second speaks of divine "deliverance" (the Hiphil of *nṣl*). V. 30, which uses both of the thematic words, links the two arguments together. The people should not be deceived by Hezekiah who makes them "trust" that the Lord will "deliver" them and the city from Sennacherib (cf. v. 22).

Each of the arguments follows a discernible plan. In vv. 19b-22, the Rabshakeh makes two points: Egypt is unreliable (vv. 19-21), and so is Yahweh (v. 22). Each claim is then reiterated in the same order (vv. 23-24, 25) to yield an AB/A'B' structure built on the theme of misplaced "confidence." Similarly, in vv. 29-30 the Assyrian officer implies that the Jerusalemites hold two convictions: Hezekiah will save (v. 29b) and Yahweh (who stands behind Hezekiah) will deliver the city from its peril (v. 30). Each of these beliefs is then refuted with implicit counterclaims. It is Sennacherib who actually will deliver you (explicitly, do not listen to Hezekiah, accept Sennacherib's "peace," vv. 31-32). Neither the gods nor Yahweh can work deliverance (explicitly, where are the gods? vv. 33-35). In v. 32b the Rabshakeh summarily joins the idea of Hezekiah's deception with the thematic word "deliver" (Hiphil of *nṣl*), and thereby binds both refutations to the introductory statement of vv. 29b-30 where the same ideas are associated with one another.

Moreover, the alternation of singular and plural suffixes in the Rabshakeh's first speech exactly delineates the imagined situation. When statements are put to Hezekiah through his emissaries, the speaker uses singular forms of address (vv. 20-21 and 23-24). When the Rabshakeh anticipates that Hezekiah's servants might offer a counterargument on their own initiative, he addresses them directly with plural suffixes (v. 22). The writer-narrator maintains this same distinction, for he has the Rabshakeh ask in v. 27, "Has my master sent me to speak these words to *your master* and *to you* . . . ? (the last is a singular suffix, but it obviously refers to Hezekiah's three servants; see v. 27aα).

All these observations suggest that the narrative as it has come down need not be read as inconsistent or roughly composed. One may therefore investigate its unified form and implicit intentionality, while leaving unresolved the issue of whether one author or several redactors produced final coherence in the text.

The episode falls into two main divisions: (1) a report of Sennacherib's deputation from Lachish (18:14, 17) which essentially depicts one speech delivered in two phases, each with its response (I.B and C, vv. 19-27, 28-36); (2) an account of Hezekiah's effort to deal with the situation by appealing to Isaiah (II, 18:37–19:7). Brief sections of narrative prose provide minimal settings (vv. 17-18; 18:37–19:1) and chart the flow of speech between persons. (Note the somewhat different outline by Wildberger, *Jesaja*, 1384.)

The Rabshakeh challenges Hezekiah to abandon his misplaced trust in Yahweh and surrender to Sennacherib's power (I.B.2, vv. 19aβ-25). When the king's servants suggest that this Assyrian official keep such upsetting counsel from the people on the city wall (I.B.3, v. 26), the Rabshakeh defiantly aims a second wave of temptation at them anyway (I.C, vv. 28-36). Refusing all these rhetorical inducements to surrender, Hezekiah appeals directly to Isaiah (II.B.2, 19:3-4) and receives a promise that Sennacherib's attempt to take Jerusalem will fail (II.B.3, 19:5-7).

The writer carefully constructs a setting for this action in vv. 17-18. Three highly placed Judean officials face three similarly ranked Assyrian emissaries, as though the contest begins with evenly matched opponents. For Hezekiah's officials, see 1 Kgs 4:6 ("head of the palace" [*RSV* "household"]); 4:3 ("scribe" [*RSV* "secretary"]; and "archivist" [*RSV* "recorder"]). Although the Hebrew writer treats Tartan, Rabsaris, and Rabshakeh as Assyrian proper names, they are in fact titles of high-ranking royal officials and mean respectively "second-in-command," "commander-in-chief" (lit., chief eunuch), and "chief cupbearer" or "butler." (See H. Tadmor, "Rab-saris and Rab-shakeh in 2 Kings 18," in *The Word of the Lord Shall Go Forth* [*Fest.* D. Noel Freedman; ed. C. Meyers and M. O'Connor; Winona Lake, IN: Eisenbrauns, 1983] 279-85; Cogan and Tadmor, *II Kings,* 229-30.)

Agents confront agents, and in this dramatic setting action goes forward as a series of messages meant to be transmitted from principal to principal: Sennacherib to Hezekiah, Hezekiah to Isaiah, God to Hezekiah. (Note the language of commissioning, 18:19a; 19:6aβ; and the messenger formulas, 18:19bα, 29a, 31aβ; 19:3aα, 6bα.) The distinctions, of course, are artificial. The Rabshakeh and Isaiah at times fade behind the words they carry, and both project in their speech the force and personality of their respective masters (cf. A. Vater, "Narrative Patterns for the Story of Commissioned Communication in the OT," *JBL* 99 [1980] 365-82, esp. 375-78). Moreover, the narrator-writer emphasizes the substance of speech rather than descriptive prose or the formalities of emissarial protocol. We are thereby privy to things which officials do and say, but we also are led by the writer to construct a dramatic struggle for dominance between Sennacherib and God, the two principals who are arrayed as antagonists but who make no appearance in the narrative (Fewell).

The Rabshakeh's first speech challenges Hezekiah to face the weakness of those upon whom he "relies" for his confident resistance (*bāṭaḥ ʿal,* "rely upon," and *biṭṭāḥôn,* "confidence," B.2, vv. 19aβ-25). Following the commissioning and messenger formulas, v. 19a, two rhetorical questions set the theme: "On what do you rest this confidence [*biṭṭāḥôn*] of yours . . . on whom do you now rely [*bāṭaḥtā*] . . . ?" (vv. 19bβ-20b). Then the Rabshakeh builds his two-staged argument on a pattern of thesis (the belittled opinion attributed directly or implicitly to the Rabshakeh's opponent) and counterthesis (the refutation offered by the Rabshakeh).

The Rabshakeh refutes two claims: that Hezekiah (and his armies) rely on Egypt to bolster their rebellion and that they expect Yahweh to support their king. We may visualize the literary structure as a set of twice-repeated claim and counterclaim (AB/A'B'): Egypt is unreliable; Yahweh may not be counted on. A thematic word "rely" *(bāṭaḥ)* ties everything together.

A **thesis:**
  "you rely [*bāṭaḥtā*] on Egypt," v. 21a

 counterthesis:
  "broken reed of a staff . . . such is Pharaoh to all those who rely [*habbōṭĕḥîm*] on him," v. 21b

B **thesis** (attributed to Hezekiah's men):
  "We rely [*bāṭaḥnû*] on the Lord our God," v. 22a

 counterthesis (implied):
  "is it not he whose altars . . . Hezekiah removed?" (Hezekiah has offended Yahweh), v. 22b

A' **thesis** (implied in proposed wager):
  "two thousand horses . . . to set riders upon them" (Hezekiah has military reserves), v. 23

 counterthesis (implied in rhetorical question):
  "How can you repulse a single captain . . . when you rely [*wattibṭaḥ*] on Egypt?" (Hezekiah cannot raise the requisite number of riders), v. 24

B' **thesis** (implied in rhetorical question):
  "is it without Yahweh that I have come?" (Yahweh is with Hezekiah), v. 25a

 counterthesis (implied):
  "Yahweh said to me, 'Go up against this land'" (Yahweh is with Sennacherib, not Hezekiah), v. 25b

The Rabshakeh darts from statement to innuendo, to proposition, to direct claims of special mission (cf. the outline by De Vries, 70, which obscures the dialogic flow of thought). As messenger, he speaks for the Assyrian king, who in turn asserts divine commission for his actions, v. 25. This is a feature of commemorative royal inscriptions among Israel's neighbors, for example the Moabite Mesha's statement, "Chemosh said to me, 'Go, take Nebo from Israel!' " (*KAI* I, no. 181 [*ANET,* 320-21]; cf. the same idea in Isa 10:5-6). Yet, the Rabshakeh also breaks strict emissarial conventions. He cajoles, tempts, and imagines hypothetical counterarguments. He invents his speech with the freedom of a negotiator who looks for any means to persuade and who thoroughly knows the intentions of his master.

The writer characterizes the Rabshakeh as one who also knows Israel's affairs intimately, and yet — from the reader's perspective — comically mis-understands them (cf. the similar irony in 1 Kgs 20:23). Yahweh is not to be relied upon. Why? Because Hezekiah offended him by destroying rural shrines (the "high places") and supporting (exclusively, it is implied) the Jerusalem cult ("You shall worship before this altar in Jerusalem," v. 22). This same God now charges Sennacherib, not Hezekiah, with a holy mission (v. 25). Of course, what the Assyrian sees as offensive to Yahweh, the Dtr writer takes as a pleasing sign of obedience. (Later, what the Rabshakeh claims here as divine commission will be dismissed as arrogant overreach, 19:25-28.) Through this unwitting Assyr-ian's words, the writer assures Hezekiah his place of distinction alongside Josiah. Both of these Judean kings are remembered for their commitment to the Mosaic teachings, and their championing of centralized worship in Jerusalem (see Deut 12:1-14; on Josiah, see 2 Kgs 22:13; 23:3, 4-14, 21-23).

Realizing the effectiveness of the Rabshakeh's arguments, and assuming that Jerusalem's defenders are wavering, Hezekiah's men request that negotia-tions be carried on in Aramaic, not in the "language of Judah" (I.B.3, v. 26). In reply, the Rabshakeh self-consciously and defiantly turns from the king and his officials to "all the men sitting on the wall" (v. 27). To these hapless defenders, all of whom are "doomed . . . to eat their own dung and to drink their own urine" (cf. 6:26-29), he aims a second verbal assault (I.C, vv. 28-36). Beginning with admonitions that imply his opponents' convictions (vv. 29-30), the Rab-shakeh presses the city's guards to surrender. The flow of thesis/counterthesis again helps us visualize the speech's rhetorical structure:

Admonitions
A   **thesis** 1 (implied):
       Hezekiah can save us, v. 29a

B   **thesis** 2 (implied):
       Yahweh can save us, v. 30

Refutations
A   **counterthesis** 1 (implied in appeal to surrender)
       Sennacherib, not Hezekiah, can save you, vv. 31-32

B **counterthesis** 2 (implied in rhetorical questions)
Yahweh cannot save Jerusalem, vv. 33-35

Although admonitory in form, the Rabshakeh's first words amount to a statement of his opponents' beliefs which are to be disputed with counterclaims. The cautionary "Do not let Hezekiah deceive you" (v. 29a) and the direct claim, "he will not be able to deliver you out of my hand" (v. 29b), imply that the men hold to exactly what the Rabshakeh warns against. A second cautionary statement, v. 30, suggests that the defenders also rely upon Yahweh to deliver the city. In these opening admonitions, the Rabshakeh actually voices the main theme of his second argument: the folly of thinking that Hezekiah or Yahweh can "save" or "deliver" Jerusalem (Hiphil of *nṣl,* vv. 32b, 33, 34, 35). Together, the exhortations imply the basic opinion (an opponent's thesis) which the Rabshakeh will systematically and serially refute (his counterthesis). Each refutation opens with an identical cautionary word, "Do not listen to Hezekiah" (vv. 31-32a, 32b-35).

Presented in the form of invitation and promise, the first counterclaim suggests that while Hezekiah cannot save the city, Sennacherib will do so. The Jerusalemites have only to seize the future envisioned in his words, "Make a blessing with me" (v. 31; *RSV* "make your peace with me"). The exact meaning of this invitation is uncertain. Some translate "salute me" (Montgomery, *Kings,* 489), or "make a peace with me" (so the Targum, accepted by *RSV* and many scholars; see J. Scharbert, *TDOT* II, 298-99). Perhaps the expression refers, as synecdoche, to a treaty (Mitchell, 44) or to a mutual undertaking that each party seek the good, the "blessing," of the other (A. Murtonen, "The Use and Meaning of the Words *lĕbārek* and *bĕrākāh* in the Old Testament," *VT* 9 [1959] 158-77, esp. 173-74). In any case, the phrase which follows, "come out to me," indicates that the Rabshakeh really speaks of capitulation, plain and simple (cf. 1 Sam 11:3, "we will come forth to you" [*RSV* "give ourselves up"]). Yet he seductively softens the harshness of surrender, hints at mutuality, and promises that material abundance in the manner of "blessings" will flow from the benevolence of Assyria (cf. the affluence of Solomon's rule, 1 Kgs 4:25-26, and the link between "blessing" and prosperity in Deut 30:19; 28:8, 12). The writer-narrator may also allude ironically to the blessings of Israel's own promised land (Deut 8:7-9; cf Hobbs, *2 Kings,* 259).

The Rabshakeh introduces his second refutation at v. 32b by reverting to the exhortation of v. 31aα, "Do not listen to Hezekiah," and linking it to the main leitmotif of the whole argument: "he [Hezekiah] misleads you by saying, 'The Lord will save us'" (*yaṣṣilenû;* cf. v. 31aα). Finally, a series of rhetorical questions in vv. 33-35 imply that Yahweh cannot deliver Jerusalem from Sennacherib. Why? Because none of the various national gods has heretofore prevented Assyria's military triumphs, and thus there is no ostensible reason why Israel's God should do so now.

The conquered countries — Hamath, Arpad, Sepharvaim, Hena, and Ivvah — are conventionally associated with Assyrian military prowess (cf. Isa 10:9; Jer 49:23). This particular enumeration may also recall 17:24, 30-31, where three of the nations (Hamath, Sepharvaim, and Ivvah [the last is probably the Avvâh of 17:24] are included among those captive peoples who resettled the northern kingdom after its defeat by Shalmaneser. However, the allusion to ch. 17 is not exact. One implication of 18:34 might be that these peoples were not simply captive-settlers as 17:24 has it, but that they had earlier tried unsuccessfully to defend their countries against Assyrian conquest. If one takes this larger literary context seriously, the Rabshakeh suggests that these gods could not, or chose not to, save their own peoples, and so naturally could not save Samaria either. In this light, one may read v. 34b not as a rhetorical question but as a scornfully sarcastic statement: "Sure, they have delivered Samaria from my hand!" (reading asseverative *kî;* see Williams, *Hebrew Syntax* [2nd ed.; Toronto: University of Toronto, 1976], § 449). If not exact history (these captive-settlers of Assyria would hardly have been defending Samaria against Assyrian armies), the allusion nonetheless accords well with the Dtr writer's desire to view Hezekiah and Judah against the backdrop of the northern kingdom's defeat (see 18:9-12).

The next section of the narrative describes how Hezekiah copes with the threat posed by Sennacherib (II, 18:37–19:7). As background, we are told that the king had commanded the people to keep their counsel before the Rabshakeh (v. 36b may be understood in the sense of English pluperfect). In distress, "with their clothes rent," Hezekiah's officials report the "words of the Rabshakeh" to the king, who, in a similarly conventional show of public mourning, withdraws to the temple and sends his own deputation to Isaiah (cf. 1 Kgs 21:27; 2 Kgs 5:7-8; 6:30; 22:11, 19). This descriptive prose introduces the dialogic center of the episode, Hezekiah's appeal for help (II.B.2, vv. 3-4), and Isaiah's oracular response (II.B.3, vv. 5-7).

The typical patterns by which commissioned messages are reported seem a bit confused in this scene. V. 3, "they [the royal officials] said to him . . . ," implies that the emissaries already stand before Isaiah delivering their message, while v. 5, "And the servants of King Hezekiah came to Isaiah," suggests that only now do they arrive with a word for the prophet. The *RSV* and *NJPS*, "when the servants . . . came to Isaiah," supply a temporal subordination that is not explicit in the Hebrew; Fricke (*2 Könige,* 270) speculates that v. 5 refers to a second visit to Isaiah; Hobbs (*2 Kings,* 265) turns v. 5 into a summarizing remark, "Thus did the servants of Hezekiah come to Isaiah."

However one might explain this lapse in clarity, we may appreciate that the writer emphasizes the content of dialogic speech rather than the formalities of its delivery, and in so doing, begins to transform our perception of events. Having overheard the provocations of Sennacherib and said nothing, Hezekiah now appeals to Isaiah in words that suggest a familiar tradition of theological interpretation. In characterizing the crisis as a "day of distress" (*yôm-ṣārâ,* 19:3a), the king associates the threat to Jerusalem with those archetypal days of divine punishment, eschatological catastrophe, or generalized troubles from which Israelites will find deliverance in Yahweh (Jer 16:19; Obad 12, 14; Nah 1:7; Hab 3:16; Zeph 1:15; Ps 20:2 [*RSV* 1]; 50:15). It is also a "[day of] disgraceful things" (*nĕʾāṣâ),* a phrase by which Hezekiah hints at moral rebuke, not of the victims who suffer, but of those who victimize. For example, see Ezek 35:12, words against Edom which conquered Judah: "I have heard all your *disgraceful things* [*RSV* 'revilings']. . . . You magnified yourself against me with your mouth, and multiplied your words against me." (Cf. Neh 9:18, 26 where the sense is "blasphemy" against Yahweh.) The situation in Hezekiah's Jerusalem is ominous, but not without solace. When assimilated to this archetypal pattern, the circumstances stir the memories and hopeful expectations of the righteous, or of a king who typically "held fast to the Lord" (18:6).

Having evoked these suggestions of a traditional moral equation, Hezekiah then lays the groundwork for his appeal by musing that God may have heard what he himself had heard, namely — and here Hezekiah again characterizes his opponent — the words of the Rabshakeh, "whom his master the king of Assyria had sent to mock [*lĕhārēp*] the living God" (v. 4). At this point, Hezekiah defines the issue as blasphemy against God, not military threat against Jerusalem. He colors the situation with still another traditional motif, the blasphemer of God, an enemy of Israel whose self-aggrandizing words offend the sanctity of Israel's Holy One. Cf. David's pious and confident belittling of Goliath: "I come to you in the name of the Lord of hosts, the God of the armies of Israel, whom you have mocked" (*hēraptā*, 1 Sam 17:45; or Isaiah inveighing against Assyria, Isa 10:5-6; Ezekiel against Edom in Ezek 35:10-15; and Daniel against Belshazzar, Dan 5:23; see Childs, 88-90). When Isaiah responds to the king's delegation, 19:6-7, he will express an identical viewpoint. The Rabshakeh's words constitute the basic problem; they represent a "reviling of the Lord" (*gdp*, which is parallel to *hrp* at v. 22), of which one need have no fear, least of all God himself. Hence, Isaiah promises deliverance for Jerusalem by announcing the failure of Sennacherib, and in the end, his violent death (v. 7).

By the conclusion of this scene the writer has guided us to see Sennacherib's deputation according to a traditional theological pattern. The Rabshakeh speaks with the typical ceremonial bluster of ancient Near Eastern kings — there are many royal inscriptions that glorify the king's unrivaled and stupendous successes. His words are then shaped by suggestion and direct claim into an instance of archetypal struggle. Sennacherib is a boastful giant of a man who unwittingly offends the God of Israel. This notion sets the theme of all that follows (cf. vv. 16 and 23), and points the reader to that moment when Hezekiah's and Isaiah's theological view will be vindicated. Through the emissarial speech of Isaiah, Yahweh himself will dispute, and finally defeat, Sennacherib (19:21-34).

Genre

This unit is an episode within a larger narrative, which is best characterized as LEGEND. See Deutsch (p. 105), who calls 18:19-32a an "edifying legend" centering on the pious king.

Some critics emphasize reputed historical elements within the episode and so distinguish it from its counterpart in 19:9b-35 (the so-called B$_2$ narrative) on the grounds that the latter, like a legend, depicts exemplary religious types and strives to edify its readers. For example, Gray (*Kings*, 675) describes 18:17–19:7 as "historical narrative . . . freely rendered by the Deuteronomistic compiler." (Cf. Childs, 93, who, while not entirely clear, appears to argue for something directly historical in the Rabshakeh's speeches; Montgomery, *Kings,* 517: "prophetic story" but with "content of exact historical detail"; Rofé, 92, includes this narrative as an example of "prophetic historiography.") Cohen (p. 47) moves furthest along this historicizing track and claims to find the "actual words of the Assyrian official" in the biblical text.

Such predilections rest on questionable conclusions drawn from literary parallels in Assyrian documents (see Deutsch, 105-7, and fuller remarks below), and from questionable assumptions about the correspondence between realistic language and historical reliability. (Rofé, 92, is entirely typical: "[the story's] wealth of detail lends it an air of authenticity and indicates that it was not written much later than the events it describes.") Such critics also tend to discount that 19:1-7, both in its surface form and conceptual associations, already moves within the realm of ideal figures, edifying themes, and legendary archetypes (e.g., the devoted king who leads the way out of crisis by turning to God's prophet and intercessory prayer; the trusting king who reduces Sennacherib to his own antitype, a blasphemer of Israel's God; cf. 1 Sam 17:41-50).

Two large portions of direct speech, 18:19b-25, 29b-35, are DISPUTATION, a form of dialogue (often implied rather than explicit) in which two or more parties argue differing points of view (see Childs, 81: "diplomatic disputation"; cf. Preuss, *Verspottung,* 143). While disputation may assume various rhetorical forms, and typically may involve a variety of smaller literary genres, formulas, or stereotyped motifs, all examples include three basic elements within their conceptual logic: a thesis (which is stated or implied), a counterthesis (stated or implied), and refutation of the opponent's point of view. Perhaps at home in the wisdom traditions (see the book of Job), many examples of disputation occur in the prophetic literature, and hence often include invectives, accusations, threats, and prophecies of salvation or judgment. For examples, see Isa 10:5-15; 49:14-21; Ezek 33:23-29; Mal 1:2-5, 6-9; 3:6-12 (Murray; Graffy; Begrich; Westermann).

Further parallels to both the form of the Rabshakeh's disputation and its narrative setting have been noted in Assyrian letters from Nimrud (Saggs). Two letters recount to the king of Assyria the efforts of his officials to persuade people in Babylon to support Assyria against one Ukin-zer, who had revolted against Assyria's rule. The similarities to the Bible are so striking as to warrant extensive quotation. Saggs's translation follows:

> On the twenty-eighth we came to Babylon. We took our stand before the Marduk-gate (and) argued with the Man of Babylon. *So-and-So* the servant of Ukin-zer was present at his side. When they came out they were standing before the gate with the Babylonians. We spoke to the Babylonians in this way: "*Why* do you *act hostilely* to us for the sake of them?", (adding): "Their *place* is in the midst of *Chaldean tribesmen* . . . . Babylon indeed shows favor to *a Chaldean!* Your citizen-privileges have been set down (in charter)".
>
> *I kept going* to Babylon: we used many arguments with them. . . . They would not *agree* to come out, they would not argue with us: they (just) kept sending us messages.

We said to them: "Open the great gate! We would enter Babylon". He was not willing, (and answered) thus: "We should only let you enter Babylon for our own submission". (I replied to them) thus: "When the king himself comes, what shall I say to the king? When the king comes they will open the great gate". They did not believe that the king would come, (so) we spoke to them in this manner: "*So-and-So* and the servants of Ukin-zer have indeed *misled* you. We are certainly *staying* in Kar-Nergal until the royal household comes". We argued *in the presence of* the Babylonians: "What message are we to send to the king about the report *of hostility?*". (Saggs, letter no. 1, p. 24)

A second letter deals with similar efforts:

We could not enlist a thousand *with us*. I sent Iasubaia to them as a messenger with cavalry, (to say) thus: "*Leave your settlement and* come out!", (and) also: "Why do you cower in (your) settlement?", (and) also: "If you will not go against Ukin-zer", then "Go as far as Marad!". (Furthermore I made an offer) thus: "I myself will come from in front of you (and) will enlist (my regular forces) in amongst you".

Iasubaia went back (and) repeated (it) to them, (but) they were unwilling (and) would not come out. Iasubaia came back again (and) duly made (his) report about them, saying: "They argue thus: 'If there are any forces, when they come we shall see (them and) then we shall go out from the city; but on the other hand if troops do not come — that is to say, there are none — we shall not go out. We are holding the city, we are not cowering in (our) settlement'". (Saggs, letter no. 2, p. 28; cf. also letter no. 3, p. 33).

A monumental stela from Pharaoh Kamose, who reigned shortly before 1570 B.C.E., describes a similar situation of military assault. Kamose twice addresses a city under siege. He boasts, taunts, and threatens the city's defenders, and then goes on to summarize his victorious campaign and triumphal return to Thebes. The Pharaoh's quoted speeches show a "carefully articulated form that at least betrays drastic editorship, if not *ex post facto* composition" (Smith). In short, they render a stylized picture of bellicose posturing before battle which is, incidentally, a typical feature of many ancient Near Eastern royal inscriptions (see *ANET,* 554-55).

While all these texts offer problems for interpretation, they at least indicate that both the situation of the Rabshakeh's disputation and its bellicose style partly follow a long-standing literary tradition of representing diplomatic practice (Wildberger, "Die Rede der Rabsake," 44; see further references in Cogan and Tadmor, *II Kings,* 242). Other influences, perhaps, may be located in the Bible itself, as, e.g., traditions and motifs from Isaianic theology (see Childs, 84-85; Isa 10:5-11; 30:2-3; 31:3). One may hardly attribute historical veracity in any exact sense to these speeches, and even less so in order to establish the nonlegendary character of this portion of the so-called B_1 narrative (against Childs, 82-83, and Cohen; note Deutsch, 105-8). At best we may assert that the biblical writer's presentation of the Rabshakeh's disputation accords with literary convention found in other types of contemporary historiography (e.g., royal inscriptions) and historical materials (e.g., letters). The scene may or may not have been fictionalized in ways familiar to us from a few Greek and Roman historians, who invented credible speeches for their literary personages (see Montgomery, *Kings,* 487).

A second important genre of direct speech in this unit is the PROPHECY OF SALVATION, 19:6b-7, with its typical messenger formula ("Thus says the Lord") and often attested reassurance formula ("Do not fear"; see Conrad), followed by the announcement of salvation. The events to come will mean health, restoration, victory, and the like for those addressed by the prophecy. The divine word is part of a conventional narrative sequence which recounts (1) a situation of extreme duress, to which a prophetic figure (or sometimes the deity himself) responds; (2) a prophecy of salvation consisting of an exhortation that expresses protective reassurance and the announcement of salvation (cf. A. Schmitt, 45-49). See Exod 14:13-14; Josh 8:1-2; Isa 7:1-9; 2 Chr 20:1-17. Also cf. examples which are given without narrative setting, and presumed related to cultic practices, e.g., Isa 41:10-13, 14-16; 43:1-7 (Begrich; Gunkel).

Schmitt (pp. 34-41) points out a similar pattern in two letters from Mari in which a writer transmits to the king certain prophecies concerning his rule: *ARM* X, 7, and *ARM* X, 50 (*ANET,* 630-31). Reports of king-warriors receiving such pronouncements from their god are also known from Mesopotamian historiographic and ritual documents. One ritual text prescribes that for the Babylonian New Year festival the king be ritually stripped of all trappings of power, recite his good deeds, and be restored to his rule through the following words, spoken by a priest: "Have no fear. . . . The God Bel [will listen to] your prayer . . . he will magnify your lordship . . . he will exalt your kingship" (*ANET,* 334). In times closer to Judah's monarchy, Assyrian scribes preserved collections of prophecies that bolstered their kings' rule and enjoined upon the king faithfulness and pious deeds (cf. Harner, who has a somewhat different understanding of these texts). For Esarhaddon, ca. 680-669 B.C.E.:

> (i.5) "[Esarhad]don, king of the lands, fear not! *That* wind which blows against you — I need only say a word and I can bring it to an end. . . . (ii) . . . (This oracle is) from the woman Rimute-allate of the town of Darahuya, which is in the mountains: Fear not, Esarhaddon! I, the god Bel, am speaking to you. I watch over your inner heart as would your mother who brought you forth. . . . I am Ishtar of Arbela; I have turned Ashur's favor to you. . . . Fear not! Praise me! Where is there any enemy who *overcame* you while I remained quiet?" (*ANET,* 605)

See similar texts reporting oracular dreams for Ashurbanipal, ca. 668-627 B.C.E. (*ANET,* 450-51, 606). Also cf. a Babylonian didactic poem, "Ludlul Bēl Nēmeqi," in which a nobleman dreams that he receives a prophecy of restoration from his earthly calamities: "a young woman of shining countenance, A queen of . . . equal to a god. She entered and [sat down] . . . 'Speak my deliverance . . .' 'Fear not,' she said, 'I [will] . . .' She said, 'Be delivered from your very wretched state, whoever has seen a vision in the night time'" (W. G. Lambert,

Babylonian Wisdom Literature [Oxford: Oxford University, 1960] 51; *ANET,* 596-600, esp. 599). See also Weippert.

Setting

Since this unit is an episode within a larger legend, we need not speculate about a setting apart from its present literary context (but see Deutsch, 94, who believes the original tradition was associated with prophets in Israel). The narrative depicts the first of two deputations from Sennacherib, and the first of two petitions which Hezekiah put to God (or his prophetic representative) in response to the threat against Jerusalem.

Intention

As presently situated, this episode portrays a major event during Hezekiah's reign, and shows Hezekiah to be a paradigmatic faithful king who depends on God for his own strength and the safety of Jerusalem. In contrast, Sennacherib — who is a presence on stage only through the words of the Rabshakeh — seems to be something of a comic figure. He is ridiculously proud, and as interpreted through the piety of Hezekiah and Isaiah, egregiously disrespectful and ignorant of Yahweh. By the conclusion of the scene, it is clear that the real protagonists are Sennacherib and Yahweh (in spite of, or in the view of the writer, because of, the Assyrian's claim to be commissioned by Yahweh himself to menace Jerusalem). It remains for the second deputation, 19:8-37, to complete this picture.

Bibliography

See bibliographies at 2 Kgs 1:2-17a; 18:1–20:21, Canonical Framework; 18:13–19:37, Canonical Framework. J. Begrich, "Das priesterliche Heilsorakel," *ZAW* 52 (1934) 81-92 (= *Gesammelte Studien zum Alten Testament* [TBü 21; Munich: Kaiser, 1964] 217-31; C. Cohen, "Neo-Assyrian Elements in the First Speech of the Biblical Rab-Saqe," *Israel Oriental Studies* 9 (1979) 32-48; E. Conrad, *Fear Not Warrior: A Study of 'al tîrā' Pericopes in the Hebrew Scriptures* (BJS 75; Chico, CA: Scholars Press, 1985); H. Gevaryahu, "The Speech of Rab-shakeh to the People on the Wall of Jerusalem," (Hebr.) in *Studies in the Bible Presented to M. H. Segal* (ed. J. M. Grintz and J. Liver; Jerusalem: Kiryat Sepher, 1964) 94-102; A. Graffy, *A Prophet Confronts His People: The Disputation Speech in the Prophets* (AnBib 104; Rome: Biblical Institute, 1984); H. Gunkel, *Einleitung in die Psalmen* (2nd ed.; Göttingen: Vandenhoeck & Ruprecht, 1966) 177-78, 245-47; P. Harner, "The Salvation Oracle in Second Isaiah," *JBL* 88 (1969) 418-34; C. Kuhl, "Die 'Wiederaufnahme' " (→ 2 Kgs 13:1–14:29); C. W. Mitchell, *The Meaning of BRK "To Bless" in the Old Testament* (SBLDS 95; Atlanta: Scholars Press, 1987); D. Murray, "The Rhetoric of Disputation: Re-examination of a Prophetic Genre,"

JSOT 38 (1987) 95-121; H. Preuss, *Verspottung fremder Religionen im Alten Testament* (BWANT 92; Stuttgart: Kohlhammer, 1971); W. Rudolph, "Zum Text der Königsbücher," *ZAW* 63 (1951) 201-15, esp. 214; H. W. F. Saggs, "The Nimrud Letters, 1952 — Part I," *Iraq* 17 (1955) 21-56; H. S. and A. Smith, "A Reconsideration of the Kamose Texts," *Zeitschrift für Ägyptische Sprache* 103 (1976) 48-76; W. von Soden, "Sanherib vor Jerusalem 701 v. Chr.," *Antike und Universalgeschichte (Fest.* H. Stier; ed. R. Stiehl et al.; Münster: Aschendorff, 1972) 43-51, esp. 46-48; M. Weippert, "Assyrische Prophetien der Zeit Asarhaddons und Assurbanipals," *Assyrian Royal Inscriptions: New Horizons in Literary, Ideological, and Historical Analysis* (ed. F. M. Fales; Orientis Antiqui Collectio 17; Rome: Istituto per l'Oriente, 1981) 71-115; C. Westermann, *Basic Forms of Prophetic Speech* (tr. H. C. White; Philadelphia: Westminster, 1967) 201; H. Wildberger, "Die Rede des Rabsake vor Jerusalem," *TZ* 35 (1979) 35-47 (= *Jahwe und sein Volk* [TBü 66; Munich: Kaiser, 1979] 285-97).

SENNACHERIB'S THREAT FROM LIBNAH, 19:8-34

Structure

I. Deputation from Libnah	19:8-13
A. Setting	8-9a
B. The challenge to Hezekiah	9b-13
1. Narrative introduction	9b
2. Commissioning of messengers	10-13
a. Commissioning formula	10a
b. Message (disputation)	10b-13
1) Admonition (implied thesis: Yahweh will save Jerusalem)	10b
2) Refutation	11-13
a) Concerning Assyrian victories	11a-bα
b) Rhetorical questions (implied counterthesis: God cannot save)	11bβ-13
II. Hezekiah's coping with the threat	14-19
A. Narrative setting	14
B. Hezekiah's appeal to Yahweh	15-19
1. Narrative introduction	15aα
2. Prayer of petition	15aβ-19
a. Invocation	15aβ-b
b. Petition	16-19
1) General requests	16
2) Basis for petition	17-18
3) Main petition	19
III. God's response: three prophecies	20-34
A. Narrative introduction	20a
B. Message for Hezekiah	20b-34
1. Messenger formula	20bα

2.	Message proper (prophecy)	20bβ-34
	a. Acknowledgment of petition	20bβ
	b. Prophecy of punishment	21-28
	1) Introduction	21a
	2) Disputational prophecy of punishment	21b-28
	a) Taunt	21b
	b) Disputation	22-26
	c) Accusation	27
	d) Announcement of punishment	28
	(1) Reason for punishment	28a
	(2) Announcement proper	28b
	c. Announcement of sign	29-31
	d. Prophecy of salvation	32-34

The beginning of this unit abruptly leaves the arena of private communications between Hezekiah and Isaiah, and returns to the public movements of the Rabshakeh, last heard from in 18:35. Some take vv. 8-9 as describing action that takes place concurrently with Hezekiah's appeal to Isaiah, vv. 3-7, as though the writer were now reverting to the sequence of events left off at 18:37 (so Hobbs, *2 Kings,* 265; cf. *NJPS*). Most take vv. 8-9 as subsequent to Isaiah's prophecy. In either case, the writer describes a new turn in public events that will lead to a deputation from Sennacherib, vv. 9b-13, 14a. The ending of the episode, which moves from threatening speech, to Hezekiah's petition to God, to Isaiah's response, comes naturally with the conclusion of Isaiah's oracle, v. 34.

Those scholars who accept the hypothesis that two independent narratives lay behind chs. 18–19 assign this unit to a B$_2$ source (see 18:13–19:37, Canonical Framework). On the basis of differing content, style, and form, most critics agree that vv. 21-34 consist of three distinct oracles: vv. 21b-28 (a poem of taunt and punishment; cf. Ezek 28:2-10); vv. 29-31 (a prophetic announcement of sign; cf. Jer 44:29-30; 1 Kgs 13:3); and vv. 32-34 (an announcement of salvation; cf. 2 Kgs 22:18b-20; Ezek 39:25-29). Many scholars suppose that vv. 21-31 were inserted between vv. 20 and 32-34, the original reply to Hezekiah, and the only one explicitly linked to the wider narrative situation (so, e.g., Würthwein, *Könige,* 425-31; Clements, 57; Hentschel, *2 Könige,* 93; Deutsch, 22-30; Robinson, *2 Kings,* 183; Childs, 96-97, with only minor differences). Major disagreements surface in explaining the process by which the present text came to its present form.

One may recognize these smaller literary units and accept that they probably are of diverse origin and now reflect a complicated history of composition. But none of these considerations materially affects the formal logic of the canonical text (e.g., the supposed originally separate prophecies are now presented as one oracle delivered on the same occasion in response to a situation of great distress; cf. 1 Sam 7:3-11; 1 Kgs 8:22-53 + 9:3-9; Jer 15:15-20). Nor do considerations of redactional history lessen the fruitfulness of investigating coherence and implied intentionality in the redacted text (e.g., the thematic words "mock" and "revile" in vv. 22a, 23, recall the same in vv. 4, 6, and 16; and in v. 23, "messengers" alludes to v. 9; see Fewell).

The structure of the episode is straightforward. Sennacherib's deputation from Libnah to Hezekiah poses a threat to Jerusalem (I, vv. 8-13). In context, this is the second embassy sent from a new location during an ongoing siege, although the translation of *wayyāšob*, v. 9b, as "again" is only one possibility. Hezekiah copes with this threat by appealing directly to God (II, vv. 14-19), and his action results in Isaiah's three-stage prophecy which provides Yahweh's answer to the king's prayer (III, vv. 20-34). In the light of ch. 18, the words which now build up between Hezekiah and Yahweh dispute Sennacherib's claims and imply a disabling strike against the Assyrian's arguments as well as his military power.

The setting for the first scene, vv. 8-9a, is somewhat confusing, as abruptly shifting subject matter and points of reference leave the interpretation of some clauses in doubt. Taking v. 9a (lit., "and he heard concerning Tirhakah king of Ethiopia, saying, 'Behold, he went out to fight with you'") as dependent on v. 9b, most translators supply subordinating words to imply that Tirhakah's threat motivated Sennacherib's deputation to Hezekiah. Hence, the *RSV* reads, "and when the king heard . . . [v. 9a], he sent messengers again to Hezekiah . . . [v. 9b]." Cf. *KJV, JPS, NEB*. Alternatively, v. 9a might continue the thought of v. 8b, in which case one would understand that the Rabshakeh found Sennacherib at Libnah (v. 8b) because he (Sennacherib) had heard that Tirhakah had come out to attack him there (cf. Robinson, *2 Kings*, 179).

Choosing between these alternatives is not easy because most of the verbs carry a nonspecific "he" as subject, and force one to decide from context whether the Rabshakeh or Sennacherib is the active agent (e.g., the *RSV* supplies "the king" in vv. 8bβ and 9aα). This matter is critical at v. 9b, which reads in the Hebrew: "and he returned [*wayyāšob*] and he sent messengers." Who is the subject of *wayyāšob* — the Rabshakeh (cf. v. 8a) or Sennacherib? Most choose the latter, and in the light of 18:19-35 translate the verb *wayyāšob* as denoting repeated mission: "And he [Sennacherib] again sent messengers" (cf. Gen 26:18; 2 Kgs 1:11, 13). This is a reasonable translation and has the advantage of suggesting a sequential relationship to the deputation previously sent from Lachish; it also suits those scholars who look upon the syntactical ambiguity at v. 9b as arising from a redactional join between two separate accounts of Sennacherib's mission. (Some Hebr. MSS, however, and the parallel Isa 37:9b, omit *wayyāšob*, either smoothing out the rough place or never reflecting it.)

However, this virtual consensus obscures a second possibility: read the second instance of *wayyāšob* as authorial intention rather than editorial join or a case of "resumptive" repetition (*wayyāšob* in v. 9b resumes the Rabshakeh's action broken off at v. 8aα; see Kuhl). In this case, one might understand vv. 8aβ-9a as a writer's parenthetical remark framed by the repeated *wayyāšob* and designed to explain how it was that the Rabshakeh (and the deputation to Hezekiah) came to be associated with Libnah. Visualizing the framing effect, the sense would be as follows:

8aα And the Rabshakeh went back [*wayyāšob*]
    8aβ and he [the Rabshakeh] found the king of Assyria fighting against Libnah, for he [the Rabshakeh] had heard that he [the king] had left Lachish;

9a for he [the king] had heard concerning Tirhakah king of
Ethiopia as follows: "Behold, he has come out to fight
against you."

9b And [so] he [the Rabshakeh] went back [wayyāšob].

This interpretation offers an explanation for the repetition of wayyāšob as
a simple literary device. And there are no problems of internal unity either. V. 9a
clearly functions in semantic relation to v. 8, but is not stylistically incongruent
with v. 9b. This in turn makes moot a problem created by assuming that v. 9a
originally joined to v. 36 in some earlier B₁ version; that assumption leads to
the idea that Sennacherib, according to the B₁ writer, returned to Nineveh
because Tirhakah opposed him (Šanda, Könige II, 267, discusses the implausi-
bility of that notion). By the same token, one need not assume with most
commentators that, owing to clumsy adjustments of two versions, Sennacherib's
embassy to Hezekiah (v. 9b) now appears to have resulted from his troubles
with Tirhakah (v. 9a), a turn of affairs just as puzzling as his departing for
Nineveh before the armies of Tirhakah.

We suggest that vv. 8-9a be read as a typical framing repetition which
interrupts forward motion in the main plot and allows the writer to fill in
background information after the fact, hence with a pluperfect temporal sense
(Long). Normal sequentiality resumes in v. 9b: "and he [Sennacherib] sent
messengers to Hezekiah." But now a reader knows that the threat to Jerusalem
remains pretty much as it has been, except that Sennacherib will press his
demands from Libnah while engaging there the Ethiopian forces (were these the
Egyptian allies of Hezekiah mentioned in 18:21?). In other words, the threat to
Jerusalem is not at all diminished.

Whereas the deputation from Lachish was styled as a confrontation between the Rabshakeh and Hezekiah's officials, this second embassy seems less
direct. We watch something like a scene of commissioning (see v. 10a) and hear
the tidings that the Assyrian messengers are to carry. But we read nothing of
their actual delivery (cf. Gen 32:3-5; 1 Kgs 12:23-24; 14:7-11; 2 Kgs 1:2).
Indeed, v. 14 indicates that the narrator quotes the content of a letter in vv. 10-13
as though it were direct speech between sender and recipient. Against Childs
(p. 97), there is nothing odd about this biblical convention. (Cf. Jer 29:25-28,
29; Pardee, 174; similarly, the distance of emissarial protocol sometimes shades
into direct dialogue, 1 Kgs 5:15-23 [RSV 1-9]; 2 Kgs 10:1-4, 5, 6-7.) Such
conventions are consistent with the preference of many Hebrew writers to create
scenes out of direct speech rather than descriptive prose (see Alter, 63-87). In
effect, the writer emphasizes the substance of, and dramatic tension within,
communication between parties.

Like the Rabshakeh's speeches in ch. 18, Sennacherib's message, although
much briefer, follows an implicit pattern of rhetorical argument: an opinion held
by an opponent (thesis) is disputed and countered by new claims (counterthesis).
Implying that Hezekiah relies upon Yahweh to deliver Jerusalem, v. 10b, the
messengers (the letter) turn allusion to past Assyrian victories into an inference
that the various national gods, including the God of Judah, cannot save their
devotees from Assyria's might: "And shall you be delivered?" (v. 11bβ). It is

as though Sennacherib speaks directly to the confidence generated by Yahweh's private promise to Hezekiah (19:7). In contrast to ch. 18, Sennacherib narrows the issue to one: Yahweh has promised to deliver Jerusalem, but can he be trusted (so Childs, 98)? It is not a question of Hezekiah being out of favor with Yahweh (18:22), or of Yahweh having abandoned Hezekiah and placed Sennacherib in the yoke of service (18:25). It is not even a simple question of Yahweh's weakness against Sennacherib's power (18:33-35; 19:11-13 alludes to this motif in the Rabshakeh's first deputation but intensifies its meaning; an unusual verb, *lĕhaḥărîm*, apparently rooted in the Israelite, not Assyrian, ideology of holy war, denotes the act of destroying the spoils of victory as holy sacrifice to God; see Hobbs, *2 Kings*, 277).

Sennacherib now draws himself up directly against Yahweh, whom he accuses of deceiving Hezekiah, and so grows to the legendary size of a brash, overreaching blasphemer. This was precisely Hezekiah's opinion of the man as expressed privately (v. 4) and confirmed by Isaiah (v. 6). Hezekiah will reiterate his view when he asks God, "Save us!" (vv. 16-19), and Yahweh will vigorously assert a similar characterization of Sennacherib (v. 22). Sennacherib's letter, therefore, is sent and received in a highly charged context, both within the world of narrative, and within the reader's awareness as pressed and formed by the writer. One cannot help but view Sennacherib as an archetypal blasphemer, one whose self-aggrandizing words are interpreted in Israel as "mocking" or "blaspheming against" God (cf. Ezek 28:1-10; 35:10-15; Jer 48:28-33; Isa 10:12-19; see Childs, 88-89).

In contrast, Hezekiah is cast as the pious and good king, who, contrary to all that the Rabshakeh has insinuated, acts as though he really does trust Yahweh, and only Yahweh (cf. 19:3-4; 18:5-6). Thus, when threatened, Hezekiah turns to Yahweh. Reading the letter from Sennacherib (the MT refers to plur. "letters" but some of the early VSS have the singular), Hezekiah goes to the temple, spreads the document "before God" (here the MT reads a singular), and asks God for deliverance (II, vv. 14-19). The situation hints at customary patterns of cultic practice, e.g., ceremonies of penitence and lament, in which individuals or cultic officials offer up petitions for relief (cf. Joel 1:14-20 and Psalm 3). More distant parallels are attested elsewhere in the ancient Near East as letter-styled petitions deposited, perhaps as memorial inscriptions, in sanctuaries (see Borger; Hallo; W. von Soden). Stylistically, Hezekiah's prayer is like many others in the DtrH and later historiography (cf. 2 Sam 7:18-29; 1 Kgs 3:6-9; 8:22-26; Neh 9:6-37; Dan 9:4-19; 3 Macc 2:1-20; 6:2-15 [*The Old Testament Pseudepigrapha,* vol. 2 (ed. James Charlesworth; Garden City, NY: Doubleday, 1985), 517-29]). In short, the king prays a traditional prayer, traditionally.

The king invokes God with familiar hymnlike epithets: "enthroned above the cherubim" (cf. Ps 80:2 [*RSV* 1]; 99:1; 2 Sam 6:2); "thou art God, Thou alone" (cf. Neh 9:6; Ps 83:19 [*RSV* 18]; 86:10); "all the kingdoms of the earth" (cf. Isa 23:17; Jer 15:4; 24:9; 25:26; 29:18); "thou hast made heaven and earth" (cf. Neh 9:6; Ps 115:15; 121:2; 124:8; for this theme in Isaiah, see C. Stuhlmueller, "The Theology of Creation in Second Isaias," *CBQ* 21 [1959] 429-67). It is this creator God alone that Hezekiah addresses in the formulaic plea of all those ever in distress, "Save us!" (Ps 106:47; Jer 17:14; Ps 3:8 [*RSV* 7]; 6:5 [*RSV* 4]; 7:2 [*RSV* 1]).

Yet despite these and other motifs associated with conventional cultic prayer, the petition in vv. 16-19 continues the argumentative, disputational style of ch. 18. Silent in earlier direct confrontation (18:36), the king now has his rebuttal and delivers it with high moral tone. For the reader (presumably God would need no persuasion in this matter), Hezekiah refutes the claims of Sennacherib and strongly affirms that Yahweh alone is God. Yes, he admits disarmingly, the kings of Assyria have laid waste the nations and overpowered their gods, just as Sennacherib claimed in his letter (vv. 11-13; cf. 18:33-35), but these were in fact no-gods, the work of merely human artisans (cf. Jer 16:20; Hos 8:6). Simultaneously, the narrator has Hezekiah seek to compel God's direct intervention. It is a question of honor, the king's prayer implies; listen to Sennacherib's words that "mock" or "blaspheme" (*lĕḥārēp*, v. 16, the theme word for the whole episode). And it is an opportunity for Yahweh to demonstrate his power and singularity: "save us . . . that all the kingdoms of the earth may know that you, O Lord, are God alone" (v. 19; cf. 1 Kgs 18:36-37; 20:13, 28; Ps 59:14 [*RSV* 13]).

The appeal proves irresistible. God responds through his prophet Isaiah, addressing himself to Hezekiah but implicitly confronting Sennacherib (III, vv. 20-34). For Hezekiah the message of these three distinct prophetic words, vv. 21b-28, 29-31, 32-34, is one of comfort in prospect. For Sennacherib, it implies that failure is a just punishment for an arrogant blasphemer.

God acknowledges Hezekiah's prayer, and this already implics that a favorable reply to his petitions is forthcoming (cf. vv. 20bβ with 2 Kgs 20:5; 22:19; 1 Sam 25:35b; cf. Exod 3:7; 6:5; 1 Sam 12:1; 1 Kgs 5:22 [*RSV* 8]; 9:3 [= 2 Chr 7:12]). Words concerning Sennacherib, vv. 21b-28, 32-33, amount to an announcement, supported by a "sign" (vv. 29-31), that the Assyrian assault will fail. Yahweh himself will defend Jerusalem for his private reasons, v. 34 (this particular formulation, using √*gnn*, "defend," appears only in 20:6; Isa 31:5; Zech 9:15; 12:8, but a similar idea of God as "defender" or "shield" may be found, e.g., in Deut 33:29; 2 Sam 22:3, 31; Gen 15:1).

The first prophecy, vv. 21b-28, is a rather complex dramatic poem. Hebrew poetic meter, and even the definition of poetry, remain matters of dispute among modern critics (see Kugel). Nowadays, we do not feel as confident as did an earlier generation in our ability to reconstruct poetic lines in some hypothetical purity of style and meter (for the history of research, see Wildberger, 1430-31; note also Budde; Meek). Most recently scholars have focused on sense lines and sought to appreciate the artistry reflected within structures of repetition, notably parallelism, which many still consider a feature of high poetic style (see, e.g., Alter; Watson; Berlin).

The prophecy is narrated as an oracle reported to Hezekiah that "concerns," or is "against," Sennacherib (*'ālāyw,* "concerning him," v. 21a). This places a double burden on us. We must observe the poem's literary features and conceptual integrity, while at the same time grasping its function as part of a wider narrative. In many similar poetic oracles against/concerning foreign nations, the writer creates a variety of dramatic situations involving different speakers and abruptly shifting points of view (see, e.g., Jer 48:1-8). Here the imagined situation is less complex. God addresses Sennacherib directly (cf. the similar Ezek 28:2-10), and only once complicates that posture by quoting a speech of Sennacherib, vv. 23b-24.

The poem in part develops a taunting rhetorical argument (esp. vv. 22-26), but at the end evolves into prophetically styled accusation and punishment (v. 28). V. 27 is a transition between these stylistic and functional divisions (we cannot say with any certainty that the writer wrote stanzas). V. 21b, the opening bicolon, invokes an image of a morally and physically vanquished foe and sets the tone for all that follows.

Through these words, Yahweh enters into a highly mediated confrontation with Sennacherib. It is an oracle for Hezekiah, but concerning Sennacherib; it is styled as address to Sennacherib, but is never delivered to him. Partly because of its argumentative style and partly because of its conceptual content, the poem implies for the reader that Yahweh answers those arguments put forth earlier in Sennacherib's name (vv. 10-13; 18:19-35). Yahweh joins word-battle with Sennacherib, but it is a battle waged entirely within the reader's consciousness.

The structural center of the poem consists of two speeches. One is speech within speech, Sennacherib's self-aggrandizing boasts, vv. 23b-24. Another is Yahweh's answer to those claims, vv. 25-26, in which Yahweh engages in a little boasting of his own to claim superior power and knowledge. As Hezekiah and Isaiah have done, God refines the issue to a single complaint: Sennacherib's arrogant blasphemy (see vv. 22-23a, "mocked the Lord," and v. 27, "ragings against me"). The poem concludes with a simple announcement of punishment in v. 28.

An opening bicolon uses a sort of limping synonymous parallelism (abc//b'c') to summon up the arresting image of maiden Jerusalem scornfully taunting her Assyrian adversary:

$$a \qquad\qquad b \qquad\qquad c$$
She despises you, she scorns you — the maiden Zion.

$$b' \qquad\qquad c'$$
After you she wags her head — the daughter of Jerusalem.

The tone of these first lines rules the whole poem. God will yield none of these moral heights to Sennacherib, who is characterized throughout as willfully arrogant (vv. 22-24), unwittingly manipulated (vv. 25-26), and thoroughly found out (v. 27).

The rhetorical questions that follow ironically extend this opening image. Sennacherib is accused of arrogant and presumptuous raising of his voice, as though God, like maiden Zion, now wags his head and tongue in derision (v. 22). The questions and answers form parallelistic patterns within which two verbal roots, "blaspheme" *(ḥrp)* and "raise up" *(rwm)*, define a thematic center.

Against whom have you *blasphemed* [*ḥēraptā*] and reviled?
Against whom have you *raised* [*hărîmôtā*] voice?
You lifted your eyes *on high* [*mārôm*] against the Holy One of Israel;
By your messengers you *blasphemed* [*ḥēraptā*] the Lord.

The figurative sense of √*rwm*, to be lifted up in arrogance, governs the center of this section (cf. Isa 10:12, also referring to the king of Assyria; Jer 48:29; Mic 2:3; Ps 89:43; Num 31:28). This trope leads us to understand the very next lines ironically. Sennacherib depicts his own exemplary prowess with the same root word: "I ascended the heights [*mĕrôm*] of the mountains, the farthest recesses of Lebanon." The poet mimics the first-person style of ancient Near Eastern monumental displays. See, e.g., for Tiglath-pileser I (ca. 1114-1076 B.C.E.): "I climbed up after them to the peaks of high mountains and perilous mountain ledges where a man could not walk . . . I pushed through rugged paths and perilous passes, the interior of which no king had previously known" (Grayson, *ARI* II, §§ 19 and 30; cf. § 216; see also § 468). But in the biblical poem, the rhetorical questions of the preceding lines lead one to evaluate Sennacherib negatively. Contrary to ancient Near Eastern convention, his actions are not praiseworthy and awe-inspiring, redounding to his glory and legitimacy, but simply illustrate his arrogant blasphemy. On this switch of the typical rests the tone of the entire poem. Maiden Zion is derisive (v. 21b) and the poet triumphalist.

The actual speech of Sennacherib in vv. 23-24 resumes the abc//b′c′ parallelism of the poem's opening lines. Widely attested in biblical, Akkadian, and Ugaritic writings (see Watson, 174-75; 1 Sam 18:7b; Hos 5:8; 7:1), this device thrusts our attention onto the counterpart images of the b′ and c′ elements to build an edifice of thematic specificity and intensification (cf. Alter, 62-84). Thus, one imagines Sennacherib to have sent a message, appropriately using the first personal pronoun in emphatic position, but in context now suggesting self-important inflation (v. 23):

>   a   b   c
> It is I who ascended the heights of the mountains,

>   b′   c′
> the far recesses of Lebanon,

>   a   b   c
> that I might fell the tallest of cedars,

>   b′   c′
> the choicest of cypresses,

>   a   b   c
> that I might enter the farthest retreat

>   b′   c′
> the densest forest.

A final couplet loosens the form, repeats the emphatic pronoun, and draws this string of superlatives toward an even more wondrous achievement (v. 24):

> It is I who dug and drank foreign waters,
>   and I dried up with the sole of my foot all the streams of Egypt.

God meets this boast with a declamation of his own in vv. 25-26. The lines at first continue a pattern of parallelism in the rhetorical question and answer, and then develop an extended metaphor to suggest the terrifying results of Yahweh's control of Sennacherib.

> Have you not heard?
>
>   a   b
> From long ago I determined it,
>
>   a'   b'
> From days of yore I shaped it.
>
> Now I bring it to pass
>   that you should turn into ruins the fortified cities
>   while their inhabitants, shorn of strength, are dismayed
>   and confounded.
>
> They become plants of the field,
>   green herbage, shoots on the rooftops
>   but scorched without a chance of growing.

In form, these lines are similar to Isa 40:21-24, 28-31; 48:6-8. In effect, they boast a counterclaim to Sennacherib's trumpeting of royal accomplishment, and in wider context answer the messengers' and the Rabshakeh's brazen attempt to weaken Hezekiah's confidence in Yahweh's power. Sennacherib is nothing on his own; he is a tool of Yahweh-Creator who determines all (cf. Isa 46:10; 48:3; 45:21). The poet alludes to Yahweh's creative activity ("make" or "determine" [ʿśh], "form" or "shape" [yṣr], "bring forth" [Hiphil of bôʾ]), and as elsewhere in the prophetic traditions, extends the metaphor to cases of divine election (cf. Gen 2:7; Isa 45:18 [creative activity] with Jer 1:5; Isa 43:1; 45:1-7; 49:5 [divine election]; see W. L. Holladay, "The Background of Jeremiah's Self-Understanding," *JBL* 83 [1964] 153-64). The ironic truth about Sennacherib's exuberant declarations of victory (19:11-13) is that developments concerning these vanquished peoples, a sweetly promising growth now shrivelled with the sun's blight, also conform to Yahweh's will. Nothing is outside his ken (cf. Ps 139:16).

In this light, the lines that follow, v. 27, make a transitional turn away from rhetorical claims and counterclaims toward accusation and punishment. The motif of "knowing" is the pivot.

> Your sitting down,
>   your goings and comings,
> I know — and your ragings against me!

Flowing from vv. 25-26, these lines have the connotation that Yahweh controls earthly affairs (cf. Ps 139:2-6; a similar motif appears in Egyptian hymns in praise of Amun-Re; see Wildberger, 1434). But the very last phrase wrests the thought from this mooring, recapitulates the poem's view of Sennacherib, and, anticipating v. 28, brings us abruptly to a climactic idea: Yahweh also "knows" of transgression. (Some critics take "and your ragings against me" as a dittography from v. 28, but without any support from the Hebrew MSS or the early VSS.)

Thus, the thought turns naturally to accusation and punishment. The poet resorts to opening patterns of parallelism again:

> Because you raged against me,
>   and your arrogance has risen to my ears,

>   a   b   c
> I will put my hook in your nose

>   b′   c′
>   and my bit in your mouth,
> And I will send you back in the way you came.

The punishment for a warrior-king is defeat at the hands of Israel's divine warrior-king (cf. Exod 15:3; Ps 24:7-8; F. M. Cross, "The Divine Warrior," in *Canaanite Myth and Hebrew Epic* [Cambridge: Harvard University, 1973] 91-111). Linking up with the language of v. 33, Yahweh announces that Sennacherib himself will be a captive of war, taken by the nose, and turned back the way he came. The imagery is typical of ancient Near Eastern inscriptions and iconography. See Ezek 38:4; 2 Chr 33:11; for Tiglath-pileser I (ca. 1114-1076 B.C.E.): "I attached to their noses ropes (and) took them to my city" (Grayson, *ARI* II, § 69); a stone relief that accompanies an Esarhaddon inscription at Sinjirli illustrates the practice (*ANEP,* no. 447).

A second prophecy from God comes abruptly in vv. 29-31. According to its narrative setting, Yahweh now addresses Hezekiah through Isaiah and announces a sign to confirm that his word about the Assyrians (vv. 27-28) will come to pass (cf. 2 Kgs 20:9-10; Isa 7:14-17; 1 Kgs 13:3; Jer 44:29-30). Apparently styled as prose (but note the elevated language of parallelism in vv. 30-31), the prophecy in context reverts to the main narrative situation — Jerusalem is under siege and short of food. God promises abundance of new growth, new crops without cultivation, and in a third year, fully restored tillage. It will be a sign in nature of a people's rejuvenation. Like that withered field growth scorched by Assyria's fury, a remnant of Judah, starved and stunted in growth, will miraculously "take root downward, and bear fruit upward" (v. 30).

The "surviving remnant" assimilates Jerusalem's specific plight under Hezekiah (cf. 19:4) into a theological archetype of cosmic and eternal significance. The threat from Sennacherib will come to naught, for the situation is really another occasion for a band of escaping survivors to experience deliverance by the "zeal of the Lord, by God's power alone" (cf. Isa 9:6 [*RSV* 7]). They will experience in the concreteness of their history the transcendent energies of salvation that flow repeatedly from God through all time, "out of Mount Zion." (On the importance of Jerusalem to this theological idea, cf. Isa 2:3; Mic 4:2; Zech 14:8; on the remnant, cf. Ezek 6:8-10; Isa 10:20-22; 46:3; Jer 42:2, 15, 19; 44:14; 47:4-5; G. Hasel, *The Remnant: The History and Theology of the Remnant Idea from Genesis to Isaiah* [Andrews University Monographs 5; Berrien Springs, MI: Andrews University, 1972].)

Letting the curtain fall across this vision of eternally recurring deliverance, a third and final word in the series of prophecies fixes on the concrete situation of Hezekiah's Jerusalem. As though it were a conclusion based on previous statements ("Therefore . . ."), Isaiah announces that Sennacherib will fail in his designs on Jerusalem. He will not breach its walls, or shoot an arrow; indeed, he will not even mount a siege against it, but he shall return by the way he came (vv. 32-33). What is the reason for such a turn of affairs? Yahweh, the divine warrior, defends the city for his own honor (an Isaianic motif, cf. Isa 43:25; 48:11), and for the sake of a promise to the Davidide dynasty (a DtrH motif, cf. 1 Kgs 11:13, 32, 34; 15:4; 2 Kgs 8:19; cf. 2 Samuel 7).

Looking back on all of vv. 21-34, one sees that everything aims toward this promise of deliverance. The ground is prepared by dismissing Sennacherib's claims to self-sufficient power, especially over Israel, as ill-founded blasphemy against Israel's God. For this offense Sennacherib will be punished (vv. 21-28). A miraculous sign will confirm the truth of Isaiah's (God's) words (vv. 29-31). Alluding once again to the broader narrative context — the oracle came in response to Hezekiah's petition during Jerusalem's siege — Isaiah at the last promises deliverance from this "king of Assyria." This is the logical and actual result of all that has transpired, and, of course, it encourages a reader to expect that a fulfillment will be narrated (see exactly this in vv. 35-37).

Genre

This unit is an episode within a larger narrative that is best described as LEGEND. As in 18:17–19:7, the main personages are edifying types. Hezekiah shows no weakness of resolve in the face of the Assyrian threat and no inclination to rest upon military might for his protection. He simply turns to God in prayer, and puts the problem with God alone, who of course is properly addressed in praise and adoration. Sennacherib for his part, even though he makes no appearance in the episode, projects the very opposite characteristics: he overthrows the gods, trusts in himself, and suggests that Yahweh deceives his people. Backed by Isaiah and God himself, the pious Israelite king puts a special interpretation onto this legendary type: Sennacherib is a blasphemer who "mocks" and "reviles" Yahweh. These two exemplars of attitude — the one is deeply and quiescently religious, the other vigorously this-worldly and vested in his own might — these two opponents compete in the arena of God's honor, trustworthiness, and power. Legend poses godliness against godlessness and Israel's God against no-gods.

Genres of direct speech are important building blocks for this unit. The messengers of Sennacherib are sent off with a COMMISSIONING FORMULA, v. 10a, but the writer depicts their letter-written message, vv. 10b-13, not as (→) letter but as DISPUTATION (see 2 Kgs 18:19b-25, 29-35, and discussion there). In response, Hezekiah utters a PRAYER OF PETITION (vv. 15aβ-19; see full discussion at 1 Kgs 3:4-15, in Long, *1 Kings*, 65). In reply to Hezekiah's prayer, Isaiah offers an ORACLE introduced by the typical MESSENGER FORMULA (vv. 20b-34).

This oracle consists of at least three distinct literary units, all now prefaced by two formulas: (1) the ACKNOWLEDGMENT OF PETITION (v. 20bβ; cf. 1 Sam 25:35b; 2 Kgs 20:5; 22:19; and full discussion in Long, *1 Kings*, 109); (2) the ANNOUNCEMENT OF ORACLE, "This is the word" (v. 21a; cf. Isa 16:13; Jer 38:21).

In the first section, Isaiah delivers a PROPHECY OF PUNISHMENT (vv. 21b-28), the main parts of which include an accusation of some offense and an announcement of punishment (cf. 1 Kgs 13:21-22; Long, *1 Kings*, 151). Good parallels may be found at Isa 10:13-19; Ezek 28:2-10; Isa 47:1-15. All these texts and this particular example in 2 Kings shade over into (→) disputation. Note the style and tone of vv. 22-26 in which the speaker argues against the grounds for taking any pride in Sennacherib's exploits. However, the rhetorical questions (vv. 22, 25), the BOAST (vv. 23b-24), and argumentative claims (vv. 25b-26) serve to reproach more than persuade, and support the accusation that Sennacherib "mocks" and "reviles" God (vv. 23, 27). Functionally, these elements belong with prophecies of punishment, not with discourse aimed at disputing opinion, or effecting a change in belief or behavior (see Hayes, 151, who labels 2 Kgs 19:21-28 as a "speech of judgment"; on Ezek 28:2-10 as a similar "judgment oracle," see W. Zimmerli, *Ezekiel 2* [Hermeneia; Philadelphia: Fortress, 1983] 74-76). Of course, taken in its narrative context, such a prophecy of punishment for Sennacherib amounts to stating the grounds for Israel's deliverance in vv. 32-34 (cf. Isa 47:1-15 and C. Westermann, *Isaiah 40–66* [OTL; Philadelphia: Westminster, 1969] 188-90).

Designating vv. 21b-28 as taunt song or the like gives too much independent weight to the TAUNT in v. 21b (cf. 1 Sam 17:43-44; 1 Kgs 12:10b; 20:11). This couplet is important as a kind of thematic proem to the prophecy, but it does not finally determine the character and function of the whole (against Robinson, *2 Kings*, 185; Fricke, *2 Könige*, 274; Hentschel, *2 Könige*, 94; Gray, *Kings*, 688; Würthwein, *Könige*, 430; Montgomery, *Kings*, 494).

After this first subsection, the composite oracle moves to a PROPHETIC ANNOUNCEMENT OF SIGN (vv. 29-31; cf. 1 Kgs 13:3 and full discussion in Long, *1 Kings*, 150). Behind the particular formulation of v. 30 may be an ancient formula of (→) curse (Gevirtz), turned here of course into a positive motif in the vision of Judah's survival. See *ANET*, 662 (Eshmun'azar). The oracle then concludes with a PROPHECY OF SALVATION (vv. 32-34), a prophetic speech which announces to an individual or a whole people deliverance, healing, health, or restoration. Typically beginning with a (→) messenger formula, the prophecy announces salvation variously with statements about God's intention to intervene, the effects and results of such intervention, and sometimes notes the reasons for God's action (cf. 2 Kgs 7:1; Isa 7:7-9; Jer 28:2-4; Amos 9:11-12).

Setting

This episode is now part of a larger narrative. There is some evidence to persuade many critics that it was at one time an independent tradition of Sennacherib's deputation to Hezekiah at Jerusalem. Even if that were true, there is hardly any way of determining with reasonable assurance what its original setting might have been. (For possible cultic influences on the writer's way of depicting Hezekiah's actions, see above; and Hallo.) It is most important to grasp its present literary context, as part of the canonical picture of Sennacherib's threat to Jerusalem. In this light, the episode represents the Assyrian's second deputation, and leads directly to the rather brief ending to the whole affair, vv. 35-37.

Intention

It follows that the writer's main purpose as implied in the present form of the text is to depict a second sequence of events, corresponding roughly to those reported in 18:17–19:7. Sennacherib tries to weaken Hezekiah's resolve to defend Jerusalem, Hezekiah turns to Yahweh, and on the basis of his petition, he receives a promise of deliverance. This second episode, however, is not just a simpleminded repetition of the first. It extracts a thematic essence from the first, Sennacherib's arrogant posturing, and interprets it in terms of a single theological problem, blasphemy against Yahweh. This is partly accomplished with strategically placed statements that characterize Sennacherib's actions as "mocking," "reviling" (19:16, 23), and "ragings against Yahweh" (19:27-28). It is partly accomplished by shifting the dramatic image — from two kings facing each other through intermediaries as 18:17–19:7 imagines it, to Yahweh confronting the blaspheming foreigner. In this, God matches Sennacherib's blustery affront in both style and magnitude of claims. It is a drama of words between blustery foes, raised to a new level of intensity in which Yahweh defends his honor and his holy city Jerusalem. To the implied question "why?" the DtrH supplies a favorite answer: for the honor of God, and for the sake of God's promise to David (v. 34; cf. 8:19; 1 Kgs 11:36; 15:4).

This point, however, must be read in the light of subsequent events which an ancient reader would have already experienced. The kingdom in fact comes to an end, and David's last reigning scion was carried into exile (2 Kings 24–25). We therefore view this theme of Jerusalem's defense and its connection with Yahweh's favor toward the Davidic monarchy in terms of its literary placement within the whole Dtr history. We view it not as a fixed ideological principle, but as a statement about God's actions and attitudes on specific occasions in the course of a long story. In time, even Hezekiah's legendary sheen becomes dulled a bit (see 20:12-19). And the religious situation shortly becomes so desperate that the DtrH expresses the prophesied certainty of God's change of heart and the kingdom's ultimate collapse (see 21:10-15; 23:26-27; 24:2-3, 20).

Bibliography

See bibliography at 2 Kgs 18:13–19:37, Canonical Framework. R. Alter, *The Art of Biblical Poetry* (New York: Basic Books, 1985); A. Berlin, *The Dynamics of Biblical Parallelism* (Bloomington: Indiana University, 1985); R. Borger, "Gottesbrief," *RLA* III (1971) 575-76; K. Budde, "The Poem in 2 Kings xix 21-28 (Isaiah xxxvii 22-29)," *JTS* 35 (1934) 307- 13; R. Deutsch, "Hiskia-Erzählungen" (→ 2 Kgs 18:1–20:21, Canonical Framework); S. Gevirtz, "West-Semitic Curses and the Problem of the Origins of Hebrew Law," *VT* 113 (1961), 137-58, esp. 149-50; W. W. Hallo, "The Royal Correspondence of Larsa: I. A Sumerian Prototype for the Prayer of Hezekiah?," in *Cuneiform Studies in Honor of Samuel Noah Kramer* (ed. B. L. Eichler; AOAT 25; Neukirchen-Vluyn: Neukir-chener, 1976) 209-24; idem, "The Royal Correspondence of Larsa: II. The Appeal to Utu," in *Zikir Šumim. Assyriological Studies Presented to F. R. Kraus* (ed. G. van Driel et al.; Leiden: Brill, 1982) 95-109; J. H. Hayes, "The Oracles Against the Nations in the Old Testament" (Diss., Princeton Theological Seminary, 1964); J. Kugel, *The Idea of Biblical Poetry: Parallelism and Its History* (New Haven: Yale University, 1981); C. Kuhl, "Die 'Wiederaufnahme' " (→ 2 Kgs 13:1–14:29); B. O. Long, "Framing Rep etitions" (→ 2 Kgs 4:8-37); T. J. Meek, "The Metrical Structure of II Kings 19:20-28," *CrozQ* 18 (1941) 126-31; D. Pardee, *Hebrew Letters* (→ 2 Kgs 10:1-27); W. von Soden, "Zwei Königsgebete an Ištar aus Assyrien," *AfO* 25 (1974-77) 37-49; W. G. E. Watson, *Classical Hebrew Poetry* (JSOTSup 26; Sheffield: JSOT Press, 1984).

HEALING OF HEZEKIAH, 20:1-11

Text

In v. 11 the *RSV* translation "dial of Ahaz" lacks convincing support. The phrase means literally "steps of Ahaz." LXX[B] omits the expression, but the parallel version in Isa 38:8 attests to it, and in addition 1QIsa[a] includes *'ălîyat* to yield "steps of the upper chamber [*'ălîyat*] of Ahaz" (cf. 2 Kgs 23:12). But see, to the contrary, Cogan and Tadmor, *II Kings,* 256.

Structure

I. Hezekiah's illness	1-3
A. Narrative setting	1a
B. Prophetic oracle for Hezekiah	1b
1. Narrative introduction	1bα

A redactional join, "in those days," and the abrupt shift in subject matter mark the beginning of this unit (cf. 1 Kgs 14:1; 2 Kgs 8:7). The end of the section comes in v. 11, which concludes the report of a sign-event for Hezekiah. Vv. 12-19 probably reflect an originally independent tradition (so virtually all commentators; but see Hobbs, *2 Kings,* 286).

Many critics treat vv. 8-11 as a later expansion on a brief tradition, vv. 1-7, which ended in the past indicative, "and they took [the cake of figs] and laid [it] on the boil, so that he recovered" (so *NEB;* Montgomery, *Kings,* 507; Gray, *Kings,* 697; Würthwein, *Könige,* 432; Ackroyd, 344; Rofé, *Prophetical Stories,* 137-38). As presently found in the MT, the addition makes Hezekiah's request for a sign appear awkward and out of sequence. The LXX and Syriac VSS (cf. Isa 38:21), possibly reflecting an attempt to overcome the difficulty, read at v. 7b "that he might recover" *(wayyeḥî),* and so imply that the narrative continues (cf. *RSV*). The *NJPS* translation seizes an expedient middle ground: all of v. 7 is parenthetical and thus effectively denied its power to disrupt the narrative's temporal sequence. (Cf. Cogan and Tadmor, *II Kings,* 257, who take v. 7 as an independent element whose position remains unexplained.)

It is impossible to choose among these alternatives without some degree of arbitrariness. Since in any case the supposed expansion is a narrative fragment and presupposes the prophecies of healing, it would hardly have existed independently of vv. 1-7. Thus, one may concede that redactional developments left their mark in the chronological tension between vv. 7 and 8 (if the MT is the preferred reading at v. 7b), but look to the resulting canonical text as the important formal unit for analysis. This requires that we understand vv. 8-11 as offering supplemental information that carries us back to a moment before Hezekiah recovered. Cf. a similar interpretation given the supplements in Isa 38:21 by the *RSV* and *NJPS* translations. (Rofé, *Prophetical Stories,* 138; Würthwein, *Könige,* 433-35; and Hentschel, *2 Könige,* 97-98, propose more complex hypotheses of redactional history. They rest their opinions on dubious literary [Würthwein] or history-of-religions [Rofé] convictions that an original thaumaturgical version of this account must have been transformed into a more complex narrative, or into one with more elevated moral sentiment.)

The structure of the unit reflects a slimly developed plot. A brief narrative consisting of two scenes and a reportorial conclusion (vv. 1-3, 4-6, 7) tells of Hezekiah's illness and cure, while an afterword reports a confirming sign. When Hezekiah falls sick, Isaiah pronounces him to be terminally ill, at which point the king pleads with God that he be spared (I, vv. 1-3). Scarcely has the prophet left the ruler's sickbed when he is commissioned by God — Yahweh has responded favorably to Hezekiah's plea — to deliver a prophecy of salvation to the king (II.A, vv. 4-6). Presumably carrying out his commission (the narrator does not mention it), Isaiah then effects a cure (II.B, v. 7). We then learn that Hezekiah (had) also asked for a sign that Yahweh would in fact accomplish what he promised. In response, Isaiah cries to God and makes the then-lengthening shadow on the "steps of Ahaz" move backward (II.C, vv. 8-11).

The first scene focuses on Hezekiah. With a directness and economy of language that is typical of many OT narratives, the writer sketches the situation in just five words (v. 1a; cf. 1 Kgs 14:1; 2 Kgs 8:7). The phrase "in those days" is an imprecise marker in itself, but v. 6 makes clear that the writer envisions this event to have taken place before the withdrawal of Sennacherib's armies from Jerusalem, and thus still during the fourteenth year of Hezekiah's rule (18:13). On his sickbed, with his capital city under siege, Hezekiah is instructed by divine oracle to set his house in order, or "give last injunctions" before his death (Gray, *Kings,* 697; Montgomery, *Kings,* 512; cf. 2 Sam 17:23). The king falls immediately into a kind of proleptic mourning. Hezekiah does not "sulk" (against Hobbs, *2 Kings,* 290, who thinks the story portrays Hezekiah with growing disenchantment). The motifs of turning one's face to the wall and weeping bitterly create an impression of intense grief (cf. 1 Sam 1:10, in connection with Hannah's prayer; 2 Sam 3:32-34; Gen 27:38; 37:35). Through these tears, and with the strongly emotive language of entreaty (*'ānnâ yahweh zĕkor nā'*: "Please, oh please, Yahweh, remember"), Hezekiah implores God to recognize and weigh his pious deeds and inward faithfulness. His highly stylized words suggest the kind of devotion reserved by Israel's historians for few people and situations. For example, "walked [continuously] before Thee in faithfulness" recalls three important DtrH scenes: David's charge to Solomon (1 Kgs 2:4), Solomon's memory of David (1 Kgs 3:6), and Joshua's exhortation to the people at Shechem (Josh 24:14). By mentioning his having "done what is good in thy sight" Hezekiah suggests the Deuteronomic idea of obedience (Deut 6:18) and paraphrases the DtrH's measure for some of Judah's kings (cf. 2 Kgs 12:2; 14:3; 18:3; 22:2). The expression "with a whole heart" is used in Chronicles to describe priestly faithfulness in administering religious law (2 Chr 19:9) and, negatively, what King Amaziah lacked (2 Chr 25:2). In short, the writer portrays Hezekiah as an ideal king, grieving over his plight, but asking God to take special account of his heartfelt religion, i.e., to dam the flow toward death with the recollection of God's own personal attachment to this same king who rules within the Davidic covenant (on this dynamic sense of "memory," see Exod 32:13; Jer 14:21; Ps 25:6; 1 Sam 1:11; Judg 16:28; see Childs; Schottroff; H. Eising, *TDOT* IV, 64-82).

The second scene, vv. 4-6, brings another divine word. Before he has departed the middle "court" (accepting Qere *ḥāṣēr* with most commentators), Yahweh commissions Isaiah to deliver a prophecy of healing and deliverance to Hezekiah. Acknowledging the king's prayer, which usually implies that a favorable response will be given (cf. 2 Kgs 19:20; 1 Sam 25:35), Yahweh promises that Hezekiah will recover, go up into the temple three days hence (a traditional formula), and enjoy fifteen more years of life. Remarkably, these personal matters have now been joined to a public concern: God will deliver Hezekiah and Jerusalem from the hand of Assyria (cf. 19:34). As in v. 3, the language suggests royal ideology, but with its institutional dimension clarified. Isaiah is to bring a message of national continuity; it is a word from Yahweh, "God of David your father," to Hezekiah, who is called "prince of my people" (cf. 1 Sam 9:16; 13:14; 2 Sam 6:21; 7:8; 1 Kgs 1:35; 14:7; 16:2; see the latest review of the term "prince" [*nāgîd*] by B. Halpern, *The Constitution of the Monarchy in Israel* [HSM 25; Chico, CA: Scholars Press, 1981] 1-11). The fifteen years of additional life, when added to the fourteen already brought to focus in the year of Jerusalem's siege (18:13), constitute the DtrH's total reckoning for Hezekiah (18:2), not in terms of personal triumph but as encapsulated in the preservation of Jerusalem; the capital city will be defended not because of Hezekiah's personal piety — that was the first impression given by vv. 3 and 5 — but because of "David my servant" and Yahweh's honor, "for my own sake" (cf. 19:34). It is hardly that Hezekiah's egocentric concern with his own achievements is being "corrected" (against Hobbs, *2 Kings*, 291). Rather, the fate of Hezekiah, the ideal king, is bound up with that of Jerusalem, the ideal "city of God" (see Ps 87:3; 48:2, 9 [*RSV* 1, 8]). The king's private morality and reward seem important to the writer only in relation to the public institutions of state (God's people) and kingship (Davidic covenant).

The scene closes with a brief report of Hezekiah's healing (v. 7). On the orders of Isaiah, people apply a poultice of fig cake to the inflammation (*RSV* "boil"; cf. Exod 9:9-11; Lev 13:18). The king then recovers full health (cf. 1 Kgs 17:22; 2 Kgs 1:2). The writer's matter-of-fact tone and acceptance of Isaiah's simple curative powers tie the royal theology with its promise of miraculous deliverance to the mundane efforts of a folk healer. Isaiah must do his part in the making of miracles or else God's word goes unrealized.

Perhaps one is urged to see the final section, vv. 8-11, in this context of joining the transcendent to the ordinary. Reading this episode as filling a gap in the earlier narrative, we may understand that before his recovery Hezekiah (had) asked for a sign to confirm that he would be healed by Yahweh and again ascend into the temple. The response to his request comes not as a typical announcement of a sign (cf. 19:29-31; 1 Kgs 13:3; Jer 44:29) but as rhetorical dialogue in which he and Isaiah choose the materials of the world in which transcendent power might be felt. Isaiah asks the king to choose his miracle — a shadow that shortens or one that lengthens on the "steps of Ahaz." (That these stairs [not "sundial"; cf. text note above] perhaps led to a roof chamber associated with non-Yahwistic sacrifices [2 Kgs 23:12] bears no particular weight in the story; Gray, *Kings,* 699, supposes that astral worship is in mind.) Hezekiah selects the more difficult option, Isaiah "cries out to Yahweh," and he (God or the prophet, or both together) make the shadow shorten by ten steps (the MT is very clear about the active, causative force of the verb).

One is left, finally, with the idea of a prophet who collaborates with God to bring about the divine purpose (vv. 7, 8-11; cf. 2 Kgs 4:33). This subverts somewhat the suggestion that God effects deliverance of Hezekiah and Jerusalem for God-specific reasons (vv. 5-6). There may be nothing invidious in the contrast; there may be no contrast at all. The transcendent joins with the mundane; God needs human powers focused on earthly matters to affect the events of royal history. Hence, it may not have been to fault Hezekiah that the writer records that the king asked for a "sign," since God's miracle, like his *tôrâ,* is inoperative in the abstract, and dead apart from human effort. (Note how just the refusal to ask for a "sign" seems to count against Ahaz in Isa 7:11-13.)

Genre

This unit is a LEGEND, a story which is concerned primarily with the wondrous and exemplary. Parallels to the motifs of sickness and cure may be found in 2 Kgs 4:18-37; 1 Kgs 17:17-24; healing stories in the Gospels. (Cf. Rofé, "Classes"; idem, *Prophetical Stories,* 138; he proposes that an early "simple legend" of healing was transformed over time into a more complex "ethical [or 'didactical'] legend"; De Vries, 56, classifies this story as legend of a specific type, the "superceding oracle narrative" in which one oracle is countermanded by a second.)

We may note other generic elements of importance to the narrative. At v. 1aβ, the narrator includes a prophetic ORACLE, introduced by the typical MESSENGER FORMULA, in which Isaiah announces God's future for the ailing Hezekiah (cf. 2 Kgs 1:4; 3:16; 7:1). A prophet's COMMISSION (vv. 4b-6), which includes a PROPHECY OF SALVATION (vv. 5aβ-6), embodies God's task for Isaiah, but also informs the reader that Yahweh intends to rescue both Hezekiah and Jerusalem. For full discussion of the form, see Long, *1 Kings,* 139. The dramatic dialogue in vv. 9-11 is a variant on the PROPHETIC ANNOUNCEMENT OF SIGN (cf. 1 Sam 2:34; 1 Kgs 13:3; 2 Kgs 19:29-31; Jer 44:29). Constitutive elements of the genre structure the scene: formulaic (→) declaration of sign, v. 9a, identification of some event which is to function symbolically, vv. 9b-10, and the word "sign" (*'ôt*). These elements emerge in dialogue and in effect announce the sign, which then of course comes to pass (v. 11). For full discussion see Long, *1 Kings,* 150-51; also Childs, *Exodus,* 56-60.

Because of its opening entreaty, "Remember, now, O Lord" (*zĕkor . . .*), Hezekiah's PRAYER in v. 3 is reminiscent of the standard plea in the (→) complaint song, both of individuals (cf. Ps 25:6, 7) and of the community (Ps 74:2,

18, 22; Jer 14:21; cf. Jer 18:20 and 1 Sam 1:11; Gerstenberger, *Psalms,* 11-14). Several facts suggest a possible connection with royal cultic practice in the ancient Near East. First, the parallel version of this incident in Isaiah 38 depicts Hezekiah offering a Thanksgiving Song after he has recovered from his illness (J. Begrich, *Der Psalm des Hiskia: Ein Beitrag zum Verständnis von Jesaja 38:10-20* [FRLANT 25; Göttingen: Vandenhoeck & Ruprecht, 1926]; Wildberger, *Jesaja,* 1454-58). That a redactor referred to this psalm as *miktāb* (Isa 38:9), "writing," suggested to H. L. Ginsberg ("Psalms and Inscriptions of Petition and Acknowledgment," in *Louis Ginzberg Jubilee Volume* [New York: American Academy for Jewish Research, 1945] 159-71) that Hezekiah's prayer was actually published. Second, *miktāb* possibly means "letter" in 2 Chr 21:12. With just a further small step, one might associate both the occasion and the prayer of Hezekiah with Old Babylonian letter-styled petitions that resemble biblical laments and thanksgiving songs and that were published as monumental or statuary inscriptions (at least one example was written on the occasion of the king's illness; see Hallo; von Soden). This line of thought is suggestive, but hardly definitive. Even though the 2 Kings text gives no hint of the matter, it would not be surprising to learn that Judean and Israelite kings had such emblems of royal piety similarly displayed.

Corresponding to the petitionary form of Hezekiah's words, God's reply to Hezekiah, although part of the prophetic commissioning, begins with a formulaic ACKNOWLEDGMENT OF PETITION, v. 5b: "I have heard your prayer, I have seen your tears." Cf. 2 Kgs 19:20; 1 Sam 25:35; cf. Long, *1 Kings,* 109, where the same formula is less aptly called "declaration of favorable response."

Setting

Legends flourished in various societal contexts. Because this particular example highlights the piety of Hezekiah as much as the power of Isaiah, it could have originally had its typical setting in the royal court or among the ordinary folk who admired prophetic figures. More important is to evaluate the literary context that the exilic DtrH gave to the story. Vague temporal phrases clearly link it to the accounts of Jerusalem's deliverance (18:13–19:37) and to the embassy from Merodach-baladan (20:12-19). Thus, in reading one moves back in narrative time to a point before Jerusalem had been delivered (cf. v. 6 and 19:35-36). In terms of narrative sequentiality, we meet redundancy, but in terms of theme, the DtrH has constructed thematic association.

Intention

A main purpose of the writer is to press an analogy between the deliverance of Jerusalem and the healing of Hezekiah. As one grasps the fortunes of Hezekiah, so one understands something of the fate of Judah (Ackroyd, 344-45). Jerusalem had been spared partly because of God's attachment to David (19:34) and partly as punishment for an absurdly blasphemous Sennacherib (19:28). Personal healing of Hezekiah flows from similar God-specific reasons (20:6b). For the sake of David and God's own honor, God will defend the capital city. Inseparable from this rescue is the grant of personal recovery and additional life to Hezekiah. In this, God acknowledges that the king embodies the Davidic (and DtrH's) ideal of religious kingship. He also confirms the historian's general evaluation of Hezekiah (see 18:5-6). From the vantage point of the DtrH, who after all claims inspired knowledge of Yahweh's desires, one may detect just a hint that the well-being of Judah's remnant depends on something like the fierce devotion and "whole heart" to which Hezekiah made appeal (Ackroyd, 346). Proffered deliverance, however, can be qualified or even withdrawn. Hezekiah's dealings with Merodach-baladan in the immediately following section will dim, but not extinguish, the flame of Hezekiah and the hopes of Judah's exiled remnant.

Bibliography

See bibliographies at 2 Kgs 1:2-17a; 19:8-34. P. R. Ackroyd, "An Interpretation of the Babylonian Exile: A Study of 2 Kings 20, Isaiah 38–39," *SJT* 27 (1974) 329-52; B. S. Childs, *The Book of Exodus: A Critical, Theological Commentary* (OTL; Philadelphia: Westminster, 1974); idem, *Memory and Tradition in Israel* (SBT 1/37; London: SCM, 1962); E. S. Gerstenberger, *Psalms, Part 1; with an Introduction to Cultic Poetry* (FOTL XIV; Grand Rapids: Eerdmans, 1988); A. Rofé, "Classes in the Prophetical Stories: Didactic Legenda and Parable," in *Studies on Prophecy* (VTSup 26; Leiden: Brill, 1974) 143-64; W. Schottroff, *'Gedenken' im Alten Orient und im Alten Testament. Die Wurzel zākar im semitischen Sprachkreis* (2nd ed.; WMANT 15; Neukirchen-Vluyn: Neukirchener, 1967); H. Wildberger, *Jesaja* (→ 2 Kgs 18:13–19:37); Y. Zakovitch, "2 Kings 20:7 — Isaiah 38:21-22," *BethM* 50/3 (1972) 302-5 (Hebr.).

HEZEKIAH AND THE DELEGATION FROM BABYLON, 20:12-19

Text

In v. 12 the *RSV* supplies "envoys" since the idea of a personal delegation must be assumed from vv. 13 and 14; following some earlier critics, and probably a Greek variant at Isa 39:1, Burney (*Notes,* 351) emends *sĕpārîm,* "letters," to *sārîsîm,* "eunuchs." The change is unnecessary, but adds a touch of irony because Isaiah envisions that some of Judah's royal sons will be taken off to serve the king of Babylon as "eunuchs" (v. 18).

In v. 13 the *RSV* "welcomed them" reads *wayyiśmaḥ* with certain MSS, VSS, and Isa 39:2 for MT *wayyišma'*. Virtually all critics follow this tradition of interpretation (see Targum); one may retain MT *wayyišma',* "and he heeded [the words and implicit demands]," because it accords well with the sense of the story that Hezekiah made a political pact with Babylon (see Begg, "Reading," and discussion below).

Structure

Probably originally independent of its present context, this tradition was joined to vv. 8-11 with the vague connector, "at that time" (so virtually all critics, but see Hobbs, *2 Kings,* 294). On the basis of two expressed attitudes toward Babylon, Würthwein (*Könige,* 435-36) supposes that a brief report friendly to Babylon, vv. 12-13, was supplemented with DtrH and post-Dtr material of a negative tone (vv. 14-19a and portions of vv. 12b, 19b, respectively). A similarly reconstructive approach leads to differing results in Hentschel, *2 Könige,* 99. There is little roughness in the text to suggest such a redactional history, however. Vv. 20-21, which close out the whole regnal epoch, obviously mark the unit's outer limit.

The writer hangs a simple plot on a dialogic skeleton. Hezekiah receives and responds favorably to a delegation from Merodach-baladan (I, vv. 12-13), and Isaiah meets this fact with a word of judgment developed out of dialogue with the king (II.A-B.1, vv. 14-18). At the end, dialogue seems to become interior monologue, as Hezekiah responds privately to Isaiah's prophecy (v. 19b; on the ambiguity, however, see below). In hearing these successive dialogues and supplying the unstated premises, a reader comes to understand that Hezekiah strikes a bargain with the Babylonians which God abhorred, and that God will bring punishment on his kingdom, not in Hezekiah's time — he had previously been granted fifteen more years of rule, v. 6 — but during the years of his sons.

We learn nothing directly about the purpose of the Babylonian delegation (for what follows, we follow substantially the lead of Ackroyd, 332-43). Mention of the occasion — Merodach-baladan had heard that Hezekiah had been ill — forces a connection with vv. 8-11, when Hezekiah was sick to death in the midst of Jerusalem's life-threatening siege (see discussion above). Yet Hezekiah "heeded them" (the letters and gifts brought by envoys) and willingly opened his treasures to the Babylonians' gaze. The writer emphasizes this action: "he showed them all his treasure house . . . all that was found in his storehouses and kingdom; there was nothing Hezekiah did not show them in his house or in all his realm" (v. 13).

The second scene reveals this last action to be of great importance. In a twofold sequence of question and answer, Isaiah elicits the king's version of events (vv. 14-15). However, the writer reports matters selectively, as perhaps Hezekiah himself would have done. We do not hear what the envoys said (this question of Isaiah remains unanswered), but that they had "come from a distant land, from Babylon." The words already evoke associations of an archetypal distant place, the exile to which the punished will go, wherein they will remember Jerusalem (Jer 51:50), and from which their deliverance will arise (Jer 46:27; Zech 6:15; see Ackroyd, 338, and cf. Solomon's prayer of dedication, 1 Kgs 8:46). Isaiah comes quickly to the main issue: "What have they seen in your house?" The king's answer virtually duplicates the narrator's words of v. 13b, even to the emphatic mode of speech: "Everything in my household they saw — there was nothing I did not show them in my storehouses" (v. 15b).

Evidently, the envoys do not come with gifts and letters in hand simply to cheer up a sick monarch (cf. 2 Sam 10:2; *ANET,* 29b-30a), and Hezekiah is not just playing the part of appreciative host. But what exactly does the give-and-take of action imply?

By situating this incident historically, many scholars suggest that Merodach-baladan was proposing an alliance against an expected assault from Assyria (so, e.g., Burney, *Notes,* 350; Robinson, *2 Kings,* 196-97; Šanda, *Könige* II, 307; cf. Würthwein, *Könige,* 436; Montgomery, *Kings,* 510; Gray, *Kings,* 701); Cogan and Tadmor (*II Kings,* 262) state more conservatively that the mission proposed to maintain goodwill with the strongest of Assyria's western vassals. Even without invoking this historical scenario, it seems likely that Hezekiah's "heeding" the envoys in v. 13 alludes to a first act of accepting a diplomatic overture (Begg, "Reading"; cf. 1 Kgs 15:18; 2 Kgs 16:8). But what is meant by "showing" one's treasures? Perhaps the action is analogous to an exchange of property between seller and buyer (so Ackroyd, 340, citing D. Daube, *Studies in Biblical Law* [Cambridge: Cambridge University, 1947]). Possibly Hezekiah confirms that he has in fact agreed to something (Begg), or demonstrates that he would be a powerful ally for Merodach-baladan (Fricke, *2 Könige,* 292-93; Wildberger, *Jesaja,* 1475-76).

The symbolism may be a good deal stronger, however. In a nearly contemporary Assyrian royal inscription, the scribes of Shalmaneser III (ca. 858-824 B.C.E.) report the king's military conquest and subjugation of an enemy as follows: "I entered the towns Sahlala and Til-sha-Turahi and brought my gods/images into his [the foe's] palaces. . . . I opened (his) treasury, inspected what he had hidden; I carried away as booty his possessions" (*ANET,* 278b). An inscription of Adad-nerari II (ca. 911-891 B.C.E.) reads similarly: "That fellow [a rebel king] I brought down from his palace. I personally inspected his property, precious stone of the mountain, chariots, horses, his wives, his sons, his daughter — (all) his valuable booty. That fellow together with his brothers I fastened in bronze clasps (and) brought (them) to my city Ashur" (Grayson, *ARI* II, § 427).

It may be that Hezekiah's "heeding" and "showing" imply that command of resources willingly or unwillingly (the story suggests the former) has passed from a vanquished or compliant state (Judah) to a dominant power (Babylon). Compare 1 Kgs 20:1-3, where giving up ownership of royal property is demanded of Ahab, who takes this as a sign of vassalage, and does not "heed" (*šmᶜ*) or "consent" (Long, *1 Kings,* 214).

If our interpretation is correct, Isaiah elicits from Hezekiah an admission that he has submitted to a foreign power in diplomatic concordat. Everything in effect belongs to Babylon. This point is brought to full closure when Hezekiah in v. 15b reiterates both the theme and emphasis of the narrator's own version of events (v. 13).

Not yet divulging the king's purpose in making this agreement, the writer has Isaiah immediately announce Yahweh's judgment on the kingdom and royal house. The prophet offers no reason for God's action — we must surmise this from the narrative; nor does he utter accusation and rebuke. Isaiah simply pronounces Judah's dismal future in two parts: (1) all the kingdom's riches will be actually, not ceremoniously, taken to Babylon (a formulaic "says the Lord" punctuates this first word); and (2) Hezekiah's sons will be carried to Babylon to serve as palace eunuchs or servants. Isaiah suggests ironic reversal in repetition and wordplay. As nothing in Hezekiah's stores was concealed from the Babylonian envoys (*wayyar'ēm . . . kol-'ăšer nimṣā' bĕ'ôṣrōtāyw*, v. 13b), so everything in the king's house that had been stored up would be taken away (*wĕniśśā' kol-'ăšer . . . 'ăṣěrû 'ăbōtêkā*, v. 17). As there was nothing that Hezekiah refused to show the Babylonians (*lō'-hāyâ dābār 'ăšer lō'-her'ām* [*hir'îtim*], vv. 13b, 15b), so nothing shall remain to Hezekiah in this exile of Judah's inheritance (*lō'-yiwwātēr dābār*, v. 17b). Moreover, the king's sons, his very own issue (Isaiah's phrasing is emphatic here), will become servants in the Babylonian palace, conceivably to be sent out on missions like those envoys whom Hezekiah had received (*sārîs*, "eunuch," may mean simply an official in service to the king; see 1 Sam 8:15; 1 Kgs 22:9; 2 Kgs 8:6).

Hezekiah reacts to this prospect of devastation with aplomb and acceptance: "The word of the Lord which you have spoken is good" (v. 19a). But immediately, the speech becomes murky, for the sense of v. 19b is far from obvious (an old Greek tradition omits it altogether, and Isa 39:8b offers a simpler form). One cannot even be sure whether the writer means to describe speech or thought. If the latter, then it is not difficult to infer duplicity, or at least self-protective smugness, in Hezekiah's inner attitude. See *RSV* "For he thought, 'Why not, if there will be peace . . . ?' " and Hobbs, *2 Kings*, 285; cf. Cogan and Tadmor, *II Kings*, 260. (Würthwein, *Könige*, 438, attributes such a negative characterization of Hezekiah to a late glossator.) However, one may also take the words less negatively, as a counterpart to v. 19a and in accord with Isa 39:8b, which reads "for [surely] there shall be peace and security in my time" (*kî yihyeh šālôm we'ĕmet bĕyāmāy*). If the divine announcement is to be accepted, Hezekiah seems to say, then "is it not so, or surely, that there will be peace and security in my time?" (Ackroyd, 337-38, cites Gen 4:7, where the Hebrew construction *hălô' 'im* means "is it not true that?"; similarly, Gray, *Kings*, 703; Montgomery, *Kings*, 510; Burney, *Notes*, 352).

In the larger narrative context, however, the writer allows these somewhat enigmatic words to suggest a purpose behind Hezekiah's "heeding" the Babylonian envoys. While Jerusalem was under siege (v. 12a, "at that time"; cf. vv. 1 and 6, which place the events before Jerusalem's deliverance), and thus while he was seeking Yahweh's aid (see 19:19), Hezekiah sought to protect Jerusalem by agreeing to an alliance with Babylon. Neither his action nor his words in 20:19b need necessarily discredit Hezekiah in the writer's eyes, but they may indeed do so (so Gerbrandt, 87-88; Hobbs, *2 Kings*, 294-95; and others who condemn Hezekiah's moral and religious failings). At the least, the king acknowledges that God's promise, along with Babylon's strength, assures Judah's survival in Hezekiah's own time. Of course, the DtrH took Hezekiah's piety as cause for praise, and his godly actions as interwoven with God's own reasons for delivering both king and kingdom.

The writer, or the narrative as it stands, denies us a precise determination of what Hezekiah's response finally means. If his exact words bring no discredit to him, the prophetic announcement clearly subverts any naive approval. God looks to trouble ahead, and announces its approach with images that reverse whatever good might accrue to Judah from Hezekiah's alliance with Babylon. The king may be spared personally — after all, Yahweh has already promised him fifteen additional years of rule, 20:6 — but Isaiah foresees eventual punishment falling upon the kingdom, even in this moment, this fourteenth year of Hezekiah, when Jerusalem gains her deliverance.

Genre

This unit is a REPORT, i.e., a brief self-contained narrative, less developed in plot and characterization than (→) story, and telling of a single event or situation in the past. (Contrast De Vries, 55, who assigns this narrative to the category of legend.) As De Vries rightly saw, the emphasis falls on Isaiah's prophecy, an ANNOUNCEMENT OF JUDGMENT. The word is doubly introduced by the formulaic CALL TO ATTENTION ("Hear the word of the Lord") and INTRODUCTION TO AN ANNOUNCEMENT OF FUTURE EVENTS ("Behold the days are coming"). The announcement itself is normally part of a longer (→) prophetic judgment speech (see Mic 3:9-12; Jer 11:9-12), but can stand alone, especially in prose narratives.

Setting

Since reports can have many societal settings depending on their content, the important issue is the literary context which the DtrH has provided this particular example. As mentioned above, the temporal phrase "at that time" (v 12), combined with a similar formula at 20:1, constrains us to place this incident and Hezekiah's recovery (vv. 1-11) within the reference points of Jerusalem's siege and deliverance (18:13–19:37). This aspect of the DtrH's composition means that everything noted about Hezekiah and his reign has been built around this one central event.

Intention

In this canonical context, we may take the experience of Judean exile to have been somewhat cryptically foretold and legitimated in prophetic judgment. The complete loss of goods and royal sons anticipates the implication one might draw from the final narrative in 2 Kings that nothing of significance remained to Judah after Nebuchadnezzar's crushing assault (see 2 Kgs 25:9-21). In this, the report is in accord with the more overt patterns of prophecy and fulfillment in the Dtr history (Ackroyd, 341-42). Read as a kind of reflection on the siege of Jerusalem, this and the immediately preceding narrative unite to offer the exilic DtrH a paradigm of deliverance and judgement, analogous to the portrayal of Jerusalem under threat and subsequently relieved. If Hezekiah's illness and recovery stress God's attachment to the Davidic household, then the impugned alliance with Babylon suggests that deliverance is not to be taken for granted, or separated from covenantal obedience. Placed in the maelstrom of Jerusalem under siege, as though watching a storm through a glass, a reader may sense the worsening fury — the confusion and destruction that is to end the larger story (cf. Begg, "2 Kings 20:12-19"). Such an awareness is already encouraged at 2 Kgs 17:19-20. At the close of Hezekiah's reign, it disturbs the feelings of relief that the stormy fury of Assyrian conquest and Hezekiah's illness have passed. Everything — not a thing is left behind — will be sent to a far off land in some future whirlwind. Later, such dis-ease will fix on Manasseh's evil and become an ideological justification so powerful as to overwhelm any comfort that might arise from Josiah's pious deeds (see 2 Kgs 21:1-15; 23:26-27). God's protection and defense of his covenant people, his chosen royal house, and his dwelling place in Jerusalem is forever tenuous because it is forever bound up with human action. To the exilic DtrH, judgment and hope belong together and are offered as paradigms in his story of Hezekiah, as indeed in all the stories concerning the monarchs of Israel and Judah.

Bibliography

P. Ackroyd, "Interpretation" (→ 2 Kgs 20:1-11); C. Begg, "The Reading at 2 Kings xx 13," *VT* 36 (1986) 339-41; idem, "2 Kings 20:12-19 as an Element of the Deuteronomistic History," *CBQ* 48 (1986) 27-38; S. DeVries, *Prophet* (→ 2 Kgs 1:2-17a); G. Gerbrandt, *Kingship* (→ 2 Kgs 18:1–20:21, Canonical Framework); H. Wildberger, *Jesaja* (→ 2 Kgs 18:13–19:37, Canonical Framework).

THE REIGN OF MANASSEH, 21:1-18

Structure

I. Introductory regnal resumé	1-9
A. Regnal information	1
B. Theological evaluation	2-9
1. General appraisal (did evil in God's sight)	2
2. Specific offenses	3-8
3. General appraisal (did evil in God's sight)	9
II. Report of a prophecy of punishment	10-15

This unit is a typically structured regnal epoch that begins and ends with customary formulaic summaries. (See 1 Kgs 14:21-31 and full discussion of stylistic elements in Long, *1 Kings,* 158-65.)

Because vv. 8 and 10-15 presuppose the Judean exile while summarizing the reign of a preexilic king, many critics assume, with minor differences, that the material has gone through at least two redactions. Typical is Gray (*Kings,* 705), who takes vv. 1-7, 16-18 as preexilic and vv. 8-15 as postexilic supplement (so also Burney, *Notes,* 352; Robinson, *2 Kings,* 203; Nelson, 65-70; cf. Šanda, *Könige* II, 324-25, who assumes two exilic redactors, but distributes the material between them quite differently). Würthwein (*Könige,* 440) and Hentschel (*2 Könige,* 101-2) defend triple redaction, but disagree with each other on some of the details. Yet Hoffmann (pp. 155-67) and Hobbs (*2 Kings,* 300-301) argue that the unit was written by a single author.

Whatever its history may have been, the resulting canonical text seems formally and thematically coherent. In presenting Manasseh's regnal epoch, the Dtr writer uses the conventional plan: introductory and concluding summaries (I, IV, vv. 1-9, 17-18) frame an event, in this case a prophetic word, which characterizes the reign (II, vv. 10-15). Furthermore, in vv. 3-7 we may observe an alternating pattern of locating Manasseh's transgressions (Hoffmann, 160):

    illegitimate worship, without localization (v. 3)
      altars built, in Jerusalem and its temple (vv. 4-5)
    illegitimate practices, without localization (v. 6)
      image of Ashcrah, in temple (v. 7)

In this ordered composition, only v. 16 seems awkwardly placed, since it appears to resume the enumeration of Manasseh's failings that now, in the retrospective experience of reading, seems to have been interrupted at v. 9 (note the *wĕgam,* "and also" [*RSV* "moreover"]).

However, certain motival repetitions counteract this sense of formal clumsiness. The phrase "do evil in the sight of the Lord" (*'āśâ hāra' bĕ'ênê yahweh*) appears four times. In vv. 2 and 16 it defines a first and last judgment on Manasseh, as though a reader were to enter and exit Manasseh's rule through this single thresholding idea. Inside the framing regnal summaries, the same phrase combines with another (Manasseh "did much evil in the sight of the Lord, provoking him to anger [*lĕhak'îs*]," v. 6) and this remark finds its intensifying recapitulation at the close of prophecy at v. 15: "because they [the people led

astray by Manasseh] have done evil in my sight, and have continually provoked
me to anger" *(wayyihyû mak'isîm 'ōtî)*. The effect of this fourfold repetition is
to provide an outer framework (vv. 2, 16) around two sections (vv. 3-9, 10-15)
which are in turn linked together by the repetition of "doing evil/provoking to
anger." In this way, the writer ties together the two main sections of the unit,
evaluation (vv. 3-9) and prophecy (vv. 10-15).

Moreover, these divisions within the unit are yoked together in substance
and tone because the report of prophecy, vv. 10-15, serves less to record a
freestanding occurrence than to comment on and evaluate Manasseh's transgressions. The introduction (v. 10) already points to the typical, not the specific. It
is not one prophet who speaks, but many (v. 10; cf. 17:13, 23). They also speak
with one voice, i.e., the writer epitomizes what they say, just as he presents some
of the specific transgressions of Manasseh as ongoing typicalities that mar the
king's fifty-five years of rule (e.g., vv. 3b, 6).

In short, a consistent evaluative tone and commentarial substance govern
the whole presentation of Manasseh's reign, despite its formal divisions. First
we read of Manasseh's personal failings (vv. 2-7), then of punishment for
transgressions committed by the people whom the king led astray (vv. 10-15).
These two foci merge in a transition, vv. 8-9, wherein the writer returns in
narrative time to an earlier divine word in which God had stated the condition
under which king and people were to live in the land. Of course, the condition
has been violated, as vv. 10-15 show. Finally, at the close of the unit, the writer
focuses again on the king's own transgressions but emphatically restates his
double guilt (v. 16).

Manasseh is a pivotal figure in the history of the monarchs. The writer's
gaze shifts back and forth, between predecessor kings and later descendant
monarchs, from northern kingdom to southern, from the ideals of a Davidic
people of God to the pitiless destruction of the last remnant of Judah. Manasseh
goes against God as Ahaz and the punished and scattered northern peoples had
done, for he behaved "according to the abominable practices [*tô'ăbōt*] of the
nations whom Yahweh had dispossessed on Israel's behalf" (v. 2b; 16:3; cf.
17:8). Now, as illustration, there follows a list of transgressions: he rebuilt the
illegitimate shrines (*RSV* "high places") which Hezekiah had destroyed, and
about which a pointed satirical blow had been aimed at Sennacherib in telling
about Jerusalem's rescue (18:4, 22; see discussion at 18:17–19:37); he built
altars for Baal, and made an Asherah, the cultic symbol of Baal's consort (see
J. de Moor, *TDOT* I, 438-44; see fuller discussion at 23:4-20); he worshiped
celestial gods and goddesses, all the "hosts of heaven" (v. 3), and engaged in
all manner of illicit divinatory activities (v. 6; the catalogue is standardized
rhetoric, cf. Deut 18:10-11; "mediums and wizards" refer apparently to forms
of necromancy; cf. 1 Sam 28:7; H. Hoffner, "Second Millennium Antecedents
to the Hebrew '*ôb*," *JBL* 86 [1967] 385-401). These actions, the Dtr writer
claims, assault Judah with the viral infection of Ahab (and of Jeroboam I) that
coursed through the northern kings' bloodstream and finally destroyed the body
politic (v. 3; 1 Kgs 16:32-33; 2 Kgs 17:10, 16). It will be these sins of Ahab,
now perpetrated in the south by Manasseh, that Josiah especially will put right
(23:4, 7b, "altars to Baal, and the Asherah"; 23:8, "high places"; on this special

link to Josiah, see Hoffmann, 156-67). Josiah will also overcome Manasseh's desecration of the Jerusalem temple with foreign altars (vv. 4, 5; 23:12), as indeed the practice of offering human burnt sacrifices to the deity (v. 6a), attributed first to Ahaz (16:3; 23:10), and also the practice of consulting non-Yahwistic and prophetic mediums (v. 6b; 23:24). As for the sculptured figure of Asherah (*pesel,* v. 7), Josiah will remove and destroy that too (23:6-7).

In sum, Manasseh is something of a structural antagonist to Josiah. In this position he distills and pours out in Judah the essence of the northern kingdom's misguided apostasies, those ways which had insidiously entered Judah by marriage (8:18, 27) and by his mimicking Israel's ways (16:3; 17:19). The basic and most grievous offense is against the singularity of Jerusalem's temple in cultic affairs. This claim corresponds to the exclusivity of Yahweh himself. In Jerusalem and in the temple connected with David and Solomon (1 Kgs 11:32, 36), God chose to lodge his empowering presence ("my name," vv. 4, 7; 1 Kgs 9:3; 14:21; Deut 12:5, 21; 14:24). It is this taboo of holiness associated with Yahweh's name that Manasseh has violated. Moreover, he has "seduced" the people to follow his ways even as they live under the condition that faithful obedience to God in this place will prevent a relapse into the stateless (and godless) disorder of wandering, refugee-like, outside the ancestral land (v. 8; see Ps 36:12 [*RSV* 11, "drive away"]; cf. Ps 59:12 [*RSV* 11], LXX [BDB, 626; *NJPS* "make wanderers of them"]). For his part, Josiah will purify that sullied space again, restore the priority of Jerusalem and its temple worship, and bring the kingdom of Judah back to its covenantal attachments to Yahweh and *tôrâ*-heartedness (see fuller discussion at 23:4-20).

This structural and thematic opposition between Josiah (and to a lesser extent Hezekiah) on the one hand and Manasseh (and somewhat Ahaz) on the other, offers a thematic middle point from which the Dtr writer takes his measure of the direction in which Judah is headed. Josiah will be praised for his submission to *tôrâ*-centeredness, while Manasseh is condemned for his "abominations," a thematic word of vv. 2-7; the people under Manasseh, led astray but nonetheless guilty, are under threat of dispersion (v. 14); and we shall see that this punishment will not be waived, so egregious is Manasseh's fault (23:26-27; 24:3).

The message is one of disaster, and the messengers, God's "servants the prophets" (II, vv. 10-15). As though summarizing the substance of many oracles, the writer presents in stylized Dtr language the reason for judgment (v. 11), the proclamation of punishment itself (vv. 12-14), and, as a framing closure, he repeats the justification for coming disaster (v. 15). The point is as astonishing as it is unmistakable. Alluding to Ahab in v. 13 (and recalling v. 2, along with the judgment against Samaria in 17:7-23), the "prophets" announce that God intends to reject the remnant of his "inheritance," i.e., the land-people Israel of sacralized borders, covenantal attachment, and *tôrâ* obedience (Deut 9:26, 29; 1 Kgs 8:53; Isa 19:25). What remains of that theologically defined community in Judah — the literary context presupposes the demise of such a reality in the northern body politic — will be cast off (cf. Jer 12:7-8, 9-13; see S. Sandmel, "Israel, Conceptions of," *IDBSup,* 461-63; H.-J. Zobel, *"yĕhûdâ,"* TDOT V, 482-99; and idem, *"yiśrā'ēl,"* TDOT VI, 397-420).

Genre

This unit is an editorial composition consisting of introductory and concluding REGNAL RESUMÉ (vv. 1-9, 16, 17-18) and a constructed PROPHECY OF PUNISHMENT (vv. 10-15). For discussion of the former, see 1 Kgs 14:21-31 (Long, *1 Kings*, 158-64). On the latter, see full discussion at 1 Kgs 13:20-22 (Long, *1 Kings*, 151); cf. 1 Kgs 14:7-11; 21:20b-22; 2 Kgs 1:16; 22:16-17.

Setting

This unit probably originated with the exilic Dtr writer, who organized this recounting of the Israelite and Judean kings and positioned Manasseh in thematic opposition to both Hezekiah and Josiah.

Intention

It follows naturally that the writer's intention is to present the reign of Manasseh as antitype to Hezekiah and Josiah. He is the archetypal bad king in Judah who, far more than some of his predecessors, embodies the faults of the apostate, punished, and now exiled northern kingdom. Now ruled by her own version of Ahab, Judah is in terminal decline (Hobbs, *2 Kings,* 303). Composing from his exilic vantage point, the writer takes up earlier hints of Judah's demise (2 Kgs 8:16-24; 12:17-18; 14:1-14; 17:13, 19-20; 20:12-19) and for the first time explains his and his readers' primary experience of catastrophic loss. Because of Manasseh, Judah will go (has gone) the way of the north, into exile (vv. 14-15). It remains for the point to be reaffirmed during the reign of Josiah. The shadowed cloud really is without its sun-lined edge (see below, chs. 22–23).

Bibliography

H.-D. Hoffmann, *Reform* (→ 2 Kgs 3:1-3); R. D. Nelson, *Double Redaction* (→ 2 Kgs 17:1-41).

THE REIGN OF JOSIAH: CANONICAL CONTEXT, 22:1–23:30

Structure

I. Introduction (introductory regnal resumé)   22:1-2
II. Account of events (Josiah's pious acts)   22:3–23:24
   A. The book of *tôrâ*   22:3-20
     1. Concerning repair of the temple
       (finding book of *tôrâ*)   3-11

As is usual for the Dtr history, the regnal epoch of Josiah opens and closes with typical summaries (I, III.B, 22:1-2; 23:28-30). Inside this framework, the writer has assembled various materials to depict a series of events as totally motivated by Josiah's commands (22:3, 12; 23:1, 4, 21) but arranged in a concentric pattern of repeated motifs. At the center are Josiah's cultic reforms (II.C, 23:4-20), framed by idealized ceremonies promulgated on the basis of the "book of the covenant [*bĕrît*]," 23:1-3, 21-23. These interlocking segments are in turn framed by material explicitly linked to the "book of the teaching [*tôrâ*]," 22:3-20; 23:24. At the outermost edges stand evaluative remarks, both of which allude to the *tôrâ* of Moses, directly (23:25) or indirectly (22:2, "left or right"; cf. Deut 17:20; Lohfink, "Cult Reform"). In short, the writer provides chiastic structure to the regnal materials of Josiah:

A   positive evaluation (implicit *tôrâ*) 22:2
   B   "book of *tôrâ*" 22:3-20
     C   "book of covenant" 23:1-3
       D   acts of reform 23:4-20
     C'   "book of covenant" 23:21-23
   B'   "book of *tôrâ*" 23:24
A'   positive evaluation (*tôrâ* of Moses) 23:25

The point of the arrangement is clearly to single out Josiah as a reformer of the cult quite unsurpassed in Israel's parade of kings. Whatever their origins may have been, the various narratives and reports now suggest that the king's efforts, depicted thematically as repentance and reform, took place in his eighteenth year (22:3; 23:23) and fundamentally in response to, and in accord with, the "book of *tôrâ*," the teaching of Moses discovered in the Jerusalem temple.

Because of their importance to many historical issues in OT study, these Josiah materials have been subjected to sustained and intense research. Assuming that the book which the high priest found in the temple was some earlier version of the canonical Deuteronomy (2 Kgs 22:8), many scholars believe themselves able to investigate the relative dating of the pentateuchal sources and other crucial aspects of Israelite religion and politics. (Note, however, A. D. H. Mayes's well-argued thesis that the connection with a "book of law" is a late Dtr literary fiction ["King and Covenant"; idem, *Deuteronomy*, 85-103].) The Josiah unit has also figured centrally in debates about the composition and redaction of the Dtr history, since such discussions revolve around issues of chronology, how the history work relates to the time of Josiah, and various shifts in ideological perspectives. Different scholars have interpreted the selfsame text as having resulted from two redactions, or from one writer-editor who wrote during the exile. Recent discussion has concentrated on modifying the latter idea by identifying traces of at least two, possibly three redactions, carried out before and after the exile. (See Long, *1 Kings*, 14-15; see the fuller review of recent research in Gerbrandt, 1-18; and the exhaustive and sensible discussion by Mayes, *Story of Israel*, 106-32.)

These hypotheses of composition and editing are attempts to explain certain difficulties within 2 Kings 22–23 that are taken as signals of literary disunity. Critics note the following main points:

(1) the storylike language of 22:3–23:3 contrasts with the largely enumerative form of 23:4-23; whereas the former involves dramatic scenes and plotted action, the latter consists largely of brief reports arranged without a strong sense of drama;

(2) *wāw* plus simple perfect verb *(wĕqāṭal)* intermingles with the more usual *wāw* plus imperfect forms *(wayyiqṭōl)* to express consecutive action in 23:4-20; this grammatical feature never appears in ch. 22;

(3) 23:4-25 appears somewhat disjointed and lacks smooth transitions at, e.g., 23:15, 21, 24; also 23:16-18 abruptly departs from the surrounding enumerative style and alludes directly to 1 Kings 13;

(4) 23:26-27 limits the power of Josiah's goodness and seems at odds with the rather extravagant praise of the king in ch. 22 (note esp. vv. 2, 19) and 23:25;

(5) the report of Josiah's death in 23:29-30 seems intrusive within the normal concluding formulas; it also suggests that Josiah suffered an ignoble and violent demise, and thus contradicts the impression given by Huldah's prophecy in 22:20;

(6) parts of 22:3-7 recall 2 Kgs 12:10-15, and v. 9 seems to continue vv. 3-7 while interrupting the flow from v. 8 to v. 10;

(7) 23:13 reproduces in large measure 1 Kgs 11:5, and 23:24 seems an afterthought with 2 Kgs 21:6 in mind.

These observations suggest to most critics that 2 Kgs 22:1–23:30 consists of at least two blocks of tradition which have been variously edited, supplemented, and brought into relation to each other. (The modern discussion is still much indebted to Oestreicher's classic formulation.) There is a narrative telling about discovering the "book of *tôrâ*" in the temple and its consequences (A = 22:3-20 + 23:1-3, 21-23) and an account of Josiah's cultic reforms (B = 23:4-20). Some scholars suggest that at the base of "A" was an account of temple repairs, 22:3-7, 9 (possibly constructed out of 2 Kgs 12:10-15) into which was fitted the narrative about finding a book (e.g., Dietrich, "Gesetzbuch," 18-22; Mayes, *Story of Israel*, 128). Others argue that Huldah's oracle, 22:15-20, in whole or in part, was added to tradition "A," but the premise itself is disputed (e.g., Mayes, *Story of Israel*, 128-29) as well as fundamental details, such as whether vv. 16-17 or 18-20 are the more original, even pre-Dtr, elements (see Dietrich, "Gesetzbuch," 25-29; Würthwein, "Josianische Reform," 402-6; Weinfeld, *Deuter-*

onomy, 25-26; Nelson, *Double Redaction,* 76-78). Tradition "B" has been variously understood as composite and perhaps supplemented with vv. 16-18 and 24-27, but consensus is elusive. (Cf. Hollenstein; Jepsen, "Reform des Josia"; and Nelson, *Double Redaction,* 79-85; note the skepticism of Mayes, *Story of Israel,* 130, toward recovering a redactional history of this section, and Lohfink's admission ["Cult Reform," 464-65] that aside from allowing for a few interpolations, he cannot reconstruct a pre-Dtr reform report.)

The details of such recent criticism and the wide disagreements among critics often depend on whether one assumes (1) a doubly redacted Dtr history (Cross; Friedman; Gerbrandt; Isbell; Lohfink; Nelson; among commentaries, see Gray, *Kings,* 713-15); or (2) a triple redaction (Dietrich, "Gesetzbuch"; idem, *Prophetie;* Smend; Spieckermann; Würthwein, *Könige,* 446-64; idem, "Josianische Reform"; cf. Hollenstein, who imagines that the original version of the reform report was written in Josiah's time under priestly influence, then subsequently edited by the DtrH, and finally revised by a post-Chronicles redactor). Other problems arise out of the inevitable ambiguity in the textual evidence. Even advocates of one or the other of these main hypotheses have difficulty achieving consensus. For example, Isbell believes most of the material in chs. 22–23 to have belonged to a Josianic, preexilic Dtr[1], while Nelson distributes whole and partial verses between Dtr[1] and postexilic Dtr[2]. Würthwein divides the same tradition into three redactional layers (an original DtrH; a "nomistic" [Dtr[N]] and a prophetic [Dtr[P]] redactor), but differs substantially from Spieckermann who sifts every word and phrase through an even finer triple-redaction screen. Hoffmann (pp. 169-270) reverts to something like Noth's hypothesis of a single Dtr writer by exposing Josiah's place in a coherent system of cross-references within 1–2 Kings that center on royal acts concerning the cult. (Burney, *Notes,* 355, earlier had taken the Josiah material as a unified narrative.) From this completely different theoretical base, Hoffmann explains as intentional literary allusion many of the motifs in the Josiah materials that trouble redaction-critical scholars. Examples are 22:4-7 (cf. 12:9-16), 23:13 (cf. 1 Kgs 11:5-6), 23:24 (cf. 21:6).

Such radical disagreements suggest that further gains toward achieving consensus are unlikely within the current paradigms of understanding. (Cf. Hobbs, *2 Kings,* 319, who simply decides to concentrate on the canonical form of the text.) In fact, the points of roughness and tension within the traditions may have been overstated; and in some cases the problems a critic finds seem too much dependent upon, rather than explained by, a particular theory of redaction (e.g., Nelson, *Double Redaction,* 79).

In any case, other alternatives suggest themselves when we consider again the main literary tensions scholars have seen in the Josiah materials.

(1) The differences in style between traditions "A" and "B" are striking, but not so sharp as to exclude all continuity between them (see esp. Hoffmann, 208-11; and note Isbell). For example, storylike detail mingles with reportorial style in the account of both southern (23:8-9) and northern (23:16-18) reforms, and action is plotted on a geographical plan — Josiah moves from Jerusalem and environs (22:3–23:14) to Bethel, Samaria (23:15-20a), and

back to Jerusalem (23:20b). Cf. a similar mix of reportorial and dramatic prose in 2 Kgs 11:9-16 + 17-20, a text that has been taken as composite, but does not yield easily to theories of source divisions. (See discussion above at 2 Kings 11, Installation of Joash.) Also, the characters at 23:4 are the same as in ch. 22, and both sections of the Josiah materials have in common a date (22:3; 23:23) and terms for the book that Hilkiah found in the temple. In fact, the end of the account of reform — unless we arbitrarily exclude vv. 21 and 24 — weaves together the various expressions that have been used separately elsewhere. "Book of the *tôrâ*" (22:11), "words of the book that was found" (22:13), and "book of the covenant" (23:2) reappear as "book of the covenant" (23:21) and "words of the *tôrâ* written in the book that Hilkiah the priest found" (23:24).

(2) The grammatical feature, simple *wāw* plus perfect used to express normal narrative consecution, offers uncertain support to theorists of redactional development. First, it is not exclusively found in late texts as some critics have argued, and thus may not be used to identify supposed late redactional layers. (See Spieckermann, 120-30, for the most thorough recent discussion of this issue.) Second, the device is not limited to enumerative prose, and on that account cannot bear a lot of weight in attempts to distinguish a finding-of-the-book narrative from the account of reforms. (See 1 Kgs 21:12; 2 Kgs 8:10; 12:10, 12.) Third, use of the perfect with simple *wāw* does not appear to be an "unerring signal of a literary layer" (against Spieckermann, 130), since it appears regularly intermingled with *wāw*-conversive forms of expression, and in material which is not on independent grounds obviously composite (e.g., 1 Kgs 6:32, 35; 12:32; 14:27; 20:27; 2 Kgs 18:4).

(3) To feel the dissonance between 23:26-27 and the more dominant praise of Josiah in these materials, we must assume that one biblical writer translated a high regard for Josiah into expectations that the king's merit would spare Judah its destruction, and that another editor or writer was scandalized by actual events (23:29-30) which then demanded explanation by means of editorial revision (23:26-27). (See, typically, Nelson, *1– 2 Kings,* 252; idem, *Double Redaction,* 84; Frost, 372, 380.) The circularity of argument is both unabashed and ignored. It is the assumption of double redaction that creates the inconsistency found in the narrative, which is then invoked to support the theory of double redaction. Without that assumption, the problem disappears, for a writer of Huldah's oracle (22:16-20) could already have distinguished between the fate of the nation, which is condemned, and that of Josiah, who is praised, and simply have reaffirmed that viewpoint in 23:26-27.

(4) Is 23:29-30 disruptive of the concluding formulas? It is difficult to claim such, for these regnal summaries in 1– 2 Kings often include nonformulaic detail which, in relation to the bulk of the tradition that represents a given reign, may seem to us extraneous or appendant. See, e.g., 1 Kgs 14:30; 15:23; 22:39; 2 Kgs 14:28; 15:16; 20:20; 24:7. In at least one case, the additional information is rather extensive (1 Kgs 22:47-51 [*RSV* 46-50]). The reputed contradiction between 23:29-30 and 22:20 is also question-

able. Because the reference to Josiah's death and burial in 22:20 has no exact parallel, it resists all scholarly efforts to clear up its ambiguity. M. Rose (pp. 58-59) expresses a near consensus that the metaphor "be gathered to your fathers" means to die a natural death after a full and satisfying life (Gen 15:15). By analogy, the argument goes, 2 Kgs 22:20 must mean something similar, and therefore stands at odds with 23:29-30 where Josiah suffers a violent death. Yet, Hoffmann (pp. 183-85) takes Gen 15:15 as evidence that the phrase "gathered to the fathers," in some cases at least, segments the event of death from the rites of burial (see Gen 49:33 and 50:1-2, 4; Deut 32:50). Thus, the phrases "I will gather you to your ancestors" and "you shall be gathered to your grave in peace" in Huldah's prophecy are parallel in form but different in meaning (so also Dietrich, *Prophetie*, 58; and Mayes, *Story of Israel*, 129). In this reading, the prophet announces only that Josiah will die, but not *how*, and comments further that his burial will be with honor, "in peace," the very opposite of those people and kings who experience God's punishment (1 Kgs 13:22; 14:11; 16:3-4; 21:21-24; Deut 28:26). We may add that 23:30b possibly signals its own commentary on the matter by specifying burial in the king's "own tomb" unlike the last three kings of Judah (see this emphasis elsewhere only at 2 Kgs 9:28 and 21:26).

(5) The objections to the integrity of 22:3-11; 23:13, 16-20, 24 can be persuasive only if one has established multiple redactions on independent grounds. Using an alternative theory, Hoffmann takes them as indicators of an implicit authorial connection between larger parts of the Dtr narrative. A more serious difficulty is felt by Mayes in ch. 22, where the connection between vv. 8 and 10 is broken by v. 9, the continuation of vv. 4-7 (*Story of Israel*, 128). The elliptical style does create a problem, and Mayes's solution, that vv. 8 and 10 came into the temple repair account when the book finding account was joined to it, seems appealingly plausible. Yet ellipses are not uncommon in biblical narrative, and obviously they do not necessarily mark source or redactional seams. Far more significant is the lack of consensus and consistent argument among scholars. Nelson, a double-redaction advocate, sees no problem here (*Double Redaction*, 76-77), like Spieckermann (pp. 46-53, 423), who otherwise vigorously pursues minute signs of triple redaction. On the other hand, Dietrich ("Gesetzbuch," 18-22) finds elements of his proposed three redactional levels, while Hoffmann (p. 192, n. 5) defends the unity of vv. 1-11.

The inherent ambiguities of evidence and wide disagreements on all these matters do not inspire confidence in our abilities to reconstruct with much assurance the redactional or compositional history of the Josiah materials. We may assume such a history, but — as the studies of Lohfink and Hoffmann suggest — we now have a text whose coherent form requires explanation and analysis. (Burney, *Notes*, 355, takes 22:3–23:25 as "continuous narrative.") It seems probable that a writer drew upon at least two different sorts of material — a story of discovering the "book of the *tôrâ*" in the temple, and various reports of reforms carried out by Josiah. We do not exclude the possibility that certain elements were simply created anew by the writer-editor. These traditions still retain something of their original independence, although it is plain that as they now stand in the Dtr history, they have been arranged to suggest that the discovery of the *tôrâ* book inspired Josiah's reforms, and that these corresponded to concerns raised in all other accounts of cultic action in the books of Kings (Hoffmann, 251-63).

The canonical account brackets Josiah's actions with evaluative statements (22:2; 23:25) and sets most events in the king's eighteenth regnal year. Major episodes are presented as a series of sequential actions, each one motivated by a decisive action, a command or a commission, from the king. (For most of what follows, see Lohfink, "Cult Reform"; idem, "Bundesurkunde.") Josiah "sent" *(šālaḥ)* Shaphan to the temple (22:3), and this leads to the king's receiving word of a "book" found by the high priest (II.A.1, 22:3-11). Josiah responds and takes a series of actions in accord with the discovery (II.A.2 + B-E, 22:12–23:24). The king presides over each of these subsequent events as monarch, a royal priest like Solomon, and chief instigator of reform:

22:3-11	Josiah "sent" *(šālaḥ)* Hilkiah
22:12-20	he "commanded" *(ṣwh)* the oracular inquiry
23:1-3	he "sent" *(šlḥ)* and presided over a covenant observance
23:4-20	he "commanded" *(ṣwh)* reform measures
23:21-23	he "commanded" *(ṣwh)* a Passover observance

This series of royal actions, moreover, has been arranged in a chiastic pattern that graphically locates cultic reform at its center, and every strand of ideological authority in the "book" that Hilkiah found in the temple.

A   Finding and dealing with book of *tôrâ* (22:3-20)
  B   Covenant by book of *běrît* (23:1-3)
    C   Cultic reforms (23:4-20)
  B'   Passover by book of *běrît* (23:21-23)
A'   Last reforms by book of *tôrâ* (23:24)

Implicit within this formal structure is a simple narrative plot. Finding the "book of the *tôrâ*" leads to penitence and reform, which of course is meant to characterize Josiah's regnal epoch. A religious question provides still another principle of coherence to the unit (Lohfink, "Cult Reform"). Can Judah, threatened by the curse of Yahweh, be rescued? Finding the book in the temple sets off a kind of panic; Huldah, the prophet, looks for the worst, and her oracle postpones Yahweh's punishment while keeping the threat of it alive (22:15-20). Josiah's actions of covenant making, Passover celebration, and cultic purification throughout the land seem to aim at warding off disaster, quite in keeping with the familiar idea that prophecies of disaster are opportunities for repentance (1 Kgs 21:27-29; Jer 26:18-19; 36:1-3; Jonah 3:1-10). Yet, the generalized note toward the end (III.A, 23:25-27) recalls for us the essential problem posed by Manasseh, Josiah's predecessor, in the ongoing story of the kings (cf. ch. 21). Will his transgressions be blotted out now that Josiah has cured the religious disorders of south and north, of Ahaz (23:12), Manasseh, Solomon (23:13), and Jeroboam (23:15)? The answer finally is no. One departs Josiah's regnal period with a sense of foreboding already generated at 21:10-15. It is reaffirmed here and will finally burst into public tragedy at 24:2-3. Josiah's death at Megiddo, so laconically reported as part of the concluding resumé (III.B, 23:28-30), seems to anticipate the national disaster that awaits Judah.

Genre

This unit is an editorial construct comprised of materials which conform to several distinct genres. Major space is given to HISTORICAL STORY (22:3-20) and related episodes presented in the style of REPORTS and ACCOUNTS (23:1-3, 4-20, 21-24). There is also the familiar REGNAL RESUMÉ (22:1-2; 23:28-30) and a brief THEOLOGICAL REVIEW (23:25-27).

Setting

This editorial unit probably stems from the work of the exilic Dtr historian.

Intention

As is typical of the books of Kings, the main purpose for such a compilation is to summarize and to characterize a regnal epoch in ways that are consistent with the larger aims of the Dtr history work. Josiah is presented as a king who is unsurpassed in penitent submission to God's teaching (23:25). In his singularity, he is to be understood in the context of Hezekiah, whom the Dtr writer similarly realized as a paradigm of unrivalled "trust" in God (18:5; see discussion at 18:1–20:21, Canonical Framework). These two kings, paragons of prayer/attachment and submission/obedience, or in short, of royal priesthood, form a constraining image around Manasseh (21:1-18), who is the main exemplar of apostasy in the south, and the reason the DtrH gives for Judah's destruction. The structural relations among these three kings is a constant factor in the Dtr writer's picture of Josiah and in his purpose to present this regnal period as a high point in the larger story of religious politics that failed (see Hoffmann, 146-67, and detailed analysis below).

Bibliography

See bibliography at 2 Kgs 8:28–9:28. F. M. Cross, "Themes of the Book of Kings and the Structure of the Deuteronomistic History," in *Canaanite Myth and Hebrew Epic* (Cambridge: Harvard University, 1973) 274-89; W. Dietrich, "Josia und das Gesetzbuch

(2 Reg. XXII)," *VT* 27 (1977) 13-35; R. Friedman, *The Exile and Biblical Narrative: The Formation of the Deuteronomistic and Priestly Works* (HSM 22; Chico, CA: Scholars Press, 1981); S. B. Frost, "The Death of Josiah: A Conspiracy of Silence," *JBL* 87 (1968) 369-82; G. Gerbrandt, *Kingship* (→ 2 Kgs 18:1–20:21, Canonical Framework); H.-D. Hoffmann, *Reform* (→ 2 Kgs 3:1-3); H. Hollenstein, "Literarkritische Erwägungen zum Bericht über die Reformmassnahmen Josias 2 Kön. XXIII 4ff.," *VT* 27 (1977) 321-36; C. D. Isbell, "2 Kings 22:3–23:24 and Jeremiah 36: A Stylistic Comparison," *JSOT* 8 (1978) 33-45; A. Jepsen, "Die Reform des Josia," in *Festschrift Friedrich Baumgärtel* (ed. L. Rost; Erlanger Forschungen 10; Erlangen: Universitätsbund, 1959) 97-108; C. Levin, "Joschija im deuteronomistischen Geschichtswerk," *ZAW* 96 (1984) 351-71; N. Lohfink, "Die Bundesurkunde des Königs Josias (Eine Frage an die Deuteronomiumsforschung)," *Bib* 44 (1963) 261-88, 461-98; idem, "The Cult Reform of Josiah of Judah: 2 Kings 22–23 as a Source for the History of Israelite Religion," in *Ancient Israelite Religion: Essays in Honor of Frank Moore Cross* (ed. P. D. Miller et al.; Philadelphia: Fortress, 1987) 459-75; idem, "Die Gattung der 'Historischen Kurzgeschichte' in den letzten Jahren von Juda und in der Zeit des Babylonischen Exils," *ZAW* 90 (1978) 319-47; idem, "Zur Neueren Diskussion über 2 Kön 22–23," in *Das Deuteronomium, Entstehung, Gestalt und Botschaft* (ed. N. Lohfink; Bibliotheca Ephemeridum Theologicarum Lovaniensium 68; Leuven: Leuven University, 1985) 24-48; A. D. H. Mayes, *Deuteronomy* (New Century Bible; repr. Grand Rapids: Eerdmans, 1981); idem, "King and Covenant; a study of 2 Kings chs. 22–23," *Hermathena* 125 (1978) 34-47; idem, *Story of Israel* (→ 2 Kgs 17:1-41); R. P. Merendino, "Zu 2 Kön 22,3–23,15," *BZ* 25 (1981) 249-55; R. D. Nelson, *Double Redaction* (→ 2 Kgs 17:1-41); idem, "Josiah in the Book of Joshua," *JBL* 100 (1981) 531-40; Th. Oestreicher, *Das Deuteronomische Grundgesetz* (Beiträge zur Förderung Christliche Theologie 27; Gütersloh: Bertelsmann, 1923); M. Rose, "Bemerkungen zum historischen Fundament des Josia-Bildes in II Reg 22f.," *ZAW* 89 (1977) 50-63; J. Rosenbaum, "Hezekiah's Reform" (→ 2 Kgs 18:1-8); L. Rost, "Zur Vorgeschichte der Kultusreform des Josia," *VT* 19 (1969) 113-20; R. Smend, "Das Gesetz und die Völker. Ein Beitrag zur deuteronomistischen Redaktionsgeschichte," in *Probleme Biblischer Theologie* (*Fest.* G. von Rad; ed. H. Wolff; Munich: Kaiser, 1971) 494-509; H. Spieckermann, *Juda unter Assur in der Sargonidenzeit* (FRLANT 129; Göttingen: Vandenhoeck & Ruprecht, 1982); M. Weinfeld, *Deuteronomy* (→ 2 Kgs 8:16-24); H. G. M. Williamson, "The Death of Josiah and the Continuing Development of the Deuteronomic History," *VT* 32 (1982) 242-48; E. Würthwein, "Die Josianische Reform und das Deuteronomium," *ZTK* 73 (1976) 395-423.

INTRODUCTION TO JOSIAH'S REIGN, 22:1-2

Structure

This unit consists of the usual formulas that introduce distinct regnal periods throughout the books of Kings. See full discussion in Long, *1 Kings*, 158-64.

Of particular interest is a variant on the typical. Not only did Josiah do "what was right in the eyes of Yahweh" and walk "in all the way of David his father" (such positive appraisals are rare and used only of Judean kings, e.g., 1 Kgs 15:11; 2 Kgs 18:3), but he "did not turn aside to the right hand or to the left," v. 2bβ. The last remark amounts to a special commendation of Josiah's moral and religious uprightness. The phrase is applied to no other king in the Dtr history, and seven of its eight occurrences with this connotation are in Dtr materials (Deut 5:32; 17:11, 20; 28:14; Josh 1:7; 23:6; 2 Kgs 22:2). In one case, the statement is associated with the "book of the *tôrâ*" (Josh 1:7-8), in another with the *tôrâ* of Moses (Josh 23:6), and in a third with God's instructions for kingship, i.e., the conditions by which a king rules in Israel (Deut 17:14-20). When the king sits on his throne he is to "write for himself a copy of the instructions [*tôrâ*] in a book, from that over which the Levitical priests have charge; and it shall be with him, and he shall read it all the days of his life so that he may learn to revere Yahweh his God and to abide by all the words of this *tôrâ*, and to keep these statutes . . . that he may not turn away from the commandment, to the left hand or to the right" (17:18-20).

Genre and Setting

This unit is an introductory REGNAL RÉSUMÉ, an organizing and evaluating device of the exilic Dtr writer. See full discussion in Long, *1 Kings*, 154-58.

Intention

This introductory regnal resumé brings the report of Josiah's reign into the ongoing story of the monarchy, and, with the concluding summary, 23:28-30, it forms the editorial framework that demarcates the report of his regnal years. In view of the associations of the phrase "he did not turn aside to the right hand or to the left," it seems likely that the Dtr writer intended that from the beginning the reader associate Josiah with the noble tradition of idealized *tôrâ* observance (see Gerbrandt, 49-50). Thus, it should seem perfectly natural that this king responds with agitated and fervent devotion when the "book of the *tôrâ*" is read to him (22:11-13, 19; 23:25), and that he carries out all his religious reforms to "establish," i.e., to put into practice, the *tôrâ*'s requirements (23:24).

Bibliography

G. Gerbrandt, *Kingship* (→ 2 Kgs 18:1–20:21, Canonical Context).

JOSIAH AND THE BOOK OF THE *TÔRÂ*, 22:3-20

Text

In v. 5a *RSV* "repairing the house" may misconstrue the syntactical relations in the sentence. The sense seems to be that Josiah gives money to the workmen so that they can repair the temple. Note the similar construction at the end of v. 6. Thus, we translate: "Let it be given into the hand of the workmen . . . to repair [*lĕḥazzēq*] the temple." (See *NJPS*, and discussion below.)

Structure

I.	Josiah arranges finances to repair temple (finding the book of *tôrâ*)			3-11
	A.	Josiah's instructions		3-7
		1. Narrative introduction		3
		2. Instructions proper		4-7
	B.	Results (instructions carried out)		8-11
		1. Concerning a book of *tôrâ*		8
			a. Hilkiah's report of book's discovery	8a
			b. The book's conveyance/reading	8b
		2. Report to Josiah		9-10
			a. Concerning payment to repair workers	9
			b. Concerning the book of *tôrâ*	10
			1) Shaphan's report of book's reception	10a
			2) The book's reading	10b
		3. Josiah's immediate response (gesture of distress)		11
II.	Josiah's further response to the book (mission of oracular inquiry)			12-20
	A.	Josiah's instructions		12-13
		1. Narrative introduction		12
		2. Instructions proper		13
	B.	Execution of Josiah's instructions		14-20
		1. Audience with the prophet Huldah		14-20a
			a. Meeting	14
			b. Oracle	15-20a
			1) Narrative introduction	15aα
			2) Oracle proper	15aβ-20a
			a) Messenger formula	15aβ
			b) First commissioning speech	15b-17
			(1) Commissioning formula	15b
			(2) Message (for Judah)	16-17
			(a) Messenger formula	16aα
			(b) Prophecy of punishment	16aβ-17
			c) Second commissioning speech	18-20a
			(1) Commissioning formula	18a

(2) Message (for Josiah)	18b-20a
(a) Messenger formula	18bα
(b) Announcement of reprieve	18bβ-20a
2. Report to Josiah	20b

This unit includes two of five action sequences that constitute the account of Josiah's reign (see discussion at 2 Kgs 22:1–23:30, Canonical Context). Each of the five sequences follows a directive of the king, and, in these first two, the writer describes scenes built on a pattern of (1) royal commission with instructions quoted, followed by (2) a report of its being carried out, and (3) a report of the results (cf. Hoffmann, 191; Lohfink, "Bundesurkunde," 264-70; idem, "Gattung," 319-22). We may envision the pattern as follows:

I, vv. 3-11
A. "the king sent" *(šlḥ),* v. 3

B. (orders carried out)
C. "he reported" *(šûb dābār),* v. 9

II, vv. 12-20
A. "the king commanded" *(ṣwh),* v. 12

B. orders carried out, vv. 14-20a
C. "they reported" *(šûb dābār),* v. 20b

This formal structure supports a simple plot line. Josiah sets out to arrange payment for repairs to the temple, and while his instructions are being carried out (we must assume this from the ellipsis at v. 8), Hilkiah discovers a book of teachings *(tôrâ)* in the temple. He reports this finding to the king's scribe, who subsequently carries the writing to Josiah along with the report that the king's original directives have been carried out. Greatly disturbed upon hearing the book's contents, the king directs that an oracle be sought ("inquire of the Lord," v. 13) and receives back a prophecy of punishment for Judah (vv. 16-17) and a promise that he himself will not witness the disaster (vv. 18-20a).

The first scene begins routinely enough. Josiah is depicted as the good and pious king who, in his eighteenth year, attends to official religion (cf. Solomon, 1 Kings 6–9) and continues the procedures established during Jehoash's reign for assuring that adequate funds be gathered to repair the temple (cf. 2 Kgs 12:12-13 [*RSV* 11-12] and 22:4-7). Indeed, the account seems based upon 2 Kgs 12:8-15 (*RSV* 7-14; see Hoffmann, 193-96; Dietrich, "Gesetzbuch," 18-21; Würthwein, "Josianische Reform," 400-401). The use one makes of this literary relationship to explain redaction and composition is less important than seeing an important thematic connection within the canonical books of Kings. Josiah's way has been prepared by the boy-king Jehoash, whose place on the Judahite throne and Yahwistic education was secured by Jehoiada, a Yahwistic priest (2 Kgs 11:4-16; 12:3 [*RSV* 2]). Josiah continues this submission to the guardians of the Judean royal cult, or rather, his wishes naturally coincide with the interests of the Judean religious. He relies upon Hilkiah, the "high priest," to carry out his orders (the rank of Jehoiada was not given in the Jehoash materials). As an agent of the king, the priest is to reckon the money that is collected in the temple and give it to the supervisory workmen, who then are to pay for labor and materials. (The meaning of the verb *wĕyattēm,* "bring to an end," hence "sum, reckon," is not attested elsewhere. Perhaps we are to envision "silver" being melted down and "poured out" [reading *wĕyattēk*] as items of monetary exchange. Cf. v. 9 and 2 Kgs 12:11, 14 [*RSV* 10, 13]; among commentators, see Burney, *Notes*, 356; Montgomery, *Kings*, 527; Gray, *Kings*, 723; Hobbs, *2 Kings*, 153-54; Würthwein, *Könige*, 446.)

As one surmises from v. 9, the king's orders are carried out. Meanwhile, the writer diverts our attention to another matter which, by its duplicated reference (vv. 8, 10), completely overshadows the piety of temple repair. Hilkiah discovers a "writing" of holy teachings (*tôrâ;* probably in scroll, not in book form), gives it to Shaphan, who reads it *(wayyiqrā'ēhû)*. Shaphan in turn repeats the action. He announces the writing ("Hilkiah . . . has given me a writing"), and reads it *(wayyiqrā'ēhû)* before King Josiah. Their actions follow exactly the paradigm of obedience envisioned in Deut 31:9-13 (cf. Neh 8:1-8), which Jehoiakim violates in the Dtr-styled Jeremiah 36. Josiah similarly announces this "book" by reading it before the assembled peoples (23:2). This image of taking to heart the contents of the *tôrâ* clearly dominates the entire account. It is expressed first in the actions of Hilkiah and Shaphan, both of whom treat a casual discovery in the idealized Dtr way as an urgently provocative event, and second in the actions of Josiah, who reacts to the reading of the words with typical gestures of distress (v. 11; cf. 2 Kgs 5:7; 6:30).

The term *sēper hattôrâ*, "writing (book) of the Teaching," is frequent in Dtr traditions. To the Dtr writer of Kings, it refers to those commandments and instructions that God presented, Moses wrote, and that Israelites are enjoined to accept as duties of heart and action. Herein was defined the covenant people, a "kingdom of priests and a holy nation" (Exod 19:5-6; see Deut 17:18; 28:58, 61; 29:19-20, 26 [*RSV* 20-21, 27]; 30:10; 31:24, 26; Josh 1:8; 8:31, 34; 23:6; 24:26; cf. Ezra and Nehemiah). Despite the virtual consensus among biblical critics that the writing which Hilkiah found was an earlier form of the canonical Deuteronomy, the fact remains that we are limited in such historical reconstructions by the literary style and interests of the Dtr writer. (For a convenient summary of the issues, see Montgomery, *Kings*, 543-44; updated in Gerbrandt, 195-96.) Obviously the account does not divulge the exact contents of the "book." Emphasis falls instead on dramatizing the responses to it. We are guided to assume that the "writing" generated feelings of penitence (vv. 11, 19) and of foreboding (v. 13b). Living in relation to this document, but in disobedience to it, implies a threat to the continuity of both religious community and body politic (cf. vv. 16, 19, 20, "bring evil upon this place . . . a desolation and a curse," with Deut 28:15, 37; the Dtr prose in Jer 19:8; 24:9; 25:9, 11, 18; Weinfeld, *Deuteronomy*, 348-49; Hobbs, *2 Kings*, 327; Gray, *Kings*, 727). In describing Josiah's reaction, the writer later implies that the king understands the writing as a broadly aimed exhortation. It was not simply "teaching" or instructional commandments *(tôrâ)*, but word of prophecy in accord with the notion that "prophets" persistently "warned" Israel and Judah, "Turn from your evil ways and keep my commandments and my statutes, in accordance with all the *tôrâ* which I commanded your ancestors, and which I sent to you by my servants the prophets" (2 Kgs 17:13). In this view, even Moses, the archetypal intermediary of *tôrâ*, is considered a prophet (Deut 34:10-12).

In the next section of the narrative, the writer reports Josiah's further responses to this "writing of *tôrâ*" (II, vv. 12-20). The king sends a delegation to "inquire of Yahweh," i.e., to seek, in this ominous situation, some direction, prediction, advice, or all of these, from God (cf. 1 Kgs 14:1-5; 22:5-9; 2 Kgs 3:11-19; 8:7-9). (The detailed enumeration of the names and patrilineage of Josiah's men, along with similar descriptive matter about Huldah in v. 14, suggests a picture of social and economic identity among royal, priestly, and prophetic families.) The king's men carry out their charge, receive an oracle from Huldah, and dutifully report back to their monarch (vv. 14-20).

The writer gives pride of place to Huldah's oracle. Her prophecy appears to have been carefully integrated into its narrative context, crafted for rhetorical effect, and set like a jewel in the ring of the Dtr history. Her words address multiple levels of hearing. They constitute a message for Josiah, address the reader in the author's voice, and offer — as indeed happens elsewhere in the Dtr work — those interpretative perspectives that transcend a particular moment in the narrative and express the main purposes of the DtrH.

Josiah's charge to his subordinates, vv. 12-13, anticipates in both form and content Huldah's prophecy (see Hoffmann, 190-91). The king asks for guidance on behalf of the people and himself. Correspondingly, Huldah's oracle falls into two self-contained phases, one addressed to the nation (vv. 16-17) and one to Josiah (vv. 18-20). The king expresses his concern, perhaps pious fear, and attributes the trouble to his forerunners' failure to "obey" *(šmʿ)* the words of the book and to "do" *(ʿśh)* according to what was written in it (v. 13; *RSV* "our fathers" in the Dtr view probably refers to previous kings). Both the sentiment and the language appear again in Huldah's oracle, vv. 16-17. Compare especially "for great is the wrath of Yahweh that is kindled against us" *(kî-gĕdôlâ ḥămat yahweh 'ăšer-hîʾ niṣṣĕtâ bānû)*, v. 13, with "my wrath is kindled [*wĕniṣṣĕtâ ḥămātî*] against this place," v. 17.

Aside from its close relation to narrative context, Huldah's oracle seems carefully composed for rhetorical effect (cf. Hoffmann, 170-89, who takes the speech as the climax to the entire narrative; Lohfink, "Bundesurkunde," 272, n. 2, sees the climax in the covenant ceremony, 23:1-3, but notes the oracle's impressive formal unity). Within double commissioning of Josiah's men (vv. 15b-17, 18-20a), the writer embeds a two-phased prophecy, each with its own prophetic messenger formula, "Thus says the Lord." Of course, everything Huldah says is considered to be a prophecy. Hence, this same emissarial claim at v. 15aβ governs the entire speech, including, somewhat oddly, the specific commissioning formula, "Tell the man who sent you. . . ." By such a threefold repetition of this formula, the writer demarcates precise horizons for which divine authority is being claimed and punctuates formal divisions within Huldah's words. (Cf. other cases in which charges to messengers carry within them prophetic oracles, e.g., 2 Kgs 1:3-4; 1 Kgs 14:7-11.)

Within the announcement that concludes the entire oracle, v. 20 hides a reprise of Huldah's first word. Concerning the nation, Yahweh proclaims, "I will bring evil upon this place" *(hinnî mēbîʾ rāʿâ 'el-hammāqôm hazzeh)*, v. 16. Now, Huldah announces that Josiah shall be spared, his "eyes shall not see all the evil which I will bring upon this place" *(bĕkōl hārāʿâ 'ăšer-'ănî mēbîʾ ʿal-*

263

hammāqôm), v. 20aβ. Also, the reason given for Josiah's reprieve in v. 19 carries within it an echo of the punishment previously announced for the nation. Thus, the statement "when you heard how I spoke against this place, and against its inhabitants, that they should become a desolation and a curse," refers in the first instance to v. 16a (so Hoffmann, 176).

These parallel and cross-referential motival relationships may be visualized as follows:

Prophecy 1 (vv. 16-17)	**Prophecy 2 (vv. 18b-20a)**
1. Messenger formula	1. Messenger formula
2. Announcement of punishment ("bring evil on this place")	
3. Reason for punishment	2. Reason for reprieve
4. Announcement of punishment ("wrath . . . kindled against this place")	3. Announcement of reprieve ("bring evil on this place")

Huldah's first prophecy, vv. 16-17, begins and ends with the announcement of punishment that Judah will suffer God's "evil" and "wrath." At the midpoint, Huldah utters the justification for punishment, the direct accusation that the people have forsaken Yahweh, v. 17a. The more usual arrangement of such discourse moves from a statement of offense to punishment (see 1 Kgs 13:21-22; 14:7-11; 16:2-4, but cf. Jer 2:26-28; Amos 8:9-14). One effect of this variation from the typical is to emphasize at the outset that punishment is related to the writing which has been brought to Josiah, and, moreover, that offenses are measured by the book's contents (vv. 16b, 17a). A deviation from pattern at the beginning of Huldah's second oracle serves a similar end. There we read an unusually expansive messenger formula: "Thus says the Lord, the God of Israel, concerning the words which you have heard" (v. 18b, accepting a proposed emendation that removes the awkwardness in the MT; E. Nicholson, "2 Kings 22:18 — A Simple Restoration," *Hermathena* 97 [1963] 94-98, esp. 97-98; see Hobbs, *2 Kings,* 314). The phrase "concerning the words which you have heard" apparently refers to Huldah's first oracle and thus binds together the two parts of the prophecy. They also allude to the wider narrative context, to the "words" which have been read to King Josiah (v. 13aβ-b), and which cry out now like a curse about to materialize into physical symptoms (cf. v. 19a, "desolation and curse"; cf. Deut 28:15; 29:19-20 [*RSV* 20-21]).

Binding all this together is a theme word, *šmʿ* ("hear, heed, obey"), which pivots between forging internal coherence within the oracle and external ties with the larger narrative. As the king "heard the words" in that first encounter with the "writing of the *tôrâ*" (v. 11), he realized that his predecessors had *not* "heard" them with due responsiveness (*RSV* "obeyed," v. 13b, but the Hebrew word is *šmʿ*). Now, in Huldah's oracle concerning his own fate, Josiah learns that with respect to the words he has "heard" (*šāmāʿtā,* v. 18bβ), i.e., those the prophet just conveyed in vv. 16-17, and those that had confronted him as a written teaching — when he humbled himself upon "hearing" (*bĕšomʿăkā*) how God spoke against the kingdom in these *tôrâ* words — with respect to all this,

Yahweh now says, "I also have heard you" (wĕgam 'ānōkî šāmaʿtî, v. 19b). While leading into the announcement of reprieve, this last expression emphatically conveys a sense of correspondence between Josiah's and God's responses. As Josiah repented upon hearing the words of the tôrâ writing, so does Yahweh "acknowledge" (šmʿ) Josiah's penitence and turn back some measure of his wrath. The king at least is to be spared the sight of the nation's devastation. He will die full of days, and be buried with honor, "in peace" (so Fricke, 2 Könige, 320; Hoffmann, 183-85; Dietrich, Prophetie, 58; Nelson, Kings, 257; against Mayes, Deuteronomy, 93; Rose, 59; see discussion at 22:1–23:30, Canonical Context).

A simple notice brings the scene to an end and completes the narrative movement begun at v. 12. Having been commissioned to inquire of Yahweh, and having received the response, "they brought back word to the king" (v. 20b).

One must assume that the punishment for the nation is unconditional. Not even Josiah, who swerved neither to the left nor to the right of the archetypal David (v. 2), can hold back this onrushing night. He can only be spared the final lapse of day's light (see Hoffmann, 186-87). Huldah's oracle plainly announces the catastrophic end of Judah for the first time in the Dtr history. The writer alluded to this catastrophe while presenting a moral and theological explanation of northern Israel's defeat (2 Kgs 17:19-20), and the dedicatory prayers of Solomon had allowed for this possibility as a hypothetical condition of need (1 Kgs 8:46-53; cf. 9:6-9). In Josiah's reign, the matter has come to expression not as possibility but as prophetic prediction. The writer will return to the point at 23:26-27.

In prophecy, it seems, Huldah speaks for the DtrH, and uses typical Dtr language (on vv. 16-17 as a Dtr composition, see Würthwein, "Josianische Reform," 404-6; Dietrich, "Gesetzbuch," 25-29; and esp. Rose, 52-54, n. 16). At the same time, the prophet portrays Josiah's reprieve as reward for his deeply felt outpouring of penitence. She looks back clairvoyantly, as it were, at the event which the narrator barely mentions at v. 11, and describes it as a ritual of penitence, a tearing of clothes, weeping, and humbling of heart that leads to "inquiry" (dāraš) of God (v. 19; Hoffmann, 179; Lohfink, "Bundesurkunde," 271). Cf. the Dtr-styled texts which similarly depict times of need: Josh 7:6-9; Judg 20:23, 26; 21:2-4; 1 Kgs 21:27; Jer 36:24; the still later Ezra 9:3, 5 (cf. Ezra 10:1) describes an elaborate ceremony of repentance.

Genre

As received, this text is not easy to assign clearly to a single literary type. For critics the difficulty arises in part from differing definitions of the literary unit to be studied, and in part from diverse features and tendencies within the narrative itself. Including 23:1-3 + 23:21-23 within his purview because of source and stylistic considerations, Lohfink calls the narrative a "historical short story," specialized as a "story of covenant making" (Bundesschlusserzählung; see his "Gattung," 321-22, and his latest statement on the matter, "Cult Reform," 463-64). This is a slight change from an earlier term, "covenant renewal report"

(*Bundeserneuerungsbericht;* see his "Bundesurkunde," 275-77), with which he tried to shift scholars' attention from *tôrâ* book to covenant ceremony as the most important characterizing motif (cf. Noth, *Studien,* 86, who had earlier spoken of a "law discovery report" [*Gesetzesauffindungsbericht*]). Despite Lohfink's efforts, many critics regularly refer to the unit as "discovery legend/report." See especially Diebner and Nauerth, who cite similar narratives from widely different cultures to support the claim that discovery legends are a distinct type of literature. None of the examples, however, are very close in form to 2 Kings 22; perhaps they are better acknowledged as offering motival parallels only. (Cf. the long observed motif "discovery of a building plan" in ancient Near Eastern, particularly Egyptian, commemorative inscriptions; see Herrmann; Euringer; Naville.)

The essential choice seems to lie among the general categories of legend, story, or report. Since a rudimentary plot recounts events as they occurred according to the canons of ordinary experience (note the realistic records-oriented detail in vv. 3 and 14), we may speak of (→) historical story. However, in view of the importance of Huldah the prophet, or at any rate her words, to giving a reader an interpretation of events, (→) prophet (historical) story might be a more precise designation. Yet, much of the narrative is styled as (→) account, i.e., a series of events cast in matter-of-fact third-person style with few imaginative or artistic features. In contrast, the idealized way in which Josiah is portrayed — he is the faithful king who acts according to Dtr models — brings the narrative close to (→) legend.

On balance, it seems best to characterize this unit as HISTORICAL STORY, while recognizing its legendary and prophetic dimensions in the portrayal of Josiah and in the importance given to prophetic oracle. Good parallels may be seen at 1 Kgs 12:1-20; 20:1-43. See full discussion at 2 Kgs 8:28–9:28.

Important generic elements within this story are COMMISSIONING OF A MESSENGER, vv. 15b-20a (cf. 1 Kgs 14:7-11; 20:9; 2 Kgs 9:1-3 and K. Schmidt), now styled as a PROPHECY. The latter comprises a PROPHECY OF PUNISHMENT, vv. 16-17, and an ANNOUNCEMENT OF REPRIEVE, vv. 18b-20a, which find their respective parallels at 1 Kgs 13:21-22; 14:7-11 and 1 Kgs 21:29; 2 Sam 12:13-14; 2 Chr 12:7b-8. In addition, we may note the more general COMMISSION at vv. 4-7 and 13 (cf. 2 Sam 11:18-21; 2 Kgs 12:8b [*RSV* 7b]; 19:2-4).

The influence of more general literary patterns may also be seen in this historical story. Vv. 12-20 are similar to reports of seeking an oracle from the prophets or priests (→ oracular inquiry), which often make up portions of longer narratives (cf. 1 Kgs 14:1-18, in Long, *1 Kings,* 156). Also, a stereotyped *topos* that reports penitence followed by a divine word of reprieve, (→) schema of reprieve, seems to have been important to the composition of this same section of narrative (see Long, *1 Kings,* 227-28).

Setting

Although some examples of historical story may have had their societal setting among the tellers of folk traditions in ancient Israel, most of them probably reflect the society of literate scribes in royal or religious institutions. The background for this particular example is unclear, and it is uncertain that the narrative ever existed in substantially its present form apart from the Dtr history work. (Martin Noth presumed that the story was based on an "official memoir" [*Studien*, 86], but this is a matter of sources, not the form as we now find the narrative in 2 Kings 22. Lohfink, "Gattung," 321-22, suggests, somewhat tentatively, that this historical story originated in Shaphan's family [cf. Jepsen, *Quellen*, 29, for a similar opinion], but in its earliest Dtr form [that which preceded the composite we now have] may go back to a Josianic commission ["Bundesurkunde," 277].)

A question more easily handled has to do with the story's present literary setting in the books of Kings. As the first series of actions taken by Josiah in his "eighteenth year," the narrative assumes as important background the procedures instituted by Jehoash for maintaining the Jerusalem temple (2 Kgs 12:5-17 [*RSV* 4-16]), the legendary greatness of Hezekiah, and the desecrations associated with Manasseh (21:1-18). The story looks ahead to Josiah's cultic reforms (23:4-24) and locates the king's zealous energy in relation to this line of royal works as well as to the *tôrâ* writing.

Intention

This story presents Josiah as the obedient servant of Yahweh. He is outstanding among the kings and comparable by allusion and inference to Hezekiah, Moses, and Joshua. (On reference to Moses, cf. vv. 13, 18 with Deut 17:8-12; see also the discussion of 2 Kgs 22:2 and 23:25; Friedman, 7-10; on allusions to Joshua, see Nelson.) In the more proximate context, the writer suggests that the energy of repentance (Josiah's singular characteristic according to 23:25) is the fundamental power which leads to a renewal of covenant and a reform of religious affairs (23:1-24). Yet, a prophecy of disaster hangs over Judah's future (22:16-17). It is, perhaps ironically, reaffirmed (it was first voiced at 21:10-15) just when Josiah seeks God's directives. Nevertheless, this king receives personal acknowledgment (22:19) and, in story, a lasting testimony of his exemplary submission to the *tôrâ*.

Josiah is in fact a royal priestly figure, just as Hezekiah had been before him, and Solomon before him. The comparison turns on the notion of word and response, which is encapsulated in a multi-nuanced verb, to "hear/obey/acknowledge-with-favor" *(lišmōaʿ)*. In Josiah's view, the ancestors did not "hear" or "obey" *(šāmaʿ)* the "words of this book" (v. 13); the writer shows us that Josiah does the opposite, and for this reason Yahweh "acknowledges" him *(šāmaʿ)*, or responds favorably to him. As Josiah repents (vv. 11, 19a), so God repents of delivering a punishing blow to Josiah personally (vv. 19b-20). The same nexus of verbal ideas is central to the figure Hezekiah in the Dtr history. His encounter with Assyrian power is largely reduced to a drama of words (see discussion at 18:13-19:37). In this situation, Hezekiah's words aim at persuading Yahweh to "hear" *(šāmaʿ)* the blasphemous ragings of Sennacherib (19:4, 16) and so to save Judah from destruction. In the end, God "acknowledges with favor" *(šāmaʿ)*

Hezekiah's plea (19:20) and joins the blustery show of words directly (19:21-28). In short, Hezekiah submits the situation to God's "hearing" and God "heeds" his cry. Josiah submits to, "hears," the *tôrâ,* and God "heeds" that act. The one king prays, the other obeys in penitence. Of course, these actions are not mutually exclusive. They are aspects of the idealized Dtr image of a king-priest who is expected to submit fully to the demands of God's instruction (cf. 1 Kgs 8:14-64; 9:4-5; Deut 17:14-20).

Since this story was placed in an exilic document, one might suppose that it also aims in some way to legitimate certain religious attitudes deemed appropriate in the changed circumstances of Judah (cf. Diebner and Nauerth). Perhaps submission in penitence to God's teaching offers a way of dealing with the tragedy of desolated hopes in the aftermath of Babylonian conquest.

Bibliography

See bibliographies at 2 Kgs 8:28–9:28 and 22:1–23:30, Canonical Context. B. Diebner and C. Nauerth, "Die Inventio des *sfr htwrh* in 2 Kön 22. Struktur, Intention und Funktion von Auffindungslegenden," *Dielheimer Blätter zum Alten Testament* 18 (1984) 95-118; S. Euringer, "Die ägyptischen und keilinschriftlichen Analogien zum Funde des Codex Helciae (4 Kg. 22 und 2 Chr 34)," *BZ* 9 (1911) 230-43, 337-49; ibid, 10 (1912) 13-23, 225-37; G. Gerbrandt, *Kingship* (→ 2 Kgs 18:1–20:21, Canonical Framework); J. Herrmann, "Ägyptische Analogien zum Funde des Deuteronomiums," *ZAW* 28 (1908) 291-302; H.-D. Hoffmann, *Reform* (→ 2 Kgs 3:1-3); A. Jepsen, *Die Quellen des Königsbuches* (2nd ed.; Halle: Niemeyer, 1956); E. Naville, "Egyptian Writings in Foundation Walls, and the Age of the Book of Deuteronomy," *Proceedings of the Society of Biblical Archaeology* 29 (1907) 232-42; M. Noth, *Überlieferungsgeschichtliche Studien* (Tübingen: Niemeyer, 1957); M. Weinfeld, *Deuteronomy* (→ 2 Kgs 8:16-24).

JOSIAH RENEWS THE COVENANT, 23:1-3

Structure

I. Assembly of all Israel	1-2a
II. Covenant ceremony	2b-3
A. Josiah reads book of *bĕrît*	2b
B. Making of covenant	3
1. The king	3a-bα
2. The people	3bβ

This unit is the third of five sections in the account of Josiah's reign to open with a specific command of the king, "The king sent" (*wayyišlaḥ;* see discussion at 2 Kgs 22:1–23:30, Canonical Context). The style is straightforwardly reportorial, with no direct discourse. Josiah orders that a great assembly come together in Jerusalem. Assuming Josiah's command has been carried out, the writer describes a public ceremony in which the king "makes a covenant before Yahweh" and the people for their part join in — i.e., like Josiah, they oblige themselves to "walk after the Lord." With this symmetrical closure, the scene ends.

Since this covenant ceremony is completed without the slightest reference to Huldah's oracles, it appears somewhat discontinuous with the end of ch. 22 (see Würthwein, *Könige*, 451). Yet Josiah reads from the "book of the covenant," which the narrator clearly takes to be identical to the "book of the *tôrâ*" found in the temple. In effect, Josiah reenacts the drama of reading that took hold of Shaphan and Hilkiah, and then himself through Shaphan (22:10-11). Pledging faithfulness to the covenant, therefore, exemplifies the commitment and focused energy that the *tôrâ* book demands (see 22:13b; cf. Deut 31:9-13). In a subsequent section of narrative (2 Kgs 23:4-23), which is distinct in style and in subject matter, Josiah will direct himself toward establishing a new order of cultic purity in the kingdom, just as Jehoiada and Jehoash had done earlier (2 Kgs 11:17-18; 12:14-16). Thus, the song of covenant sounds a reprise on exemplary royal piety (22:3-20) and the first notes of cultic reformation (23:4-23).

On the basis of his own turning to God, the king makes public ("read aloud in their hearing") the newly discovered text, now called "writing [scroll, book] of the covenant [*bĕrît*]." The change in nomenclature signals a shift to the ceremonial context, and also does its part to surround subsequent reformative acts with the suggestion that Josiah's behavior conforms to a deeply traditional model: hearing and obeying (see 22:13; the expression "book of the covenant" [*sēper habbĕrît*] occurs independently only at Exod 24:7; see Lohfink, "Bundesurkunde," 288). Josiah leads a ceremony of covenant making that memorializes mutual self-obligation between God, the nation, and its people. The report concludes with a simple statement that the assembled masses join in the covenant. (The Hebrew expression means lit., "all the people stood [*'md*] in [with, for] the covenant," and may be a technical term [Montgomery, *Kings*, 528]; cf. Deut 29:14 [*RSV* 15]; Targum and *NJPS*, "entered into the covenant"; there may be some attempt to mirror Josiah's action in that of the assembled people, for of the king it is written, with the same verb, that he "stood [*'md*] by the pillar [or platform, *'ammûd*] and made a covenant.")

The narrator probably envisions a renewal of covenant rather than its first time establishment. As expressed particularly in Dtr materials, the idea is that Israel regularly healed its relationship with God at moments of crisis or epochal transition by taking on the obligations of covenant (Lohfink, "Bundesurkunde," 274-75; cf. Exod 24:3-8; Josh. 24:1-28; 2 Kgs 11:17; see K. Baltzer, *The Covenant Formulary in the Old Testament, Jewish, and Early Christian Writings* [tr. D. Green; Philadelphia: Fortress, 1971] 39-93; A. Weiser, *The Psalms* [tr. H. Hartwell; OTL; Philadelphia: Westminster, 1962] 35-51). By this act the king restores covenantal order and establishes the requisite religious and political base for the reformation that follows (23:4-25). Such is also the pattern in the account of Jehoash's accession to the throne (2 Kgs 11:17-18).

This thoroughly Dtr narrative imagines an ideal Israel personified by typical groups of people led by a priest-king (cf. Solomon in 1 Kings 8; or the

Chronicler's view of Hezekiah and Josiah, 2 Chr 29:20-36; 35:1-19; Hoffmann, 200-203). Josiah gathers together "all the elders of Judah" (cf. Deut 5:23; 31:9, 28; 1 Sam 8:4; 1 Kgs 20:7; 8:1), "each man of Judah and all the inhabitants of Jerusalem" (cf. Jer 4:3; 11:2, 9; 17:20, 25), the "priests and prophets" (cf. 2 Kgs 10:19; Jer 2:26; 4:9; 8:1; 26:7, 8, 11, 16; Neh 9:32), and "all the people, both great and small" (2 Kgs 25:26; Jer 42:8; cf. 1 Sam 30:2; 2 Chr 15:13). The assembled multitude enters the Jerusalem temple where the king replicates the action that had earlier piqued his own religious conscience. He reads from the "covenant writing" (cf. v. 2b). Insofar as "covenant writing" (*sēper habbĕrît*) may reflect Israelite ritual, the term might refer to something very specific and ceremonial such as "covenant text" (Lohfink, "Bundesurkunde," 285) or "deed of covenant" (Z. W. Falk, "Forms of Testimony," *VT* 11 [1961] 88-91). It is clear, however, that the narrative associates this "writing" with the one that Hilkiah found in the temple. As Shaphan read to Josiah, so the king now reads to the people; as Josiah asked for guidance on behalf of himself and the people, so now he enters into a covenant for himself and the ritually inclusive all Israel. From a customary place (perhaps not by a "pillar" but on a platform for royal ceremonies; cf. 2 Kgs 11:14), Josiah "makes a covenant" that obliges him to observe God's "commandments and his testimonies and his statutes . . . to establish [*RSV* 'perform'] these words of this covenant written in this book" (v. 3a; for the concepts and stereotypical language involved, see Weinfeld, *Deuteronomy*, 334-38; idem, *TDOT* II, 253-79). The people for their part agree.

With that closure, the ritual cosmos is restored to its former order, and the threat implied in the covenant writing (22:13) is properly dealt with. Josiah does not necessarily remove the threat (already 22:17 made that clear), but he responds to it as a priestly or cultic paradigm requires (see Deut 31:11-13 and 29:1-27 [*RSV* 2-28]).

Genre

This unit is a REPORT. A Dtr pattern of representing covenant making may lie in the background, as becomes clear when we observe the close similarities in viewpoint, sequence, and vocabulary between this bit of Josiah narrative and Deut 29:1-26 (*RSV* 2-27).

Deut 29:1-26	2 Kgs 23:1-3
1. assembly gathered (v. 1, *qr'*)	1. assembly gathered (Hiphil of *'sp*)
2. people "stand before Yahweh" (vv. 9 and 14, *'md*)	2. king "stands on a platform" (v. 3, *'md*)
3. language of totality (vv. 9b-10)	3. language of totality (v. 2)
4. description of covenant making:	4. description of covenant making:
a. "enter into covenant" (*'br bibrît*, v. 11)	a. "stand in covenant" (*'md babbĕrît*, v. 3)
b. "make covenant" (*krt bĕrît*, v. 11)	b. "make covenant" (*krt bĕrît*, v. 3)

c. "establish [hāqîm] his [God's] people" (v. 12)	c. "establish [hāqîm] words of the covenant" (v. 3)
5. references to tôrâ book (vv. 20, 26)	5. references to tôrâ book (v. 3; 22:8, 10)

Setting

It is difficult to imagine that this report existed or originated independently of its present literary context. It is best understood as forming a crucial link between the account of Josiah's private penitence and his public acts to cleanse the temple and the land of deviances from orthodox Dtr practice.

Intention

Indeed, one may say that this report and the allusion to the covenant making in Deuteronomy 29 help the writer to depict Josiah as a model king in Judah. He responds to the reading of the tôrâ in accord with the demands laid down in the book of Deuteronomy (Deut 28:1-68), and he renews the covenant with Yahweh on the pattern of Moses (Deut 29:1-27 [RSV 2-28]); cf. Josh 24:1-28 and Exod 24:3-8). All this is now to be read as foundation for turning the disorder that has accumulated in the kingdom into order, once more under the rule of God and of the watchful eye of the king-priest who reads and acts upon the holy tôrâ.

Bibliography

H.-D. Hoffmann, Reform (→ 2 Kgs 3:1-3); N. Lohfink, "Bundesurkunde" (→ 2 Kgs 22:1-23:30, Canonical Context); M. Weinfeld, Deuteronomy (→ 2 Kgs 8:16-24).

THE REFORMS OF JOSIAH, 23:4-20

Text

In v. 4 RSV "in the fields of the Kidron" makes little topographical sense, since the Kidron is a steep valley, but the reading is possible if one allows for poetic usage of běšadmôt (cf. Deut 32:32; Isa 16:8; Hab 3:17). Here perhaps šdmwt means "fields of death" or "cemeteries." See v. 6, where "graves of the common people" are associated with the dry streambed of Kidron (wadi; RSV, misleadingly, "brook"; cf. Jer 31:40 [Qere]). A few scholars suggest that a cultic place name related to the Canaanite god môt lies in the background (M. R. Lehmann, "A New Interpretation of the Term šdmwt," VT 3 [1953] 361-71; J. S. Croatto

271

and J. A. Soggin, "Die Bedeutung von *šdmwt* im Alten Testament," *ZAW* 74 [1962] 44-50).

In v. 12 *RSV* "broke in pieces" apparently rests on an emendation of MT *wayyāroṣ miššām*, "and he ran from there," which makes no sense in context. Taking the verb to be a form of √*rṣṣ* and the *mêm* on *miššām* to have been originally attached to the verb as a suffix, one derives *wayyĕraṣṣēm šām*, and translates more precisely, "and [he] crushed them to pieces there." (See Montgomery, *Kings*, 540.) Taking the verb as Hiphil, *wayyĕrēṣēm* (lit., "he hastened them"), to imply "removal" has also been suggested (e.g., Cogan and Tadmor, *II Kings*, 289).

Structure

This unit is set between scenes which lift up Josiah's response to the "book of covenant" (23:1-3, 21-23), and recounts the specific reformative actions that Josiah took during his eighteenth year of rule. Like each episode in the account of Josiah's reign, this one begins with a kind of narrative superscript, "and he [the king] commanded" *(wayṣaw)*, v. 4. Subsumed under this brief notice is a series of enumerative statements (in contrast to the discursive narrative style of ch. 22) that report specific royal actions taken to cleanse the land of its cultic impurities. A remark in v. 20b closes the unit and amounts to a delayed recognition that the scene in vv. 16-18 required the king's absence from the capital.

Many critics sense some disorder in the organization of vv. 4-20 (e.g., Mayes, "King and Covenant," 42-43; Hollenstein; Würthwein, *Könige*, 455). They point to such things as (1) the unusual mixture of both *wĕqāṭal* and *wayyiqṭōl* constructions used as equivalent consecutions, e.g., vv. 4bβ, 5aα and vv. 6-8a or vv. 8b, 10 and v. 11; (2) inconsistency with regard to place and kind of reforms (Jerusalem is treated in vv. 4, 6-7, 8b, 10-12, but mixed in with scattered references to places outside Jerusalem; some actions aim at purifying the Yahwistic cult, e.g., vv. 6-7, 14-15, while others concern foreign gods, with no distinction made between the two); (3) vv. 15 and 19 begin with an emphatic adverb, "and moreover" *(wĕgam),* as though expressing a parenthetical or supplemental idea; (4) vv. 16-18 break the enumerative form and develop a narrative scene that clearly alludes back to 1 Kings 13, and hence to the wider scope of the Dtr history.

These facts may reflect a history of redaction, the details of which remain obscure, and over which critics disagree (see discussion at 2 Kgs 22:1–23:30, Canonical Context). This widely shared perception of incoherence apparently induced Lohfink ("Cult Reform," 464-65) to describe the structure of vv. 4-20 as little more than a list of subject statements which successfully hides its pre-Dtr history. Nevertheless, the final form of this textual unit is not without its ordering principles and inner motival relationships. (Cf. Hoffmann, 218-53, for a similar line of inquiry that achieves somewhat different results.)

The material falls generally into two divisions. The first (I, vv. 4-9) concentrates on cleansing the land and the Jerusalemite temple largely without reference to previous kings ("kings of Judah" in v. 5 is the single exception). The second (II, vv. 10-20) enumerates various reforms linked to the repeated mention of kings, sometimes even by name. Despite this division, there is nevertheless the suggestion that the kings and their transgressions really sum up the matter with which Josiah deals (v. 5, "kings of Judah," and v. 19 at the end, "kings of Israel"). Furthermore, a few key words which express Josiah's aggressive action span both portions of the text, and, as will be shown below, constitute an elaborate system of cross relationships. Note the following: "burn" (√*śrp*, vv. 4, 6, 11, 15, 16, 20); "defile" (√*ṭm'*, vv. 8, 10, 13, 16); "break down" (√*nts*, vv. 7, 8, 12, 15); "*asherah*" (vv. 4, 6, 7, 14, 15); "high places" *(bāmôt,* vv. 5, 8, 9, 13, 15, 19).

The writer reports thirteen separate reform measures in which the king brings out, destroys, defiles, burns, pulls down, or otherwise rights the wrongs on the cultic landscape. For the most part, each reformative act is cast in a standard reportorial mold (Hoffmann, 224):

A. verb + object (the actual cultic reform)
B. subordinating word *('ăšer)*
C. a verbal or nominal clause that explains in some way the object of Josiah's action.

Verse 5 is a typical example:

A. "And he deposed the idolatrous priests
B. whom
C. the kings of Judah had ordained to burn incense."

(Cf. vv. 7, 8aβ, 8b, 10, 11, 12, 13, 15, 19, 20, 24.) In the Hebrew, an emphatic word order dominates the second division of the account (vv. 12-13, 15, 19, 24), or just those sections that single out the crimes of specific kings. Vv. 4, 6, 9, and 14 take a different form. Of these exceptions to the general pattern, it is noteworthy that v. 9 comments on events, v. 14, with mention of "bones," makes a transition to the next section (vv. 15-18), and v. 4 sets a governing paradigm, although somewhat elliptically, by which a reader is to understand the entire account. The king commands and his orders are carried out (cf. 22:3-4, 12; 23:1, 21). Like the subject in a royal commemorative inscription, the king accomplishes great deeds and to him belongs all praise.

Within part one, the writer presents the statements of reform as reduplicated pairs. We move from vessels in the Jerusalem temple (v. 4) to the illegitimate priests *(kĕmārîm,* v. 5) who "burn incense" *(qiṭṭēr,* vv. 5, 8) at the Judean shrines (v. 5), back to the temple concerns (vv. 6-7), and finally revert to the priests *(kol-hakkōhănîm)* again at v. 8, thus completing an AB/A'B' pattern (I.A, vv. 4-8). In the center of this alternation stands a double mention of "(the) *asherah*" (vv. 6 and 7; cf. v. 4), who (which) is condemned especially by the Dtr writers as the cultic symbol of Baal's companion, a fertility goddess (Judg 3:7; 1 Kgs 18:19; 2 Kgs 21:3; see J. de Moor, *TDOT* I, 438-44); *asherah,* probably as a symbol of the goddess, is associated without condemnation with Yahweh in a nonbiblical inscription from the Sinai. (See J. A. Emerton, "New Light on Israelite Religion: The Implications of the Inscriptions from Kuntillet ʿAjrud," *ZAW* 94 [1982] 2-20; M. Weinfeld, "Kuntillet ʿAjrud Inscriptions and Their Significance," *Studi Epigrafici e Linguistici sul Vicino Oriente antico* 1 [1984] 121-30; J. Day, "Asherah in the Hebrew Bible and Northwest Semitic Literature," *JBL* 105 [1986] 385-408.)

Somewhat suppressed within this structure, since the reforms of holy places receive most attention, is an implicit sequence of action concerning the priests at the "high places" *(bāmôt),* those shrines, largely beyond Jerusalem, but at the very least located outside the temple compound and thus illegitimate for the Dtr historian (note v. 8b, *bāmôt* are within the city walls). These priests are deposed (v. 5), then brought to Jerusalem and their places of worship destroyed (v. 8). At this point the writer — he is now a commentator on events — seems to speak of the priests' means of livelihood in the new order: they do not perform temple service in Jerusalem, but instead eat unleavened bread (their portions from the sacrifices, or an anticipatory reference to 23:21-23?) among their own kind (v. 9). After that comment, these Judean priests disappear entirely from the account.

In the next section (II, vv. 10-20) Josiah corrects those cultic deviances expressly attributed to the kings, first in the south (Jerusalem and its environs, vv. 10-13), then in the north (Bethel and Samaria, vv. 15-20a). The southern reform is marked off by a single verb, "defile" *(ṭimmēʾ)*, which is repeated at beginning and end, vv. 10 and 13. This enumeration of defilements amounts to reporting how Josiah removes or otherwise repairs his predecessors' brazen and apostate misdeeds. First is sacrifice by fire to Molech, a Syro-Palestinian deity at Topheth (v. 10); the Dtr writer most likely alludes to the transgression of Manasseh (cf. 21:6) and possibly Ahaz as well (16:3-4). (On the cult, see G. C. Heider, *The Cult of Molek: A Reassessment* [JSOTSup 43; Sheffield: University of Sheffield, 1985].) Second, cult objects of the sun-god (v. 11) and "altars on the roof" (v. 12a) are attributed vaguely to the "kings of Judah" (see Ezek 8:16; Jer 32:29; Gray, *Kings,* 736-37). Third, destruction of the altars inside the temple courts (v. 12aα1-β) singles out Manasseh and loops back to the imagery of vv. 6 and 8 ("pulling down" and pulverizing the material into dust, casting it into the Kidron wadi). Finally, defilement of the "shrines" built by Solomon to Ashtoreth (a Canaanite fertility goddess given the vowels in Hebrew of *bōšet,* "shame"?), to Chemosh (the god of the Moabites), and to Milcom (god of the Ammonites), v. 13. The statement directly recalls the DtrH's negative evaluation of Solomon (1 Kgs 11:5, 7), and by focusing on *bāmôt* brings us at the end of this Judean series back to one of the major concerns of vv. 4-8. On these particular deities, see Gray, *Kings,* 275-78. In short, Josiah "defiles" the work of the kings of Judah, which is to say, he purges the land and the monarchical culture of its impurities and extends the sacralizing power of the Jerusalemite temple into the farthest reaches of the kingdom (cf. 2 Kgs 11:18-20; 10:22-27).

The idea of defilement, though not the word itself, rules the very next statement in v. 14. The verse ostensibly continues the exposition of Josiah's action against the Solomonic shrines. However, the choice of words, e.g., "he broke in pieces" *(šibbar),* "pillars" *(maṣṣēbôt),* and Asherim *(ʾăšērîm),* introduces a set of non-Solomonic associations and shifts the narrative horizon. We hear in this language those Dtr formulas concerning the original Canaanite inhabitants in the land (Deut 7:5; 12:3; 16:21-22; cf. 2 Kgs 17:10; Exod 23:24), and, within the horizon of 1-2 Kings, an echo of that moment of transgression and prophecy of punishment associated with Jeroboam (1 Kgs 13:2-3). It may be that this last allusion is the important one. With this faint evocation of Jeroboam while speaking of bones that defile, the writer makes a bridge to the following incident which will take up explicitly the "high place" of Jeroboam and the legendary bones that characterize his memory (II.C, vv. 15-20a).

In this next section, Josiah turns to reform in the northern areas, Bethel and then Samaria, and particularly to correcting the transgressions associated with Jeroboam. The writer basically keeps to the style of all the preceding statements. Yet, inverted word order and a series of appositional phrases that push up against the main subject add great intensity. To catch the flavor, one should translate, "And even the altar at Bethel, the high place which Jeroboam son of Nebat built [and] by which he made Israel to transgress — even that altar and the high place he pulled down . . ." (v. 15; cf. *NJPS*).

The particular phrases recall, of course, the traditions in 1 Kings 13 (cf. Hoffmann, 262-63, for a different reading of the relationships to ch. 13). Indeed, the writer goes on to construct a short scene of prophetic fulfillment (v. 16), and then reiterates the point in a duet of royal dialogue (vv. 17-18a) and elaborating exposition (vv. 19-20a). Noticing tombs on the land's rise at Bethel, Josiah robs them of their human remains and offers a sacrilege of a sacrifice, burning the bones on the Bethel altar which, subsequent to the acts in v. 15, must be understood to be now in ruins. Sounding the theme word of vv. 10-13, the writer notes that the king "defiled" Bethel and that this act fulfilled a prophecy as spoken "according to the word of the Lord which the man of God proclaimed" (v. 16, *qārā'*; cf. 1 Kgs 13:2). It is striking that this formula of fulfillment duplicates a somewhat unusual detail in the original word's narrative setting wherein the "man of God" from Judah was said to have "cried out" *(qārā')* against the altar at Bethel. The Greek VSS reproduce even more of that context and, incidentally, remove the awkward redundancy at the end of MT v. 16 (LXX IV Kgs 23:16b) and also ease some of the sequential difficulties: "according to the word of the Lord which the man of God proclaimed when Jeroboam stood by the altar for a feast [cf. 1 Kgs 12:33–13:1]. And he turned and raised his eyes toward the tomb of the man of God who [had] proclaimed these words" (then follows MT v. 17). Whether or not the Greek reflects an original Hebrew wording that fell out of the text (see Burney, *Notes,* 361; Montgomery, *Kings,* 534-35), and whatever the literary relationship between 1 Kings 13 and 2 Kings 23 might have been, the resulting statement in the Dtr narrative implies a writer who knew, or read, and duplicated the very language of the original prophet legend. Not only is a prophecy fulfilled, but a *story* of prophecy finds its interpretative extension in this account of Josiah's action in Bethel.

A resulting dialogue in v. 17 moves further along this track. Enclosed within Josiah's question and response, the "men of the city" (who appear without introduction of any kind) offer a reprise of the original prophecy's actualization, and in closely similar wording (note the special verb of prophecy in this case, *wayyiqrā'*, "proclaimed" [*RSV* "predicted"]). But by focusing on the prophet's "tomb," the writer presupposes the ending of the original legend in 1 Kgs 13:30. Beyond reiterating fulfillment, looking back from the prophet's grave marker, the writer has Josiah agree with the old prophet from Bethel who commanded his sons, "lay my bones beside his [the Judahite man of God's] bones" (1 Kgs 13:31). For the old prophet, this was an act of honor by association, in anticipation that the word which the Judahite had spoken against Bethel would assuredly come true (1 Kgs 13:32; see Long, *1 Kings,* 143-50). Now Josiah, as if reading those events similarly, honors the Bethelite's gesture. The prophet's bones, singled out among those disinterred instruments of sacrilege, are left undisturbed. Their resting place, "yonder monument," is a graphic symbolic antithesis to the utter desecration depicted in vv. 15-16. (On this contemptuous defilement of things holy, see Num 19:11-22.) The grave is thus both reprise and coda to the prophetic word and to the legend which carries it. Both take their fullest form in Josiah's own time, i.e., in the DtrH's rendering of Josiah's praiseworthy activities.

The following statements in vv. 19-20a seem to leave all these matters aside and resume the enumeration of reformative actions (note the emphatic word order, as in v. 15, "and even all the shrines of the high places"). However, the vocabulary is again drawn from 1 Kings 13, with perhaps a cross reference to Hezekiah. Josiah "removed" (*hēsîr;* cf. 2 Kgs 18:4) the "shrines [or structures] of the high places that were in the cities of Samaria" (*bāttê habbāmôt 'ăšer bě'ārê šōmrôn;* cf. the identical phrase in 1 Kgs 13:32). The king "sacrificed all the priests of the high places who were there, upon the altars" (*wayyizbaḥ 'et-kol-kōhănê habbāmôt 'ăšer-šām 'al-hammizběḥôt,* v. 20; cf. closely similar wording in the Judahite's prophecy, 1 Kgs 13:2). And Josiah "burned human bones" upon the altars (*wayyiśrōp 'et-'aṣmôt 'ādām;* cf. 1 Kgs 13:2). Moreover, the writer considers the incident at Bethel (vv. 15-18) as a paradigm by which to measure all the wrongs that Josiah put right in the north, for "he did to them according to all that he had done at Bethel" (v. 19b). Exactly the same paradigmatic extension from Bethel to all areas of Samaria is evident in 1 Kgs 13:32. In short, in this conclusion to the account of Josiah's reforms, the writer broadens the king's activity in the north, but covertly and by allusion seems to continue elaborating that legend found in 1 Kings 13. All of Josiah's actions in Samaria finally, and simply, fulfill a strange prophecy delivered during the reign of Jeroboam of Israel.

In its way, the material on Bethel and Samaria forms a climax to the account of reform and part of a high point for the Dtr history. Here, in word-actualization, two anchoring elements in the DtrH's literary structure, Jeroboam and Josiah, have been linked together. The archetypal evil king Jeroboam, who is the measure of apostasy for the kings of Israel and to a large extent even of Judah, meets his nemesis in retrospect, as Josiah reverses what Jeroboam created. For this thematic concept, narrative sequentiality is obviously not as important as the suggestion that Josiah is a way station — his rule is not yet the end of Judah's story — from which to view the final outcome of this experiment with kingship under Yahweh.

Genre

This unit is a REPORT (Hoffmann, 208, speaks of *Reformbericht*). The listlike style is obvious throughout (i e , vv. 5-8, 10-14), but not decisive for defining the whole (against Hoffmann's term, 218-19, "enumeration" [*Aufzählung*]). The Dtr writer does not simply enumerate but provides a general reportorial sequentiality to the material (e.g., vv. 4, 20b) and includes a storylike scene at vv. 16-18 (cf. Hoffmann, 208-11).

Setting

This report may have been, or may have been based upon, an independent source (often called "archival" or "annalistic") about Josiah's reforms (see, e.g., Levin;

Gray, *Kings,* 715; Hollenstein; Oestreicher; Jepsen, "Die Reform"; Würthwein, "Josianische Reform"). Note, however, the opinion expressed by Lohfink ("Cult Reform," 464-65) and Hoffmann (p. 217) that one cannot get behind the earliest Dtr material. Hoffmann (p. 251) even doubts that there was any significant tradition at all which predated the Dtr writer's composition.

Reports could derive from a number of different sources, and be used in a variety of situations. Thus, the more important question has to do with the literary setting of this particular report. The Dtr writer placed it between covenant renewal and Passover observance, both of which are tied to the motif of "book of the covenant"; he let it stand as the central episode in the account of Josiah's eighteenth year. Sweeping religious reform, a kind of ritual cleansing, thus appears as activity that appropriately follows the restoration of covenantal order (23:1-3) and precedes the celebration of Passover (23:21-23).

Intention

This report presents Josiah's purifying of land and temple as a major consequence of his coming back to covenant and as the outworking of an old prophecy against Bethel. Because of its position in the presentation of Josiah and in the larger configuration of 1–2 Kings, the account of reforms is a kind of high point in the Dtr history. In generalized and specific references, the writer claims that Josiah put right the wrongs of previous kings, northern and southern (cf., e.g., v. 12 and 21:5; v. 13 and 1 Kgs 11:5, 7; v. 15 and 1 Kgs 12:32; generalized references in vv. 5, 11-12aα_1, 19). Josiah corrects the transgressions of Manasseh, whose misdeeds are taken up point for point as though each required its own ritual of exoneration (cf., e.g., vv. 4 and 8 and 2 Kgs 21:3; v. 12aα_2-b and 21:4-5; v. 10 and 21:6; v. 6 and 21:7; see Hoffmann, 162-63). Josiah rages against and destroys the north's archetypal "sin," the illegitimate sanctuary built by Jeroboam at Bethel (vv. 15- 20; 1 Kings 13), which evidently remained a problem even after the northern kingdom collapsed (2 Kgs 17:24-33). In this, the king fulfills prophecy and thus completes a major thematic bridge in the Dtr work. Comparable in reach to the less specific tie between Elijah and the reforms of Jehu (cf. 1 Kgs 19:15-18 and 2 Kings 9–10), Josiah's reform stands at the paradigmatic center of a motival sequence in the Dtr history that displays the cultic actions, or *mis*actions, of all the kings. It has even been suggested that Josiah is a kind of Moses *recidivus* (Friedman, 7-10) or that Moses was a literary and theological model for depicting Josiah as a royal figure (Nelson, "Josiah").

Bibliography

See bibliography at 2 Kgs 22:1–23:30, Canonical Context. H.-D. Hoffmann, *Reform* (→ 2 Kgs 3:1-3).

PASSOVER AND LAST REFORMS, 23:21-24

Structure

I. Report of Passover (by book of *bĕrît*)   21-23
   A. Josiah's command   21
     1. Narrative introduction   21a
     2. Command proper   21b
   B. Narrator's comment   22-23
II. Notice of reforms (by book of *tôrâ*)   24

This unit consists of two short reports, which were perhaps originally independent and now have been brought together to conclude the account of Josiah's reformative deeds. The first (I, vv. 21-23) opens with Josiah's order ("and the king commanded," *wayṣaw*), and thus completes a series of five reports dealing with events driven exclusively by royal command (see 22:1–23:30, Canonical Context). The explicit reference to the "book of the covenant" *(sēper habbĕrît)* is a mark of the framework that has been provided for the extensive account of reform (vv. 1-3 and 21-23 enclose vv. 4-20).

The second report (II, v. 24) stands apart from the command-action structure that the Dtr writer gave to the materials of Josiah's reign. However, it is not simply a casual appendage. If Josiah's reformative actions are set directly under the aegis of a "book of the covenant" (21:1-23), then his last act of reform expands our sense of narrative horizon back to the "book of the *tôrâ*" (ch. 22), and thus creates a more encompassing motival framework for Josiah's reforms. Here, the king clears Judah of assorted "abominations," so that "he might establish the words of the teaching [*tôrâ*] which were written in the book [*sēper*] that Hilkiah . . . found in the house of the Lord" (v. 24).

These characteristics of form and content suggest that each report provides closure to the larger body of Josianic materials in a particular way. The first concludes the central focus on cultic reform with the image of incomparable Passover celebration according to the "book of the covenant." The narrator's comment, vv. 22-23 (v. 22 is unlikely to have continued the quoted speech of Josiah), is somewhat puzzling. Although a possible construal of the Hebrew, it seems unlikely that the writer is suggesting that Passover was newly instituted in Josiah's time. (2 Chr 30:1-27 says that Hezekiah observed the festival, and 35:1-19 stresses the incomparable grandeur and *tôrâ* correctness of Josiah's festival.) The sense of the account in Kings seems to be that a Passover observed in such a manner as Josiah prescribes has not been kept previously, from the time of the early rulers (*RSV* "judges") through the reigns of all the kings of Israel and Judah. The writer's emphatic language is important — he means no such Passover "at all, except [*kî 'im*] in the eighteenth year of King Josiah" (cf. *NJPS;* also the translation by Hobbs, *2 Kings,* 329).

This attribution of exceptionality, but vagueness about the features on which the claim to uniqueness rests, has stimulated much discussion among historians of Israel's religion (see Gray, *Kings,* 741-45). As a matter of literary form, however, authorial commentary stresses that the Passover was kept as commanded "in this book of the covenant" and "in Jerusalem." The thought contributes to the general impression that Josiah acts only in obedience to God's teachings *(tôrâ)*. It also comports with the implicit ideology of centralization — one God, one *tôrâ,* one place of legitimate worship — that underlies all the king's actions, as well as with the commentarial reference to non-Jerusalemite priests eating Passover-related food among their own kind (v. 9). This is a Passover that strictly adheres to the requirements of covenant book, just as was true for the renewal of covenant (vv. 1-3). Submission to the requirements of this "book" is an image that completely surrounds and molds our reading of Josiah's cultic reforms. Keeping Passover is not just another in a series of corrections to the misguided ways of previous kings. It is a melody of submission to the "book of the covenant," a return to the *cantus firmus* of Josiah's song.

The second report, v. 24, provides a different sense of closure by identifying that song with Moses' melody, the "book of the *tôra.*" The writer reclaims the voice and tone of one who chronicles reform (cf. vv. 4-20). We hear enumerations of specific actions, imitations of the emphatic, inverted word order of vv. 15 and 19, and allusions to Manasseh just as in vv. 10 and 12. The egregious patronage of "mediums . . . wizards . . . idols" (*gillūlîm,* a general term for despised idols, related to excrement) is precisely the "sin" for which Manasseh was condemned (cf. 21:6, 11), and toward which the Dtr historian feels such abhorrence (cf. Deut 29:16 [*RSV* 17]). Indeed, Manasseh is a kind of structural antitype to Josiah. Whereas the latter is revered as a *tôrâ*-centered reformer, the former is immortalized as the worst of the southern kings (21:3), unreservedly disobedient to the *tôrâ* requirements of centralized worship (21:7-8), and more wicked than even the Amorites, whom God had dispossessed (21:11).

Yet, for all its suggestion of Manasseh's great wrongs, the report reaches back into the account of specific Judean reforms and offers a summarizing view. Josiah puts away "all the abominations [*šiqqūṣîm*] that were seen in the land of Judah and in Jerusalem" (cf. v. 13), and — here the writer slides into summarizing evaluation — he does all out of one motivation, to establish the *tôrâ* and its demands, as given in the book Hilkiah discovered. With this note, we set eyes again on the controlling image of the years of Josiah. Here, at the end of the account of reforms, and near the end of what the writer has to say about the king's eighteenth year, the broader thematic framework for Josiah's story returns. Everything that happens submits to the enveloping power of that book of the *tôrâ,* and Josiah is preeminently the king of submission, one who repents, obeys, and reforms the cult (cf. 22:11-13, 19).

Genre

This unit is an ACCOUNT consisting of two brief REPORTS.

Setting

It is doubtful that these reports originally existed independently of their present context. Many critics believe that at least vv. 21-23 would have been closely related to 22:3–23:3 in some original narrative about Josiah's public actions in response to a book of *tôrâ* (e.g., Nelson, *Double Redaction,* 83; Lohfink, "Gattung," 321-22; idem, "Cult Reform," 462-63; Gray, *Kings,* 714; Hentschel, *2 Könige,* 112-13; Levin). Hoffmann (pp. 259-60) argues that vv. 21-24 ought not to be separated from the rest of ch. 23. Whatever one decides on this question, it is clear that, as now situated, these reports form a final episode in the series of royal actions, and that they substantially conclude the main narrative about Josiah's rule. In the narrowest sense, they offer closure to the account of reform. Especially in the perspective of v. 24, and from the exilic writer's point of view, this unit loops back to the fundamental thematic center of Josiah — the "book" which marshalls so much of the king's energy toward cultic reform.

Intention

From this observation, it follows that the main purpose of the Dtr writer is to conclude the account of Josiah by drawing attention to the controlling foci for the entire presentation. The Josianic reforms proceeded according to the dictates of the "book of the covenant," and more broadly (which is the same thing to the exilic Dtr writer) from the king's energizing submission to the "book of the *tôrâ.*" In language reminiscent of prophecy fulfilled, the writer celebrates the carrying out of all commands in the temple writing and brings the narrative to its goal; it is a story of discovery, penitence, empowerment, and actualization of God's instruction (see Hoffmann, 260-61).

Bibliography

See bibliography at 2 Kgs 22:1–23:30, Canonical Context. H.-D. Hoffmann, *Reform* (→ 2 Kgs 3:1-3); R. Nelson, *Double Redaction* (→ 2 Kgs 17:1-41).

CONCLUSION TO JOSIAH'S REIGN, 23:25-30

Structure

B. Death and burial of Josiah   29-30a
C. Successor to Josiah   30b

This unit leaves behind the narrative and enumerative account of the reforms Josiah makes in his eighteenth year and takes up concluding commentary. The writer closes Josiah's regnal epoch with final evaluative comments and the usual statements regarding death, burial, and successor.

The first section (I, vv. 25-27) begins with a reprise. A positive theological evaluation of Josiah, v. 25, picks up the tone and substance of 22:2 and thus reiterates an important grid through which we are constrained to view all events. At the beginning, a reader learned that Josiah walked in the habits of David, turning neither to the left nor to the right, which means — it is implied in the idiom — never departing from the path of Moses' *tôrâ* (see discussion at 22:1-2). Now, at the end of Josiah's reign, one returns to that image, though with a slightly different specificity regarding the focus on repentance ("turn" or "return" [*šûb*] to God), but nonetheless invoking again the *tôrâ* of Moses. In effect, these two encompassing statements bracket the reign of Josiah with positive evaluation and with the idea of the king's complete obedience to God's revelation *(tôrâ)* given through Moses. This forms the outer frame within which successive repeated motifs contain and narrow our focus to the central narrative moment, Josiah commanding sweeping religious reform (see fuller discussion at 2 Kings 22:1–23:30, Canonical Context).

With v. 25, the writer's perspective on Josiah's actions is summarized. (Cf. the somewhat different analysis by Hoffmann, 204.) The writer praises Josiah the reformer without limit, at least with regard to the single point made, that this king "turned to the Lord" unlike all before and after him. He repented absolutely with the fullness of devotion that is caught in the Dtr phrase "with all his heart and with all his soul and with all his might" (v. 25; cf. Deut. 6:5). Thus, in context, we are given to understand Josiah's story as a narrative of consummate repentance that energized cultic reform.

A similarly phrased encomium for Hezekiah (18:5) also points toward a specific claim that is rooted in the particularities of the narrator's vision of his subject (cf. the DtrH's remark about Moses, Deut. 34:10). Hezekiah is said to have been unrivaled in placing his confidence in God *(bāṭaḥ bĕyahweh)*, clinging to him, and not turning aside from this single-minded devotion, and of course the presentation of Hezekiah exemplifies just those claims (see discussion at 18:1-8). For all this difference between the kings, however, the Dtr writer praises both of them for actions that negated predecessors' wrongdoings (18:4; 23:4-24) and for unwavering allegiance to the *tôrâ* of Moses (18:6; 23:25aβ). In this regard, Josiah and Hezekiah are linked together in opposition to Manasseh. Paradigmatic images of upright piety surround, hedge, and offset the prototypical depravity of Manasseh (see discussion at 21:1-18; Hoffmann, 206; 146-67).

Working within this structure of contrasts, the writer reverts immediately to antitype, to Manasseh (vv. 26-27). The quickness of reversal pivots on wordplay. Josiah is incomparable in his "turning" to God *(šûb)*, but God is immovable in refusing to "turn" *(šûb)* from his anger toward Manasseh. With this thought, the final element in a secondary plot running throughout the Josianic materials comes to expression (see chs. 22:1–23:30, Canonical Context). One arrives at the opening of the account of Josiah's rule with the startling prophetic word of 21:10-15 in mind: because of Manasseh's transgressions, Judah will fall. In line with the Dtr understanding that prophets warned and cajoled their audiences to stir them to national repentance (see 1 Kgs 21:27-29; Jer 26:18-19; 36:1-3; cf. 2 Kgs 13:4-5; 17:13), Josiah understands the book of teaching to imply a threat and responds with penitence. But in effect he acts also to forestall this particular word against Judah of which he knows nothing (the writer presents it as private information to his readers). Can Judah redirect its energies to follow the demands of *tôrâ?* The answer is yes. But to the question buried in subtext, "Can the power of Judah's [or Josiah's] repentance dissuade God of his revenge against Manasseh (and Judah)?," the answer is no.

A generalized report of divine word, v. 27, makes the point unmistakable. A single verb, repeated to create associative emphasis, connects the fate of Judah with that of the misguided northern kingdom, and simultaneously evokes memories of Josiah's (and perhaps even Hezekiah's) reforming zeal. Even the inverted word order mimics the last series of statements about reformative actions: *(wě)gam 'et* such and such, "and even the XX," he "tore down" or "removed" or "put away" (vv. 15, 19, 24). So Yahweh says, "Even Judah I will remove" just as Israel was "removed" *('āsîr, hăsirôtî),* and as Josiah "removed" *(hēsîr)* the shrines of Samaria (v. 19; cf. for Hezekiah, 18:4, 22). Josiah's attachment to *tôrâ* leads him to repent and to remove the apostate excesses of Samaria, but God's refusal to turn from his anger will lead to Judah's exile, even to the excess of casting off the "city" (Jerusalem) and its "house" (temple) wherein God's name dwells (on the Dtr phrase, see 1 Kgs 8:16, 29; cf. Deut 12:5, 11, 21; 1 Kgs 9:3; 11:36; 14:21; 2 Kgs 21:4, 7; Weinfeld, 325; on the conventional association of "city" [*'îr*] and "house" [*bayit*] to encode the totality of space wherein God is available, see D. E. Fleming, " 'House'/'City': An Unrecognized Parallel Word Pair," *JBL* 105 [1986] 689-93).

The writer subverts any bogus confidence in the power of human repentance to dissuade God of his purpose (cf. Jer 36:3). Josiah's actions delay but do not turn away the intended punishment. To this extent, summarizing and evaluating at the end of Josiah's reign, the writer concurs with the word from Huldah (22:19-20) and turns generalized prophetic words to and about Manasseh's generation (21:10-15; 23:26-27) into a hedgerow of limitations to Josiah's power.

The next section (II, vv. 28-30) closes Josiah's reign with slight variations on the usual regnal summaries. The notice of Josiah's death, presumably in military confrontation, is vague and unhelpful to the historian of state and politics (see above, pp. 254-55), but nonetheless satisfying as a literary phenomenon. The writer clearly differentiates death from burial and, perhaps in a slight redundancy, adds emphasis: "[they] buried him in his tomb." (Most Greek MSS add, "in the city of David." Cf. 1 Kgs 22:37; 2 Kgs 9:28.) Without drawing attention to it with formulas, the notice implies fulfillment of Huldah's prophecy as happens elsewhere, e.g., 2 Kgs 8:13, 15; 13:19, 25 (Hoffmann, 187-88). The king does not live to see the catastrophe that awaits Judah in the fading light of day.

Genre

This unit is a composition which consists of a number of elements that are typical of, and perhaps specific to, the Dtr history. Most obvious is the concluding REGNAL RESUMÉ in vv. 28-30 (see full discussion at 1 Kgs 14:21-31, in Long, *1 Kings,* 158-64). Embedded within the resumé is a brief REPORT that is similar to (→) battle report. The evaluative statements in vv. 25-27 are typical of THEOLOGICAL REVIEW, although in this instance their purpose is less to evaluate a king's deeds by religious standards than to reiterate and comment upon a judgment that was already pronounced against Judah. The hyperbolic praise for Josiah in v. 25, aside from parallels in 18:5 and Deut 34:10, has analogues in ancient Near Eastern royal inscriptions which primarily offer praise of the king. Particularly interesting is a late Babylonian text that enumerates the virtues of an unnamed king as lawgiver and judge, offers a catalogue of his stupendous daily sacrifices to the gods, and then states, "What no one had done like this from time immemorial, they (the gods) received from his pure hands for eternity and constantly blessed his kingship" (W. G. Lambert, "Nebuchadnezzar King of Justice," *Iraq* 27 [1965] 1-11, esp. 9-10).

Setting

This unit is part of the compositional work of the exilic Dtr writer and presents the last remarks on Josiah's reign.

Intention

From this, it follows that the main intention is to mark the closure of the account of Josiah's regnal period — his accession, his eighteenth year, his death at Megiddo. But the coloring is ominously dark, and herein the antitype which Manasseh represents to both Josiah and Hezekiah in the Dtr history finds its clearest expression and reiteration (see discussion above, and at 21:1-18). One might imagine a complete convergence of the writer's and reader's points of view. To an exilic reader who has experienced the disastrous end of Judah, hearing catastrophe proclaimed in prospect (and in disavowal of the nations' penitence) is already to experience the horrors of fulfillment. In this context, the death of Josiah, so abrupt and decisive a blow, is like a proleptic image of Judah's death which awaits her in just a few more years, or, in the reader's double consciousness, is already a fact of experience.

Bibliography

H.-D. Hoffmann, *Reform* (→ 2 Kgs 3:1-3); G. Vanoni, "Beobachtungen zur Deuteronomistischen Terminologie in 2 Kön 23,25–25,30," in *Das Deuteronomium. Entstehung, Gestalt und Botschaft* (ed. N. Lohfink; Bibliotheca Ephemeridum Theologicarum

Lovaniensium 68; Leuven: Leuven University, 1985) 357-62; M. Weinfeld, *Deuteronomy* (→ 2 Kgs 8:16-24).

THE DECLINE AND END OF JUDAH, 23:31–25:30

Structure

This unit succinctly narrates the decline that led to Judah's defeat and exile during twenty-two and a half years, as the DtrH reckons them, following Josiah's reign. The writer arranges varied materials into four discrete regnal periods, each one marked by a conventional introductory summary (23:31-32, 36-37; 24:8-9, 18-19). Due to the chaotic circumstances, of the four kings only Jehoiakim receives the usual formulaic closure to his reign (24:5-6). Standing outside this typical reign-by-reign structure, an epilogue (III, 25:22-30) deals with the fate of those who remained in Judah (they wound up exiled in Egypt) and of Jehoiachin, penultimate king of Judah (he was elevated to high privilege even while a captive in Babylon).

Discussion of source- and redaction-critical questions has been framed mostly in terms of identifying pre-Dtr sources within the text and where an original edition of the books of Kings, or, according to the more recent frame of reference, where an earlier version of the Dtr history ends and where an editorial supplement begins. Many suspect redactional layers in 24:8-17 because of internal repetitions and inconsistencies; others look upon the pedantry of 25:13-17 with its obvious allusion to 1 Kgs 7:15-50 as evidence of an intrusive addition. Because 25:22-30 falls outside the formal reign-by-reign structure of 1–2 Kings, many scholars view this section as an appendix to the whole book.

There is little agreement in the details of such considerations, however. Obviously, many of the conclusions that scholars have arrived at are highly dependent on their operative theory of redaction (e.g., opinions since mid-century tend to express the notion of a Dtr history authored by one person [Noth], two editions of the Dtr history [Cross; Nelson], or an original history with separate prophetic and priestly editing [Würthwein, *Könige*]). Despite these efforts, it remains difficult to rule out the possibility that some of the incongruities in the text that critics feel today may derive from the compositional practices of an ancient writer (see Long, *1 Kings*, 14-21).

While acknowledging multiple sources, and perhaps a history of redaction, the formal qualities of the canonical text require analysis. There are, in fact, several signs of both schematic arrangement and thematic shaping.

Most obvious is the typical division of material into regnal blocks, each of which is marked by the conventional regnal summaries. Beyond this, it is striking that the last four kings of Judah are presented not simply sequentially but as parallel pairs of vassalage and disturbed primogeniture. Jehoahaz, son of Josiah, sits for three months and is forcibly removed by Pharaoh Neco who also installs Eliakim, Jehoahaz's brother, as successor to the Judean throne. Under the Egyptian-dictated name of Jehoiakim, the new king rules for 11 years (I.A-B, 23:31–24:6). We see exactly the same pattern for the next two kings. Jehoiachin, a grandson of Josiah through the line of Eliakim, rules for three months before surrendering his authority to Nebuchadnezzar, who then promptly places Mattaniah, an uncle to Jehoiachin, on the throne. With his name changed to Zedekiah, this Davidide Babylonian vassal rules for eleven years until he is taken captive into Babylon (II, 24:8–25:21).

The writer builds a certain ideological perspective into this schematic balance that in effect transcends the limits of the usual reign-by-reign structure. A retrospective remark in 24:7 notes the end of Egyptian influence in Judah, and thus suggests that the paired sequence of Judean rulers be viewed in the context of a now mostly suppressed geopolitical drama, Judah's passage from Egyptian to Babylonian hegemony. This in turn brings closure to the "story" of Egypt's influence that began in the most recent past with an incursion that led to Josiah's death (23:29; cf. 1 Kgs 14:25). Evidently aware of the struggles between Egypt and Babylon, the writer paints the picture of Judah's loss of independence and final demise on that canvas. The emptying of Jerusalem of its spiritual power, royal family, temple, population, and religious authority is shown opposite the filling of Riblah in the land of Hamath with demons of bondage, torture, and murder (23:33; 25:6, 21).

Yet, as we have seen elsewhere in 1–2 Kings, it is not simply a matter of political history but equally, if not more, a question of citing the religious failures and prophecies that order political events into a rational universe. Thus Judah's military defeat by Babylonian and allied forces is explicitly instigated by Yahweh (24:2) for reasons already enunciated by the prophets: Manasseh's transgression must be expiated (24:3-4; cf. 21:10-15). Further, the language of explanation already foreshadows Judah's eventual exile, which also triggers a memory of exhortation and prophecy. For Yahweh's purpose in bringing up these hostile warriors is "to remove them [the Judeans] out of his sight" (lĕhāsîr mēʿal pānāyw, 24:3), as was foretold near the end of Josiah's reign (23:27aα, "I will remove Judah also from my sight," ʾāsîr mēʿal pānay) and as happened to Judah's northern sister-kingdom (23:27aβ; 17:18, wayĕsirēm mēʿal pānāyw, and 17:23, hēsîr yahweh ʾet-yiśrāʾēl mēʿal pānāyw). Nebuchadnezzar's retaliation is the beginning of Judah's end-in-exile, and it is this image that has in the course of the Dtr history become an increasingly urgent premonition (see 1 Kgs 8:46-53; 11:39; 2 Kgs 17:19-20; 20:17; 21:14; 23:26-27). From this perspective, it is understandable that the writer later characterizes his rather differentiated picture of destruction (25:4-21a) with a rather more restrictive closure, "So Judah was taken into exile out of its land" (25:21b), a phrase which also summarized the northern kingdom's experience (17:23).

In view of this narrowing of focus to the experience of exile, it is probably no accident that the subjects important to the writer when reporting events after Judah's demise (III, 25:22-30) again have to do with suppressed political questions: where is the remnant of Judah's social order, who rules it, and with what attitudes toward the real rulers, the kings of Babylon? The murder of Gedaliah at Mizpah (cf. the fuller version in Jeremiah 40–44) is finally shaped to explain the origins of a separate exile in Egypt for all those whom the Babylonians left behind. This time the trek away from homeland is self-imposed, and is a consequence of rejecting Gedaliah's counsel to accept Babylonian rule (25:24). As though accepting Gedaliah's point, the writer immediately reports how a scion of David, even in the keep of Babylon (note that the dating with reference to Babylonian rulers in v. 27 reinforces the loss of Judahite independence) fares quite well in Babylon (25:27-30). Though murdered, Gedaliah seemed correct in his urgings, and the Davidic dynasty, though robbed of its political significance, is still treated with honor and respect.

Genre

This unit is a composite ACCOUNT of Judah's last days. Of the diverse materials the writer drew upon, we may cite especially (1) introductory and concluding REGNAL RESUMÉ in 23:31-32, 36-37; 24:5-6, 8-9, 18-19; (2) abbreviated THEOLOGICAL REVIEW in 24:3-4, 20; (3) CHRONISTIC REPORT in 25:1-7, 8-12, 27- 30; (4) REPORTS in 23:33-35; 24:10-17; 25:13-17, 18-21, 22-26; and (5) ORACLE FULFILLMENT FORMULA in 24:2.

Setting

Some of the reports in this composition may ultimately stem from royal records. But since we lack good evidence on this matter, the more important consideration is the literary setting of this unit within the books of Kings and the Dtr history, writings produced by a writer, presumably Judean, in exile, in Babylon. Here the distinction between the writer's own situation and that of the characters within the narrative is finally and clearly removed. Although this gap was collapsed occasionally through affirming continuity with one's past (the testimony formula "as at this day," or "until this day"), one feels that the narrative recitation of Israel's kings reaches its end in the writer's own time, or in a past so recent as to be virtually indistinguishable from the present, especially as to its importance.

Intention

Clearly, the DtrH meant to report the end of the kingdom in Judah. Hinted at, foreshadowed, and directly pronounced with increasing frequency, the punishing blow has now fallen on Judah. She pays for her transgressions and for the misdeeds of her kings; God's moral authority is vindicated in the writer's eyes because repeated warnings, constantly ignored, have finally led to a point of no return. That is the inescapable conclusion to draw from those earlier statements about God's unshakable resolve to destroy (23:26-27) now reaffirmed as fulfillment (24:2-4, 20).

The brief report in 25:27-30 has become the center of attention as various scholars debate the purposes for which the books of Kings and the Dtr history were written. Regardless of one's theory of authorship and redaction, the question comes down to whether the last word to a reader is one of pessimism and despair or of optimism and hope. M. Noth (*Deuteronomistic History,* 97), thinking of a single exilic author, exemplifies the former option: "Clearly he [the DtrH] saw the divine judgement which was acted out in his account of the external collapse of Israel as a nation as something final and definitive and he expressed no hope for the future, not even in the very modest and simple form of an expectation that the deported and dispersed people would be gathered together." G. von Rad (*Theology I,* 343) exemplifies the opposite opinion: "But the Deuteronomist saw yet another word as active in the history, namely, the promise of salvation in the Nathan prophecy [2 Samuel 7], and it, as well as the threat of judgement, was effectual as it ran through the course of the history. Had it too creatively reached its goal in a fulfillment? The Deuteronomist's history leaves this question open. Yet, closing as it does with the note about the favor shown to Jehoiachin (II Kings xxv.27ff.), it points to a possibility with which Jahweh can resume."

Interpreters align themselves more or less with one of these two points of view. Most recent critics continue to express something like von Rad's optimism, which for a Christian reader may preserve an opening for messianic sensibilities (e.g., Spronk; Zenger; Wolff; Hobbs, *2 Kings,* 369; Nelson, *Kings,* 269). But the more strictly constructionist reading of Noth also has its followers, e.g., Cogan and Tadmor, *II Kings,* 330: "The Deuteronomistic historian(s) responsible for the final edition of Kings did not speak in these [optimistic] terms; the harsh realities of the destruction and the rigors of the exile were apparently too close at hand to entertain such high hopes. It was for others to guide the community of Israel in their search for return."

Recently, Begg ("Jehoiachin's Release") suggested that the text answered the question, "Can things go well for the Judean survivors under Babylon's rule?" with a yes. Survival while ruled by Babylonian conquerors seems to have been a matter of political debate among the Judeans. It is reflected not only in the Gedaliah incident (and in the parallel version in Jeremiah 40), but also in Jer 27:12-15, 16-22. Thus Begg's suggestion has real merit.

Naturally, the writer holds fast to the basic ideological stance that informs the entire Dtr history. Yahweh demands *tôrâ*-centered obedience from his kings and from his covenant people. From this way of living comes true life, i.e., the blessings of mutual attachment — God to people, people to God. But the story of the monarchy is finally one of failure that was prophesied and fulfilled. It is a story of broken obligations, and probably told as both record and instruction. What remains then for those who are left? Take the lesson to heart, which in this case, being exiles in Babylon, also means getting along with the Babylonians.

Bibliography

C. T. Begg, "The Interpretation of the Gedaliah Episode (2 Kgs 25,22-26) in Context," *Antonianum* 62 (1987) 3-11; idem, "The Significance of Jehoiachin's Release: A New Proposal," *JSOT* 36 (1986) 49-56; F. Cross, "The Structure of the Deuteronomic History," in *Perspectives in Jewish Learning* III (Chicago: Spertus College, 1967) 9-24; R. Nelson, *Double Redaction* (→ 2 Kgs 21:1-18); M. Noth, *Deuteronomistic History* (→ 2 Kgs 8:28–9:28); G. von Rad, *Old Testament Theology* (tr. D. M. G. Stalker; 2 vols.; Edinburgh: Oliver & Boyd, 1962-1965); K. Spronk, "Aanhangsel of uitvloeisel? Over het slot van het deuteronomistische geschiedswerk (2 Koningen 25:27- 30)," *Gereformeerd theologisch Tijdschrift* 88 (1988) 162-70; H. W. Wolff, "The Kerygma of the Deuteronomic History Work," in W. Brueggemann and H. W Wolff, *The Vitality of Old Testament Traditions* (Atlanta: John Knox, 1975) 83-100; E. Zenger, "Die deuteronomistische Interpretation der Rehabilitierung Jojachins," *BZ* 12 (1968) 16-30.

GLOSSARY

GENRES

ACCOUNT (Erzählung, Bericht). A term nearly synonymous with (→) report. Generally longer and more complex than simple report, an account may consist of several briefer reports, statements, descriptions, or even fragments of (→) story, organized according to a common theme. Accounts may aim at some degree of explanation rather than simple narration of events. Like reports, however, accounts show a matter-of-fact third-person narrative style and few literary, imaginative, or artistic features. Examples of account are Judg 1:16, 17; 1 Kgs 6:1–7:51; 2 Kgs 10:1-27; 23:1-20; 23:31–25:30.

ADMONITION (Ermahnung gegen . . .). A speech designed to dissuade an individual or a group from a certain kind of behavior. Thus, admonition is closely related to (→) exhortation, (→) parenesis, and (→) instruction, and not easily distinguished from statements which *prohibit* certain actions. Admonition is prominent in prophetic discourse (e.g., Isa 1:16-17, Jer 25:3-7; Amos 5:4-5, 6-7; and, in irony, Amos 4:4-5), but is equally at home in the didactic literature (e.g., Prov 6:20-21; 7:1-5). It is doubtful, therefore, that either prophets or wisdom teachers created this form of speech. Perhaps *both* groups drew upon a widely used genre of tribal discourse.

ANECDOTE (Anekdote). A particular kind of (→) report that records an event or experience in the life of a person. Anecdote may also show a tendency toward storylike features, such as conversation and imaginative description. It is the private "biographical" focus, however, as distinct from "public" events recounted in many reports, that is characteristic of anecdote. Examples are 1 Kgs 9:10-14; 19:19-21. Societal setting and intention for anecdote would naturally vary according to circumstances and content.

ANNALS (Annalen). A concise, year-by-year series of (→) reports, arranged chronologically and designed to record events pertaining to a particular institution, such as monarchy or temple. Although no Israelite examples exist, some OT texts may have been based on annals, but in ways finally unclear to us (e.g., 1 Kgs 3:1; 9:15-23; 2 Chr 11:5-12). Certain ancient Near Eastern (→) inscriptions may draw upon annals or even adopt annalistic style, but in themselves are not annals, since they aim at glorifying the king and commemorating his deeds (→ royal inscription; see *ANET,* 234-41, inappropriately called "annals" of Thutmose III; A. K. Grayson, "Histories and Historians," *Or* 49 [1981] 150-52). A text very close to annal would be the ancient Palermo Stone (Breasted, *ARE* I, §§ 76-167). Annals probably had their typical setting among scribes who kept records pertinent to governmental affairs.

ANNOUNCEMENT OF JUDGMENT (Gerichtsankündigung, Gerichtsansage). Ordinarily the element in a (→) prophetic judgment speech in which punishment is announced for specified reasons, this sort of announcement also occurs as an independent genre. Its essence is the statement that God is bringing disaster in the near future. Although not stated, one assumes the reason to lie with some transgression. The announcement is most frequently styled as a speech of God through a prophet, and is thus introduced by a (→) messenger formula or (→) call to attention formula, and sometimes concludes with an (→) oracle formula. For example, see 2 Kgs 9:36b-37; 20:16-18. See further Prophetic Judgment Speech.

ANNOUNCEMENT OF REPRIEVE (Ankündigung von Strafaufschub, von Strafmilderung, von Begnadigung). A type of prophetic (→) oracle which states that God intends to mitigate a promised punishment to (an) individual(s). Typically, the elements include (1) an allusion to some act of penitence taken by the person in question, (2) the reasons for God's intended actions, (3) the reprieve or mitigated punishment. See 1 Kgs 21:29; 2 Kgs 22:18-20; 2 Chr 12:7-8. All these examples occur as part of a longer narrative now arranged into a stereotyped sequence called (→) schema of reprieve. The societal setting for announcement of reprieve is unclear, beyond the general one of prophetic activity. Its history may only begin with written narrative traditions which interpret royal and national affairs as religious, divine-human drama.

ANNOUNCEMENT OF SALVATION (Heilsankündigung). Ordinarily the element in the (→) prophecy of salvation in which healing, restoration, or reward is announced because of specified reason(s). Sometimes this announcement occurs as a simple statement, especially in narratives which describe a divine speech, or as a prophetic speech. See, e.g., 2 Kgs 10:30. Its opposite counterpart is the (→) announcement of punishment, which is an element within (→) prophecy of punishment, but which on occasion occurs alone in freer form.

ANNUNCIATION SCENE (Szene einer Geburtsankündigung). A set of stereotyped motifs in a narrative that announces the imminent birth of a special child. Narrative elements are used flexibly and often with special literary effect. Examples are Gen 16:11-14; 18:10-14 (cf. 17:15-20); Judg 13:3-5; 2 Kgs 4:11-17; Luke 1:11-20, 26-36. Cf. 1 Sam 1:9-20; 1 Kgs 13:2; 1 Chr 22:9-10; and Isa 7:14. The most important parts of the scene are:

    (1) *Appearance* of a divine emissary (usually "angel" [*mal'āk*]) against the background of the woman's infertility or related troubles. The key verb is "to make oneself to be seen" (Niphal of *r'h* as in Gen 18:1 and Judg 13:3).

    (2) *Announcement of birth,* introduced with *hinnēh,* "behold," and falling into two parts: (a) prediction of conception and birth of son, usually hinting at miraculous circumstances (√*hrh,* "conceive"; √*yld,* "give birth"); (b) designation of a special name and destiny for the child.

    (3) Reactions to the announcement that vary according to the circumstances.

Following this scene, the narrator usually reports that birth (and naming) occurred just as announced.

BATTLE REPORT (Schlachtbericht). A schematic recounting of a military en-counter typically organized around the following elements: (1) the con-frontation of forces, (2) the battle, (3) the consequences of battle, whether defeat or victory, usually with summarizing and characterizing statements. Examples are: Num 21:21-24; Josh 7:2-5; Judg 3:26-30; 8:10-12; 2 Sam 10:15-19. Often, the report will include a scene of consultation with priests for divine guidance (as in 1 Sam 23:2-4; 14:36-37; [→] report of oracular inquiry) or words of encouragement (e.g., Josh 8:1-2). We have little or no evidence for the typical societal settings for this type of report. All the examples in the OT are now integrated into larger narrative contexts of varied contents.

BATTLE STORY (Schlachterzählung). A type of (→) story whose main theme and action serve to tell of a military encounter. It differs from (→) battle report in the sophistication of the narrative art: it shows narrative exposition, characterization, and plot. Like report, it tends to emphasize a "historical" aim: what the battle was and how it happened. Examples are Josh 8:1-29; Judg 9:34-41. → Prophetic Battle Story.

    While some battle stories may derive from official literate circles, many belong to the folk and may incorporate motifs and techniques drawn from popular culture. Thus settings and intentions vary widely, depending upon circumstances of origin, narrator, and occasions for telling.

BEATITUDE (Seligpreisung, Gratulation). At its simplest, beatitude is a short, formulaic speech which extols the fortunate or blessed state of an in-dividual or whole people, such as Israel. Typically, the utterance begins

293

with *'ašrê,* "fortunate" or "blessed," followed by the subject and any special qualifiers, often in the form of relative clauses. So 1 Kgs 10:8, "Happy [*'ašrê*] are your wives! Happy [*'ašrê*] are these your servants who continually stand before you." See Ps 2:12; Prov 8:34; 16:20. These basic elements can be expanded with the addition of elaborate clauses (e.g., Ps 1:1-2; Prov 3:13-14), or worked up into more lengthy collections of sayings, as in the NT (e.g., Matt 5:3-11). Beatitude is related to (→) blessing and (→) praise speech but remains distinct. It does not invoke God's blessing or utter his praises, but describes one who is fortunate by reason of upright behavior or blessings already received from God. Egyptian parallels are known. Beatitude perhaps was originally a type of spontaneous exclamation. Most examples in the OT, however, suggest that it became a form of wisdom teaching, a description turned into didactic example or precept by those "wise men" whose instructions and learning live on in the books of Proverbs, Ecclesiastes, and certain of the Psalms.

BIOGRAPHY (Biographie). A type of (→) history which is concerned to record events of an individual's life over its duration. Biography may include evaluations of a person's achievements or importance in a larger view of a national history, and it may give its subject heroic or legendary proportions to some degree. Yet, the characteristic feature is that the narration purports to relate real events, organized and ruled by the chronology of a life. There are no genuine biographies in the OT — not even the narratives about Jeremiah (see Jeremiah 26–45), which claim that what the prophet experienced had didactic, edifying significance for others. The Jeremiah traditions live in a world of (→) legend, biography in the arena of (→) history.

BLESSING (Segen, Segnung). A pronouncement cast in either the imperative or indicative mode, designed to call down divine power through the spoken word. Blessing can be introduced or concluded with a formula employing the participle *bārûk,* "blessed," followed by the person who is to be blessed. Good examples are in Gen 24:60; Num 24:5-9. Blessing derives from a tribal ethos (so Gen 24:60; 27:27-29) but was also at home in organized cultic affairs (e.g., 1 Kgs 8:14). Blessing should be distinguished from (→) beatitude (e.g., Ps 2:12; 1 Kgs 10:8), which acclaims blessings already deemed to have been received and becomes a type of didactic saying — as indeed some formulas with *bārûk* have become (e.g., Jer 17:7). Blessing is also different from (→) praise speech (e.g., Ps 72:18; Exod 18:10), which, though beginning with a *bārûk* formula, always has God as its object, and so offers praise to *God* rather than invokes his blessing upon *people.*

BOAST (Prahlwort, Prahllied). An utterance which appraises some person or thing as superior to another. See 1 Sam 18:7; 1 Kgs 20:10; or Cant 6:8-9; perhaps also 8:11-12. Boast seems to have no fixed literary form; the term refers to the motivation, effect, or even the intent of one's speech. Thus,

1 Kgs 20:10 is in the form of (→) oath, but the effect is clearly to boast of one military commander's superiority over another. Or 1 Sam 18:7 takes the form of a proverbial saying, but means to boast of David's superior strength over against Saul.

CATALOGUE (Katalog). A list which enumerates items according to a systematic principle of classification. Decisive for the form is the scholastic and systematizing character of the material. Thus, catalogue is not simply a random (→) list, a summary, or a (→) register, which orders items according to the needs of governmental control. Nor is it simply a form of record keeping. Catalogue results from a particular kind of intellectual activity which seeks to order reality into systematic and classifiable bodies of knowledge. Possibly created by scribes, catalogues would have been used by priests in Israel. Examples of catalogue in the OT are Leviticus 11; Exod 25:3-7. Texts which perhaps are based upon catalogues are Gen 6:19-21; 7:2-3, 8, 9; 1 Kgs 7:40b-44, 48-50. For earlier ancient Near Eastern examples, cf. *ANET*, 205 (catalogue of gods), 276 (catalogue of tributes), 328-29 (catalogue of execrations).

CHRONICLE (Chronik). A prose composition consisting of a series of (→) reports, normally in third-person style, or selected events arranged and dated in chronological order. Chronicle differs from (→) annal in that the former may offer somewhat fuller prose, does not include entries for *each* successive year, and thereby moves away from record keeping toward selective recollection of history. Unlike commemorative (→) royal inscriptions, chronicles simply summarize events over discrete periods of time, whether for the purpose of genuine (→) history or for propagandistic "re-telling" of past events. There are no examples of chronicle in the OT (the books of Chronicles are better called [→] history), though references to "the book of the things of the days" (*RSV* "Book of the Chronicles," 1 Kgs 14:29; 15:7; etc.) may refer to Israelite writings of the type found in late Assyrian and Neo-Babylonian times. (For the latter, see Grayson, *Assyrian and Babylonian Chronicles* [Locust Valley, NY: J. J. Augustin, 1975].) Perhaps 2 Kings 25 and Jeremiah 52 are drawn from Israelite chronicles. Chronicle is clearly a product of a centralized government which employed scribes to keep records and produce monumental inscriptions, king lists, and the like.

CHRONISTIC REPORT (Chronistischer Bericht). A type of brief (→) report explicitly dated by regnal year and thus having the character of (→) chronicle. One might speak equally of "annalistic" report, since (→) annals also characteristically employ regnal dating. Examples in the OT are 1 Kgs 14:25-28; 2 Kgs 12:7 [*RSV* 6]; 17:6; 18:9-12, 13-15; cf. the various units within 2 Kings 25, demarcated by regnal date formulas.

COMMISSION (Beauftragung, Sendung). An authoritative charge given by a superior to a subordinate. Commission may include a variety of elements

such as direct command or specific instruction, depending upon the particular role which the order-giver envisions, e.g., military envoy (2 Sam
11:18-21, 25), messenger (Gen 32:3-5; 1 Kgs 14:7-11), royal official
(2 Kgs 19:2-7). Commission is often found in narratives about prophets
(e.g., Exod 3:7-10; 1 Kgs 12:22-24; 19:15-16; 21:17-19; Amos 7:15-17)
and in the prophetic vocation accounts (e.g., Isa 6:9-10; Jer 1:4-10; Ezek
3:1-11). Thus, commission became an important way to represent the
prophet as God's messenger and to organize collections of prophetic
words. In this context, (→) reports of a prophet's commission typically
show (1) the prophetic word formula, "the word of the Lord came to . . .";
(2) the commissioning formula, which often has the imperative, "Go,
speak"; (3) the messenger formula, "Thus says the Lord"; and (4) the
message itself, usually some kind of oracle addressed to individuals or
nations. See Isa 7:3-9; Jer 2:1-3; 7:1-7; 26:1-6; 1 Kgs 12:22-24; 19:15-18;
21:17-19; cf. 2 Kgs 9:1-3.

COMMISSIONING OF A MESSENGER (Aussendung eines Boten). A narrative representation, usually as (→) report, which tells of the sending of a messenger with a message. The emphasis falls upon the (→) commission,
which takes the form of direct instructions concerning where to go and
what to say. Commissioning appears as part of a larger narrative in Gen
32:3-5; 1 Kgs 14:7-11; 20:9; and in (→) official reports, e.g., 2 Sam
11:18-25. It also takes on great importance in describing the prophet's (→)
commission as messenger of God.

COMPLAINT SONG OF THE INDIVIDUAL (Klagelied des Einzelnen). A song sung
by or on behalf of an individual in distress, complaining to God of the
person's dire situation and petitioning for relief. Such a complaint song
typically includes (although not in any rigidly fixed order) the following
elements: (1) invocation to God, (2) confession of transgressions or pro-
testations of innocence, (3) affirmations of confidence in God's power,
(4) complaints to God about one's condition, (5) imprecations of enemies,
(6) petition to God for help, (7) vows. The petition for help is the center
of the song; other elements may be expanded or omitted. Examples are:
Psalms 3–7; 11–13; 17; 22. Presumably, such complaint songs would have
been performed in cultic settings, at shrine or temple, or in the individual's
home. A clear picture cannot be gained, however. The intent was to bring
about a change in the person's situation by tapping into the divine powers
made available through qualified cultic officials.

CONFESSION OF GUILT (Schuldgeständnis). A statement in the midst of juridical
proceedings or in situations conceived judicially, in which a defendant
formally acknowledges his or her guilt. At its simplest, the confession of
guilt consists of a formulaic (→) plea of guilty (expressed mostly as ḥāṭā'tî,
"I have transgressed/sinned," Exod 10:16; 1 Sam 15:30; 2 Sam 12:13;
24:10). In more complex examples the speaker refers to the offense (Josh
7:20-21; 1 Sam 15:24; 2 Sam 19:20-21 [RSV 19-20]; Ezra 10:2), and

includes a (→) petition or a pledge that in some way puts the situation right (1 Sam 26:21; 2 Sam 19:21 [*RSV* 20]; Exod 9:27-28; 2 Kgs 18:14). Thus the speaker's intention is usually to effect mercy or a turn for the better (e.g., Exod 9:27-28; 10:16-17; 1 Sam 15:30; 2 Kgs 18:14). Proximity to the judicial setting and language associated with trials accounts for the first person singular style of the confession (but see Ezra 10:2).

CONSTRUCTION REPORT (Baubericht). A type of (→) report which tells of building, manufacture, or fabrication of cultic and/or official state objects and edifices, along with descriptions of size, materials, ornamentation, etc. Simple verbs (e.g., *bnh*, "build"; *'śh*, "make") convey the action, and nominal clauses state in listlike fashion descriptive details. Examples are 1 Kgs 6:5-6, 8, 16-18, 20a, 23-26; 7:2-5, 6, 7; Exod 36:8-9, 14-15, 20-30; 37:1-9, 10-16. Related are the less specific reports of large-scale building activities associated with certain kings (e.g., 1 Kgs 12:25; 16:24, 34).

Archival records possibly stood behind these reports. In their present literary form, however, they seem to have been produced by scribes and priests whose aim was to record with prescriptive overtones many matters pertaining to cult and royal edifices. Probably some of these reports would have been included in the no longer extant (→) chronicles of the kings.

CONTEMPORIZING SUMMARY (Vergegenwärtigende Schlussfolgerung). A comment in the iterative or frequentative mode *(wyqtl)* which concludes a brief report, encapsulates the reported action or its outcome, and, with the (→) testimony formula "until this day" *('ud hayyôm hazzeh)*, affirms the continuance of effects into the time of the narrator. Examples are 2 Kgs 8:22a (= 2 Chr 21:10aα): "And Edom has been revolting from the rule of Judah to this day." See also 1 Kgs 12:19 (= 2 Chr 10:19) and 1 Macc 13:30. Such a summary validates the truth of the writer's claim and establishes a continuity between past and present which is important for cultural, national, or religious reasons. Contemporizing summary belongs to the style of ancient historians, and so appears frequently in historiographical works. Parallels may be seen in Herodotus *Histories* 2.154, 182; 4.11; 5.77; 6.14. Other parallels are cited in Childs ("A Study of the Formula 'Until this Day,' " *JBL* 82 [1963] 279-92). Contemporizing summary may be compared with self-contained statements which, while not concluding a longer report, make claims about cultural or national facts of antiquity and, with the formula "until this day," assert their continuity and relevance to the narrator's time. (See, e.g., concerning territorial claims, Deut 2:22; 2 Kgs 16:6; 1 Chr 4:41, 43 [cf. 5:26]; or ethnic groups, Gen 19:37-38; Josh 16:10; 2 Sam 4:3; 1 Kgs 9:21 [= 2 Chr 8:8]; evaluative remarks, 1 Kgs 10:12; 2 Kgs 10:27; 17:23, 34, 41; custom, Gen 47:26; 1 Sam 30:25; or religious object, 1 Kgs 8:8. Besides being a regular feature of historical accounts, this type of brief comment frequently concludes an etiological report or narrative (→ Etiology).

DECLARATION OF ALLIANCE (Erklärung, Proklamation eines Bündnisses). A statement of solidarity and commitment between two parties, such as kings of equal rank or a king and vassal, that implies the taking on of obligations, one to the other. Formulations vary in the narrated examples preserved in the Bible. See, e.g., "I am as you are, my people as your people, my horses as your horses" (1 Kgs 22:4 and 2 Kgs 3:7); "I am your servant [vassal] and your son" (2 Kgs 16:7; cf. 1 Kgs 20:32-33); "[Let there be] a covenant [treaty] between me and you" (1 Kgs 15:19). Presumably these declarations were important in managing official relations between states, and could be incorporated into written treaties, e.g., Niqmaddu of Ugarit to Šuppiluliuma, his Hittite overlord: "I am the servant of the Sun, the great King, my lord; with the enemies of my lord, I am an enemy; with his ally, I am an ally" (J. Nougayrol, *PRU* IV, no. 17.340, lines 12-13, pp. 48-52). For other examples from the ancient Near East, see Kalluveettil (→ 2 Kgs 10:1-27).

DEDICATORY INSCRIPTION (Weihe- oder Widmungsinschrift). A type of ancient Near Eastern (→) royal inscription written on an object dedicated by the king to a deity. The objects are of a cultic nature, such as ornamental mace heads, building bricks, door sockets, statues. The inscription typically includes (1) dedicatory address (e.g., "To the god so-and-so, his lord"), (2) royal name and epithets, identifying the giver of the object, (3) dedicatory statement (e.g., "He [I] dedicated [this XX] for his [my] life"). See A. K. Grayson, *ARI* I, lxxxvi, 23; II, xcviii, 3. The OT may reflect the form of dedicatory inscription in Solomon's prayer, dedicating the temple (1 Kgs 8:13). Cf. Deut 26:10 and 1 Sam 2:28. See also → Prayer of Dedication.

DIRGE (Trauerlied, Grabgesang). A song bewailing the loss of the deceased, describing and praising his or her merits, and calling for further mourning. The most characteristic formulas employed are "How! Alas!" (*'êk* or *'êkâ*) and imperatives such as "weep!" "mourn!" The dirge was performed by hired women or gifted individuals and was sung in the presence of the corpse as part of the preparations for burial. Examples are 2 Sam 1:19-27; 3:33-34; 1 Kgs 13:30b (fragments). The prophetic books show adaptations of the dirge with new literary effects and purpose, e.g., Isa 14:4-23; Amos 5:1-3.

DISPUTATION (Disputationswort, Streitgespräch). A general term to designate a dispute between two or more parties in which differing points of view are held. Examples may be seen in disputes among wise men (e.g., the book of Job), parties in a legal proceeding (e.g., as reflected in Gen 31:36-43), or between prophet and people (e.g., Mic 2:6-11; Jer 2:23-28; 3:1-5). A particular example of disputation may include a variety of smaller literary genres, formulas, and stereotyped motifs. Obviously the settings vary according to circumstances and usage. Most OT examples appear in the prophetic literature, especially Deutero-Isaiah.

DREAM EPIPHANY (Traumerscheinung). A type of brief and schematic (→) report which mentions that God appears in a dream (Niphal of *rā'â*, "become visible"), gives a message, and/or otherwise engages in dialogue with a human being. Such reports are part of older and younger portions of the pentateuchal narrative (e.g., Gen 12:7; 17:1-21; 18:1-33; 26:2-5, 24; 28:12-16; 48:3-4) and the "historical" books (e.g., Exod 3:2-12; Judg 13:10; 1 Kgs 3:4-15; 9:1-9) and continue into NT times (e.g., Matt 2:19-20). Reports of dream epiphany may have originally been associated with shrines; some were rooted in (→) legends circulating among visitors in and about holy sites. However, such reports now assume greater literary importance as scenes in larger narratives or as bearers of themes important for continuity in the canonical materials (e.g., promise to the patriarchs, or wisdom for King Solomon).

DREAM REPORT (Traumbericht). A type of (→) report in the first- or third-person style that recounts the principal elements of a dream experience. Such reports use the verb "dream" *(ḥālam)* extensively, especially in the introduction, and demarcate major shifts in subject matter with the particle "and behold" *(wĕhinnēh)*. Sometimes a conclusion will remark on the person's awakening and recognition that he or she was dreaming (e.g., 1 Kgs 3:15). The larger narrative contexts will often provide for a separate scene in which the dream will be interpreted. Examples of dream report are Gen 37:5-11; 40:9-11, 16-17; Judg 7:13-14. For ancient Near Eastern examples, see A. L. Oppenheim, *The Interpretation of Dreams in the Ancient Near East* (Transactions of the American Philosophical Society 46; Philadelphia, 1956). The primary setting for dream report in Israel would have been the situation in which one seeks understanding of the experience from a qualified interpreter (e.g., as reflected in Gen 41:1-8; Dan 2:1-11). Frequently, reports of dream center on an appearance of God to the dreamer and take on great importance in theological themes of canonical scope. For this aspect → Dream Epiphany.

ETIOLOGY (Ätiologie). A type of (→) story or (→) report set in either primordial or historical times, involving god(s) and/or human beings, and designed to explain the origins of certain elements of knowledge, experience, practice, custom, and the like shared by a cultural group. Developed etiology (story) is rare in the OT, but brief reports and etiological motifs imbedded in larger narrative traditions are common. A common type, etymological etiology, explains a name by associating some event with that name by means of wordplay or folk etymology; the report concludes with a formula: "Therefore one calls the name of that place . . ." or "And he called her [its, his] name . . . , for he said . . . (explanation follows)." See Exod 15:23; 2:22. Other etiological motifs may be expressed in formulas, such as (1) "until this day" (e.g., Josh 4:9), (2) "it shall be a (memory) sign for you" (e.g., Gen 9:13; 17:11), or (3) a question-and-answer pattern: "What does so-and-so mean to you?" (then follows the answer which explains origin and significance), e.g., Josh 4:6-7. Etiology and etiological motifs are popular literary forms, and hence their settings would be with the ordinary people, in diverse circumstances.

ETYMOLOGICAL ETIOLOGY (Etymologische Ätiologie). → Etiology.

EULOGY (Lobrede). An utterance, often poetic, designed to praise a person, whether living or dead. In the OT, eulogy may appear as part of a (→) dirge, as in 2 Sam 1:19-27, or be reflected in eulogistic statements for the king and his accomplishments (e.g., 1 Kgs 5:9-14). In the ancient Near East, eulogy is regularly part of (→) royal inscriptions which commemorate the deeds of the king (e.g., *ANET*, 653-54; Breasted, *ARE* IV, § 47; cf. the stylized encomiums of courtiers who respond to a king's building plans, e.g., Breasted, *ARE* III, §§ 251-81; II, §§ 131-66).

EXHORTATION (Ermahnung zu . . .). → Admonition, Parenesis.

FABLE (Fabel). A short (→) tale, usually involving animals or plants as characters, which implicitly makes a particular ideological statement or expresses a moral principle. Examples are Judg 9:8-15 and 2 Kgs 14:9.

FAREWELL SPEECH (Abschiedsrede). A first-person styled speech reported to have been delivered by a person near the time of death. The contents follow a typical sequence: (1) references to advancing age or impending death, (2) admonition(s), and (3) directives to those hearing the speech. Farewell speech may occur in the context of a full report about testamentary activities and death (e.g., Gen 49:29-30, part of 47:29–49:33) or by itself (e.g., 1 Kgs 2:1-9), followed by report of death (2:10-11; Josh 23:1-16 [a highly theological example]; 1 Macc 2:49-70; Testaments of the 12 Patriarchs, both later, very elaborate examples). Cf. Acts 20:18-35; John 13:1–17:26. Distant ancient Near Eastern parallels may be in the Egyptian (→) instruction (e.g., *ANET*, 418-19, 414-18). Originally, farewell speeches would have been delivered when a leader, family or tribal head, conscious of impending death, would have passed on his final words and bequeathed possessions to heirs. However, the OT examples deal with leaders who are prominent and important to the theological continuities in the canonical "story." In all these cases, biblical authors depict the passing of special figures as momentous events, weighted with religious, social, and historical significance.

GENEALOGY (Stammbaum, Genealogie). A type of oral or written (→) list which enumerates individual and tribal descent from an originating ancestor through intermediate persons down to the last, presumably contemporary with writer or speaker. OT examples may be linear (expressive of a single line of descent, e.g., Gen 5:1-32) or segmented (indicating multiple lines of descent, e.g., Gen 35:22b-26; 2 Sam 3:2-5). Genealogies are numerous in the OT, as well as in the ancient Near East; in the Bible they range in style and form from very simple lists (2 Sam 3:2-5) to more complex compositions which carry within them various bits of information and rudimentary narrative (e.g., Gen 10:2-32). Genealogies now appear variously integrated into wider canonical contexts. In late biblical times,

300

genealogy seemed an appropriate literary form with which to introduce very large historical compositions (e.g., 1 Chronicles 1-9; cf. Matt 1:1-17).

HEROIC SAGA (Heldensage). A type of (→) saga which focuses on events in the life of one central figure who is significant for the people who remember him or her. Typically, heroic saga includes some account of the hero's birth, marriage, vocation, death — along with displays of virtue and heroic deeds. The intention is not simply to describe the hero in factual terms, but to interpret the figure according to stereotyped, imaginative categories. An example in the OT of heroic saga is that of Moses, Exodus 1–Deuteronomy 34.

HISTORICAL STORY (Historische Erzählung). A self-contained narrative mainly concerned to recount what a particular event was and how it happened, but with more literary sophistication than is evident with simple (→) report. Typically, one finds at least a rudimentary plot running from a tension or problem to its resolution (→ story), along with dialogue and imaginative touches. The chief difference between historical story and (→) legend, fictional story or brief (→) tale, is not so much in content — which may contain fictional or even legendary elements — but in purpose. With historical story the narrator does not seek primarily to edify, entertain, or instruct, but to recount events as they occurred (whether or not the evidence is sufficiently trustworthy by modern critical standards). Examples of OT historical story are 1 Sam 11:1-11; 1 Kgs 12:1-20; Judg 9:1-21. A special type is the (→) prophet story, a developed prose narrative in which a prophetic figure plays a central role and carries themes and interpretative motifs expressive of the narrator's voice. See, e.g., 1 Kgs 20:1-43; 22:1-37. Some examples of historical story may have originated with the folk and been transmitted orally as traditional storytelling materials. For the most part, however, the biblical examples reflect literate scribal classes at work in the royal court or religious institutions.

HISTORY (Geschichtsschreibung). An extensive, continuous, written composition based upon various materials, some originally traditional and oral, others written, and devoted to a particular subject or historical period. The author of history links together materials and unifies the whole by imposing overarching structural and thematic connections. History is dominated by a concern with chronology and cause-effect relationships; it seeks to place events and how they occurred within a framework of interpretation and in relation to the author's own time. For purposes of literary definition, it is not important whether, from our modern point of view, the events actually occurred as reported. Apparently neither Egypt nor Mesopotamia produced history in this sense, although both have left us many inscriptions with historical content. Examples from Greece are known (e.g., Thucydides or Herodotus). From the OT, one may cite 2 Samuel 9–20 and 1 Kings 1–2 as fairly early work. Less disputed examples would be the books of Kings, the books of Chronicles, and from much later times,

1–2 Maccabees. History writing presupposes literacy. For this reason, it developed in Israel most fully among those scribes whose business it was to record the affairs of the royal government. Writers of history intended to document, reflect on, and organize the past in order to understand, legitimate, or define in some way the institutional and social reality of their own time.

IMPUTATION SPEECH (Beschuldigungsrede). A speech by a person(s) charging another individual or group with a fault or crime. It is characteristic of (→) disputation, either leading to legal proceedings or quite unrelated to trials. Imputation speech follows no rigid form, and its contents vary according to the diverse occasions on which it was used. Frequently, however, a formula appears: "What is this you have done to me?" (e.g., Judg 8:1; Neh 13:17; 2 Sam 12:21). Imputation speech may also be quite convoluted and indirect, as in 1 Kgs 18:9-14. Other examples are Gen 12:18-19; 16:5; 26:9, 10; 29:25; 31:26-30.

INCANTATION (Zauberspruch). Prescribed words to be recited or chanted in conjunction with symbolic actions with the aim of their working together to achieve cures, protection, or release from the malevolent effects of spirits. Incantation belongs to the world of religious and magical activity where word and act combine in ritual.

INDICTMENT SPEECH (Anklagerede, Anklageerhebung). A formal statement handed down by a juridical authority charging a person with committing a crime. It may be presented upon approval of an accusation or in its own right, directly and probably orally. OT texts which probably reflect the form and substance of such indictments are 1 Sam 15:17-19; 22:13; 1 Kgs 2:42-43; 18:17; 22:18.

INSCRIPTION (Inschrift). Characters or words written, carved, or otherwise affixed to a surface, but not necessarily for public display. The OT probably alludes to such in 1 Sam 15:12; 1 Chr 18:3 (Hebr. *yād,* "monument," or victory stela?). Also, see 2 Sam 18:18 and Isa 56:5. Many examples are known from the ancient Near East, and even from ancient Israel (*ANET,* 320, 321); most are associated with the institution of monarchy. → Royal Inscription.

INSTRUCTION (Instruktion, Unterweisung). A fairly extensive writing or discourse, chiefly in the imperative mode, which offers distilled guidance on traditional matters to an individual or group. The form is somewhat flexible, but the contents rather fixed: broad values, traditional rules for conduct, aphoristic knowledge drawn from wide experience. Instruction tends to deal with the universal rather than the particular. In Israel, instructions were probably created by persons of some official, if not aristocratic, status, such as lawgiver, priest, or even prophet (Isa 8:16-20). But instruction could also be the work of scribes and "wisdom" teachers. In Egypt, the best examples derive from scribes who formulated didactic works to summarize accepted knowledge, or in some cases produced instruction in the guise of an after-the-fact testament from a king to his successor, with propagandistic overtones (*ANET*, 414-18; 418-19; more generally, see M. Lichtheim, *Ancient Egyptian Literature* [3 vols.; Berkeley: University of California, 1973-1981] I, 58-80). Similarly, the clearest examples from the OT are in the didactic literature (e.g., Proverbs 1–9; 22:17–24:22). The settings and occasions for use of instruction must have been quite diverse. Closely related to instruction is (→) farewell speech, which often contains admonitions and specific directives appropriate to the speaker.

INVASION REPORT (Invasionsbericht). A brief report concerning an invasion and the actions taken to deal with it, or more simply, the results of the invasion. The report opens typically with an invasion formula, "X [name of a king or an army] came up against [*'lh bĕ/'al*] Y [reference to the place, often a city]." This formula is sometimes extended with verbs such as "besiege" (*ṣûr*) or "fight against" (Niphal of *lḥm*). The report may be developed with a brief statement concerning the immediate result (e.g., "he took it" [*lkd/tpś*]) or more often with a longer summary of, e.g., defeat, exile, or successful suing for relief. Good examples are 1 Kgs 14:25-28; 2 Kgs 12:18-19 (*RSV* 17-18); 16:6-9; 17:5-6; 24:10-17 (cf. Jer 39:1-10). Some examples of invasion reports, or at least certain of their literary formulas, appear in the Bible as integral parts of longer accounts of military events, e.g., 1 Kgs 16:17; 20:1; 2 Kgs 6:24. Unlike a (→) battle report, a report of invasion avoids description of battle, although occasionally it will mention the gathering of forces (e.g., 2 Kgs 6:24). The precise chronistic reckoning in 1 Kgs 14:25-28 and 2 Kgs 18:13-16; 24:10-17 suggests that invasion reports probably originated in the activities of royal scribes who maintained records of the king's actions which then could be drawn upon to write (→) royal inscriptions, (→) chronicles, (→) annals, and (→) history.

ITINERARY (Itinerar, Wegverzeichnis). A formal structure of (→) accounts or (→) reports, which relate movement by stages. Itinerary often includes special formulas, noting the point of departure ("set out from so-and-so") and/or the point of arrival in a journey ("encamped at so-and-so" or "came to so-and-so"), and thus may serve as a literary skeleton for larger collections of varied material (e.g., Exod 17:1–18:27; 19:1–Num 10:10; 1 Kgs 19:1-18). If the itinerary appears with little or no narrative materials between stages of movement, it should be understood as a type of (→) list, as, e.g., Num 33:5-37, 41-49.

ITINERARY NOTICE (Itinerarnotiz). A formulaic statement of travel that notes point of departure and/or arrival in a journey, e.g., "So-and-so went to XX [place name], and from there he [she] went on to YY [place name]." A good example appears in 2 Kgs 2:25. Such a notice is usually found as a part of schematic (→) accounts or (→) reports that relate a person's movement from place to place, e.g., Exod 17:1–18:27; 1 Kgs 19:1-18.

JUDGMENT SPEECH (Gerichtswort, Gerichtsrede). → Prophetic Judgment Speech.

JURIDICAL PARABLE (Gerichtliche Gleichnis- oder Beispielerzählung). A prose narrative, usually a (→) report, which relates a fictional though realistic violation of custom or law in order to induce the hearer, who has committed an analogous violation, to pass judgment on himself while adjudicating the fictional case. The best OT examples, all involving the king, are 2 Sam 12:1-4; 14:5-7; 1 Kgs 20:39-40. Each one is part of a larger narrative context, and in fact depends upon that context for its sense. Thus, it is difficult to know to what degree the literary device reflects customary social relations in ancient Israel.

KING LIST (Königsliste). A type of (→) list which enumerates successive rulers in a particular state. It consists of royal names, sometimes with the addition of epithets, regnal years, and filiation. Unlike (→) genealogy, which it may resemble in form, a king list need not express *kinship*. Its essential character turns on *succession*, which may or may not follow lines of kinship. King list is widely attested in the ancient Near East, where sometimes the stylistic distinction from (→) chronicle is hard to maintain (e.g., *ANET*, 265-66, 271-72, 564-67; other examples in Grayson, "Königslisten und Chroniken," *RLA*). In Israel, king list may have been a literary model for Gen 36:31-39 as well as Judg 10:1-5; 12:7-15. King lists derive from bureaucratic circles in centralized governments, and aim to legitimate an orderly succession of rulers on a line extending back through many generations, even, on occasion, to primordial times when the gods first decreed kingship (e.g., *ANET*, 265-66).

LEGEND (Legende, Heiligen- oder Wundererzählung). A narrative concerned primarily with the wondrous, miraculous, and exemplary. Legend is aimed at edification rather than merely entertainment, instruction, or even imaginative exploration of the storyteller's art. Thus legends often encourage awe for a holy place (e.g., Judg 6:19-24), ritual practice (2 Macc 1:19-22), and holy people (e.g., Gen 22:1-19; 1 Kgs 12:33–13:34; 14:1-18; 17:1–19:21; 2 Kgs 1:2-16; 2:1-25) who may be models of devotion and virtue. Legend differs from (→) history and (→) historical story in its refusal to be bound by a drive to recount real events as they happened; it differs from the more artistic (→) story in giving less attention to developed points of narrative interest, such as description, artistic structure, and plot. Legend belongs to the world of oral folklore and storytellers. Legends took varied forms and were told in the royal court, at religious shrines, in family and tribal settings, and on pilgrimages to holy sites.

LETTER (Brief). A general term for a written communication sent from one person to another. Typically, the letter begins with a prescript which identifies the sender and addressee along with a salutation or wish for blessing (e.g., Ezra 4:11, 17; 7:12). Then follows the body of the letter, opening with a transitional "and now" *(wĕʿattâ)* and consisting of diverse contents and literary genres. See Ezra 4:12-16, 18-22; 7:13-26. Apparently Hebrew letters, like those in Egypt and Mesopotamia, contained no special conclusion. Allusions to letters and letter writing, along with quoted excerpts, may be found, e.g., in 2 Kgs 10:2-3, 6; Jer 29:1-28. Letters may stand behind the narrative convention of reporting diplomatic exchanges as direct dialogue, e.g., 1 Kgs 5:23 *(RSV* 5:8). Examples from the ancient Near East are plentiful (see *ANET,* 480-81, 482-92). Letters probably developed out of the custom of instructing and sending messengers with oral communications (see 2 Kgs 19:9-14), and they obviously presuppose scribes who can read and write. Particular settings and occasions for letter writing would naturally vary according to circumstances.

LIST (Liste). In its elementary form, a simple enumeration of items without any particular principle of order. In more developed forms, a list would be ordered systematically by a main idea or principle. Commonly, it would claim to reconstruct or preserve an order of things as they exist in reality. Examples of list are (→) genealogy, (→) king list, (→) itinerary. See also OT lists of booty (Num 31:32-40), votive offerings (Exod 35:5b-9), royal mercenaries (2 Sam 23:24-39), administrative officials (1 Kgs 4:2-6). The latter texts may have been drawn from administrative lists or (→) registers.

NOTICE (Notiz). A very brief (→) report not too different from a simple (⁌) statement. See, e.g., 1 Kgs 3:1.

OATH (Eid, Schwur). A pronouncement, cast as either cohortative or indicative, which binds the oath taker to a particular course of action, attitude, or stance by invoking sanctions of the deity. An oath is typically introduced with the formula "As the Lord lives" *(ḥay-yahweh,* e.g., Judg 8:19) and/or a similar asseveration "by the life of" *(bĕḥê)* the person(s) to whom the oath is addressed (e.g., 1 Sam 20:3). Then follows what the oath taker will or will not do, the actual content of the oath. A fuller formula, and almost as common, runs "May God the Lord do so to me and more also, if . . . ," followed by the content of the oath (e.g., Ruth 1:17; 1 Sam 3:17; 14:44). The intention of oath is to impress upon parties their mutual obligations in various situations. Thus, the settings would differ according to circumstances. Some oaths would habitually be taken at shrines and associated with priests, others in various realms of social life. Literary reflexes of oath and oath taking are common in the OT and seen most commonly as (→) report(s) of oath in the midst of larger narrative contexts (e.g., 1 Kgs 1:29-30; 17:1).

OFFICIAL REPORT (Amtlicher Bericht). The representation of the transmittal of information or message by a person duly authorized and sent forth, such as a military envoy or royal messenger. Official report amounts to a narrative sequence which recounts (1) the commissioning of a messenger, (2) the going forth and reception of the messenger, (3) the message, directly quoted, (4) the recipient's reaction. In the interests of narrative economy or special effects, some of these elements may be omitted, expanded, or abbreviated. In most cases, the message from one party to another is quoted, and thus is to be distinguished from (→) report, which simply narrates in third-person style, *for the reader,* the simple course of an event. Examples of official report are 2 Sam 11:18-25; 18:19– 19:1 (*RSV* 18:33); Josh 2:1, 23-24. Fragments of, or allusions to, official report may be seen in 1 Kgs 20:2-3, 5-6, 32. Cf. 1 Kgs 5:15-16.

ORACLE (Orakel). A communication from the deity, often through an intermediary such as priest or prophet, especially in response to an inquiry (→ oracular inquiry). The OT also describes oracles as unsolicited. In all cases, the structure and content vary; oracles have to do with, e.g., salvation, healing, punishment, judgment, promise, encouragement, warning. Some oracles commission a prophet to lifelong vocation, and frequently the prophet's speeches are presented as God's own words, hence as oracle. Settings and intentions vary, according to content and circumstances. Some clue as to solicited oracles comes from (→) reports which mention dreams, prophets, priests, as involved in procedures for obtaining divine communication. See, e.g., 1 Sam 28:6; Num 22:7-12, 19-20; Josh 7:6-15; Judg 1:1-2; 1 Kgs 20:13-14; 22:5-6, 15-17; Ezek 20:1-8.

ORACLE FULFILLMENT (Erfüllung eines Orakels). A type of (→) report which notes a situation or event and concludes with a formulaic expression that the circumstances have come about "according to the word of the Lord which he spoke by so-and-so." Normally, such reports are motifs in a longer narrative, sometimes indigenous to the narrative tradition, sometimes associated with various stages in the redaction. They intend in all cases to assert the correspondence between a divine word, spoken through a prophet, and events in the human realm. Examples are 1 Kgs 16:34; 17:16; 2 Kgs 1:17a; 2:22; 4:44. For this type of report as editorial remark see 1 Kgs 15:29; 16:12; 2 Kgs 9:36.

ORACULAR INQUIRY (Einholung eines Gottesbescheides). A type of (→) report which tells of seeking an oracle from God. The basic elements include: (1) report that an oracle was sought, usually at the request of a military leader; (2) the oracle in response to the inquiry. Two forms of the report occur, one associated with priests (cf. 1 Sam 23:9) and the other with prophets.

The normally brief priestly inquiry mentions "inquiring of Yahweh" *(šā'al běyahweh),* quotes the question put to the priest, and reports the answer as a word from God. Sometimes the question is omitted, and other minor variations occur. Examples are 1 Sam 23:2, 4; 14:37; 2 Sam 2:1. This procedure for seeking oracles had its setting in war making and in priestly divination by Urim and Thummim (Num 27:21). However, schematic representations of these activities belong to storytellers and history writers. The reports are usually scenes in longer narratives.

Inquiry for an oracle from a prophet is reported at greater length. The report typically recounts: (1) the problem to be addressed by divine word, (2) an audience with the prophet during which one requests an oracle *(dāraš 'et-děbar yahweh)*, (3) the oracle, (4) report of its fulfillment. Examples are 2 Kgs 8:7-15; 1 Kgs 14:1-18; 2 Kgs 3:4-20. This sort of activity belongs to divinatory activities of prophets (cf. 2 Kgs 3:15-16). Reports of these activities are now mainly important as scenes in larger narratives which, in some cases at least, may derive from prophets and prophetic circles in Israel.

ORACULAR REPORT (Bericht eines Orakels). A message from God cited or closely paraphrased in a report from one party to another. It may be concerned with the person who reports, the recipient of the report, or a third party. In all cases the oracle is presented as doubly mediated divine speech, from God through a prophet, and reported by another. Examples are 1 Kgs 8:16, 18-19 (2 Chr 6:5-6, 8-9); 2 Kgs 9:26, 36-37.

ORDER (Befehl, Verbot). A forthright, direct expression of personal will, which may be a speech of (→) command or (→) prohibition. Orders have several settings in social life and appear in many different literary contexts in the OT.

PARENESIS (Paränese, Ermahnung gegen oder zu etwas). An address to an individual or a group which seeks to persuade toward a definite goal. It may include several genres, such as (→) admonition, (→) instruction, (→) command, and (→) prohibition, arranged in flexible structures. Examples are Deuteronomy 6–11; Zech 1:3-6; Josh 24:2-15; 1 Kgs 8:56-61. Clear evidence for the setting of parenesis is unavailable.

PETITION (Petition, Bittrede, Bittschrift). A request or plea from one person to another asking for some definite response. In ordinary day-to-day expressions, a petition would almost always include: (1) the basis for petition, (2) petition proper, expressed directly or indirectly (e.g., Gen 18:3-4; 1 Kgs 2:15-17; 5:17-20; Gen 23:4). A highly stylized petition addressed to God, thus a prayer of petition, is common in portions of the OT shaped by Deuteronomic perspectives. The form is regular: (1) statements of transgression against God or God's past dealings with important people serve as a basis for petition; (2) a transition formula, "and now" *(wě'attâ)*, leads into the petition; (3) petition proper asks God for relief from distress (2 Kgs 19:15-19), forgiveness (Exod 32:31-32), divine favor (Exod 33:12-13; 2 Sam 7:18-29; 1 Kgs 3:6-9), and the like. See Jonah 4:2-3; Neh 9:6-37; Ezra 9:6-15. All these examples form representative images of ideal, heroic, divine-human dialogue that support thematic continuities in the wider canonical texts. These stylized prayers of petition represent a literary, theological development from ordinary petition. It is not possible to identify one primary societal setting for the genre, since petitions might be uttered by anyone in almost any situation.

PRAISE SPEECH (Lobrede). A brief or somewhat elaborate formulaic utterance which offers praise and thanksgiving to God for some good fortune or happy circumstance. Praise speech follows a typical, one-sentence structure: (1) formulaic opening ("Blessed be Yahweh" [*bārûk yahweh*]), followed by (2) a relative clause describing the event, deed, or circumstance which has called forth the praise. In form, the praise speech is much like uttering the name of God with certain epithets. Examples are 1 Kgs 1:48; 5:21; 8:15, 56; 1 Sam 25:32, 39; 2 Sam 18:28; Ezra 7:27. (Cf. 1 Sam 25:33 for an extension of the form into nonreligious speech.) Praise speech is related to (→) blessing (see 1 Kgs 8:14-15), but differs chiefly in function; it does not *pronounce* blessing upon someone but *acknowledges* blessing from God. Although its usage was widespread in ordinary life and its settings varied according to circumstances, praise speech seemed to have a special place in cultic affairs (1 Kgs 8:15; 8:56 is part of [→] parenesis in cultic ceremony).

PRAYER (Gebet). Any communication of a person toward his or her God. Ordinarily, prayer is direct address to God in the second-person singular and encompasses a wide variety of expression, motivation, purpose, and societal setting. Thus, prayer may take a number of different literary forms or genres depending on content, intention, and setting. For example, (→) complaint song of the individual, (→) hymn, (→) prayer of dedication, (→) prayer of petition. Besides the book of Psalms, which contains in effect many cultic prayers, we find mention of prayer in narrative contexts (e.g., Gen 24:10-14; 2 Kgs 20:3; Gen 18:23-32) and even in (→) vision reports (e.g., Amos 7:2, 5).

PRAYER OF DEDICATION (Weihegebet). A type of (→) prayer which is spoken on the occasion of dedicating an object, person, offering, or building to God. The examples in the OT are rather stylized. There is (1) a statement of background which provides context, and (2) a simple declaration, e.g., "I bring to you [God]" (Deut 26:5-10), "I have lent him to the Lord" (1 Sam 1:28), or "I have built you [God] an exalted temple" (1 Kgs 8:13). Now related in narrative contexts, these prayers probably reflect real cultic activities. Related to prayer of dedication is (→) dedicatory inscription, a genre not directly represented in the OT. But see *ANET*, 653-58, for examples from the Syro-Palestinian area.

PRAYER OF PETITION (Bittgebet). → Petition

PROMISE (Versprechen). A statement which expresses a speaker's agreement or commitment to act in a certain way or to bring about a specific situation in the near or distant future. Promises frequently are the essential performative elements of (→) oath (e.g., 1 Kgs 17:1) and (→) prophecy of salvation (e.g., 2 Kgs 20:5-6). However, they also occur in historical narratives, particularly in passages that have to do with the dynasty and well-being of the kings (mostly the Davidides), either embedded within direct discourse in the narrative (often as God's speech), or in a writer's statement to the reader. Good examples are: 2 Sam 5:2b; 7:10-16 (1 Chr 11:2; 17:8b-14); 1 Kgs 3:13 (2 Chr 1:12); 2 Kgs 10:30; 22:19-20 (2 Chr 34:27-28).

PROPHECY (Prophezeiung). A general term for any type of announcement by a prophet concerning future events or actions of God. Prophecy is different from (→) oracle since it refers to words of prophets, whereas oracle more broadly designates utterances, solicited and unsolicited, of priests and dream interpreters as well. There are many different genres of prophecy, as indicated by various contents, forms, and purposes.

PROPHECY OF PUNISHMENT (Prophetische Strafankündigung). A prophetic word which announces disaster to an individual or group because of some offense against God. The structure follows the procedure of two actions in a legal proceeding: indictment and verdict. Thus, prophecy of punishment typically contains: (1) an accusation, where the defendant or group is directly addressed and confronted with the offense, and (2) the announcement of God's intervention in human affairs to bring about punishment. The latter usually begins with a messenger formula, "Thus says Yahweh," and is tied to the former with a logical connective, "Therefore" *(lākēn)*. Thus, offense is reason for, or justification of, punishment. The literary structure is fairly flexible, especially in those forms which have a group, or even whole nation, in view. Examples (individual) are 1 Sam 2:27-36; Amos 7:14-17; Jer 20:1-6; 1 Kgs 13:21-22; 14:7-11; 16:2-4; (group) Amos 2:1-3, 4-5; 4:1-3; Hos 2:7-9. In Isa 3:1-11; Jer 2:26-28; Amos 9:8-10, all addressed to a group, one finds the basic components, accusation and punishment, reversed. The settings for prophecy of punishment varied according to the changing and diverse circumstances in which prophets were active.

PROPHECY OF SALVATION (Prophetische Heilsankündigung). A general term for a (→) prophecy which announces salvation, healing, health, restoration. It typically begins with a messenger formula, "Thus says Yahweh," or another kind of introduction, and moves immediately to the announcement of salvation. The latter consists variously of statement(s) of God's intervention to save, the effects and results, and closing statements, sometimes with reasons for God's action. Examples are Isa 7:7-9; Jer 28:2-4; 34:4. Less constrained are Amos 9:11-12, 13-15; Mic 5:1-2 (*RSV* 2-3). Solomon's words to Shimei in 1 Kgs 2:42-45 seem to reflect both the prophecy of salvation (v. 45) and its corresponding opposite, the (→) prophecy of punishment (vv. 42-44).

PROPHET LEGEND (Prophetenlegende). A type of (→) legend which focuses chiefly on the prophet as main character and exemplar of virtue, goodness, piety, and divine favor. Its purposes would be multiple, but chiefly to edify or inculcate religious devotion. Some prophet legends probably originated among prophets, but some also among the people who dealt with prophets. Occasions of telling, the societal settings, were varied, as for legends in general. → Legend.

PROPHET STORY (Prophetenerzählung). A type of (→) historical story in which a prophetic figure plays a central role and carries interpretative motifs expressive of the narrator's interest. For further information → Historical Story.

PROPHETIC ANNOUNCEMENT OF A SIGN (Prophetische Zeichenankündigung). An announcement in the context of (→) prophecies, either of salvation or punishment, that an event will occur in the future to confirm the main prophetic word. Normally, the announcement consists of three elements: (1) a declaration of an event as "sign" from God, e.g., "This is the sign [for you] from Yahweh"; (2) a subordinate clause which gives the significance of the "sign," e.g., "that the Lord has spoken" or "that the Lord will do this thing"; (3) the description of the event which is to be taken as "sign." Sometimes the second element is missing, since the context supplies the significance. Good examples of the genre are 1 Kgs 13:3; Jer 44:29-30; Isa 38:7-8 (= 2 Kgs 20:9-10); 37:30-32 (= 2 Kgs 19:29-31). The settings of such announcements vary according to the circumstances in which prophets were active. In general, however, the main occasion seems related to the custom of soliciting (→) oracles from prophets, and also, by extension, asking for "signs" (Isa 7:10).

PROPHETIC BATTLE STORY (Prophetische Schlachterzählung). A type of (→) historical story focused on military encounter(s) in which one or more prophets assume important dramatic roles and enunciate for the reader those interpretative perspectives important to the author (→ battle story). Closely related is (→) battle report, which tells of military encounter but without those literary features characteristic of developed, imaginative (→) story, and often without reference to prophets. See, e.g., Josh 7:2-5; Judg 8:10-12. Examples of prophetic battle story are 1 Kgs 20:1-34 and 2 Kgs 19:1-37 (cf. Isa 7:1-9). Although the societal setting of this genre is uncertain, and may even have been quite varied, the intentions seem related to recounting an event in the past for historical, instructional, and explanatory reasons.

PROPHETIC JUDGMENT SPEECH (Prophetische Gerichtsrede). A speech in which the prophet as the spokesperson for Yahweh announces judgment upon an individual, group, or nation. The main elements are: (1) statement of reasons for judgment, usually offenses against God; (2) logical connective, e.g., "therefore" *(lākēn);* (3) the announcement of judgment, often introduced with a messenger formula, "Thus says Yahweh." Additional elements occur frequently. Often, but not always, the reasons for judgment are presented as the prophet's own words, and the announcement as the words of Yahweh. Examples are Mic 3:9-12; Isa 8:6-8; Jer 11:9-12. The chief difference between this genre and the similar (→) prophecy of punishment is that the latter includes direct accusation of an individual or group, and thus preserves something of literary parentage in juridical procedures.

QUESTION-AND-ANSWER SCHEMA (Frage- und Antwort Schema). A literary device which projects a question and its answer as a means of describing a future situation. One type assumes a disaster and assigns reasons and responsibility for it, thus elaborating implicit admonitions to avoid the behavior which will lead to such an end. Typical are Jer 22:8-9; 1 Kgs 9:8-9; Deut 29:21-24 (*RSV* 22-25), all from the Dtr writers who placed national destruction in the context of broken covenant and realized covenantal curses. Parallels are in the commemorative (→) royal inscriptions of Ashurbanipal (e.g., *ANET*, 300). A second type appears as a divine speech addressed to a prophet, envisions a situation in which someone will ask a question, and suggests the answer that will be given. Examples are Jer 23:33; 5:19; 13:12-14; Ezek 21:12 (*RSV* 7); 37:18-19. Literary function, of course, varies according to biblical context. Models for this device apparently derive from situations in which a person sought oracles through a prophet. → Oracular Inquiry.

REGISTER (Register). An administrative (→) list, or even a book, which records for official purposes items or persons according to the means by which they are subject to administration by institutions or corporate bodies. The purpose of a register is to record and document the basis on which persons or items can be administered. Depending on the content, the forms of a register vary. OT texts either based on a register, or themselves a register, list citizens for labor recruitment (Nehemiah 3), or for military service (Num 1:17-47); officials to administer the state (1 Kgs 4:2-6, 7-19; Num 1:5-16); booty for support of religious shrines (Num 31:32-47). Cf. references to making registers in Num 1:2-4; 2 Samuel 24. Parallels appear frequently in Mesopotamian and Egyptian (→) royal inscriptions designed to commemorate the king and his deeds (e.g., *ANET*, 242-43, 249, 260-61, 278-79). Register originated with the scribal classes whose jobs included keeping administrative records of a centralized state. If such activity did not actually begin with the monarchy, it surely grew enormously with the consolidation of the Israelite state.

REGNAL RESUMÉ (Abriss einer königlichen Regierungszeit). A formulaic summary in the books of Kings which provides information about a monarch of Israel or Judah. Regnal resumé normally appears in two parts, as an introductory and a concluding summary which form a framework around other materials relating to a particular reign. The introductory resumé typically includes: (1) the name of the king and a synchronistic formula giving the date of accession; (2) the age of the king at accession (for Judah only); (3) the length of reign and capital city; (4) the name of the queen mother (for Judah only); (5) a theological evaluation, variously

311

worded, but in general highly stylized and stereotyped. Occasionally some elements, or even the entire resumé, may be missing for a particular reign. The concluding resumé, sometimes omitted, carries: (1) a citation formula, referring the reader to other sources for regnal information; (2) notice of death and burial of the king; (3) notice of succession. Examples are 2 Kgs 13:10-13 (the complete regnal resumé); 1 Kgs 15:1-5, 33-34 (introductory); 1 Kgs 14:19-20; 2 Kgs 10:34-35 (concluding). Regnal resumé is a literary device invented by the author-editor of 1–2 Kings, though it is possible that some elements at least were drawn from his sources.

REPORT (Bericht). A brief, self-contained prose narrative, usually in third-person style, about a single event or situation in the past. There is no developed plot or imaginative characterization (contrast [→] story). Because there is usually action, however, report is different from a statement or description. Report also differs from (→) official report, which is a narrative representation of a message being transmitted from one person to another. Varying in length from the very short (→) notice to the longer, even composite (→) account, reports carry diverse contents, e.g., settlement (Judg 1:16-17), royal construction (1 Kgs 6:2-38), name (→) etiology (Gen 35:8), a leader's (→) farewell speech (1 Kgs 2:1-9), diplomatic concord (1 Kgs 5:15-26 [RSV 5:1-12]), or (→) prophecy of punishment (1 Kgs 20:35-43). Certain types of report as defined by structure and content take on special importance in the OT (e.g., [→] dream, [→] theophany, [→] vision, [→] battle, [→] symbolic action). Naturally the setting for report would vary according to content and purpose.

REPORT OF PROPHETIC COMMISSION (Bericht einer Prophetensendung). A type of (→) report which tells of a prophet's being commissioned by God to speak or act. For full discussion, → Commission.

REPORT OF PROPHETIC REVELATION (Bericht einer Prophetenoffenbarung). A type of (→) report which recounts a private message from God to a prophet. Typically, such reports open with a prophetic word formula, "And the word of Yahweh came to so-and-so" (wayhî děbar-yahweh [hāyâ] 'el-PN), and then quote the message, which may be variously command, commission, prediction, warning, and the like. Examples in narrative are 2 Sam 7:4-16; 1 Sam 15:10-11; 1 Kgs 16:1-4; 17:2-4, 8-9; 21:28-29; cf. 1 Kgs 6:11-13. In the later literature, features of this narrative reporting style came to shape prophetic words intended to stand alone as a kind of public revelation. In these cases, the introductory formula became autobiographical in form ("And the word of the Lord came to me") and functioned as a superscription to the divine message. The entire report now was much like an independent poem, a testimony revealed, rather than — as in the narrative contexts — a telling of what the prophet experienced or did. See, e.g., Jer 21:1-10; 32:1-44; 34:8-22; Ezek 14:1-11; 20:1-44.

REPORT OF PROPHETIC WORD (Bericht eines Prophetenwortes). A type of (→) report developed rather late in association with the making of literary collections of prophetic (→) oracles. Even though the report may begin with a (→) prophetic word formula and include possibly secondary narrative elements of situation, date, and circumstance, the intent is not to convey a private (→) prophet revelation, or what the prophet has done or experienced, but to preserve what the prophet has said publicly. The report stands apart from (→) story or (→) legend about the prophet and emphasizes a word of God for its own sake. Examples are Jer 21:1-10; 32:1-44; 34:8-22; 35:1-19; Ezek 14:1-11; 20:1-44.

ROYAL INSCRIPTION (Königsinschrift). A general term for those ancient Near Eastern (→) inscriptions which commemorate historical kings and/or their deeds or record their gifts dedicated to the gods. There are Sumerian, Babylonian, Assyrian, and Egyptian examples, and several different types. All are products of centralized monarchies and aim in various ways to support and preserve strong royal government. (See Grayson, *Assyrian and Babylonian Chronicles* [→ 2 Kgs 8:7-15]; idem, *ARI;* idem, *Babylonian Historical-Literary Texts* [Toronto: University of Toronto, 1975]; idem, "Königslisten und Chroniken," *RLA;* E. Sollberger and J. R. Kupper, *Inscriptions royales sumériennes et akkadiennes* [Paris: Cerf, 1971]; W. W. Hallo, "The Royal Inscriptions of Ur: A Typology," *HUCA* 33 [1962] 1-43.)

ROYAL NARRATIVE (Königsnovelle). Strictly speaking not an independent literary genre (against A. Herrmann, *Die ägyptische Königsnovelle* [Leipziger Ägyptologische Studien 10; Glükstadt/Hamburg/New York: Augustin, 1938]), but narrative portions of Egyptian (→) royal inscriptions that present the king as an ideal figure of strength, piety, and success. Literary content and form vary considerably, and examples are known from ca. 1900 through 300 B.C.E. The accounts present the king in a variety of flattering ways: interacting with worshipful courtiers to plan and build great temples and monuments; quelling rebellions and going on military campaigns with glorious success; renowned from birth and youth, chosen by the gods to rule, given beauty, talents, special prowess. Examples may be found in M. Lichtheim, *Ancient Egyptian Literature* (3 vols.; Berkeley: University of California, 1973-1981) I, 115-18; II, 57-72; Breasted, *ARE* II, §§ 131-66; III, §§ 251-81 (additional bibliography in Long, *1 Kings,* 2-3, 67). Since these accounts for the most part are portions of commemorative inscriptions carved on temple walls, their principal aims are to glorify the king and to commemorate his deeds so as to accrue divine favor and afterlife for him. This type of royal inscription may stand in the background of 1 Kings 3–11.

SAGA (Sage). A long, traditional narrative, composed of episodic units built around typical themes or topics. Saga may include originally independent shorter pieces, such as (→) legend, (→) story, (→) anecdote, and various types of poetry. These episodes tell of deeds, virtuous ancestors, and heroic events which contribute to the narrator's cultural world. Though saga may include fanciful elements, that world for the narrator is the real world, when the earth was pretty much as it is now (contrast [→] myth). OT examples are Exodus 1–Deuteronomy 34 (saga of Moses); Gen 12:1–25:10 (saga of Abraham). The settings for saga are diverse. It belongs to popular literature and thus would be composed, transmitted, and told in a range of circumstances and on many occasions. The intentions of saga would likewise vary according to the situation. Chief among the story-teller's aims would be to entertain and to educate members of the audience in the ways of their particular culture.

SCHEMA OF REPRIEVE (Schematische Darstellung von Strafaufschub, Straf-milderung, oder Begnadigung). A pattern of literary motifs characteristic of the final shape of certain heavily redacted portions of the OT. Typically, one reads: (1) a description of penitence which follows upon an event of divine punishment, or the promise of such; (2) a (→) prophecy of salvation which mitigates the punishment, or a report of such an event. The language is stereotyped. Penitents "rend" their garments *(qrᶜ bgd)*, dress in sack-cloth, and fast *(sûm)*. The prophecy, which typically includes an allusion to penitence, gives the justification for reprieve, and then announces that the punishment has been set aside or mitigated in some way. Examples are 1 Kgs 21:27-29; 2 Kgs 22:19-20; 2 Sam 12:13-14; 2 Chr 12:7-8. Al-though schema of reprieve may be a kind of "stock scene" at home with Israelite storytellers, it appears more likely that this literary schema had its origin in the redacting and shaping hands that organized large blocks of OT tradition.

STATEMENT (Mündliche oder schriftliche Aussage). A brief prose-word or -writ-ing which simply notes or describes a situation or circumstance. Unlike (→) report, it does not relate action, and it differs from direct speech. Examples are 1 Kgs 3:2, 3; 5:2-3, 4-5.

STATEMENT OF ACQUITTAL (Freisprucherklärung). A formal declaration by a juridical authority that a person charged with a crime is innocent. Reflected in narratives, such statements occur (1) as a direct address to the defendant, either by an accuser or a judge: "You are innocent" (e.g., 2 Kgs 10:9; Prov 24:24; cf. Exod 9:27; 1 Sam 24:18 [*RSV* 17]; 2 Sam 14:9; Neh 9:33); (2) as a declaration about the defendant, either by a judge to the accuser ("He has not transgressed," Job 1:22; 2:10), or by an accuser to the judge ("She is more righteous than I," Gen 38:26; cf. Jer 3:11), or by an Accuser (who also acts as judge) to the Accused (1 Sam 24:18 [*RSV* 17]). State-ments of acquittal also occur in definitions of consequences in legal materials, e.g., "He [the owner] is free from guilt" (Exod 21:28) or "He is innocent" (Ezek 18:9) or "He/she shall be exempt from punishment" (Exod 21:19; Num 5:28). The original setting for such statements is the juridical process with authorities such as elders (see Ruth 4:1-11), state officials, or the king empowered by social custom and law to establish, or to interpret, existing law.

STORY (Erzählung). A narrative of some literary sophistication which creates interest by arousing tension and resolving it during the course of narration. Its structure is controlled by imaginative plot. The narrator moves from exposition (background and setting for the action) to a problem, sometimes complications in relationships (tension), to a climactic turn of events from which the resolution flows. Finally, narrative tension drains away into a concluding sense of rest.

Since literary structures are flexible and contents varied, one may not think of rigid definitions of type. Nevertheless, it proves useful to make certain distinctions. When a narrator emphasizes imaginative creation and artistic plot less than what an event was and how it happened, we speak of (→) historical story. When a brief content is structured simply and its purpose centered on entertainment, we are dealing with folkloristic (→) tale. If the story dwells on the wondrous qualities and exemplary character of a person or place, it is a (→) legend, the primary purpose of which is religious edification. Finally, a story that moves in a fantasy world unlike that of ordinary experience is a (→) fairytale; if its content centers on primordial times when gods and people dealt directly with one another, it is (→) myth. Examples of story are Exod 2:1-10; 1 Kgs 1:1-53.

With the exception of some (→) historical stories, most OT examples of story derive from and belong to the folk. They are folktales which incorporate motifs, scenes, and narrative techniques out of popular culture and oral tradition. Settings and intentions vary widely, therefore, depending on the story type, narrator, and occasions for storytelling.

SUMMARY OF PROPHETIC ORACLE (Kurzbericht eines Prophetenspruches, Zusammengefasster Prophetenspruch). A statement in third-person reportorial form that aims to summarize very briefly the content of a prophet's (→) oracle. Occasion, circumstance, and scene are unimportant; the prophet is usually unidentified. Emphasis falls upon the generalized content which floats free of narrative moorings somewhat like a commonly known or invented saying. Examples are 1 Kgs 21:23 (cf. 2 Kgs 9:36); 2 Kgs 10:30; 14:25-27; 17:13; 21:11-15. Such summaries are literary devices and stem from the writing and collecting activity of scribes who put together the books of Kings.

SYMBOLIC ACTION REPORT (Symbolische Handlung). A type of (→) report in first- or third-person style that recounts incidents in which the prophets accompanied their pronouncements with actions understood to be symbolic demonstrations of their messages. Such reports of symbolic action typically contain: (1) God's instruction to perform a certain act, (2) report of that act being executed, (3) an interpretation, usually cast as a word from God. Very often, the second element is omitted, and other minor details may be added. Examples are Isa 8:1-4; Jer 13:1-11; Ezek 4:1-8; cf. 1 Kgs 11:29-39; 22:11. Reports of symbolic action evolved from early accounts of magical activities. In their present literary contexts, however, they are similar in function to (→) reports of prophetic words. They communicate an oracle from God to humans spoken by and enacted through the prophet.

TALE (Volkstümliche Geschichte). A short, folkloristic type of (→) story. Originally a part of oral tradition, a tale is characterized by a minimum number of characters, one or two scenes, and a simply constructed plot. Typically, a tale briefly sets out the circumstances for its action (exposition) and develops a point of dramatic tension as the problem to be resolved in the narration. Length varies somewhat, but in all cases the plot remains uncomplicated. Tale derives from popular storytellers and the varied situations of storytelling. Hence, the OT examples still show their relative independence, being incorporated into longer collections of narrative, (→) saga, or still resisting full integration into their written context. Examples are Gen 12:10-20; 26:6-11; Exod 4:24-26.

TAUNT (Verspottung, Verhöhnung). An utterance which derides a person or thing as inferior to another. Closely related to (→) boast, taunt often appears in similar circumstances: a battle of words between opponents. Taunt has no fixed form. The term refers to the rhetorical motivation, effect, or even intent of one's speech. See 1 Sam 17:43, 44; 1 Kgs 12:10b; 20:11; Jer 22:14-15; Isa 23:15-16.

THEOLOGICAL REVIEW (Theologische Beurteilung). An editorial statement in the books of Kings which reviews, states offenses of, and evaluates a king. The structure is somewhat flexible, but the language is flat, stereotyped, and aimed at measuring a king according to religious orthodoxy. The language and style are related to that in the (→) regnal resumé, but limited to only a portion of what resumé covers. Theological review is dominated by evaluative tones, innuendos, and statements. It is characterized by generalization and lacks action or narrative interest. Theological review may incorporate (→) oracles as warning or as messages of salvation or punishment, though without narrative detail. They are oracles really carrying the author's omniscient perspective in the interest of religious evaluation. Examples are 1 Kgs 11:1-13; 2 Kgs 10:28-31; 17:7-18. Cf. Judg 2:11-15; 3:7-8. Theological review is a literary device of the author-editor of 1–2 Kings.

THEOPHANY REPORT (Gotteserscheinung). A type of (→) report, occasionally poetry, which recounts the manifestation of God, as distinct from (→) epiphany, which refers more generally to the appearance of any kind of divine being, e.g., angels, cherubim, etc. Two elements are characteristic: (1) description of Yahweh's approach, (2) accompanying natural upheavals (wind, fire, storm, etc.), along with reactions of fear and awe.

Examples are Judg 5:4-5; Deut 33:2; Amos 1:2; Mic 1:3-4; Ps 68:8-9 (*RSV* 7-8). The genre was probably influential in shaping 1 Kgs 19:9-14. Either element may be expanded with additional motifs (e.g., Isa 19:1; 26:21; 30:27-33; Nah 1:2-6; Hab 3:3-12). Possibly originally belonging to celebrations of military victory, and hence aimed at praising the God who gives victory, these reports are now found in various literary contexts, such as (→) hymn (Ps 97:2-5) and (→) prophecy of punishment (Isa 19:1-4; 26:21).

THRONE CONSPIRACY REPORT (Verschwörung gegen den Thron). A type of (→) report which tells briefly and schematically of conspiracy against the king and its outcome. It typically includes: (1) mention of conspiracy (the verb *qšr*); (2) the king is struck down and murdered (Hiphil of *nkh*, "struck/killed," and the verb *mwt*, "die"); (3) mention of conspirator who assumes the throne, often with a succession formula, "And X reigned in his stead." Examples are 2 Kgs 15:10, 14, 25, 30; 21:23. See also the more didactic, moralizing form of the report in 1 Kgs 15:27-30; 16:9-13. Similar reports appearing as part of Babylonian (→) chronicles and (→) king lists suggest that the OT examples may have been drawn from royal records or selected excerpts from such.

VISION REPORT (Visionsbericht). A type of (→) report which recounts what a prophet or seer (cf. Numbers 23–24) hears and/or sees in an inner perception. Varied in content and mostly cast in autobiographical style, a typical report includes: (1) announcement of vision, reporting essentially that the visionary "sees" *(r'h)*, or was "made to see" (Hiphil of *r'h*); (2) transition to the vision: "and behold" *(wĕhinnēh);* (3) the vision, usually beginning with juxtaposed images and continuing with scene(s), sounds, voices, dialogues, movements (sometimes the prophet is drawn into the drama).

The OT offers three main types of vision report: (1) oracle-vision, dominated by question-and-answer dialogue wherein a simple visionary image provides an occasion for oracle (e.g., Amos 7:7-8; 8:1-2; Jer 1:11-14; 24:1-10; Zech 5:1-4); the report aims at oraclelike proclamation; (2) dramatic-word vision depicting a heavenly scene taken as a portent of some future event on earth (e.g., Jer 38:21-22; 1 Kgs 22:17, 19-22; Amos 7:1-6); the report recounts a private omenlike revelation, which may or may not be acted upon; (3) revelatory-mysteries vision, aimed at conveying veiled secrets of divine activity and future events; imagery is symbolic and bizarre, and always a pattern of dialogue between divine "guide" and prophet interprets the esoteric (e.g., Zech 2:1-2, 3-4; 4:1-6a; cf. Daniel 8; 10–12).

Vision reports belong to those situations in which persons would ask a prophet or seer to divine information about God's purposes (1 Kgs 22:13-23; 2 Kgs 8:7-15; Ezekiel 14; 20; Jer 38:21-22). → Oracular Inquiry. However, most examples now are important as literary vehicles for theological claims.

317

WORD OF SELF-DISCLOSURE (Prophetisches Erweiswort). A prophetic word of salvation for Israel which at the same time announces disaster for her enemies and a means by which Yahweh will be acknowledged as God. Cast as God's speech and related by a prophet, the characteristic elements are: (1) the reason for God's intervention; (2) the means of God's intervention; (3) a formula of recognition, "And you [they] shall know [recognize, yd^c] that I am Yahweh," or "By this you [they] shall know. . . ." Thus, this oracle intends to announce not only salvation but also that Yahweh be recognized as God. The earliest setting may have been in the cultic institution of holy war (cf. 1 Kgs 20:13-14, 22, 28, 35-43). With many variations, word of self-disclosure is found in Ezekiel and Deutero-Isaiah, e.g., Ezek 25:3-5, 6-7, 8-11, 15-17; 26:2-6; Isa 41:20; 49:23, 26.

FORMULAS

ACCESSION AGE FORMULA (Formel für das Thronbesteigungsalter). Part of the introductory (→) regnal resumé, this formula simply states the age when a particular king began to reign. Allowing for minor variations, it appears as: "X years old [was] RN when he began to reign" or "RN [was] X years old when he began to reign" (lit., "a son of X years [was] RN at his reigning" or "RN [was] a son of X years at his reigning"). The formula is used only for Judean kings but is occasionally missing in the resumé. For examples, see 1 Kgs 14:21; 22:42; 2 Kgs 8:17; 12:1; 14:2.

ACCLAMATION FORMULA (Akklamationsformel). A short utterance acclaiming that Yahweh alone is God, as in 1 Kgs 18:39b: "The Lord, [he] is God" *(yahweh hû' hā'ĕlōhîm)*. Its roots seem to be in Israelite worship activities (cf. Pss 95:7; 100:3; 105:7), including religious (→) parenesis (cf. Deut 4:35, 39; 7:9; 1 Kgs 8:60).

ACKNOWLEDGMENT OF PETITION FORMULA (Anerkennung der Bitte). Variants of the following statements, singly or in combination: "I have heard . . . I have seen . . . I know . . . ," all of which signify to the hearer that a petition of some kind has been received and is about to be acted upon (usually favorably, but cf. Num. 14:27). A good example is in a scene of a petitioner before the king, 1 Sam 25:35. It also appears in narratives that represent occasions of divine speech, wherein the formula leads naturally into announcements of salvation, e.g., 2 Kgs 19:20; 20:5; 22:19; Exod 3:7; 6:5; 16:12. In short, the formula is used as part of a speaker's response to adversity, a response whose import is to correct the situation, improve it, or "save/heal."

ANNOUNCEMENT OF MESSAGE FORMULA (Formel für die Ankündigung einer Botschaft). The phrase "This is the word that PN spoke concerning . . ." *(zeh haddābār 'ăšer-dibber* PN *'al . . .)* or "Hear the word [which, of] PN [spoke] . . ." (*šm' dbr* PN). For the first variant see 2 Kgs 19:21, and for the second variant, 2 Kgs 18:28. There are many examples in prophetic oracles. The formula announces and draws attention to the "message" or "oracle" in the prophetic context that immediately follows (see Isa 16:13; Jer 38:21; etc.). It is distinct from the (→) messenger formula, which functions basically to legitimate the authority and credentials of the message bearer and which has its background in epistolary style. → Messenger Formula.

ASSISTANCE FORMULA (Beistandsformel). The formula affirming Yahweh's presence with his people or an individual. The basic form is cast as divine speech, "I am with you," with appropriate variations for human speakers and situations. Three main usages are found: (1) in an (→) oracle as part of a divine promise; in such cases the assistance formula ordinarily is introduced by the (→) reassurance formula, "Fear not" (cf. Isa 43:5; Jer 30:11; 46:28; Judg 6:12, 16); (2) spoken by people as a promise, wish, or question (in slightly different form; cf. Gen 28:20; 48:21; Exod 10:10; 18:19; Num 14:43; Deut 20:1); (3) as an assertion or confession (cf. Gen 39:23; Num 23:21; Deut 2:7; Josh 6:27; 1 Sam 16:18; 2 Chr 13:12; Ps 46:8, 12 [*RSV* 7, 11]).

ATTESTATION FORMULA (Beglaubigungsformel). An expression by which one cites information, knowledge, obligation, or facts shared with another, in order to persuade someone to act according to the wishes, or request, of the speaker. Basic elements: (emphatic pleonastic subject) "you surely know [that] so-and-so [is true]" (Gen 30:26, 29; Exod 32:22; Num 20:14; 1 Kgs 2:5; Ezek 37:3; etc.). The expression "you know . . ." (*wĕ'attâ yādaʿtā kî . . .*), with its completing information, often forms the implicit basis for a petition to be offered and received favorably — in ordinary life and business (e.g., Gen 30:26, 29), in diplomatic affairs (e.g., 1 Kgs 5:17, 20 [*RSV* 3, 6]), or in prayer (2 Sam 7:20; 1 Kgs 8:39). See also Josh 14:6. This way of speaking strengthens the speaker's position, for it subtly implicates the addressee in the common ground of shared knowledge, experience, or obligations between them.

CALL TO ATTENTION FORMULA (Aufmerksamkeitsruf, Aufforderung zum Hören, Lehreröffnungsformel). A formula which opens a public presentation or address, and intends to attract the attention of the hearers to the speech which follows. The constituent elements are an invitation to listen, mention of the addressee(s), and an indication of what is to be heard. This call would be used by, e.g., a singer (cf. Judg 5:3), a wisdom teacher (cf. Prov 7:24), or an official envoy (cf. 2 Kgs 18:28- 29). It is frequently found in the prophetic literature in various forms and is often expanded by relative clauses (cf. Amos 3:1; Hos 4:1; Mic 6:1-2; Isa 1:10; Ezek 6:3). See 2 Kgs 7:1aβ. Cf. De Vries, *1 and 2 Chronicles* (FOTL XI; Grand Rapids: Eerdmans, 1989) 437.

319

CITATION FORMULA (Zitationsformel). Part of the concluding (→) regnal re- sumé, this formula refers the reader to other sources of information about a particular king's reign. Typically, the citation consists of three ele- ments: (1) introduction, "and the rest of the acts of RN" (*wĕyeter dibrê RN*); (2) brief epitomizing allusion to the reign, e.g., "and all he did," "and the conspiracy he committed," "his wisdom," etc.; (3) citation, usually as a question, "are they not written in the chronicles of the kings of [Judah] Israel?" Examples are 1 Kgs 11:41; 14:29; 15:7; 16:14; 2 Kgs 20:20.

COMMISSIONING FORMULA (Beauftragsformel). Part of a stock scene, (→) com- missioning of a messenger, in which one person (or God) grants authority to a messenger or emissary with such imperatives as "Go, say to PN . . . ," "Thus you shall say to PN," and the like. For examples, see Gen 32:5 (*RSV* 4); 1 Kgs 14:7a; 2 Kgs 18:19; 19:6.

CONVEYANCE FORMULA (Übereignungsformel, Übermittlungsformel). A stereo- typed statement that God did, or will, hand over Israel or Israel's enemies to defeat. A typical form is "Yahweh gave/sold [will give/sell] them [Israel] into the hands of X." See the Deuteronomic summaries in Judg 3:8; 4:2. As direct address to Israel, the formula appears as part of a prophet's or priest's (→) oracle and functions to assure Israel of victory over her enemies. Here the typical form is "I [Yahweh] will give X [it/them] into your [our] hand." For examples, see 1 Kgs 20:13, 28; 22:6; Josh 6:2; 8:1, 18; Judg 1:2; 4:7.

CRY FOR HELP FORMULA (Hilferufsformel). A type of formulaic (→) petition (*hôšîʿâ* + addressee) which is often associated with the opening statement of a longer petition to someone with authority to offer help or render a judicial decision. Examples are "Help, my lord, the king!" (2 Kgs 6:26; cf. also 2 Sam 14:4 and 1 Kgs 3:17; cf. more distant 2 Kgs 4:40; cf. the religious use where God is addressed, Ps 106:47; 1 Chr 16:35; 2 Kgs 19:19). Perhaps this formula was rooted in petitions that were delivered in formal juridical proceedings, e.g., as reflected in Ruth 4:1-12 (cf. Boecker, *Redeformen des Rechtslebens im Alten Testament* [2nd ed.; WMANT 14; Neukirchen: Neukirchener, 1970] 61-66). Mostly the formula is part of a stock scene in which one petitions a higher authority. A technical term in the OT for the act of crying for help in this juridical sense is *liṣʿōq*, as in 2 Kgs 8:3, 5. See the word in narrative settings, e.g., 2 Kgs 6:26.

CRY OF DISTRESS FORMULA (Schmerzensrufformel). An exclamation expressing distress over a situation, present or envisioned. Typically, it begins with an interjection (*'ăhāh*), followed by the name or title of the one addressed and a brief allusion to the cause of distress, which may take varied rhetorical forms. Examples are Judg 6:22; 11:35; 2 Kgs 3:10; 6:5, 15; Jer 1:6; 4:10; cf. 1 Sam 4:7-8 for a related formula (*'ôy*).

DEATH AND BURIAL FORMULA (Todes- und Bestattungsformel). Part of the concluding (→) regnal resumé, this formula states in two parts that a king died and was buried. The actual wording may vary slightly from case to case. Most frequently, one reads that "he [the king] slept with his fathers and was buried [they buried him]" (e.g., 1 Kgs 11:43a; 14:31). Occasionally, one or the other element is missing (e.g., 1 Kgs 14:20; 2 Kgs 15:22). Sometimes both may be absent or supplanted by a narrative which tells of the circumstances of death (e.g., 1 Kgs 16:9-10; 2 Kgs 12:21-22 [*RSV* 20-21]).

DESCRIPTION OF HOMAGE FORMULA (Formularische Schilderung einer Huldigung). A stereotyped expression that describes one paying deep homage, even obeisance, to another. Typically one "goes" *(bô')* and "bows down" *(hištaḥăwâ)* toward the ground *('ārṣâ)*. Cf. Gen 18:2; 42:6; 43:26; 2 Kgs 2:15; 4:37.

DISPENSATORY DISMISSAL FORMULA (Entlassung in Friedenformel). The words "go in peace" *(lēk ['lh] lĕšālôm)*, which imply that the speaker (or God for whom a prophet or priest speaks) has granted a petitioner what has been asked, e.g., pardon (Gen 44:17) or blessing (Judg 18:6) or stay of avenging punishment (1 Sam 25:35b). See also 2 Kgs 5:19; Exod 4:18; 1 Sam 1:17; 20:42.

EMISSARIAL SELF-INTRODUCTION FORMULA (Formel für die Selbsteinführung eines Gesandten). The phrase "PN has sent me to you," by which an emissary or messenger introduces oneself to another and indicates the authority by which one conveys a message. See 2 Kgs 5:22; 8:9b; Gen 45:5. A person who claims to be an emissary of God, such as a prophet, uses the same formulaic language, e.g., Exod 3:13, 14, 15; cf. Jer 26:12. A parallel from the texts at Mari may be seen in *ANET,* 624.

GREETING FORMULA (Gruss-, Begrüssungsformel). A word by which one person greets another, asking about his or her welfare. The simplest form is *hăšālôm,* "is all well?" Examples are Gen 43:27; 2 Kgs 4:26; 2 Sam 20:9. Sometimes the formula takes on a nuance of anxious concern, as someone with cause of alarm inquires into another's intentions or the general situation (e.g., Gen 29:6; 2 Sam 18:32; 2 Kgs 9:11, 17). See the narrative description of greetings being offered in Exod 18:7; Judg 18:15; 1 Sam 17:22; 2 Sam 11:7.

INTRODUCTION TO THE ANNOUNCEMENT OF FUTURE EVENTS (Formel für die Einleitung einer Zukunftsankündigung). The formula "behold the days are coming" *(hinnēh yāmîm bā'îm),* which serves as an introduction to (→) prophecies of salvation or punishment. See 1 Sam 2:31; 2 Kgs 20:17; Amos 4:2; 8:11; 9:13.

INVASION FORMULA (Invasions Berichtsformel). The opening statement of an (→) invasion report. It typically states that a king or an army "came up against" (*lh b/*l) a place or city, and may include brief reference to siege and fighting (ṣûr/nlḥm). See 1 Kgs 14:25; 2 Kgs 12:18 (RSV 17); 17:5; 18:13; 24:10 (cf. Jer 39:1).

LENGTH OF REIGN FORMULA (Aussageformel für die Dauer einer Herrschaft). The standard element in an introductory (→) regnal resumé that states the number of years a particular king ruled in the capital city. For example, "he reigned X years in Jerusalem" (cf. 1 Kgs 14:21).

MESSENGER FORMULA (Botenformel). A stereotyped introduction to a message in which the speaker identifies the one who ordered the message transmitted. The most frequent form is "Thus says [kōh 'āmar] X" (e.g., Gen 32:5 [RSV 4]; 2 Kgs 1:11 [cf. v. 9]; 2 Kgs 18:29). The formula frequently occurs in the prophets' (→) oracles as "Thus says Yahweh" (e.g., 1 Kgs 21:19; 2 Kgs 1:16; Jer 6:16; 8:4; Ezek 16:59), and shows that the prophet was understood in analogy with the practice of commissioning, instructing, and sending a messenger. → Commission.

ORACLE FORMULA (Orakelformel, Offenbarungsformel). The formula nĕ'um yahweh ("says Yahweh"), which is found in the beginning, in the middle, or at the end of a prophetic word. The term "oracle" is used here in a very general fashion for any kind of prophetic utterance.

The original setting probably was the (→) vision report of a seer (cf. Num 24:3; 2 Sam 23:1). The intention is similar to (→) messenger formula.

ORACLE FULFILLMENT FORMULA (Orakel- oder Worterfüllungsformel). Part of a report of (→) oracle fulfillment, this formula asserts that something happened "according to the word of Yahweh" (kidbar yahweh), sometimes adding the clause "which he spoke by his servant PN" or, more simply, "which PN spoke." Examples are 1 Kgs 16:34; 17:16; 2 Kgs 1:17; 2:22; 4:44.

PLEA OF GUILT (Schuldgeständnisformel). An element of the (→) confession of guilt, in which the supplicant states, "I have erred/sinned" (hāṭā'tî), sometimes with a designation of the person sinned against and the circumstances. It is found in Exod 10:16; 1 Sam 15:30; 26:21; 2 Sam 12:13; 24:10 (1 Chr 21:18); 2 Kgs 18:14.

PROPHETIC EMPOWERING FORMULA (Prophetische Ermächtigungsformel). "The hand of the Lord came [fell] upon him" (wattĕhî 'ālāyw yad-yahweh) (1 Kgs 18:46; 2 Kgs 3:15; Ezek 1:3; 3:14, 22; 8:1; 37:1; 40:1; cf. Isa 8:11; Jer 15:17). It expresses the seizure and empowering of the prophet through God, the circumstance of being stricken, and thus receptive to oracle and/or vision (see Ezek 33:22). It is related to but differs from the (→) prophetic word formula, which, although used as narrative introduction to a private communication from God to prophet, is not associated with visionary and trancelike circumstances (see 1 Kgs 16:1; 17:2, 18:1).

PROPHETIC WORD FORMULA (Prophetische Wortereignisformel). A statement that "the word of Yahweh came to PN [him, me]" (*wayhî dĕbar-yahweh [hāyâ] 'el-PN*). The formula belongs to (→) stories and (→) reports about prophets and serves to convey the beginning of a private communication from God to the prophet. It is thereby distinct from narrative introductions to prophetic words which have a public audience. Examples are 2 Sam 7:4; 1 Kgs 16:1; 17:2; 18:1. The formula became a device to introduce collections of prophetic (→) oracles in the prophetic books, e.g., Jer 2:1; 14:1; 24:4; 25:1; 30:1.

REASSURANCE FORMULA (Bestätigungsformel). A statement in the imperative mode, "Do not be afraid" (*'al tîrā'*), followed by a subordinating preposition "for" or "because" (*kî*) which introduces the basis for the assurance being offered. Good examples are in Gen 35:17; 1 Sam 22:23; 2 Kgs 6:16. The formula often occurs as part of longer speeches (e.g., Josh 8:1-2), and frequently in (→) prophecies of salvation (e.g., Isa 7:4-9; 10:24-27; 2 Kgs 19:6-7).

RECOGNITION FORMULA (Erkenntnisformel). Part of a (→) self-disclosure oracle, this formula expresses the purpose of Yahweh's action. The typical form is "And you [they] shall know [*yd'*] that I am Yahweh," e.g., 1 Kgs 20:13, 28. Cf. Exod 7:17, "By this you shall know [*tēda'*] that I am Yahweh." The formula occurs in Ezekiel (e.g., 25:5, 7, 11, 17) and in Isaiah (e.g., 41:20; 49:23, 26).

SUCCESSION FORMULA (Sukzessionsformel). The last element in the concluding (→) regnal resumé, this formula states the identity of the person succeeding to the throne. Typically, the expression is "And RN . . . reigned in his stead" (*wayyimlōk* RN . . . *taḥtāyw*). Where circumstances warrant, the words "his son" or other explanatory statements are added. Examples are 1 Kgs 14:31b; 15:8b; 2 Kgs 1:17; 20:21. The formula does not appear for every monarch in the books of Kings.

SYNCHRONISTIC ACCESSION FORMULA (Synchronistische Thronbesteigungsformel). Part of the introductory (→) regnal resumé, this formula states the date of accession to the throne of one monarch with reference to the regnal year of his counterpart in the northern or southern kingdom. For Judean kings the usual form is "In the nth year of RN, king of Israel, RN king of Judah began to reign" (*bĕ* + year *lĕ* + RN *melek yiśrā'ēl mālak* RN *melek yĕhûdâ*). For example, see 1 Kgs 15:9; 2 Kgs 8:25; 14:1; 15:1. For northern kings, a slightly different formula occurs: "In the nth year of RN, king of Judah, RN began to reign [over all Israel] at X [for x years]" (*bĕ* + year *lĕ* + RN *melek yĕhûdâ mālak* RN . . . [*'al yiśrā'ēl*] *bĕ* + place X + number of years). Examples are 1 Kgs 16:8, 15; 2 Kgs 13:1, 10.

TESTIMONY FORMULA (Zeugnisformel). The phrase "until this day" (*'ad hayyôm hazzeh*), which at the end of brief reports affirms the continuing effects of a past event into the writer's own time. The formula serves mostly as a writer's personal attestation to the reliability of what has just been reported to the reader. It may not have belonged to the sources on which a writer drew. The formula is often a key element in (→) etiology (e.g., Josh 7:26; 2 Chr 20:26), (→) contemporizing summary (e.g., 1 Kgs 12:19; 2 Kgs 8:22a), and brief informational or evaluative comments (e.g., Josh 15:63; 1 Kgs 8:8; 10:12).